CAVENDISH ENCYCLOPEDIA OF THE

WATER GARDEN

CAVENDISH ENCYCLOPEDIA OF THE

WATER GARDEN

The ultimate guide to the design and maintenance of the water garden with more than 150 plant profiles

PHILIP SWINDELLS

CAVENDISH BOOKS
VANCOUVER

Published in 2000 by

Cavendish Books Inc.,
Unit 23, 1610 Derwent Way, Delta, BC
V3M 6W1

www.gardenbooks.com

email: sales@cavendishbooks.ca

1-800-665-3166

ISBN 1 55289 017 1

All correspondence concerning the content of this volume should be addressed to Salamander Books Ltd.

CREDITS

Managing Editor: Anne McDowall
Copy Editor: Ian Penberthy
Designers: Mark Holt, John Heritage
Artwork illustrations: Elizabeth Pepperell
Colour reproduction: Dah Hua Printing Press Co Ltd, Hong Kong
Printed in Spain

THE AUTHOR

Philip Swindells has more than 30 years of practical professional horticultural experience and now works as a consultant specializing in the conservation, restoration and management of historic gardens, particularly water gardens. After training at the University of Cambridge Botanic Gardens, Philip then went on to work extensively with aquatic plants, particularly at the famous Perry's Hardy Plant Farm, Enfield, at that time the largest aquatic plant nursery in Europe. He was a founder member of the International Waterlily Society and for many years edited its Journal. Currently the International Registrar for Cultivated Nymphaea (Waterlilies) and Nelumbo (Lotus), he was entered into the International Waterlily Society's Hall of Fame in 1994.

As well as lecturing and broadcasting at home and overseas, Philip has written more than two dozen books, many about water gardening, and contributes regular columns to water gardening publications. He has won a number of awards and scholarships for his services to horticulture, including one from the International Plant Propagators' Society for studies into modern propagation techniques with waterlilies. Among his writing awards have been the UK Garden Writer of the Year Award in 1985 and the Quill and Trowel international communications award by the Garden Writers' Association of America the following year.

CONTENTS

INTRODUCTION

Few other aspects of gardening are as all-consuming as water gardening. Water holds a fascination for everyone, both old and young alike. Whether it be in the quiet stillness of a pool that reflects all about it, or when tumbling and splashing over rocks, water is captivating.

For the plant enthusiast, it provides a unique opportunity to grow species that cannot be cultivated elsewhere. Aquatic plants are very special. They not only provide the water garden with long-lasting interest and colour, but also contribute to the well-being of all the creatures that live in it, for a garden pond is a miniature ecosystem where all the living entities depend upon one another for their continued existence.

Submerged plants produce oxygen and compete with algae for mineral salts in the water, while floating aquatics provide shade for the fish and reduce the incidence of troublesome blanket weed by denying it light. Deep-water aquatics, such as waterlilies, do a similar job, but primarily they are grown for their beautiful blossoms. Reeds, rushes and other marginal plants will decorate, the waterside, but also shelter myriad forms of wildlife. In the water, fish and snails deposit nutrients for the benefit of the plants, while the former control many of the insect pests that prey upon them. All is in harmony, and the gardener can look through the surface of the water, as through a window, on to a beautiful and intriguing world.

However, the prime purpose of water in the garden may not necessarily be to provide a safe haven for wildlife or the ability to grow particular plants; it may be to offer a means of caring for fish. While these are seen as the natural occupants of a traditional pond, with the soaring popularity of creatures like the nishiki koi carp, the keeping of fish alone is becoming a very important part of the water gardening hobby. Modern sophisticated filtration systems make it possible to ensure the health of quite large populations in relatively restricted circumstances. Plants rarely play a part in such ponds, as the fish are likely to destroy them.

Plants are often absent when water is used as a feature for its own sake, whether a still open 'mirror' or the kind of 'sculptures' created by fountains. Water alone can be magical, especially when moving, for wonderful effects can be created when sunlight plays upon it, all accompanied by the delightful tinkling sound as the droplets fall.

Water offers many enjoyable aspects, and while not all can be accommodated satisfactorily in a single feature, several can often be combined to give immeasurable pleasure. Through the pages of this book, I have tried to convey some of the inspiration that water has given to me, and I have set out the opportunities that are available to all. There are rules to follow, but I have interpreted them as widely as possible to give the aspiring water gardener the greatest range of options. I hope that having read this book, many more gardeners, who may have been uncertain about how to create a practical and visually pleasing water feature, will be tempted to take up the spade and join our happy band of aquaholics.

Philip Swindells

CHAPTER ONE

WATER GARDEN DESIGN

Whether it be the deep, reflective amber glow of a dew pond or the raging torrent of a mountain stream, water has a peculiar fascination for young and old alike. In the garden, however, it can be appreciated to the full: tumbling gently over rocks and splashing into a pool alive with the myriad colours of goldfish, or in a quiet corner supporting the broad verdant pads and starry blossoms of waterlilies. In the formal water garden, the reflective qualities of still water will mirror the beauty of its surroundings, echoing not only garden features, but also puffy clouds scudding across the sky and the long drawn shadows of trees. Marsh marigolds, primulas, hostas and globe flowers will dance in attendance upon the pool, extending it into the accompanying bog garden, an essential adjunct to the larger feature, tying it into the garden landscape and offering a wonderful habitat for wildlife. Where this is not felt appropriate, a water meadow can be created. This grassy patch, filled with ragged robin, cardamine and fritillaries, will recreate a riverside habitat that provides a most appealing addition to a stream. Indeed, the waterside can be as fascinating as the aquatic environment itself, each complementing the other.

Moreover, water makes a splendid free-flowing medium for the artist. It is wonderful when allowed to rest and create reflective pictures, but is equally endearing when thrust into the air or dropped from a height. Fountains and waterfalls present the gardener with great opportunities for creativity: water can be moulded into beautiful, often changing, shapes; it can be coloured by the mood of the day or enhanced by artificial light; and, when appropriate, its movement can be accompanied by music.

Water gardening is a wide-ranging and fascinating pastime, embracing the skills and imagination of the artist, yet giving full rein to the practical desires and craft of the gardener, and at the same time offering a sanctuary for wildlife.

A water garden is a wonderful place in which to relax and enjoy the beauty of nature – not only the wide and varied plant life, but also the colourful fish and myriad aquatic fauna.

THE PRINCIPLES OF WATER GARDENING

There are many reasons for adding a water feature to the garden. For most of us, however, it is the desire to grow aquatic plants or keep fish. To do either, we need to construct a pond, and when we do that, we must create conditions that are conducive to the happy co-existence of all the inhabitants, be they plants or fish. You cannot successfully integrate a specialized pond into the garden; it must be a balanced ecosystem. For example you can keep fish without plants, but filtration and oxygenation equipment becomes essential to keep them healthy. Conversely, if you grow plants alone, insecticides will be necessary to control pests.

Probably the most important factor that the newcomer to water gardening must appreciate is the interdependence of all life forms within a still water environment. With a stream, this is not as critical, although even there many elements still depend on each other. A pool is a complete, self-contained environment, but influenced from outside, not only through additives to the water, but also its surroundings. As with most life, the sun is the powerhouse, and a pool denied full exposure will be doomed to a second-rate existence.

COMBINING SCIENCE AND ART

Water gardening is a facet of horticulture where both the science and art of gardening can be observed in their richest diversity. The scientific aspect lies in understanding something of the chemistry of the water and the life cycle and habits of the plants, fish and other aquatic creatures that live in it. An artistic flair is required to ensure that the feature is not only placed sympathetically within the garden landscape, but also used to create other effects. These may not be

A well ordered water garden results from carefully chosen plants. Each makes a contribution to the natural balance of the pool and the gardener must be aware of this when creating a floral picture. Full account should be taken of fish and aquatic life as well.

While plants and fish are usually regarded as the major decorative attributes of a water garden, moving water can also make an important contribution. A foaming geyser can serve as a focal point or feature, adding magical sound as well as sparkling beauty.

purely visual, for with moving water sound is an important component. Certainly its value should be appreciated fully when a scheme is devised, whether it be the crashing fury of a mill race or the gentle trickle from a bamboo pipe. Apart from the rustling of living bamboo, there are few other natural sounds that the gardener can place and influence in quite the same manner.

Water should also be regarded as work of art and used as such. A flat placid area of water, in a formal garden, will reflect all about it. The pool will become a moody place when dark clouds cross the sky; it will exhibit stark beauty in winter when reflecting the naked branches of nearby trees; and it will be a cheery sparkling mirror when the sun shines. A properly maintained, clear formal pool can be an ever-changing picture that is like nothing else in the garden.

Such flexibility is also possible by using fountains. Regard these as sculptures in water, and take the opportunity to create a sequence of changing spray patterns. You can achieve this with a timer, which will fade one pattern into another, or you can run a particular water pattern for several weeks, then replace the fountain outlet with another to give a fresh look. Modern technology permits wonderful effects with fountains, among them 'dancing' jets of water to the accompaniment of music and coloured lights.

Such fun and fantasy do create constraints upon the pool, and while many plants will tolerate such exuberance, sadly they do not include waterlilies. Provided such restrictions are appreciated from the outset, however, there need be little disappointment with the final planted scheme.

A waterfall is a more natural-looking addition to a water feature, which will provide greater flexibility in plant cultivation if positioned at one end of the pool, leaving a relatively undisturbed area at the other. Because it recreates a feature found in nature, it should appear to grow out of the garden, rather than sit on it. If a waterfall is planned at the time the pool is constructed, this should not be difficult to achieve.

This could also be said about the water garden as a whole, and the first principle when considering such a feature should be careful planning; not just for your immediate needs, but for the future as well. This is particularly applicable to a bog garden, for a true, fully-integrated and practical bog garden can be created with a pool liner if constructed at the same time as the pool. If added afterwards, however, it can often become isolated and a potential desert, the soil being separated completely from the surrounding ground and pool by an impermeable membrane.

BASIC PRINCIPLES

Planning ahead and understanding what goes on in a pool, together with a knowledge of what is needed to make everything flourish, are the basic principles of successful water gardening. Unlike other aspects of gardening, there is much to learn before you start, but that process can be fun and will lead to a much greater enjoyment of the water garden itself. Once the practical aspects have been firmly grasped, the design elements can be addressed. On the following pages, we will discuss many of these and the influence that they have had upon the modern water garden, together with some of the key factors that you should observe. However, beauty is in the eye of the beholder, and no matter what the final result, provided it conforms with the basic principles set out here, it will be an undoubted success.

WATER GARDEN STYLES

Water has been an important part of man's gardening activities for centuries. The reasons for this, however, have not always matched those that inspire modern water gardeners: the great pleasure of growing beautiful waterlilies, fine irises and rushes, for example, or caring for brilliantly coloured goldfish or exotic koi carp. In the past, water often served practical, economic and religious purposes.

ANCIENT SYMBOLISM

Some of the earliest water features recorded were in the deserts of Egypt and Mesopotamia, where the waters of rivers such as the Nile, Tigris and Euphrates were controlled and channelled for irrigation purposes. The earliest gardens containing areas of water were designed essentially for food production, cultivating lotus, keeping fish and growing papyrus.

As time passed, the rulers of these desert kingdoms brought water into the gardens of their palaces and temples, extensive areas often being used as decorative features. The opportunities that these bodies of water afforded for nourishing trees and plants, together with their reflective and cooling qualities, led to them being regarded as manifestations of heaven on earth.

Waterlilies were revered by early civilisations, especially the Egyptians, who benefited from some of the most beautiful tropical waterlilies; *Nymphaea lotus* and *N. caerulea* were native to the area. Indeed, most of our knowledge of the early history of the cultivation of waterlilies comes from the XIIth dynasty (3000-2500 BC) and the tombs of the village of Beni-Hassan, alongside the river Nile. Here pictures of gardening scenes have been discovered that show gardeners bringing water from a pond to irrigate plants growing in square, evenly spaced beds. A narrow canal leads from the beds to a pond. It is thought that it was in such a pond that the white-flowered waterlily lotus was cultivated.

Waterlilies were not grown by the ancient Egyptians for their beauty in cultivation, although pleasing formal pond arrangements were made, but for their cut blossoms, which were used extensively in religious festivals. Offerings of flow-

Water has always played an important part in the culture and traditions of man wherever he has lived in the world. This wall painting from the tomb of Nebamun Thebes, circa 1400BC, shows the garden of an estate with ornamental water.

ers were made to the dead, or placed on altars before their gods. They were also given by noblemen to guests as a gesture of friendship and goodwill, the visitors being expected to reciprocate by holding the blooms in their hands or twining them in their hair while in the presence of their hosts.

Petals from the blossoms of both *N. lotus* and *N. caerulea* have been found in the funeral wreaths of Rameses II (1580 BC) and Amenhotep I. The custom was to lay wreaths on the mummy in concentric semi-circles, from the chin downwards, until the sarcophagus was packed with floral tributes. Both plants have been portrayed extensively in the mural decorations, pottery and furniture of the period. Later they were were grown as decorative plants for their ornamental merit alone. We know that Amenhotep IV grew them in ponds surrounded by flower beds in his famous palace gardens at Ikhnaton, while Rameses III (1225 BC) is reputed to have grown 'rushes and the lotus ... and have many tanks and ponds ... of the lotus flowers.'

Many early water gardens were very elaborate, as depicted in this illustration to Baburnama. Babur, with his architect, plans the Baghi-i-Wafa near Jalalabad, Moghul 1589.

A DIFFERENT TRADITION

Early Egyptian water features would have been very utilitarian, with an abundance of plants, but little consideration given to their arrangement or the value of open water. In Persia, a different tradition developed, which concentrated more on water for its own sake than as a means of cultivating aquatic plants. Behind the evolving water garden histories of both civilizations, however, there was a common theme: the oasis in the desert, the expression of man's desire to secure himself from his hostile surroundings.

This is best seen in the chahar bagh, or four-fold garden, a level enclosed square, which was divided into four by two intersecting canals. A pool, fountain or pavilion was placed at the centre, the canals radiating from this focal point and representing the four rivers of paradise. Adjacent to these, trees, shrubs and flowers grew freely in the four quarters of the garden, being irrigated by a series of decorative channels.

The origins of this tradition have been lost in the mists of time, but the designs can be seen in old carpets and paintings. The overall plan seems to have derived from the royal hunting parks, pairidaeza, and the protective oasis. These Persian designs were assimilated into what is regarded as Islamic garden design, no doubt as the result of the conquest of Persia by Muslim Arabs in the 7th century. The ideas and designs found in these early gardens were readily accepted, being very close to the descriptions of the garden of paradise found in the Koran.

CHINESE INFLUENCE

Water in China played two roles in the garden: as a landscape feature and as a means of growing waterlilies and lotus. The importance of plant cultivation and its symbolism is best illustrated by a passage from the writings of Chou Tun-I, a noted author of the 11th century: 'Since the opening of the T'ang Dynasty, it has been fashionable to admire the peony; but my favourite is the waterlily. How stainless it rises from its slimy bed. How modestly it reposes on the clear pool, an emblem of purity and truth. Symmetrically perfect, its subtle perfume is wafted far and wide; while there it rests in spotless state, something to be regarded reverently from a distance, and not to be profaned by familiar approach.' Such wonderful sentiments echo the feelings of all waterlily lovers.

In landscape terms, the Chinese used water much as we do today, capturing its stillness and reflective qualities or its turbulent humour in waterfall or fountain. The only use to which they put it that has never successfully invaded our water gardening culture, was to link parts of the garden by water channels that ran beside paths. These silvery guides would encourage the visitor to move from one area of the garden to another. The idea became stylish in Western gardens for a few years during the last century, but it did not persist.

The gardens of the Orient can be traced back into antiquity and have had considerable influence upon European and North American styles. While the view of what a garden should be and the whole philosophy of gardens and gardening are completely different, Western culture has borrowed heavily from the East.

JAPANESE WATER FEATURES

There is something special and unique about Japanese gardens and their use of water. While they may not always suit Western tastes or understanding in their purest form, much can be borrowed from the Japanese tradition, even if the meanings and features are interpreted incorrectly.

Japanese ponds are traditionally shaped like the written character for heart and mind, kokora, although the tendency to disguise the edge or shoreline with rocks and planting can make this less obvious. No doubt, however, knowing that this shape lies beneath the rock and plant dressing is reward enough for the true Japanese gardener. In practical terms, though, the shape of the pool matters little, for all the other influences of the Orient can be brought to bear in creating a tranquil picture. This is very much what Japanese water gardening is about: creating a picture for contemplation, which brings the landscape of the countryside into the garden in a much reduced form.

Most Japanese pools contain islands that represent various features of the landscape, although not necessarily islands. Rocky features that suggest mountains should be heavily planted with evergreens, like Japanese azaleas, and there should be rocky shallows at the base. A low flat island alludes to a moor and may comprise a planting of reeds, rushes and mosses among a few prominent rocks. Cliffs are created with stark rocks that jut from the water, ideally with a small twisted pine growing between them, while a tidal island is represented by almost completely submerged rocks interspersed with a tiny grassy planting. These are all traditional significant features within a Japanese water garden, and while they are all fascinating, they do not rest easily with Western perceptions of water gardening. For most of us, if the features appeal, we will use them, irrespective of their meaning, but they are difficult to justify in anything other than a Japanese setting.

The Japanese garden also uses the shoreline creatively. Rocks and planting create niches and promontories, and where water enters a pool from a stream, the planting is always contrived to conceal that point of entry. Sometimes fire charred posts, 8cm (3in) in diameter, are grouped together and sunk into the ground along the shoreline to represent old moorings or pilings. They protrude above the water by 10-15cm (4-6in). The shoreline from just below water level to the bankside generally consists of large stones or well washed gravel in colours that complement or contrast with one another.

Running water is important too, not just in meandering streams and rills, but also through bamboo pipes in an array of configurations. In the stream bed, the strategic use of rocks has always played an important role, being positioned

Oriental water features have a simplicity which conveys peace and well being. Each part has individual significance whether it be a stone, a lantern or a plant.

Rocks and water have essential roles in Japanese gardens. Their meanings are often ignored in Western interpretations, but this restful garden style has become popular around the world.

Water is frequently accompanied by beautiful sculptures in classical Italian garden design. In addition to providing enormous pleasure, such elaborate fountains as the Hundred Fountain Terrace at the Villa d'Este Tivoli, were also prized as feats of engineering.

to create curves and ripples that have a purpose in the overall design. That purpose is to please the eye, although guidelines were set out in Sakutei-ki, the 11th-century memorandum on garden making, which state that 'the usual places to set out rocks are where the stream emerges into the courtyard, where it curves round a hillock, where it empties into a pond and where it bends in passing buildings.' This advice is still followed by purist Japanese garden makers.

THE EUROPEAN INFLUENCE

Oriental water gardening had little influence upon Western gardens until the end of the last century. European traditions owed more to the Middle East, while ultimately North America followed Europe's lead. In more recent times, however, the Japanese tradition in its purer form has found widespread acceptance in North America, especially in the West and Mid-West.

The earliest knowledge that we have of water gardening in Europe comes from Homeric times, when the Greeks were said to have constructed nymphaeums. These were grotto-like structures surrounded by trees and containing constant running water. It is doubtful that this had anything to do with the cultivation of waterlilies, despite the fact that the name nymphaea is a direct transliteration of an early Greek word used to describe these plants. Waterlilies dislike both moving water and shade, so it is likely that a nymphaeum was constructed for its decorative merits, rather than as a functional feature for growing aquatics.

It was water for its own sake that eventually took Europe by storm. The grand fountains and cascades, water staircases and geysers created spectacular effects that can still be seen today. The Italians relied heavily upon sculpture to enhance their water features and had water crashing about, while the French tended to prefer more sedate trickling cascades and vast areas of still open water. These traditions have led to the modern water gardener's desire for sculpture fountains and other ornamentation, and for multiple and twisting jets of water, which can be enhanced still further by lighting to create an even more spectacular experience.

Water gardens have a long tradition in Britain, not as we know them today through our great enthusiasm for plant diversity and penchant for exotic fish, but as features in their own right. This interest grew largely from the leads provided by the Italians and French.

THE ENGLISH RENAISSANCE

The renaissance, or rebirth, of interest in classical antiquity came to England after the War of the Roses in 1485, the enclosed medieval garden gradually being replaced by the Renaissance pleasure garden. Much of the influence was French, and although the term 'formal' was not adopted until the end of the 19th century, much of what was witnessed at that time, and in the gardens where it remains today, can confidently be described as formal. Indeed, in the pursuit of ideas for the modern garden, much can be learned by visiting some of the great English houses, such as Chatsworth in Derbyshire. Of course, such water features are laid out on an enormous scale, but the principles behind many of them are just as relevant when the concept is translated to the small suburban plot.

One of the great amusing features of the time, which can be recreated readily in the domestic garden is the trick, or joke, fountain. This is not a true fountain, but a device constructed from piping to startle the unwary visitor. A simple modern trip mechanism can cause the water jet to squirt as someone passes, a prospect that delights children. A tree fountain is another possibility, and an excellent example is the wonderful willow tree creation at Chatsworth. This consists of copper tubing welded into the shape of a willow tree, from which water cascades delightfully, the epitome of inventiveness from the Renaissance period. No doubt, something more modest could be achieved by the innovative do-it-yourself enthusiast.

The trick fountain, which was often disguised as a tree or other natural feature, startled the unwary visitor by producing jets of water. It was activated as they passed by.

ENGLISH LANDSCAPE TRADITION

The great landscape tradition followed people like Lancelot 'Capability' Brown and Humphry Repton. These renowned gardeners used the landscape like an artist's canvas, creating

The great English landscape tradition depended for its success on the extensive use of water. Usually this was unplanted or only sparingly so, in order that the wonderful combinations of trees and garden structures could be reflected in its stillness.

wonderful, expansive and well balanced visions. The achievements of Brown and Repton are unlikely to be repeated in most gardens today, however, which may be to the good. Indeed, it could be true to say that we never want to see their likes again, for although they created great masterpieces, they also destroyed much of what earlier gardening generations had achieved. Repton's only saving grace was that he permitted the use once more of fountains, which had been swept away and virtually outlawed by Brown.

Historically, the influence of Brown and Repton on water gardening is interesting, but it has little relevance to the gardeners of today, except those with spreading acres at their disposal. All that those of us with smaller plots can learn is the importance of proportion, for without doubt the balance that they achieved between water and uncluttered planting is a lesson to us all.

THE MODERN WATER GARDEN

It is difficult to determine when water gardening, as we know it today, began, although Philip Miller was probably a major influence. In his Gardeners' Dictionary (1731), he stated: 'In some gardens, I have seen plants cultivated in large troughs of water, where they flourish very well and annually produce great quantities of flowers.' At that time, few people had any awareness of the myriad tropical waterlilies that were being cultivated abroad. This only occurred when Sir Joseph Paxton, head gardener to the Duke of Devonshire at Chatsworth, began hybridizing tropical waterlilies and, in a blaze of publicity, flowered the giant Victoria waterlily for the first time in England. Following the presentation of the first blossom to the Queen, the waterlily was named in her honour. This sparked an interest in water gardening among the aristocracy which, together with the successful production of coloured hardy waterlilies by innovative Frenchman Joseph Bory Latour Marliac towards the end of the century, secured its future as an integral part of modern gardening tradition.

Not everyone was convinced, though, for Reginald Farrer, one of the greatest English gardeners and plant collectors, stated in his classic Alpine and Bog Plants: 'Advice to those about to build a water garden – DON'T.' William Robinson, that other great English gardener, concurred. Writing in his English Flower Garden (1895), he says: 'Unclean and ugly pools deface our gardens; some have a mania for artificial water, the effect of water pleasing them so well that they bring it near their houses where they cannot have its good effects. But they have instead filth that gathers in stagnant water and its evil smell on many a lawn.'

Fortunately, these perverse views were short-lived, and with the advent of modern pool liners and pre-formed pools in the 1960s, a water gardening revolution took place.

It was not until the end of the 19th century that water gardens as we popularly enjoy them today became fashionable. Until then water was used for its own sake, uncluttered by planting and demonstrating its beauty in fountains and water staircases.

THE FORMAL WATER GARDEN

In the formal water garden, the art of gardening is at its zenith. Even so, basic scientific principles must be observed to ensure that the water remains clear and brightly reflective, whether this be achieved by planting or through the use of chemicals. As a picture, however, the formal water garden is contrived art, combining the best of man's innovative and constructional skills with the great beauty of nature.

PERSPECTIVE AND SCALE

The size of a formal water feature will determine its success. Although it is possible to create a pool that is too large and out of keeping with its surroundings, for the most part, the maxim should be the bigger, the better. Water can create wonderful illusions, and even the tiniest courtyard will benefit and appear larger through its carefully planned presence. Its reflective qualities are the key to its success.

Obviously, budgetary constraints will come into play when deciding upon the size of a pool, but there are aesthetic and practical reasons for making it as large as possible. The greater the area of water, the more opportunities there will be for wonderful reflections and also for creating a stable balance of pond life. A large body of water experiences slow temperature changes which, in turn, affect the appearance of water discolouring algae. If water clarity can be maintained by virtue of scale and natural means, so much the better, for clarity is vital to a formal pool's success.

Although scale and proportion are important, with a formal pool it is generally a case of the bigger, the better. Such a feature can create illusions of space and wonderful reflections.

When deciding on the pool's size, bear in mind that by extending its surface area, you will not necessarily increase the financial outlay in direct proportion. Much of the cost involved in pool construction is absorbed by the initial laying out and the materials. By doubling the surface area, you will only increase the perimeter by half; turning a planned rectangular pool into a square one, by lengthening the narrow sides, can be very cost effective.

From the visual point of view, the greatest difficulty arises when working with the small garden, especially if it is a courtyard. Quite often, such gardens have restricted access, while it is virtually impossible to achieve the correct proportions if constrained by an existing lawn. On a larger plot, a lawn can provide a pleasing surround to a pool, but in a confined area, it can look silly. Moreover, a small lawn running up to the pool is likely to become worn, and if a fountain is installed, the grass may become wet and muddy. It is far better to remove the lawn completely and lay paving.

The variety of paving materials is so diverse that even the most unimaginative gardener can create a pleasing pool surround. Use a variety of textures and colours to contrast with and complement the pool, laying out patterns that will accentuate its shape and size. This will integrate the pool into the garden, rather than making it look out of place, as is often the case when surrounded by a tiny patch of turf.

Interest can be added with potted plants, perhaps evergreens like camellias or neatly trimmed conifers. Containers can be a great help when attempting to give the pool a sense of scale and perspective. These aspects do not have to depend merely upon the shape and size of the pool.

Scale and perspective can be greatly altered by changing levels. These are quite critical in the small enclosed garden. In such cases, empasise different levels in the design with steps and walls, constructed in materials that link with other garden structures and the house itself. A more extensive design will offer a greater opportunity to provide contrasts, but whatever you decide to do, regard changing levels as an asset, rather than a hindrance.

The larger scheme offers many advantages when it comes to deceiving the eye. This is particularly so when planning a flat body of water. A long narrow garden can be made to appear wider by a pool that runs across it, rather than down its length. Conversely, an illusion of greater distance can be created by making a rectangular pool narrower towards its far end. The great designer Sir Edwin Lutyens was a master of this effect, creating canal-like pools that looked symmetrical, but which were narrow at the far end.

A formal water feature can rest easily in an informal garden by the careful treatment of the surroundings. The pots have formality themselves, but are grouped informally and spill over into the pool surrounds, happily linking the various elements.

MOVING WATER

When considering scale, do not forget moving water, especially fountains. The entire appearance of a formal water feature can be altered by a fountain. It must be in proportion with the open body of water, not just visually, but also practically. Its fall should remain within the confines of the pool, even when there is a gentle breeze. A fountain is a vertical water feature that should be regarded in a similar manner as an open body of water. Remember, however, that while the pool is dark, placid and still, the fountain is transparent and widely variable in effect, depending upon the light and its position.

This water feature appears to be larger than it really is by the shape that is employed and the fact that it is raised. This is an ideal formal pool design for a small city garden.

Although a pool with a fountain precludes the cultivation of most aquatic plants it does create a cool spacious feel to an otherwise confined area. This is a classic Moorish design.

SUITABLE SHAPES

Essentially, a formal water garden should be designed around regular shapes. Squares, oblongs, circles and semi-circles can all play a part in the configuration of a pool and should be tied in with other features in the garden landscape. These should be looked at in broad outline as shapes or combinations of shapes, for the pool must either complement them or contrast quite radically. Without an over-view of the features' outlines, this will not be easy to achieve.

Straight paths and walls suggest oblong or square bodies of water in close proximity, although it is quite acceptable for a semi-circular pool to abut a wall. Straight-sided pools are very suitable for raised water gardens, too. Not only are they visually pleasing, but they are also much easier for the enthusiastic do-it-yourself gardener to construct than semi-circular or circular features.

Square and oblong pools look more pleasing in paved areas as well. Again, construction is simpler, while a satisfactory finish is easier to achieve, as the lines of the paving and edging can be used to enhance the effect of the pool. Laying paving around a circular pool can lead to a messy overall appearance unless considerable care is taken in its design.

Interlinking pools is also more practical with square and oblong shapes, working well in paved areas. With careful pre-planning, the shapes of the paving slabs, which need not necessarily be of uniform size, can be linked to the shapes of open water. These can be linked directly with a small straight cascade, or be on the same level and offset in relation to each other, so that although they give the appearance of separate pools, in fact the body of water is one entity. This will be an invaluable aid to its successful management.

The interlinking of pools of uniform size has two main practical purposes: to spread water evenly and attractively across a narrow or awkwardly shaped site; and to allow a water feature to be enjoyed throughout a site of changing levels. Integrated into such a design can be square pockets of waterside planting that will soften the appearance of the feature, yet not detract from the overall defined shape. This method also permits the plant enthusiast to indulge his or her passion, for formal water gardens do not provide the best facilities for growing aquatic plants.

If there is anything worse than the formal design for the plant grower, it is the formal pool with a fountain, for not only does the water feature depend upon its shape and plant-free open water for its attractiveness, but the constant movement of water from a fountain also precludes plant cultivation. In this aspect of water gardening, the use of water becomes an art form, which does not cater for the practicalities of horticulture. Consequently, chemicals must be used to maintain water clarity.

Circular and semi-circular pools are the most popular for use with fountains. Indeed, a fountain looks much more appropriate in a circular pool than in a square or oblong one. This may be because of the shape of the spray, which mostly takes a rounded or arching configuration. Certainly, only small fountains or white-water geysers really associate well with square and oblong water features.

As circular pools are quite difficult to fit into hard surfaced areas, they should be considered for use in open sites, perhaps surrounded by grass. It is possible to buy edging stones and slabs that are cut specially so that they make a neat circle, but these generally look much better when used to produce a clean edge in a lawn, rather than being combined with the square slabs of a patio.

Circular ponds tend to have to stand alone as focal points, especially if their central features are fountains. A semi-circular pool, as indicated earlier, will associate happily with the straight lines of a wall. It also makes an ideal feature for the base of a wall, especially where space is limited. This not only allows water to be satisfactorily accommodated visually, but also provides an opportunity for the introduction of a water spout or mask. This is attached to the wall and discharges into the pool. Such a feature offers the enjoyment of moving water in a restricted space, and because of its position and the minimal water turbulence it creates, provides the greatest opportunity for the successful cultivation of marginal and deep-water aquatics in a formal setting.

Of course, a formal water garden need not be restricted to one shape or a series of the same shapes. Provided the outline is balanced, semi-circles can be added to oblongs or squares, and both triangles and hexagons introduced. The secret of success lies in assessing the surrounding landscape, then incorporating shapes that are complementary or contrasting in both size and proportion.

A formal pool should present a balanced appearance, the construction providing an opportunity to enjoy uncluttered open water, but at the same time allowing for the strategic use of sculptural plants. For the best effect these should all be of the same variety.

THE INFORMAL WATER GARDEN

The purpose of an informal pool is to look natural and blend into the garden landscape. Unlike a formal pool, which will often form a focal point and stand isolated in the middle of a lawn, an informal water feature should appear to be an integral part of the surrounding garden. The area of open water, alight with waterlilies, may be a focal point, but it will also be the centre-piece of the planting scheme, which will flow naturally outwards into the garden.

Much of the success of an informal water garden will be determined by the plants and features that tie it to its surroundings. The most common means of linking the pool to the landscape is either a rock garden or bog area. In many cases, the former results from a reluctance to dispose of the spoil from the pool, rocks being placed on the mound, which is then planted with alpines. This arrangement is rarely satisfactory, for it is not natural.

The informal water garden provides an opportunity to learn from nature. Indeed, disregard for the way in which water occurs naturally will be directly reflected in the effectiveness of the feature. Here the lessons of nature have been learned.

It is not only the configuration of the water feature that may be informal, but also the surrounding materials, such as cobbles, and the restrained but effective planting.

It is principally the careful selection of plant material and its arrangement in an unrestricted manner which gives a pool or other water feature its informality.

In fact, the excavated soil should be removed and any rock feature built independently. To take on a natural appearance, it should be designed to reproduce the characteristics of a moraine, an accumulation of rocks and free draining soil in which alpines may be grown. Rarely will it appear natural, or provide a suitable home for alpines, if it takes the form of a heap of sub-soil with protruding rocks.

NATURAL EFFECTS

Any rock feature should grow out of the landscape and not merely end at the water's edge. It will be easier to achieve a natural effect if there is a sloping area behind the pool and, in some cases, the spoil from the pool can be redistributed to create a suitable land form from which a rock garden can be developed. This will look quite effective if allowed to spill into the water, provided a hard rock like millstone grit, which will not flake if frosted, is used.

Any adjacent bog area should be developed as the pool is constructed. Not only will it be easier to incorporate such a feature at this time, but also deciding upon the scale will be a simpler task if the pool is not already in place. For any bog garden to be effective, it should have an area at least half that of the pool, although there is no reason why it should not be twice or even three times the area of open water.

An informal pool can have almost any shape and configuration, but kidney and dumbbell shapes are the most popular of the pre-formed types. However, this type of water feature is also relatively easy to construct by other methods, which provide good opportunities for tasteful planting and ensuring that the pool rests easily in an informal setting.

Another essential element in achieving success with an informal pool will be the thoughtful use of natural materials. It is wholly inappropriate to lay concrete or concrete paving in close proximity to the pool, since these materials will destroy any informal effect. Natural stone should be employed to provide visual relief or background, as necessary, and particularly where the relative formality of a path or edging is required. Genuine York paving, even though of formal appearance, blends quite naturally with an informal water garden design.

In many ways, the manner in which the edge of the pool is treated will determine the natural look, or otherwise, of the feature, whether it is disguised by planting or accentuated by hard landscape materials. Natural paving and rocks are good choices, but wood should not be rejected out of hand, while consideration can also be given to a cobble beach. If used discreetly, all such natural materials can add much to an informal water feature.

PLANTING

Of course, the planting scheme will determine whether or not an informal water garden is a success, for unlike other designs, it is the arrangement of plants in an unrestricted manner that gives the feature its informality. Indeed, provided the shape of the pool is compatible with good plant cultivation, the scale is suitable for the size of garden, and it is linked to its surroundings by an integral bog garden or rock feature, it could be said that planting is everything. A well planned informal water garden will provide the opportunity to grow a wide range of plants. In fact, the main reason for the feature's existence may be for the enthusiastic gardener to take advantage of this diversity of plant life.

An informal pool must appear to be a relaxed and untroubled feature, the plants all growing in a carefree manner. At first sight, this may seem easy to achieve, but behind such success there must be considerable attention to detail.

The plants must be in proportion and of a vigour that is compatible with the space available. With a small pool, the undoubted desire to grow the bold, brown poker-like heads of the reedmace, or typha, should be restrained. At least, the typical tall growing species should not be entertained, for it dislikes life in a small container and, unless carefully secured, will topple into the pool at the slightest breeze. Instead, plant the shorter growing *Typha minima,* which rarely exceeds 45cm (18in) in height, and enjoy its fat brown poker heads. These will be produced freely on plants that are easy to manage; there is no point in fighting nature.

Likewise, avoid those plants that creep and may jump from basket to basket. Using a creeper like *Lysimachia nummularia* to disguise the top of a container is fine, but having water mint (*Mentha aquatica*) or brooklime (*Veronica beccabunga*) leaping around could cause problems. These plants can invade a well planted margin, even when isolated in containers, and will swamp the unrestricted planting of a soil covered margin completely.

If such plants are avoided, and those that seed freely deprived of their flower stems immediately, management will be greatly simplified. Beware of musk, or mimulus, and the various water plantains, beautiful plants though they may be. Along with some of the common rushes, these are very generous in producing self sown seedlings.

Deciding on which plants should be grown together is very much a matter of personal taste, but several are quite beautiful and look natural in an informal setting. Contrasts of flowers, as well as flowers and foliage, should be considered, along with the beauty that a solitary example can display against a watery background, particularly in the centre of the pool. A waterlily will look majestic on still amber water, but will simply become part of a floral mix if fighting for its place among encroaching marginal plants or exuberant floaters.

With an informal setting, where the margins of the pool are likely to be heavily and colourfully planted, often extending into a surrounding marsh or bog area, simplicity in the water is the keynote. Choose a waterlily with plain green leaves and single-coloured blossoms. Avoid those that have mottled foliage or flowers that change colour with age, resulting in several blossoms of different colours on one plant at the same time. A simple white or pink waterlily, especially if it is also heavily fragrant will provide stability, dignity and an essential focal point for the water feature.

The margins of the pool are rather like the frame of a picture, but with an informal water garden, they often reach out into a bog garden. Wherever possible, the two should merge and not be obviously separate entities, although by their very nature, they will be managed as such. Some plants, like the marsh marigolds, umbrella leaf and Himalayan cowslip, will easily bridge the gap, since they may be grown in both bog and margin without difficulty.

The choice of plants for an informal water garden must take into account their vigour and the space available. Waterside irises will not advance into the deeper water and will comfortably restrain the spread of other more exuberant moisture loving plants.

Of these plants, the marsh marigolds are the most useful, for they are among the first to flower in spring, bringing sparkling colour to a dull landscape. Use their bold mounds of gold and white blossoms as focal points, but position them so that as blossoms fade and the leaves start to look jaded, other vegetation takes over.

Follow these plants with aquatic irises: bold sentinels that produce lovely flowers in a wide array of colours during midsummer. Use their upright clumps of bright green, sword-like leaves for summer structural planting, and do not clutter them with a tangle of other plants of looser habit.

BEST CONDITIONS

Where the main purpose of the water garden is to provide a means of growing as many different plants as possible, the primary aims are to create the best conditions for the well-being of the plants and to ensure that they will live in harmony together. For the most part, these objectives are not difficult to attain, for the soil and water conditions that suit the broad range of aquatic plant life are easy to achieve and leave few plants wanting. A few aquatic and bog garden plants, such as the cotton grass (*Eriophorum angustifolium*) and the clematis-flowered iris of Japan (*Iris ensata*), demand acid conditions. However, these can be achieved easily by isolating the plants' root systems, which can be done without being obvious.

THEMING

Although the keen plant enthusiast's pool often becomes the equivalent of a stamp collection, it need not look unattractive. While drifts of plants, which can create wonderful effects with their simplicity, may be excluded, by theming the plants, it is often possible to develop a collection that lives in visual harmony. The secrets of success lie in the flowering times and in associating plants by what they can do for each other, rather than for their colours and contrasts.

This means considering how mid-season plants can complement early flowering varieties, and later ones disguise the untidiness of both. Of course, it is not simply a matter of planting vigorous plants, of progressively later character, next to one another, for although hiding fading flowers and foliage is important, the plants should not be swamped. All plants require sufficient light during their growing period to perform and develop properly.

When choosing plants, it is also useful to have an overall theme in mind. Although the collection may be extremely diverse, it can be unified somewhat by careful planting. For example, all the bog garden ferns could be grown in a gloomy area, or candelabra primulas could be placed on a sunny peninsular. Large-leaved skunk cabbages can contrast with the substantial foliage of the giant Brazilian rhubarb (*Gunnera manicata*), while moisture loving grasses and decorative reeds and rushes can be kept together. This kind of theming can turn a disparate collection of plants into a scheme that is much more pleasing to the eye.

Careful thought should be given to the attributes of each plant, not only so that can they be arranged attractively, but also so that they will complement each other seasonally, as here.

OPEN WATER

Space is also important, especially in the open water. Waterlilies, water hawthorn and the water fringe look very effective when surrounded by open water. It need not be much, but it should be retained, and any encroachment by floating foliage dealt with regularly. Keep submerged aquatics, such as water crowfoot (*Ranunculus aquatilis*) and water violet (*Hottonia palustris*), away from deep-water aquatics, for these punctuate the water surface with floating leaves and blossoms. Although charming in their own right, they can detract from the general scene and produce a very cluttered appearance.

Floating plants can also be a distraction and, if possible, should be contained in one area of the pool. Although this may not always be practical, they should not be allowed to invade the space of other inhabitants of the open water. With a plant enthusiast's pool, the open-water element, even if sparse, provides the opportunity to make the pool attractive and, to some extent, allows the background of margins and bog to be a little less ordered without looking too awful.

With the marginal shelves and bog garden, initial consideration should be given to structural planting, using visually important characters like the giant-leaved *Gunnera manicata*, the majestic royal fern (*Osmunda regalis*) and the decorative rush (*Schoenoplectus lacustris tabernaemontani* 'Albescens'). If these can be planted so that they provide a background or focal point, to an extent, the other plants can be regarded as dressing.

THE SEMI-FORMAL WATER GARDEN

In design terms, the semi-formal water garden is neither one thing nor another. However, in small gardens, where it is not always easy to create a completely formal or informal scheme, it can play an invaluable role. It can often link different areas of the garden, the pool itself providing a focal point. One part of the garden may be of formal design, the approach to the pool being of a strictly regimented nature, while on the other side, the planting may be more liberal and informal.

In an ordinary domestic setting, the semi-formal pool can be most appealing, having a comfortable lived-in air that is denied those who have water gardens on a grand scale. Not unlike the family home compared to the stately property, it may not be as perfect technically or artistically, but it will be much loved, well used and very functional.

On such a modest scale, where most functions of a water feature are desired, the semi-formal pool offers the greatest versatility. Whether you want to introduce a fountain or waterfall, a collection of aquatic plants or fish, or simply some amusing ornament, each can be integrated successfully and arranged in a semi-formal setting without offending the eye unduly.

The semi-formal pool is often the best option for the family, for it can embrace aspects that satisfy all ages and interests. It can become the focus of outdoor activity, providing an interesting feature to sit around and perhaps eat and drink, or simply enjoy the antics of the fish.

The semi-formal water garden embraces the best of all worlds, although skill is needed to ensure harmony. Carefully consider not only the pool, but also the planting around it.

USE YOUR IMAGINATION

The configuration that a semi-formal water garden takes will be restricted only by your imagination. For example, one side of the pool may be formed by a border, path or patio, and the other by a lawn or groundcover. The edge of the pool does not have to be uniform throughout, and materials as diverse as timber decking and paving can be incorporated in the same feature. Planting can be used to remove the harshness of the edge where desired, although a straight clean line can also prove attractive, and peripheral planting can be set back in spaces created by removing the occasional paving slab. The opportunities for innovation are innumerable.

While it is generally agreed that a pool should be level, the surrounding ground does not have to match. Sometimes, the differing levels of a garden are major attractions, and the pool must be fitted into undulating terrain. This is often easier if a semi-formal shape is adopted, for part of the pool can be raised while the rest is set into the ground.

A partially raised pool can also link with raised and partially raised beds or borders. There is no reason why water cannot be simply one of a series of interconnected planting features; provided the structure is level overall, water can be fully integrated into a series of planted designs. This is not only appropriate where the land slopes and options are limited, but is also useful for the less able, who can enjoy the water feature at a more convenient height.

However, a semi-formal water garden does not have to be raised to be linked to other features, for planting designs can be equally successful on the flat. More often, under such circumstances, the water forms a thread that runs through a planted area: an angular channel or shape within an informal grouping of plants or, conversely, an irregular configuration among a more formal and rigid planting scheme. Each can affect the other, either reducing stiffness and rigidity or sharpening liberal informality.

PERSONAL TASTE

A semi-formal water garden relies on surrounding plants rather more than either a formal or informal design. With these, the water feature can be self contained, a formal pool utilizing the open water and strategic planting, while the informal pool is of tangled informality. In a semi-formal setting, there are no rules. The reflections of surrounding plants and their relationship with the waterside planting, together with the reflective nature of the pool, must be taken into account from the outset. The result will be very personal, echoing the taste of the individual.

However, if the pool is to stand alone, it can become very confused, for the temptation is to utilize the freedom of expression that a semi-formal feature offers and to create what amounts to a compendium of water gardening, incorporating all that is good in a single feature. To reduce some of the fussiness that can arise in this situation, and provide greater planting opportunities, it is useful to extend the water feature into a bog garden.

IMPORTANT CONSIDERATIONS

When planning a semi-formal water garden, consider it from every point of view: the practical and the aesthetic, as well as the pleasurable. Ensure maximum enjoyment by installing outdoor lighting, which will transform a modest pool and patio into an evening wonderland. Design the planting around the pool to accommodate the lights so that they are not intrusive during daylight, and arrange any fountain or waterfall so that it can be accentuated by the lights.

A semi-formal pool is one of the most exciting types of water feature, but also one of the most challenging. However, because it does not have to conform to particular design ethics or planting criteria, it is unquestionably the most variable and interesting. The only rules that you need to follow are those pertaining to the plants and fish in the context of a balanced environment. Otherwise, do your own thing.

Although plants are important in softening rocks and stones, it is the latter that give this water garden its appeal. Address the blending of hard landscape materials carefully.

This semi-formal water garden is almost like an oasis and depends heavily for its attractiveness upon the surrounding planting, using only sufficient plants to create a balance.

THE KOI POOL

In some cases, a pool will meet a very specific requirement, for some water gardeners are so focused on a particular aspect of water gardening that this takes precedence over all others. In the majority of cases, these are the koi carp enthusiasts; koi are beautiful playful creatures, and it is easy to fall under their spell.

A koi pond is not a normal garden pool, for its primary purpose is to keep the fish happy and healthy. Their welfare takes priority over garden aesthetics, but it should become an integral part of the garden scene nevertheless. The construction of a koi pond is very different to that of a normal garden pool, for an appropriate filtration system must be accommodated, together with any necessary drainage system. Consequently, fitting it into the garden landscape comes relatively low on the list of priorities.

For security and maximum enjoyment, the pool should be close to the house. It can be set into the ground or raised, the latter providing the greatest opportunity for enjoying the fish at close quarters. However, it must be at least 1.5m (5ft) deep, ideally straight-sided and devoid of any obstruction that may damage the fish as they swim about. Plants are precluded, for not only do koi tear them apart, but they also uproot them, scattering stones and soil into the water and creating an unsavoury situation that is not easily controlled.

Open clear water is necessary in order to enjoy a koi pond to the full. The peripheral planting is important visually, but generally has to be of more vigorous species in order to survive; koi carp are notoriously destructive of plant life.

In order to maintain a generous population of colourful koi and to ensure crystal clear water, a filtration system is essential. Any plants should be considered for their visual attributes rather than serving a functional purpose.

ESSENTIAL REQUIREMENTS

Unless the number of carp that will be accommodated is very modest, an elaborate filtration system will be necessary. This usually takes the form of a substantial container or containers, which must be situated close to the pond. Easy access for servicing is also essential, but this can make it difficult to incorporate the unit discreetly into the garden landscape.

If a raised formal pool is being constructed, the filter can often be built into the walled structure without being obvious. Most problems occur when attempting to adapt an existing garden pool to the needs of koi. In this situation, substantial restructuring may be required.

An informal koi pool is even more difficult to contrive if it is to retain some sympathy with the landscape. A sloping site may allow the filtration system to be placed alongside the pool and integrated into the slope, while careful planting with shrubby evergreens could help reduce its intrusion. The latter would look best in an informal landscape.

Modern koi pools often incorporate a bottom drainage system, which feeds water from the pool bottom into the filter. The pump in such systems is positioned in the filter, with water passing through the bottom drain by gravity. This has the considerable advantage that any debris is not pulverised by passing through the pump before it is removed by the filter. The design and construction of such specialised systems is best left to professionals.

CHOOSING A SUITABLE SITE

One of the best places to site a koi pool is alongside a wall, if possible near the house, for security and easy access. If no suitable wall exists already, it may be worthwhile constructing one as a garden feature, which will enable the pool to become fully integrated into the landscape. A dividing wall within the garden, which can provide a backdrop for tasteful planting, can be a boon to the water garden, for it can act as one side of the pool.

The pool itself can be constructed so that its floor level is significantly higher than the ground level on the other side of the wall, thereby ensuring that drainage will present few problems. The filtration system can also be concealed by the wall, which does not have to be substantial, but merely sufficient to ensure suitable provision for services and to tie the pool visually into the garden design. It can also be useful in providing an opportunity to add further decorative features, such as a spout or wall mask.

Any wall will help tie the pool into the landscape, even if it cannot be used to conceal the necessary services. A pool built against a wall, particularly in a confined area, will help to put more emphasis on the perimeter of the garden, creating an illusion of greater space.

WATER FOR WILDLIFE

The garden pool is an important asset for nature conservation. Even when established in an urban garden, where there may not appear to be any obvious wildlife, it has a role to fill. Surprisingly, in such extensive conurbations, there will be aquatic species that will welcome it as a safe retreat. Where they come from is often a mystery, but it is quite likely that other garden pools provide watery havens and act rather like stepping stones across a developed landscape.

Of course, pools are also important in the countryside. Many may believe that water gardens have no part to play in conservation in rural areas, but the rolling fields and woodlands are an agricultural desert. Field ponds have been drained in the name of progress, and very little natural water is to be found on farmland compared with fifty years ago. Garden pools are the last retreat for many species that have largely been driven from their traditional habitat.

A wildlife pool does not need to contain a wide range of native aquatic plants. The construction of the water feature to provide varying habitats, and the use of plants with a range of growth and behaviour ensures that it is well used by the local fauna.

STUDY YOUR SURROUNDINGS

If the main objective of your garden pool is to conserve native wildlife, it is essential to study the plants and creatures that are common to your area. Providing an additional facility for the plants, birds, insects and amphibians of your immediate locality will be much more fruitful than trying to represent the native flora and fauna of the entire country. For example, it is not truly natural conservation to bring together the cotton grass (*Eriophorum angustifolium*) and arrowhead (*Sagittaria sagittifolia*) when it is unlikely that these species would be found growing close to each other in the wild.

While purists may insist that the plants you grow should be truly local to ensure genetic purity, it may be difficult to obtain suitable material legally. The law of many countries precludes the taking of any such stock from the wild and introducing it to your garden, unless threatened by some other legal human activity.

With widely distributed species, the danger of polluting the local genetic base is seen by botanists as undesirable, but in reality, this may occur, for gardeners who wish to plant for wildlife conservation will use horticulturally raised stock. By its very nature, this is likely to be clonal: propagated originally from an individual and, when increased vegetatively, without diversity. Such plants are also likely to be the most appealing visually, as gardeners select for appearance and, naturally, choose individuals that are most attractive from which to propagate. Only in very recent times has there been an awareness of the importance of variation within a species in nature. This has led to the availability of non-selected stock, but only in very limited quantities, which is the next best thing to obtaining local plants.

By utilising native aquatic plant species, the maximum benefit can be given to indigenous fauna. Such plants are often invasive and best contained by pond contouring.

CONSERVING WILDLIFE

In reality, native plant conservation is best left to the bodies that manage nature reserves. However, water gardeners can play a useful role in conservation by providing havens for aquatic insect life and amphibians. These are not creatures that you introduce, but which appear quite naturally if your pond is set up correctly. They will be indifferent to the origins of the plants upon which they may depend, provided that these are of the appropriate species.

Deciding to conserve specific types of wildlife is pointless, for they will naturally find you if the conditions are correct. Such conditions can be created by carefully observing what grows in the ponds and wetlands of your locality. You may have little idea of the diverse aquatic fauna on your doorstep, but this will not be important if you incorporate appropriate planting. A mixture of local species will bring in migrating wildlife quite quickly, as will any body of open water, no matter how small.

LIKELY APPEARANCE

When considering a true wildlife water garden, an early appreciation of its likely appearance must be obtained. To be truthful, most creations of this kind are untidy. It is not simply the tangled growth of largely dull plant species that creates this appearance, but also the fact that the plants must remain largely undisturbed to be successful in attracting aquatic fauna. There can be none of the regular manicuring that is associated with the decorative garden pond.

However, some management is necessary, although this should be subtle and minimal. For example, one plant species must not be allowed to encroach upon another, while floating species should be prevented from obscuring the surface of the pool and reducing the light beneath, which would cause the demise of the essential submerged aquatics. In a pool with native species that grow naturally in the surrounding countryside, a variety of life will evolve, but not always to the advantage of the wildlife that you may wish to conserve and enjoy. The entire project will be fulfiling, but there must be an awareness that with such a feature, beauty is very much in the eye of the beholder.

A wildlife pool need not be dull. With careful planning it can be as attractive as a pool established solely for decorative purposes. Not every plant needs to provide a mecca for a particular insect species; some should be included for their great beauty.

TYPES OF WILDLIFE WATER GARDEN

There are two very distinct forms of wildlife gardening. One is based on the dogged desire to do something for the immediate area by providing a haven for local species, ensuring their continued diversity and well-being. This is not so much gardening as nature conservation. On the other hand, there is wildlife gardening in celebration of nature in all its wonder. This is exemplified by the water garden where aesthetics are important, but not overbearing, and where wildlife is the focus of interest and attention, whether it be attracted by a native rush or a rare bog orchid from China.

Although some may consider that the second course of action produces a vulgar assembly of wildlife hot spots, it will provide the maximum attraction and pleasure for the owner while fulfiling much of the function of the purist's enterprise. The purpose of such a water garden is to combine what is most productive from a wildlife point of view, using visually attractive species wherever possible. There is no need for this type of feature to be dull. Indeed, with careful planning, it can be as attractive as a pool established for purely decorative purposes. The secret of success is not to insist that every species must be a mecca for a particular creature. Some may be of little merit in this respect, yet will serve a useful function because of their outstanding beauty.

A prime example is the waterlily. It provides beneficial shade for creatures living in the pool, and a place for aquatic snails to deposit their eggs, but the flowers evolved originally to be pollinated by beetles of a kind that died out during the Ice Age. The waterlily survives and continues to prosper because it reproduces freely vegetatively, while other non-specific insects, which visit the flower, sometimes pollinate it accidentally. So while it is of relatively limited value to aquatic fauna, it is an essential visual ingredient of the well ordered wildlife pond.

IMPORTANT CONSIDERATIONS

The structure of a wildlife pool is quite important if it is to be a success. All the requirements of a conventional garden pool must be met, but with the addition of other beneficial features. The shape and size are not critical, except in the context of the available space and the role that the water garden will play as a feature. If you have no preconceived notions in these respects, it is a case of the larger, the better.

Two of the most important factors in ensuring a stable and diverse aquatic ecosystem are the volume of water and its associated surface area. Most of a wildlife pool must be 30-45cm (12-18in) deep, but it need not be deeper, the overall surface area being much more crucial. Most aquatic fauna functions in the upper 45cm (18in) of water, and there is a danger of greater depths functioning separately and in a manner that is not conducive to the overall well-being of the pool, particularly in the case of large bodies of water.

Shallows are very important, for they provide an escape route for mammals, such as the hedgehog, which may periodically take a tumble. They are also vital for frogs, toads and newts when they wish to leave the pond. Birds love to bathe in the margins, and while there are risks involved in encouraging them to do this, especially if they bathe having just returned from a recently sprayed field, they do provide enormous pleasure. Fish, of course, are very vulnerable if you provide a shallow area, for the heron will come fishing. This handsome bird will appear in the most urban of settings, walk into the pool and take the fish until all have gone. Despite this potential hazard, shallows are invaluable in both attracting and retaining wildlife.

An island will also be an asset, unless the pool is tiny. In this case, it can create visual clutter and restrict the area of open water unnecessarily. In a large pool, however, an island can make a safe haven for wildlife and, if constructed as a free floating structure, its shadow will offer a private and safe retreat for fish. It is also a place in which more boisterous plants can be isolated, their spread being controlled by the surrounding deep water.

As with other informal pool features, a wildlife water garden should extend beyond the bounds of the pool. It is even more important for planting to spread from dry land, through moist soil, to bog and subsequently the margins. Wildlife diversity comes with habitat diversity, and while open water will attract an enormous number of interesting creatures, thoughtfully planted surroundings will offer accommodation to all kinds of life that is attracted to water.

It is also essential to regard the wildlife water garden as a year-round feature: it need not close for the winter. Birds, in particular, can add greatly to the pleasure it provides, especially if seeding heads of reeds and rushes are allowed to remain. However, few will be ground dwelling birds, and all will appreciate a place to perch, so incorporate some woody structural planting to keep them happy and to provide some visual backbone in the gloomy days of winter.

While a diversity of plant material is essential for a successful wildlife water garden, so too is the nature of construction. While some deep areas are desirable, shallows are equally important to allow for birds and mammals to use it as a place to both bathe and drink.

A pool is a focal point for the bird population, offering a place for drinking, but also swimming. In the decorative pool ducks are tiresome, but in the wildlife pool they are an important focus, adding life and interest and controlling invasive plants like duckweed.

ATTRACTING BIRDS

Where space permits, there will be great opportunities to develop water features for attracting birds. While the general mixed wildlife water garden will certainly attract its complement of visiting birds, there are ways of turning a pool into a miniature bird sanctuary. In addition to the expected range of wild birds, which just come for a drink or to bathe, it is possible to attract waterfowl or, indeed, introduce your own ducks. Careful thought must be given to the latter, however, for although ornamental ducks are fascinating creatures, in all but the largest expanses of water, they will paddle down the margins of the pool and permit very few of the desirable and popular aquatic plants to prosper. They can be very destructive unless thoughtfully catered for.

Few gardeners have the kind of water garden that will sustain bird life permanently. In general, they will be visitors. This does not mean that they will move on from one pond or feeding site to another and be replaced by others. For the most part, they will return time and again, going off to roost or preen elsewhere. Nesting is a very territorial activity, so it is unlikely that more than a couple of pairs of unrelated species will be persuaded to nest in close proximity.

Despite these shortcomings, much can be done to attract birds. The water garden cannot be all things to all birds and, to a great extent, the area of open water will determine whether waterfowl are a viable proposition. Anything less than about 15x16m (50x20ft) will be generally unsuitable.

Where waterfowl are expected, or will be introduced, shelter must be provided, along with a place for them to rest and preen. There should be a gentle slope into the water, ideally a stone beach so that when it rains, the birds' droppings will be washed harmlessly away. This problem should be addressed early on, for not only will the droppings be unpleasant, but they will also cause the pool to turn very green by providing abundant nutrients for water discolouring algae. To some extent, the problem can be addressed by substantial planting, which will mop up much of the excess nutrients. However, where there are waterfowl in quantity, green water will always be a potential problem, which ultimately may have to be addressed by the use of algicides.

The shelter required by ducks will be minimal, but if they are to be encouraged to stay, some shrubby planting nearby will help by providing them with privacy. Where the pool is large enough to warrant an island, this will often encourage the birds to nest, although not all ducks are ground nesters; some prefer to inhabit burrows.

Planting plays an important role in keeping birds happy, and although plants can be difficult to sustain, this is by no means impossible if some form of protection is provided early on, especially for the more resilient reeds and rushes. Schoenoplectus of all kinds offer good cover, as does the spire reed and the various bur-reeds. These also provide a limited amount of food, but it is plants like the arrowhead and the Canadian wild rice (*Zizania aquatica*) that water fowl regard as delicacies. The overwintering buds, or turions, of the arrowheads are popularly known as duck potatoes, being scooped from the mud by the birds during winter, while the seeds of zizania provide a reliable and much appreciated food resource from autumn into winter.

OTHER CREATURES

While birds are the most visible forms of wildlife to be attracted to a natural water garden, many other creatures will live there, too. For these, there are other aspects to consider. Unless a pool that is home to waterfowl is of a substantial size, it is unlikely to offer a suitable environment for amphibians. These like clean water and abundant plant growth, especially underwater vegetation, in which they can hide and which offers some protection for their tadpoles.

Frogs, toads and newts may not always occupy the same body of water, but one or more species will often live happily together. They will appear quite naturally and suddenly if the conditions are correct, although it is quite possible to introduce them as tadpoles and allow them to naturalize.

The only problem with a pond devoted to wildlife lies in ensuring that it looks good. While the fascination with ducks or amphibians can become all consuming, their home should also have a pleasing aspect. Although the plants will be essentially functional, to retain some dignity and beauty, they should be planted in bold drifts or groups. Not only are they likely to be more appealing, but also of greater value than when planted in isolation. A wildlife water garden will never look stunningly attractive, but there is no reason why it should not be pleasing to the eye if the essential plants are positioned carefully and, where possible, the best decorative variety of each species is selected.

Toads are welcome additions to the garden, preying on insect pests. They enjoy clear water and abundant plant cover.

A pool devoted to wildlife should be generously planted if it is to remain pleasing to the eye. Choose vigorous reliable plants and arrange them boldly. A natural balance is often difficult to achieve in a wildlife feature, especially where ducks are present.

THE NATURAL WATER GARDEN

A gardener contemplating a water feature for the first time may believe that a natural water garden is the ultimate goal: an open body of water that has been created by nature and which is, therefore, in total harmony and sympathy with its surroundings. Although visually this may appear to be the case, in practical terms, a natural water garden can be the most difficult type of water feature to both organize and maintain.

There are two kinds of natural water garden: the true naturally occurring body of water, and that which is created to have the appearance of a natural water feature. The genuine article is usually satisfactory visually, for its location will have been decreed by natural forces. While its general outline may merit some development, in all other respects, it is likely to be at a suitable point in the landscape.

Although the position of a naturally occurring pond may be satisfactory for an open-water feature, it may not be perfect for plants. Shade from nearby trees, for example, may preclude a balanced planting. Such a pool may not necessarily be a clean and healthy body of water when left to its own devices, so some adjustments to the immediate environment may be required.

However, provided there is a constant water source and the water levels do not fluctuate substantially, this type of feature can be one of the most rewarding to manage. There are so many opportunities for artistry in planting when working with a natural pond. As long as the behaviour of various plant groups is understood, an easily maintained picture can be created. Only when planting with ill-mannered species are problems likely to arise.

A natural pool is usually visually pleasing, but not always the best for plants. Waterlilies demand full sunlight and a pool which can retain a constant water depth if they are to prosper.

Often, a naturally occurring pond will need some subtle landscaping to ensure that it is practical to manage. This usually involves providing a more gentle marginal slope so that the edges can be planted satisfactorily. Sensitive grading of the surrounding soil can greatly enhance the appearance of a natural body of water, without affecting its ecology or stability.

CONTRIVED NATURE

An artificially contrived, natural looking water feature is probably the most difficult for the water gardener to create. Most domestic gardens are unnatural in their position and design, and here we are trying to introduce a natural countryside feature. Considerable skill is needed to get it right, but, with care and an understanding of how water appears in a natural landscape, it is possible to achieve such a feature.

Primarily, water only appears at a low point, so when deciding how it will fit into the garden, it is vital to consider the existing landform and determine how water can be introduced, either by using existing features, or creating the minimum of disturbance. Careful ancillary planting should always be considered before moving earth. Often, this can produce a deception that suggests the pond is in a natural setting and at an appropriate level in the landscape, when in fact that is not the case.

Natural bodies of water rarely produce constricted or sharp edges. Water erodes the soil in these situations, while the surrounding contours are always smooth and gentle. Steep sides only occur naturally where the ground around the pond is immovable, normally when it consists mostly of rock and the water has washed out the soft soil between.

LARGE WATER FEATURES

Some natural water features are extensive and provide their own particular benefits and problems. The greatest benefit is the minimal change in water temperature and, therefore, the greater ease with which an ecological balance can be maintained. Rapid temperature changes encourage the regular development of algae, a potentially major problem in small bodies of water. In large areas of water, where algae appears to be troublesome, the problem is often caused by the run-off of agricultural fertilizers from surrounding land, which introduces additional nutrients.

Wave action is probably the most important factor to be aware of with a large body of water. A surprising amount of erosion can be produced by the action of waves created by the wind. In some cases, netting must be fastened to banks and planted through to ensure a stable edge. This may even be necessary where the land slopes gently into the water.

As with a small pool, nature generally creates its own slopes, which are the result of natural erosion. With large bodies of water, the edges are often much shallower than those of ordinary ponds, and in many cases consist of stone beaches. These are formed because the soil is gradually washed away until only an accumulation of stones remains. When constructing a very large pool or lake, it is prudent to incorporate such unplanted beach features, especially at the main potential points of erosion. Planted edges are good for general stability and the prevention of sheet erosion, but they can be undermined by strong eddies and currents.

Larger water features benefit from relatively slow changes in water temperature and are therefore less likely to suffer severe algal problems, although such open bodies of water are susceptible to damage from wave action and erosion.

THE BOG GARDEN

A wide range of interesting plants, which cannot normally be cultivated elsewhere, can be grown in a bog garden. It is a natural adjunct to a water garden, neatly linking the pool to the surrounding garden and providing great opportunities for extending the season of plant interest.

Many of the plants that are popularly grown in bog gardens can often be seen in mixed or herbaceous borders, but unless they happen to be growing in damp spots, they will be mere shadows of their true selves. Daylilies, or hemerocallis, revel in wet soil, along with astilbes and hostas. There are even bulbs that love damp conditions, such as the summer snowflake and the quamash, or camassia. All give a peak performance in a richly-organic wet soil. Conversely, some of the plants that are grown as marginal subjects will adapt to bog garden conditions. Marsh marigolds always look more robust when growing in damp soil, rather than standing water, while water forget-me-not and brass buttons are equally content in the bog garden. Some plants, however, are specifically bog garden dwellers: for example, the brightly coloured candelabra primulas, the clematis-flowered iris of Japan and the umbrella leaf.

SEASON-LONG COLOUR

For the majority of gardeners, the main objective with any feature is to achieve season-long colour and interest, and a bog garden is no exception. Here, the aim is easier to achieve than with a pool, for woody plants are available that provide year-round height and structure, as well as winter colour.

A bog garden provides an opportunity to grow a wide range of plants that cannot be successfully cultivated elsewhere. It can be either created as a self-contained feature or provide an attractive adjunct to a pool or streamside.

Many bog gardens or streamside plantings can look bold and strident if flowers alone are considered to be a priority. The most attractive planting associations are created when the soft colours and textures of foliage plants are harmoniously incorporated.

The coloured-stemmed cornus are classic examples, producing bright red, purple or yellow stems that sparkle in the winter sunshine. Provided that they are cut down each season just before they burst into leaf, they will come up trumps every year. The same applies to some of the willows, not the large weeping types, but wonderful restrained characters with bright upright stems.

Sprinkle the ground around such plants with *Primula rosea*, a very early spring flowering primula, much like an exotic, iridescent pink primrose. This makes a contrast with the colourful stems just before they are pruned, and provides a convenient link with the short growing double marsh marigold (*Caltha palustris* 'Flore Pleno'). Although grown primarily in the margins of the pool, it will make a lovely golden hummock in the spring bog garden.

The umbrella leaf (*Peltiphyllum peltatum*) also associates well with marsh marigolds. Its globular heads of rose-pink flowers, borne on naked stalks, wander across the bog garden by means of stout rhizomes. These smother the fading remains of early flowered subjects with green and bronze leaves as spring turns to summer, but rarely cause them any harm. As their leaves unfurl, the undoubted stars of the bog garden burst into flower. Hot on the heels of the lilac, blue or white drumstick primulas come their candelabra counterparts. Few late spring or early summer displays can surpass the sight of their tiered whorls of blossoms. Plan to grow these easy-going plants in a way that will permit self seeding, not crowding them with other plants, but planting in groups of the same variety so that they form spreading colonies.

FOLIAGE AND FORM

Such planting schemes can look bold and strident on their own, so it is a good idea to soften them with foliage. The moisture loving ferns are ideal for this, especially the ostrich feather fern (*Matheucia struthiopteris*) with its pea-green, fiddle-like heads, which transform rapidly into luxuriant shuttlecocks. The sensitive fern (*Onodea sensibilis*) creeps and forms a pale green understorey, but starts off rose-pink as the fronds unfurl. It spreads harmlessly among clumps of perennials, tumbling over the poolside into the water. For a focal point of architectural foliage there is the majestic royal fern (*Osmunda regalis*), a giant of a plant with handsome bright green fronds that turn bronze at the first hint of frost. This looks superb at the water's edge, its regal presence being reflected in the still clear water.

However, the most magnificent foliage effects in the bog garden are created by hostas, such is their diversity of colour and stature. Formerly referred to as plantain lilies, in recent years, these easy-going plants have enjoyed a cult following, but justifiably so, for their handsome broad leaves and occasional striking flowers make them some of the most versatile plants for wet conditions. They look best when planted in groups or drifts, as few as three plants of a kind producing a pleasing effect. Their exotic appearance can be used to suggest a tropical environment.

A bog garden will be a tremendous asset, particularly when developed as an integral part of a water garden. However, even without an accompanying body of water, it can become a valuable feature in its own right.

THE STREAMSIDE

It would be easy to confuse the streamside with the bog garden, for it appears that similar conditions exist, with plants growing beside water. In reality, the conditions beside a stream are almost the complete opposite of those found in a bog garden, so careful consideration must be given to the plants that will be grown and how they will be presented for maximum effect.

A natural streamside will be extremely difficult to plant successfully, but once this has been achieved, there will be few more beautiful sights. The major problem is the water level, for whereas a bog garden has a consistent and adjustable moisture level, and adjacent bodies of water can be controlled to maintain the ideal conditions, a stream has a will of its own.

Few plants occupy the stream bed, especially if it is fast flowing. Peripheral planting is not only important to provide colour and interest, but makes major contribution to the prevention of erosion and also disguises the often untidy edges of the feature.

In winter, particularly after snow melt, a stream is likely to become a raging torrent. Unless securely rooted, any streamside planting may be dislodged, while the banks may suffer scouring and sheet erosion. Of course, the plants will not require too much water in the winter, and in the summer, they will need keeping damp at a time when the stream may be reduced to a trickle.

THE ARTIFICIAL STREAM

If an artificial stream is constructed, particularly if made from a liner, it will enable true bog plants to grow on a permanently wet site. The liner should be passed under the area to be planted, allowing the soil to be kept damp. This can also be done with a natural stream, the bed being lined along with the adjacent banks. However, this produces a hazard that is not present when the stream is controlled by a pump, for in a winter surge, great sections of bank may be swept away. Although the plants will stabilize some of the soil, they will not secure it completely, owing to the sandwich effect produced by the liner.

However, where the arrangement does work, this kind of streamside can be magnificent, for it can be developed as an extended bog garden. The plants will prosper in the damp soil, and interesting reflective effects will be created in the stream, provided that it is not flowing too quickly. With a natural streamside that is improved in this way, a certain amount of care must be taken to ensure that the plants do not dry out if there are seasonal variations in the water level. In such a case, leaving the banks without a waterproof membrane may be preferable, particularly if watering will be difficult to arrange.

THE NATURAL STREAM

Where planting takes place directly into the stream bank, care must be taken not to encourage erosion, and also to select plants that will tolerate drier conditions, as well as winter inundation. In such circumstances, species that are usually regarded as border perennials, but that grow better in a bog, should be the first choice. Astilbes, with their plumes of brightly coloured flowers, are most adaptable, so too are the various filipendulas. These might look weary under very dry conditions, but they are tolerant of ordinary moist garden soil and really come into their own when it is wet.

Purple loosestrife (*Lythrum salicaria*) is a similar proposition, along with its brightly coloured named varieties, while the exotic and easily grown musks, or mimulus, do well in all except the most spartan of conditions, their height and lushness of foliage being related to the amount of moisture that is available to them.

Mix these with various grasses if the going is tough, for the very tolerant *Phalaris arundinacea* 'Picta' looks almost the same as the moisture-dependent variegated water grass (*Glyceria maxima* var. *variegata*). It is easy to cheat by using some of the drought-tolerant stipas instead of rushes. They do not bear close examination, but the overall effect is similar. The important point to remember is that an effective streamside planting is achieved by the arrangement of flower, foliage and form that grow well. It has nothing to do with doggedly persevering in the cultivation of plants that technically may be streamside plants in nature, but everything to do with producing a convincing picture.

Bulbs are excellent for planting into the established bank of a natural stream without causing disturbance and encouraging erosion. Rockwork also provides great stability.

ADDITIONAL OPPORTUNITIES

Streamside planting offers additional opportunities for the skillful garden artist if the unpredictability of soil conditions is used to advantage. Bulbs can be introduced, where they would be impractical in a bog garden. Daffodils, scillas and chionodoxa are all easy-going, will tolerate a wide range of soil conditions, and are not seriously bothered by temporary flooding. Plant them among other perennial streamside plants to create a spring show before the former break into growth. Only the cuckoo flower, or cardamine, is likely to create any unexpected contrasts, while the summer flowering perennials will disguise the fading bulb foliage with their burgeoning leaves.

Of course, a streamside does not have to be cultivated. Some of the most effective features have grass right down to the edge. This may not be easy to mow, and it is inevitable that some grass cuttings will enter the water, which may lead to problems. However, where slopes are carefully adjusted to accommodate a mower, a really classy effect can be created.

Plain grass to the water's edge can look startling, but remember that this can be highlighted with bulbs, such as the shorter growing, early flowered kinds that die back swiftly and do not produce bulky leaves. The Greek windflower (*Anemone blanda*), with its bright starry blossoms, is superb, as are the bunch-flowered crocuses. These are available in both spring and autumn flowering forms, which will extend the natural streamside season.

THE WATER MEADOW

A genuine water meadow is a natural extension of a river, being the winter flood plain which, during summer, is often constantly damp and produces a lush crop of grass. Traditionally, water meadows have been grazed, and the plants that live in them have either benefited from the grazing or have been bypassed by the animals. They are places where self seeding occurs and there is a natural regeneration of the attractive flowering plants.

In many ways, a water meadow is akin to an alpine meadow and, like that habitat, is predominantly a spring and early summer feature. This is an advantage, for it will be well into summer before the floral show in the water garden itself really gets under way. However, a potential problem is that it is difficult to keep a water meadow looking tidy from mid-summer onwards: if the meadow is to flourish naturally, you will need to establish some sort of compromise between allowing the decorative plants to seed into the sward and keeping the grass under control.

The double cuckoo flower is a wonderful spring blossoming perennial for the water meadow. It is easily and quickly established as a plug or pot grown plant.

Much can be done to make the situation tolerable by cutting neatly around and through the area to create sculpted shapes in the grass, in the same way that a lawn containing naturalized bulbs would be mown. This leaves long grass, but neatly manicured edges, and with an occasional swathe cut through for a path, the meadow can become an interesting addition to the garden. This is particularly true if you are interested in wildlife, for the natural mix of vegetation will encourage insects, especially tiny moths and butterflies.

As an adjunct to the water garden, the water meadow is superb, allowing the tangled informality of the natural pond to spread out into the garden. When linked to a wildlife water feature, it rarely looks scruffy or ill at ease. Only if you try to incorporate a meadow with the more manicured water garden, especially the formal water feature, will it look alien.

Provided that the sward is predominantly grass and not a mixture of weedy vegetation, a water meadow can be very beautiful. The grass should be of a type that can be mown satisfactorily, for although in the countryside clumps of tussock grass and rushes will invade the water meadow, they are rarely appealing in a garden setting and will cause mowing problems. A good clean cut towards the end of the summer, and consistent mowing until the first sharp frost, will ensure recovery of the turf, guaranteeing a wonderful green foil for the early flowering plants of spring.

SUITABLE PLANTS

There can be few more beautiful sights than the cuckoo flower (*Cardamine pratensis*), with its pale lilac flowers and fern-like foliage, spreading from the bog garden into the water meadow. Allow it to mix with the snakeshead fritillary (*Fritillaria meleagris*), planted in informal groups right up to the water's edge. Few gardeners consider bulbs as plants for wet places, but the snakeshead fritillary always looks its best when scattered among lush grass in very damp conditions.

Ragged robin (*Lychnis flos-cuculi*) is the star of the summer water meadow, with its strong wiry stems and starry, somewhat spidery red flowers. The foliage is rarely noticeable when growing among grass, which is useful since it is not particularly attractive. Allow ragged robin to spread naturally, scratching away a few patches in the turf, during late summer, into which it can self seed. Use water avens (*Geum rivale*) as companion plants to ragged robin; they are so different in habit and appearance that they complement each other beautifully. They are not fiercely competitive and will grow happily together, both requiring the same regime to prosper. A spreading perennial with rather coarse leaves, the geum produces nodding blossoms in shades of orange or pink on wiry green stems.

Carpet around the geum with the marsh bird's foot trefoil (*Lotus uliginosus*) for a most pleasing effect, allowing the small-leaved creeping stems to spread freely. These will be smothered in yellow and often red tinged flowers, not unlike those of a miniature sweet pea, and followed by masses of tiny pods during late summer.

Such a contrast of water meadow plants can be most effective in a very small garden where a true water meadow cannot be created satisfactorily. Indeed, it is possible to combine the most popular wild waterside plants in a rough-and-tumble floral carpet, which has many of the attributes of the water meadow, but is not a true re-creation of this natural feature. For a small patch by a wildlife pool, this is a perfect compromise, offering a diversity of plant life of benefit to wildlife, which otherwise would be difficult to produce. However, it will need very careful managing if it is to look tidy and cared for throughout the year. Regularly removing the worst of the dead and dying flower heads is important, not least of all to prevent undesirable self-seeding.

REGULAR REPLACEMENTS

Of all the water garden features, a water meadow is probably the most difficult to contrive and maintain naturally. If you want to create such a spectacle, you will have to take a very pragmatic view, particularly with regard to natural regeneration. In theory, it should work for all except the tiniest of areas, but in practice it may not. Be prepared to replace plants regularly, inserting them into the turf in the autumn or spring. It is possible to adopt a management regime under which the meadow is mown quite closely, immediately flowering is over and the patch looks untidy, any adverse effect on the reproduction and longevity of the flowering plants being tolerated and made good with new stock.

A water meadow is usually created as the result of periodic flooding or a high water table associated with a stream or river. It offers damp conditions and the association of grass, which if carefully maintained produces a sustainable environment.

THE INDOOR POOL

If there is sufficient light and warmth, a wide range of beautiful and exotic aquatic plants can be grown in an indoor pool, turning it into a tropical extravaganza. In a heated conservatory, the pool can provide an almost year-round cavalcade of colour, although with dull winter skies and shorter days, some of the most spectacular aquatic plants may sulk.

CREATING AN EXOTIC EFFECT

Of all tropical aquatic plants, one of the best known and easiest grown is the Egyptian papyrus (*Cyperus papyrus*). This is a towering plant of somewhat spidery palm-like appearance, which retains its character throughout the year if the correct temperature is maintained. It would be too tall for a small pool, but the shorter growing garden variety, 'Haspan', can be used to almost equal effect and may even be grown in an indoor tub or aquatic planter.

The banana-plant-like thalias offer similar benefits and, while looking regal and tropical, are really quite tough. Grow these alongside the papyrus for a truly exotic tropical effect, disguising their containers by planting around them with parrot's feather (*Myriophyllum proserpinacoides*), a hardy scrambling plant that responds well to warm conditions.

Indoor pools are often small and complemented by moving water. Although this places some constraints upon planting, the surrounds can be successfully dressed with a range of attractive flowers and foliage. Container grown, they are easily maintained.

As with an outdoor pool, waterlilies will be the centrepiece of an indoor water feature. The tropical forms will only grow well in still water, so a fountain or cascade cannot be allowed. However, the great beauty of these plants will compensate for the lack of moving water, especially when it is realised that their glory can be enjoyed day and night.

Tropical waterlilies are divided into two main groups: the day flowering and the nocturnal. Of all aquatic plants, the night blooming waterlilies are the most spectacular. Imagine sitting beside a pool in the evening, with exotic blossoms up to 30cm (12in) across unfurling as the sun sets. These big velvety blooms can also be picked and used as indoor table decorations for a special dinner party. Although of exotic appearance, if kept consistently warm, tropical waterlilies are not difficult to cultivate, but they are rarely a year-round proposition, benefiting from a dormant period when they should be lifted and stored in cool frost-free conditions. For the best results, they should be treated rather like tuberous begonias, being started into growth afresh each spring.

Lotus, or nelumbos, should be treated in a similar manner when grown in the confines of an indoor pool. Although they do not have to be lifted each autumn, doing so will provide the opportunity of replacing the compost each spring when replanting takes place. This is sensible, for the lotus is a gross feeder, but it is also a rapid grower.

Lotus are legendary plants of tropical water gardens, being known to gardeners and non-gardeners alike. In some parts of the world, they have religious significance, and they also play an important part as a food source. In the main, however, they are prized for their decorative value.

The common sacred lotus (*Nelumbo nucifera*), which is the parent of most modern hybrids, is a large plant that rarely can be accommodated in a modern conservatory pool. Where there is sufficient space, it makes a spectacular sight, with its huge plate-like leaves and deep rose or pink blossoms. It is best replaced by one of the shorter growing types, such as the double-carmine-flowered 'Momo Botan', which rarely exceeds 45cm (18in). and will even produce beautiful flowers in a tub kept in a conservatory.

TUB CULTURE

Consider the tub and similar containers as viable options for indoor aquatic cultivation. Many of the popular varieties can be grown successfully as solitary specimens in tubs of water with soil or aquatic compost on the floor. Do not try to create a balanced aquatic environment by mixed planting: enjoy the individual plants for their own sake.

If there is room for several containers, they can be assembled as a water feature. Group them together and, provided that they are of similar height, surround them with a length of log roll. This is sold in garden centres for edging paths and beds. It comprises short logs, of uniform length and diameter, held together with strong wires. The log roll will provide a neat edge to the feature. Being flexible, it can be adjusted as necessary to allow the removal of any tub that has finished flowering and looks untidy.

Of course, even smaller features can be planted to good effect, being placed in the conservatory or living room. Large terracotta or earthenware vases and bowls, intended for outdoor planting, can be used for growing individual plants. Often, they are decorated with oriental designs, which can be tastefully matched with appropriate looking plants to produce a special effect. Tropical aquatic plants need not be solely the prerogative of the indoor pool owner; they are sufficiently versatile to be enjoyed by anyone, irrespective of circumstances.

An attractive sunkenconservatory pool filled with tropical waterlilies. It is necessary to maintain a display of this kind artificially, by using either filtration or algaecides, as it could not be sustained naturally.

MOVING WATER

FOUNTAINS AND GEYSERS

Fountains have decorated pools for centuries, but only in recent times have they become readily available to the domestic gardener, and economical to run. Until the advent of the submersible pump, the establishment of a fountain was largely the prerogative of the landed gentry and the wealthy. The modern pump has not only brought fountains within the reach of ordinary working people, but its compactness and versatility has also made possible water acrobatics that, in the past, would have been rather difficult to arrange.

Fountains can serve as focal points, often appearing as watery sculptures. They are also ever changing in the light and bring a magical sound to the garden.

FOCAL POINTS

Fountains are best employed as focal points, making use of their wide and varied plumes of spray and, where the opportunity arises, the sculptures from which they can be induced to play. A fountain that emanates directly from the water's surface will only be a feature while the pump is switched on, but one that flows from a wood nymph or dolphin leaves behind an attractive feature.

The position for a fountain must be chosen very carefully, taking into account not only the effects of any breeze and the height and spread of the spray in relation to the pool, but also light and shade. Observe the proposed site over a period of two or three weeks, assessing the light, particularly direct sunlight, at different times of the day in varying weather conditions. Always choose a sunny spot for a fountain, but wherever practical, arrange for it to be seen from the main viewing point through shade, especially when employing a plume of water or geyser. This will help make it stand out dramatically.

It is also important to look at the fountain's surroundings, considering how the spray will appear against the various backgrounds that will be seen from all the viewing points. A fountain is an almost transparent sculpture, so much of what is behind it will be seen through the spray and, perhaps more importantly, may detract from its decorative effect. Even the sky can cause extreme displeasure to the owner of a badly sited fountain.

Of all the possible backgrounds, a plain hedge or wall is best; this will allow the fountain to be the focus of attention. With large plumes or geysers, it can be pleasing to frame them, and the edge of the picture formed by the garden as a whole, with the tall straight trunks of trees or pencil-like conifers. More modest arching sprays can be complemented very successfully by the rounded shapes of small bushes. For the most part, the scene should be uncluttered; even within the pool, the stately foliage of reeds and rushes should be the only distractions.

In most cases, fountains will look best when combined with artificially constructed water features. They are so definitely man-made that they do not rest easily in a natural landscape. The large plume of water, which appears from beneath the surface and suggests, although it does not imitate, a geyser, is the only configuration that really works in a pool that is intended to appear natural. However, if this is not a practical proposition, consider a waterfall or cascade.

FORMAL SITUATIONS

Fountains belong in formal situations and can be either modern or classical. In most domestic gardens, the classical look is still preferred, with sculpted maidens and nymphs of the last two centuries finding the greatest favour. In many cases, they do not look at home in their settings. Although made of reconstituted stone or imitation lead, which can be very convincing, the contrast they make with modern brick, concrete and tile leaves a lot to be desired. Where the pool is an adjunct to a modern patio or terrace, consider using up-to-date materials such as steel and chrome for the fountain structure. If this does not appeal, simply use the water on its own, tossing it into the air to form an aquatic sculpture. A fountain pushing up a jet from just below the surface of the water associates well with most materials and surroundings.

OTHER ATTRACTIONS

In addition to the visual aspect of fountains, the sound that they create can be used to advantage. Indeed, for many gardeners, the sound of moving water is as great an attraction as its movement and the play of light upon the spray. A gentle tinkling in a small patio pool is charming and lends much to a sense of tranquillity, while the gushing of a plume of water brings excitement and a desire to stand, stare and listen.

Of course, not all fountains are so flexible and such independent features. Where space is limited, a wall fountain can be employed. Although offering far fewer possibilities than the traditional kind, this does provide an option for the gardener who has no pool, nor the room to install one. So, irrespective of the size of your garden and personal circumstances, there is a fountain to suit, but its success will rely very much upon the initial planning given to the project. Like a cascade, a fountain must be a carefully considered integral part of the water garden, not an appendage that is a convenient means of enjoying moving water.

It is not necessarily the moving water itself which provides a focal point. Many fountains are integrated into statuary and art in all its configurations, the moving water complementing the handiwork of man.

A water feature need not be extensive in order to be attractive. The simplicity of this channel with its precisely placed fountains gives this small garden an air of grandeur.

SPRAY PATTERNS AND SEQUENCES

The fountain unit creates the means by which elaborate sprays can be produced. For most pool owners, the source of its power is a simple, totally submersible pump to which jets offering various spray patterns can be attached. The choice of spray shapes and patterns is enormous and, as experience is gained, a range of interesting configurations can be created. For the newcomer to water gardening, it is best to select a simple jet initially, bearing in mind the principles of design that determine the most suitable arrangement.

With a circular pool, a single, thin vertical jet will be the most effective. However, this would look ill at ease in an oblong pool, where two or three evenly spaced jets, running down the centre, would complement the longer shape. Another possibility for the rectangular pool, and also for any long, canal-like feature, would be to arrange for a jet of water to rise from each corner and be directed into the centre. Although this arrangement works well in theory, there are practical constraints when dealing with large pools, for it would be impossible to operate the system from a single submersible pump. Therefore, several would need to be employed, or a larger surface pump installed. As with all

A quiet corner tastefully planted to enhance the stillness of the water which is only punctuated by two simple sprays. A well conceived idea which has produced a welcome retreat from the pressures of modern life.

aspects of water technology, the practical limitations must always be addressed thoughtfully.

HEIGHT AND SPREAD

Tradition dictates certain rules about the height and spread of a fountain spray, but these cannot take into account individual circumstances, especially concerning the exposure of the pool and the constraints imposed by the wind. Most gardeners agree that in a windy garden, it is prudent to restrict the height of a fountain jet to half the radius of the pool. Although very practical, this may not produce a very appealing feature, in which case, the fountain should be given extra height by using a statue or similar ornament, to which the pump can be connected. If conditions are generally calm, as may be the case in an enclosed walled yard, the jet of water can be equal in height to the diameter of its pool or basin. While a simple single jet of water can be used very successfully as a focal point, it can also be utilized to divide a space or interrupt a vista, encouraging the visitor to pause before moving on. Alternatively, a single-jet fountain can be incorporated in an asymmetric design to offset and balance another garden feature nearby.

If a single jet, with all its simplicity, is rejected in favour of a multiple-patterned fountain spray, the rule book can be discarded, as anything goes. Today there are so many different configurations available that it is almost impossible to provide guidelines for their use. The only advice that can be given is that if it looks right, it probably will be right.

When selecting a suitable spray arrangement, consider the possibilities of combining it with lighting. Few garden features can compare with a pool in which a fountain is illuminated at night. Although most lighting systems are installed completely separately, some fountain units not only incorporate a lighting attachment, but also have a special automatic control that will switch from one colour to another. However, for the ultimate in sophistication, equipment is available that will make beautifully lit fountain jets dance to a programmed musical recording.

Doubtless, the majority of gardeners would find such innovation too much, but careful consideration should be given to the options that are available among the spray patterns and sequences. It is possible to buy special sets of jets that allow variations in pattern to suit the gardener's mood and circumstances. With modern submersible pumps, these are readily interchangeable, being merely snapped on and off the outlet pipe.

SPECIFIC SHAPES

The spray patterns available include some very specific shapes. Of the more popular examples, the silver arch is considered to be the most beautiful. This produces twelve ribbon-like jets of spray, which shoot into the air, forming an inverted central cone, then fall gracefully into the pool in a glistening circle. The crystal cone offers a similar pattern: a vertical inverted cone comprising a profusion of crystal-like droplets. The droplets soar upward from the fountain jet in a rotating widening cone, appear to hesitate, then fall back musically into the water.

Bursting-star spray patterns are equally popular and consist of a vertical cone of water, which soars upwards and is supported by a second level of up to six plume-like streams. The water droplets burst from the two rotating levels, falling back into one another.

In many parts of Europe, a traditional pattern has been the fleur-de-lis, which has retained its popularity despite all modern innovations. With either a two-tier or three-tier configuration, it looks at home in most pools, even those of modern design. However, for it to be really successful, it must be placed in a pool at least twice as wide as the spray is tall.

Whatever initial decision is taken with regard to a fountain, changes can always be made with very little effort. There can be few other parts of the garden where it is possible to alter the appearance so dramatically by doing something as simple as slipping a new fountain jet onto a tube. This versatility enables the gardener to create a specific mood or to match a change in the water garden's surroundings whenever required.

Water is used imaginatively in this tiny pool to produce a moving, twisting focal point unspoilt by peripheral planting. The mood of the fountain will change with the light and breeze.

WATERFALLS AND CASCADES

When it comes to creating dramatic effects, waterfalls and cascades, even modest examples, offer great opportunities. The power of water as it tumbles over rocks gives the impression of something that can be awesome and unstoppable, but at the same time of great beauty. That beauty changes, too, being affected not only by the strength of the flow of water, but also by the effect of light on the moving water.

FOLLOW NATURE

The character of a waterfall or cascade should be copied from nature, even if it will not be created from natural materials. An understanding of how waterfalls are formed is essential if the right ambience is to be created.

Waterfalls and cascades occur where the ground level changes, and can be created by swirls of water cutting through soil and stone. However, the most spectacular effects, and the kind of features that the majority of gardeners desire, result from water wearing relentlessly through solid rock and washing it away.

The strength of character that a natural waterfall or cascade can convey should be translated in the garden. Be bold and make a generous feature. Nothing looks worse than a small fall, fed by an inadequate pump. Indeed, pump technology can make or break a waterfall. An adequate pump with spare capacity is essential if the correct effect is to be created. With the range of modern equipment at the disposal of water gardeners, there is no excuse for producing anything other than a moving spectacle.

The character of the waterfall should be copied from nature, even when it is not constructed wholly from natural materials. An understanding of how water falls is essential.

SUITABLE MATERIALS

The materials from which a waterfall can be constructed are many and varied, but most water gardeners choose rock. Provided that this is sufficiently tough to withstand the battering meted out by a waterfall, there is no doubt that it is the safest material to use from a design aspect.

In the majority of gardens, a waterfall will form part of a rock garden, which is a particularly suitable arrangement. At the same time, it will often provide a perfect niche for plants that might be slightly difficult to grow. For example, the hardy moisture loving maidenhair fern, which loves life in a rocky pocket, will revel in the constant moisture from the spray produced by the waterfall. Dwarf mimulus, such as 'Whitecroft Scarlet', will be in their element in these conditions, too. So apart from being a natural link between the rock garden and pool, the waterfall allows the establishment of plants with special requirements.

To create a natural-looking waterfall, the rock must be carefully selected and the feature built so that all the strata lie in the same plane. The waterfall should appear to be an integral part of the rock garden, and not something imposed upon it, which is a major problem when preformed plastic or fibreglass cascade units are employed. Blending these into a rock garden waterfall is extremely difficult; they are more suitable for setting into a soil bank, where they can be disguised by heavy planting that will spread over the edges.

A waterfall in a rock garden outcrop need not necessarily be of the same material. It is quite possible to incorporate what, at first sight, may be considered an alien material if the rock feature is regarded as the stage, and the waterfall is tucked in behind. Under such circumstances, an obviously artificial waterfall can still be very appealing and will not detract from the natural surroundings. It can be likened to adding a sculpture to the garden. Many materials are suitable, but slate and marble are often recommended, although indulging in the latter will require a deep pocket.

For a really unusual material, choose glass, which, along with steel, is being used increasingly in modern formal gardens. While glass may not be to everybody's taste, it must be remembered that there are many kinds to choose from, the slightly opaque reeded glass and dusky smoked varieties offering great artistic possibilities. The flow over a modern glass, or glass and steel, waterfall or cascade need not be as turbulent as over a fall that attempts to re-create nature. However, a constant, consistent flow, which will send water over the lip evenly and cleanly, is absolutely vital for a satisfactory effect. Make sure that a drip channel is cut into the underside of any flat glass spill to prevent the water from running back beneath it.

INTEGRAL ELEMENT

Whatever style of waterfall or cascade is eventually decided upon, take care to integrate it into the garden landscape. There is a great danger of the waterfall becoming an appendage to the water garden: something that is imposed upon it because of a desire for moving water. While the latter is very desirable, it must look as though it belongs. To ensure that this is the case, employ a waterfall or cascade as a linking element that will lead the eye gently down a slope, or cause it to drop and follow a sudden change in level. Where appropriate, strengthen the line of a path or steps by running such a feature alongside.

A waterfall should be an integral part of the garden landscape rather than an appendage to a garden pool. Here the waterfall provides the main focus of attention.

This water feature demonstrates the many ways in which moving water can be enjoyed in the modern garden. Gently flowing or frothing and tumbling, it can create moods and ambience that are unachievable with any other medium.

STREAMS, RILLS AND CHANNELS

Streams can take on a number of aspects, depending upon their position and how they are constructed. A naturally occurring stream will be a great pleasure and, if long established, can rarely be improved upon, although radical changes to its surroundings may mean that some adjustments to it become necessary.

Often, a natural stream may have flowed through fields for centuries before housing development completely alters the way in which it contrasts with and complements its surroundings. Doubtless, the way in which such a stream has contoured the landscape in its immediate vicinity will be appealing, but this must be carefully considered within the overall plan for the garden landscape. Small alterations to the flow, or a dam or diversion, can make all the difference to a natural stream's appearance, although it is unwise to alter the flow of water into or out of a property without con-

The contours of a naturally occurring stream are generally pleasing and only require dressing with colourful moisture loving plants. Care must be taken when planting not to disturb the banking so that soil erosion begins.

sulting the relevant local authorities and anyone else who may be affected, such as your neighbours.

An artificial stream is much easier to deal with, and can often be readily accommodated in the garden landscape. However, it must have definite points to flow to and from, but should not end up as a simple straight or curved channel. If contriving a beginning and an end is difficult, use planting to disguise the arrangement.

A pool will often form the focal point, but it need not be at the end of the feature, as with a waterfall. It can easily be the point from which a stream flows and disappears behind a shrubby planting. If the level of the ground is awkward, cleverly arranged planting will make it possible to feed the stream underground and, by means of a simple submersible pump, persuade it to appear as a spring elsewhere.

Such a stream provides the sound of moving water, a wonderful environment for aquatic insect life, an opportunity to discreetly incorporate a filter, and a great chance to indulge in extensive waterside planting. If space is limited in the margins of the pool, a stream will make it possible to extend marginal planting throughout its length, for with an artificially constructed stream, creating reliable wet waterside growing conditions will be quite easy.

When introducing an artificial stream into the garden, take care in blending it into the landscape, especially with regard to the distribution of excavated soil. It may be tempting to dig out the stream and place the soil on the banks. In some cases, this may be acceptable, but for the most part, it creates a very artificial appearance, making the stream look like a canal. Observe natural streams in the countryside and try to emulate them. They have evolved as a result of water running through the softest or lowest ground, and have gradually carved out their passage. An artificial stream, even if intended to look man-made in a more formal setting, should still obey this simple rule if it is to be pleasing to the eye.

A tumbling stream creates the best effect; not only does it plays with the light, but it also creates more musical sounds. Placed alongside a path it encourages the visitor to explore.

CROSSING POINTS

When considering a stream, do not forget the opportunities that it will provide for adding stepping stones or a bridge. Neither will be functional without flowing water, and their value as additional garden features should not be underestimated. Whether the simple stone clapper type or an elaborate oriental structure, a bridge can bring as much interest to a garden as a gazebo. If it is to be elaborate, make it a focal point and design your stream to meander beneath it.

Stepping stones are useful for crossing a stream, although few domestic gardeners will have a stream of sufficient size to warrant more than a couple. However, the stones themselves can be very pleasing to the eye and, in addition, may be cunningly employed to vary the flow of the stream and appearance of the water.

PRACTICAL CONSIDERATIONS

In terms of construction, a stream will look best if created in levels. In other words, the floor of the stream should be level for a certain distance before dropping, by means of a small waterfall or merely the depth of a stone, to a new level, and so on. The water will be pushed along by a pump, which may be switched off from time to time. When this occurs, it is very important for the appearance of the stream that it retains a certain amount of water. This also has a practical purpose, since the capacity of the stream system and pond will exceed that of the pond, leading to flooding if all the water is allowed to drain into the pond.

The same applies to rills and channels. The latter are very formal features, while the former are normally more natural looking, although they can be either. With a channel, everything will be much clearer and angular. Use it rather like a stream, but where appropriate, be eccentric. It is an artificial feature and can be employed to great advantage, especially in guiding visitors around the garden. Place a channel beside a path to lead the visitor on, but create side channels and surprises, dressing the feature with carefully selected plants to tease the eye.

CONSIDERING YOUR BUDGET

The construction of a water garden can be a very expensive exercise, so not only is it important for everything to be correct from the beginning, but consideration should also be given to the most economical way of handling the task. In some cases, this should be to obtain a quotation from a local builder or landscaper, for if you are not a practical person, the job should be handed to a professional.

It is essential that you know what you want, both visually and to ensure the well-being of the fish and plants. An expert builder is unlikely to be an expert pondkeeper, so an understanding must be gained of all the principles involved in establishing and sustaining aquatic life. A detailed brief of your requirements should then be provided for the builder. Do not tell him his job, for he will know much more about how the concrete should be mixed and laid or the brickwork built, but it is important to ensure that your requirements for the fish and plants are met, and that expedient building techniques do not compromise your brief.

It is wise to engage a builder to undertake substantial hard landscape construction. Rarely are builders pondkeepers and so a happy compromise between the requirements of the fish and plants and the constraints of construction should be agreed.

In most cases, when a water feature is built from brick or with concrete, engaging a professional will ensure a better and more cost-effective result than doing it yourself. Only the skilled do-it-yourself enthusiast is likely to produce a feature that looks right and works properly. Although the job may appear to be cheaper if you do not count the cost of your own labour, it certainly will not be more economical if your carefully laid concrete leaks. When seeking a professional, make sure that he belongs to an appropriate trade organization, which will not only indicate that he knows what he is doing, but will also provide a means of obtaining some redress if things go wrong.

FORWARD PLANNING

Careful planning is the key to economy when employing a contractor or adopting the do-it-yourself approach. It is essential to know exactly what is required and to make no compromises about it. If using a pond liner, dig the excavation first, then purchase the liner. So many gardeners buy a liner first, then attempt to create a hole for it – a recipe for disaster. In such cases, the pool is unlikely to look right, and wastage of material is almost inevitable.

Quality is also very important: you get what you pay for with liners, as with everything else in life. If you plan to remain in the same home for the foreseeable future, durability will be vital. When a lined pool will be planted with aquatics in containers and have a soil-free floor, a top-quality manufactured pool liner will be better value in the long term. On the other hand, if a wildlife pool is to be created and the liner will not be seen because it will be covered with a layer of soil, a considerable saving can be made by purchasing a stack or truck cover. These are waterproof sheets of varying size and often bright colours, but they are as good as the real thing and about a third of the price.

Economies are difficult to make elsewhere, for equipment like pumps and lighting, which are necessary if a pool is to be enjoyed to the full, must be paid for at the going rate. Again, quality is important, and with a pump, choosing a slightly more expensive model with a larger capacity than is required initially will be a good investment. Apart from the fact that as enjoyment of the pool develops, greater demands are likely to be made upon the pump, operating it at less than its full capacity will ensure a long and trouble-free life.

A successful water garden depends upon sound structural planting. The main focal plants should be established quickly, then followed by those that are essential for the pool's well being.

Of course, moving water need not be introduced to the pool immediately; you may not be able to afford everything at once. However, careful planning before any work begins will ensure that such improvements can be made easily at a later date. For example the conduit that will carry the cable to the pool can be laid during construction. Simply thread a string through it so that when the time comes for the cable to be installed, it can be tied to the string and pulled through.

One thing that your budget must allow for in the first year is essential planting. Certain plants, especially submerged aquatics and deep-water subjects like waterlilies, must go in during the first season. They will ensure a reasonable balance within the pond from the outset, guaranteeing that fish and other aquatic life can be introduced with safety later.

When contemplating a water garden, your budget must embrace any costs involved in running services to the site, the provision of a liner or prefabricated shape, and the basic plants to enable a satisfactory natural balance to be achieved. Everything else can be added after this, as money becomes available. However, it is worth considering the inclusion of a bog garden at an early stage when a lined pool is being planned, for it is much simpler and cheaper to create such a feature from an extended pool liner than to add it later.

If, in the short term, economics really do not permit you to indulge in a fully fledged garden pool, consider a tub garden. An enormous amount of pleasure can be derived from such a simple water feature for a minimal outlay.

PROBLEM-SOLVING

CHOOSING A STYLE

I have quite a small garden, so my water garden has to fit into it neatly. I would like to draw out a plan so that I can create different effects before I decide on one that I like, but I do not know how to go about it. Please advise.

Each site is different, offering a variable amount of space for the comfortable accommodation of the pool and its associated features. When making a plan, it is important to include all the features that can be seen from the water garden and, equally, the features from which the pool can be seen. With a small garden, this may comprise the entire plot.

When transferring the positions of the existing features within a garden to the plan, the first task is to establish a base line. This is a fixed line from which points can be measured accurately so that they can be plotted on paper without difficulty. A wall or path makes a good base line, but if such a feature does not exist, you will have to use pegs and string. The base line should be marked off at 1m (1yd) intervals, using pegs.

From the base line, measure out to each feature, which may be a tree, the edge of a border, etc. The measurement must be taken at right-angles to the base line, and the easiest way to check this is with a large builder's set square. This can be cut from plywood, making the sides 3, 4 and 5 units long to ensure a right-angle.

All this information should be set down on squared paper, taking each square as having sides of 1m (1yd). Plot and mark in the measured points, where appropriate joining them together to give accurate representations of borders, paths, etc. When adding trees to the plan, make sure the spread of the canopy is represented accurately and, with the exception of fastigiate trees or conifers, also regard this as the root spread.

If you already have a plan showing the positions of services like water, electricity and gas, include these as well. If not, locate the points at which they enter your home and, if possible, where they end up in the street (sometimes, a small cover will give an indication of this). When this can be discovered, assume that the pipes run in direct lines and draw them in. There is nothing more frustrating than hitting a water pipe during excavation and having to rethink your scheme completely.

Shade is also critical. Draw in areas that are heavily shaded during the summer months, for it would be unwise to include any part of a water feature at these points.

In a small garden it is essential to plan carefully before introducing a pool. Draw everything out on paper, incorporating features such as sitting out areas.

Although a professionally drawn plan would include the ground levels, for the home gardener who will be very familiar with his or her own garden, this will be unnecessary. For the purposes of this exercise, levels can be remembered and, if required, checked on the spot.

Once the plan is complete, you can decide where the pool is to be located. Take a sheet of tracing paper or, better still, acetate and place it over the plan. Draw the pool on this, arranging its size, shape and position to give the most pleasing effect visually and accommodate the requirements of the plants and fish. The proportions and position can be changed as often as necessary until you achieve the best arrangement. Once the position has been decided upon, the precise dimensions of the pool and any surrounding bog garden can be drawn on the plan. Having done this, take the part of the plan that embraces the water garden and scale it up on another sheet of squared paper, making the squares, say, three times as large. This will allow you to draw in items like edging and marginal shelves.

Is it possible to design a pool that is both functional as a garden pool and, if large enough, suitable for use as a swimming pool?

There are all kinds of potential health hazards to address in using a garden pool as a swimming pool. However, if there is no possibility of fertilizers or other chemicals seeping in, which would not be appreciated by the fish either, there is no reason why this should not be done if the pool is deep enough. Certainly, dual-purpose ponds are becoming very popular in central Europe, and articles about their construction may often be found in gardening and home care magazines from that part of the world.

The important factors are the depth and the marginal plantings. It is undesirable to have too many waterlilies in the centre of the pool, as they may impede a swimmer's progress. Consequently, a depth of 2m (6ft) is desirable, as this will only permit certain very vigorous kinds to be established successfully. The sides of the pool must also be vertical, except in the shallows where the marginal plants are to be established. This effectively root prunes them and confines their activities to clearly defined areas.

The best swimming and garden pools are natural features that are spring fed. It is more difficult to achieve a happy association of plants and humans in an artificial pool, unless it is of considerable size. Planting should follow similar principles to the ordinary garden pool, although if a filtration system is added, much of the underwater vegetation may be unnecessary.

Finally, if you decide to create a pool like this, remember that swimmers must be able to get in and out easily. A simple handrail or support may be required.

The latest development in outdoor swimming pools incorporates a water garden. These are pleasingly planted and yet provide a deep central area for recreation. They are now appearing in many temperate parts of the world.

CHAPTER TWO

BUILDING A POOL

It is vitally important that the construction of a water garden is right from the beginning. If you put a rose bed or herbaceous border in the wrong place, or make an error in the preparation or planting, it will not be too tiresome to start again. However, if you put a concrete pond in the wrong place, or omit any of the essential practical design elements, correcting your error will be a major task.

So consider the design very carefully, particularly the portion that is below water. This should not only accommodate all the plants and fish so that they live in harmony, but also make essential maintenance as easy as possible. While only those elements of the pond that are above the water will be seen, from the construction angle, it is the pool's profile that enables the gardener to achieve the plant effects he or she desires.

If the profile is right, the material used to construct the pool will not be critical; all will produce equally good growing and living conditions for plants and fish. However, cost and, perhaps more importantly, your practical ability and inclination will all play important parts in helping you decide which material to use.

A flexible liner is generally considered to be the easiest to install, followed by a pre-formed shape, and lastly concrete, which in most cases should be entrusted to a professional. Clay puddling is another option, although it is rarely satisfactory unless a bentonite blanket is used. Again, this is probably a job for an expert.

One of the most useful things to do, when assessing the best material to use, is to take a look at some established pools of different construction. Since the finished feature will remain for many years, its quality should be paramount. Therefore, provided the material you choose will produce the best visual and practical returns, whether you undertake the construction yourself or not will be of less importance.

A successful water garden results from the careful design of the structure to accommodate all the necessary plants for an ecological balance, and from choosing the correct position for it.

SITING A WATER FEATURE

The position in which a water feature is placed is absolutely crucial to its well-being and the appearance of the garden around it. In nature, water is usually found at the lowest point in the landscape, which is where it looks most natural, even if the garden surrounding it is manicured and formal. Why this should be is difficult to say, but no doubt the reason has something to do with light and the reflective qualities of the water. A water garden pool placed where it is higher than the surrounding ground will look ill at ease and, like the mountain tarn, will appear to be impatient to tumble to a lower level.

A formal raised pool is an exception, however. There is no reason at all why water should not be brought closer to the gardener. Indeed, one of the great pleasures of a raised pool is being able to sit beside it in comfort and close proximity to the fish and plants, observing the busy life that every water feature embraces. When formally contained, it does not look alien to the landscape, for all formality is alien to nature, and as such, we are looking at a contrived picture, rather than what is intended to be a natural experience.

CONSIDERING VIEWPOINTS

Despite the desirability of placing a water feature at the lowest point in the landscape, it may not always be practical to comply with this ideal. The lowest point may be beneath a chestnut tree, which would provide totally unsuitable conditions for the pool's inhabitants, or it may be completely removed from the direct line of sight from the house. So a compromise may be necessary. This can be achieved by redistributing excavated soil so that the pool appears to be at the lowest point in the landscape, or by the cunning use of plants to deceive the eye over the lie of the land.

One of the most important considerations, when positioning a pool, is that it should always look its best from the

The position in which a water garden in placed is vital for its success. It must be in full uninterrupted sunlight and away from overhanging trees. It should also rest easily in the lower part of the landscape, only formal water features like this defying such a rule.

centre of all activity, the house, whether it will be seen from the living room, the kitchen or the patio. Sometimes, however, when the garden is on a larger scale, it may be desirable to place the pool in a hidden corner where you come upon it unexpectedly, but this is a luxury that most of us cannot afford the space to accommodate. Separate garden rooms and secret places are not so easy to fit into a modern domestic garden, and with the pool providing a focal point, most gardeners would rather flaunt it than hide it.

Remember that a pool will be seen from several different viewpoints. Obviously, one will be used more than the others, but do not overlook its appearance from any upper rooms in your house. When viewed at ground level, some pools are a delight, but when seen from above they are near disasters. If you are only likely to look at the pool from upstairs through the bleary eyes of early morning, this may not be so significant, but if you spend a considerable amount of time living upstairs, the view of the water garden from above will be very important.

Bear in mind, too, that whatever you do to the pool to make it look good from one viewpoint will affect the way it appears from other positions around the garden. You will be creating a three-dimensional work of art, which will be observed with varying degrees of frequency from different angles, and the best face possible must be put on each.

If the pool is required for the mirror-like qualities of the water, rather than as a place in which to grow aquatic plants and keep fish, there is the additional consideration of reflection. Careful observation must be made of anything that, through reflection, might impinge upon or improve the picture. The proximity of buildings can produce an ugly intrusion, while the stark presence of trees, especially during the winter when they are leafless and the pool is a cool, still glassy mirror, can be an absolute joy.

COPING WITH TREES

Trees can be a great blessing, in a garden where there is a pool, providing a lovely foil and often reflective contrasts, but equally they can be a nuisance. Obviously, the annual discarding of their leafy canopy, in the autumn, creates potential problems. The leaves fall into the water and decompose, causing all kinds of unpleasantness. Fallen leaves can be coped with reasonably easily by netting the pool in advance

ESSENTIAL REQUIREMENTS

Aesthetically, the correct siting of a water garden is crucial, but even more important is the effect the position has on the well-being of the plants and fish. If you get that wrong, the whole project will be a disaster. It must be in an open situation, receive plenty of sun and have sufficient depth, and variation of depth, of water to accommodate all the plants and creatures that are necessary to make the water garden a balanced, viable proposition.

The pool will be viewed from several points in the garden and so should fit comfortably into the landscape from all angles. Here a sitting out area is softened by pot grown plants.

In some gardens it is more pleasing to come upon the pool unexpectedly. Here it is discreetly surrounded by planting.

of autumn and regularly sweeping them up. However, other undesirable aspects, which are less obvious, must also be taken into account from the outset.

The disruptive nature of some tree roots to a pond must not be underestimated. Some of the more vigorous species, such as willow and poplar, can certainly lift a pre-formed pool, crack concrete, and disrupt a liner. Many gardeners like the idea of growing weeping willows beside their pools, but do not be tempted, for the foliage of willows contains a toxin akin to aspirin which, if it gets into the water in quantity, can harm the fish. Willows are trees of the riverside, where their fallen leaves are washed away by the current. If your thoughts turn to a weeping flowering cherry, rather than a willow, think again. All cherries and plums are potential hosts for over-wintering waterlily aphids, which are the bane of the pondkeeper's life.

Respect the beauty of trees, but regard them all with suspicion, and think very carefully before introducing them, not least because of the potential shade that they may cause as they develop. Remember that a pool must have full uninterrupted sunlight to be a success.

SOIL AND GROUNDWORKS

Having come to a conclusion about where the pool is to be placed to be most pleasing on the eye, and having acquired full knowledge of what the plants and fish will require to prosper, you will need to give consideration to the realities of the site. Although, for the most part, a pool will look most at home in the lower areas of a garden landscape, it is these that are often naturally wet.

The first reaction to this is that it is an obvious advantage, but when modern construction materials are used, it can be a mixed blessing. Even when a natural form of pond construction, such as clay puddling or bentonite linings, is proposed and the pool is to become a natural feature, fed by natural water, disasters can occur. Even if such a material is used to contain the water, remember that it is still a waterproof membrane and, as such, embraces most of the physical attributes of pool liners and concrete.

The problems associated with a naturally low lying area will become most apparent during winter. Without the formal excavation of a pool, a very wet, or even flooded, pool-like area will appear, forming a quiet placid splash of water

A natural low lying area may seem to be the ideal place for a pool. Visually this is so, but it is very important that appropriate drainage is provided and a proper construction is made. The advantage of surrounding damp ground can be seen here by the bush vegetation.

on the garden landscape. Once an excavation has been created, however, its true nature will be revealed.

During winter, the water table of the ground rises dramatically. This is the body of water within the soil, which effectively acts like a sponge. The amount of winter rain determines how soaked the 'sponge' becomes. On occasion, the soil will be completely saturated, and water will lie on the surface. This water appears through pressure from below, and it is not quite the same as water that is unable to drain away because of surface compaction. Although not apparently under any pressure, soil water from the water table is deceptively powerful. In fact, it is so strong that it can disrupt the best constructed ponds.

Unless your pond is extensive, unrelieved ground water pressure can push the pool liner into the pond, almost like a balloon. It can also cause a small prefabricated pool, which is not well secured around the edges, to pop out of the ground like the cork from a bottle. Such is the pressure of ground water. So an awareness of this potential problem, and finding a method of dealing with it, should be high on the agenda when deciding where to place a pool.

Land drains will not resolve the problem in a part of the garden that frequently floods and is saturated. Under such circumstances, any idea of establishing a pool in that area should be abandoned. However, land drains can resolve most of the problems that very wet soil has the potential to create. So if you are thinking of putting your pool in a part of the garden that is often very wet, lay some suitable land drains before you begin construction.

The soil structure can also have an influence upon the construction method used. Most gardeners have a preconceived idea of how they will build their pond, long before they have finalized the site. In most cases, the structure or quality of the soil will be unimportant, but some soils do place constraints upon construction methods.

It is difficult to fit a liner into a free flowing sandy soil because the excavation is unlikely to retain its shape. On the other hand, it is much easier to fit a pool liner into an excavation dug out of clay or a heavy loam soil, where the slicing spade cuts through the ground like cheese. However, clay soils expand and shrink, depending on their moisture content, which is not good news for anyone contemplating a concrete pool. The often quite marked soil movements beneath the concrete, especially during a hot dry summer, when shrinkage can be considerable, may cause the even the most expertly laid concrete to fracture. If you are uncertain of what lies beneath the surface of the soil, it is a good idea to dig a small trial hole in the proposed site of your pond and examine the soil structure carefully before committing yourself to a particular pool construction method.

A pool that is heavily shaded will never prosper. All aquatic plants demand maximum sunlight in order to function properly and produce a healthy balance in the water.

SERVICES

Apart from providing drainage, you should take care in identifying services; not just those that might be required, but also those that already exist in the garden. Nothing is more frustrating than deciding upon a site for all the right reasons, then discovering that a gas or water main passes right through the middle of it. Modern service installations will often be deep enough to pass harmlessly beneath the area that you want to excavate, but older systems may not be far beneath the surface. Apart from the danger of disrupting your domestic supply through accidental damage during construction, it is not desirable to have them close to your water garden.

Of course, some services will be essential. If moving water will be part of the feature, an electricity supply will be vital, and if you want to top up the pool to compensate for evaporation, a discreetly placed tap will be useful. Thus, before finally deciding upon the exact position of the pool, the presence of any existing services must be determined, and you must be sure that it is practical to establish any that are required.

DESIGNING FOR SUCCESS

The aesthetics of a water garden are largely determined by the configuration of the open water area, whether this is intended to complement the planting or is the main reason for the pool's construction. Plants are also important in providing colour, form and height. Put these together and the overall effect of the water feature is achieved.

KEEPING FISH HAPPY

Fish are as much a part of a water garden as plants, although some gardeners do not rate them highly. It is true that a well planted garden pool will not be ideal for a fish fancier who wants to practise selective breeding, but it will be a pleasant haven for a modest selection of decorative fish that will live and breed happily with little attention.

Even though some gardeners have no intention of becoming fish fanciers, introducing fish to a water feature is worthwhile. Not only do they add life to the pool, but they also act as a fine biological control of most aquatic insect pests.

When planning a pool it is important to take the requirements of fish fully into account. They ideally require a minimum depth of 45cm (18in) and plenty of surface area.

Common goldfish and shubunkins, golden orfe and green tench are all quite resilient. They will survive the winter in as little as 30cm (12in) of water, although 45cm (18in) is preferable. This will also protect any fancy goldfish, such as fantails and moors, which would be at risk in shallower water. However, it is not only the depth of water that is critical; the surface area must be as large as possible to permit gaseous exchange.

A well planted pool generally provides sufficient cover for ornamental fish, especially when submerged aquatics are liberally introduced. Although fish enjoy basking in the sunshine, in really hot weather, they require some respite, and submerged and floating foliage can offer this. Such plants also give some protection from predatory cats and herons, but only during the active growing season; in the winter, the pool will be bare and the fish exposed. To protect fish when the pool is devoid of foliage, a few rocks should be placed on the floor of the pool so that the fish can shelter beneath them. This will not interfere with any planting in the pool. Such shelters are available to buy ready-made for small water gardens.

Apart from the generous introduction of submerged aquatics, the positioning of marginal plants is also quite important. As far as possible, make sure that the entire marginal shelf is planted. Any vacant spots will be quickly spotted by birds and used as bathing places, often with disastrous results. In country areas, birds often bring pesticides with them on their feathers; even a small trace of such chemicals can kill fish. If birds are permitted to bathe freely, this becomes a very real threat. To counter this, provide them with their own separate bird bath and make sure the margins are full.

BEARING WILDLIFE IN MIND

Whether your pool is a deliberate wildlife feature, or merely attracts wildlife in the way that pools inevitably do, some consideration should be given to their presence. A pool will often be the watering hole of many small animals, including hedgehogs. If its margins are heavily planted to exclude birds, there is a great danger that deeper areas will be used for drinking with the attendant risk of some of these animals taking a tumble and drowning.

Hedgehogs and other small mammals can usually swim for a short time, so if an escape route is provided, such tragic accidents are less likely to occur. Some pre-formed pools incorporate a small ramp to allow escape, but a similar feature is quite easy to install in any pool. A simple narrow board with small wooden cross-pieces would be perfectly adequate.

The pond profile is very important. The structure beneath the water affects considerably the appearance of the planting above. Here the irises and rushes are controlled in their spread to some degree by the arrangement of the marginal shelf and the depth of water.

THE POOL PROFILE

The design of a water feature should not only be pleasing to the eye, but also embrace all the requirements of aquatic life. Plants must be happy in the home that you have provided and, equally important, must be easy to maintain. Pest and disease control and feeding regimes should be borne in mind, too. However, the most important design element, from the practical growing and management point of view, is the profile of the pond structure. There are four groups of plants to consider, each of which has its own specific requirements.

The waterlilies and other deep-water aquatics, such as the water hawthorn, require deeper water than the marginal plants. However, this rarely need be more than 90cm (36in), for all the popular waterlilies will grow successfully in this depth of water. This is also the maximum depth at which other desirable deep-water aquatics will be happy. A garden pool does not depend upon a great depth of water for its success, but rather the balance of a sensible depth with a generous surface area.

If practical reasons dictate a shallower pool, there are many waterlily varieties that can be grown successfully in much less water; some pygmy waterlilies will even flourish in as little at 15cm (6in) of water. In fact, the majority of desirable deep-water subjects will also adapt to shallower conditions, but bear in mind the well-being of any fish before settling on a shallow depth.

A small pool which owes its open water to a carefully considered profiling. The deep central area successfully prevents incursions by the desirable but vigorous marginal plants.

PLANTING DEPTHS

It is important to designate specific areas of the pool to appropriate plant groups. Submerged plants and deep-water aquatics are grown on the pool floor, while marginal plants require a shelf. Bog plants inhabit wet areas around the pool edge.

Submerged aquatics must have sufficient depth in which to remain submerged in a water temperature that does not become too high during summer. Most popular submerged aquatics are happiest growing in 45-90cm (18-36in) of water. Beyond that depth, the water becomes dark and gloomy, impairing growth, while shallower water can heat up and cause dense submerged growth to decompose.

Most submerged plants naturally flower at, or just above, the surface of the water and, with few exceptions, they will grow to a length dictated by the water's depth. Provided this

When constructing an area of deep water, it is important to allow for both the presence of waterlilies and the reflective qualities of the water body itself. Plant interest can be increased by thronging the margins with colourful marginal and bog garden subjects.

is within the guidelines given, the majority should develop successfully. Only the likes of the consistently short growing hair grass (*Eleocharis acicularis*) will be adversely affected by excessively deep water or very shallow conditions. Conversely, there are rootless submerged aquatics, like the hornwort (*Ceratophyllum demersum*), that suspend themselves in the water at the most advantageous position, irrespective of depth.

Floating plants are not too bothered by depth, although shallow water can pose problems by heating up during the summer. Some of the smaller floaters, such as the frogbit (*Hydrocharis morsus-ranae*) resent warm water and may rot; on the other hand, fairy moss (*Azolla caroliniana*) would not object. So if circumstances force particular conditions upon you, you will need to select plants carefully to avoid problems.

Although deep water does not have any adverse effect upon floating plants, it will be colder in spring than shallower water, which will impair the re-appearance of the overwintering plants. With few exceptions, floating aquatics produce winter buds, or turions, which spend the winter on the floor of the pool. As soon as spring sun warms the water, they come to life and start to grow. Cold deep water obviously slows this process, and they may be two or three weeks later in coming to the surface.

MARGINAL AREAS AND BOGS

The marginal area of a pool provides the best opportunity for growing interesting aquatic plants. It can be of varying depth, as most marginal plants are natural stream or riverside dwellers and are used to periodic drying and inundation. Consequently, they will grow in merely damp conditions or several centimetres of water. A generous marginal shelf that will accommodate a standard planting basket, both in width and depth, and permit 5cm (2in) of water over the top of the basket is ideal.

The way in which the margins are distributed around the pool is purely a matter of taste, but they should be as long as possible if they are to co-ordinate visually as a whole. Short lengths of marginal shelf, sufficient to take a couple of baskets, look untidy. They really only have a place in a formal pool, where architectural plants such as reeds or rushes are desired in the corners or spaced along its edge.

A bog garden will be a valuable addition to most pools for, except in very formal circumstances, it will tie the feature visually to the surrounding garden. It will also offer great opportunities for growing a wide range of interesting plants that would be difficult to accommodate in other parts of the garden. Consider the bog garden from the beginning. Do not construct the pool, then decide that a bog garden would be a pleasant feature, for it will be much more difficult to add. A bog garden should be a natural extension of the pool. Particularly if you are planning to build a pool using a flexible liner, a bog garden can be accommodated quite easily and effectively (see pages 100-101).

DESIGNING FOR SAFETY

However carefully you construct and plant your pool, it will always be potentially dangerous, especially for children. While a child can drown in very shallow water, you will reduce many of the risks by making the maximum depth not more than 90cm (36in). Planting around the edge, together with the use of shallow margins and bog garden extensions, also reduces the chances of an accident through some one slipping into the water.

Obviously, the edge of the pool produces the greatest hazard, so any edging materials should be chosen with care. Paving should be sufficiently wide to accommodate a foot and, as far as is practicable, have a non-slip surface. Where visitors may be encouraged to stand to look at fish, make sure that the paving is not only secured firmly, but also that there are no gaps into which a woman's high-heeled shoe may become wedged.

Electricity can also pose a danger, so use only the recommended armoured waterproof cable when installing a pump in the pool. The latter will require removing from the pool during the winter and, if you have fish in the pool, you may want to replace it with a pool heater, so a connection close by is essential. This should be safely housed beneath a paving slab that can be removed rather like a manhole cover (see also page 151). All electricity supplied to the pool should be connected via an RCD circuit breaker.

A pool is a great attraction to children, but potentially dangerous. Teach children to respect water and the life which lives there.

KOI POOLS

Before constructing a koi pool, it is worth learning a little of the background of these remarkable fish and of their behaviour. Although the koi carp is a distant relative of the goldfish, its way of life is almost completely different. While the goldfish will swim serenely beneath waterlily pads, koi carp will thrash about and create havoc. They also have special environmental and nutritional requirements, which must be met if they are to prosper. Remember that they are highly sophisticated in-bred fish and, as such, are not as easy to satisfy as their more lowly cousins.

The environmental requirements of koi have a considerable bearing upon the pool construction. A koi pond must have filtered and constantly recirculated water with a stable pH, very low ammonia, nitrite and nitrate levels, and oxygen close to saturation point. To achieve this, the pool must have a suitable filtration system, which should function continuously. For a koi pool to be really successful, it should also be at least 1.5m (5ft) deep and have a capacity of at least 9000 litres (2000 gallons).

Traditional garden pools do not make good koi ponds, so a specialized structure is necessary. This can take the form of a raised pool, built from concrete blocks with an outer skin of facing bricks and the inside coated with a waterproof render. Alternatively, a large plastic container, as used for water storage, can be set within a brick surround. This will not only provide a more pleasing appearance, but can also

Traditional garden ponds are not good for koi as they are usually too shallow. A koi pool should ideally be up to 1.5m (5ft) deep and of at least 9000 litres (2000 gallons). Plants are used only to decorate the edge, as koi are notorious for destroying them.

add stability. For guaranteed strength, opt for a double-skinned wall, which should be tied together and built on a proper foundation.

FILTRATION

When constructing the pool, take into account the filtration requirements. Although, in principle, these are the same as for a garden pool, they will be on a much larger scale. Experienced koi keepers would expect the biological area of the filter to be at least a third of the pond area and, preferably, a half. The system will also be more efficient if this part of the filter is constructed as one chamber, rather than being divided into smaller sections. Some modern filters use less conventional designs and incorporate high-tech media with very different flow rates to the normal arrangement. If you decide to use one of these, it is essential to follow the manufacturer's instructions to the letter.

Most koi owners favour an in-ground, gravity fed filter. This is built on the same level as the pond and has large input pipes from bottom drains in the pond, the pump being situated towards the end of the system. Many pool owners contrive to construct their own systems because it seems to be more economical. However, if you are taking your first steps into koi culture, this would be folly, for without actual experience, it would be difficult to achieve the correct set-up, even with the guidance of a koi expert. A manufactured system of the correct size, fully integrated into the construction programme from the beginning, will be the most satisfactory, and almost certainly the most cost-effective, way forward. For more on filtration, see chapter six, pages 274-277.

To be successful a koi pond should have a good filtration system and through flow of water. Koi will destroy most aquatic plants and they also dislike fast moving water.

CHOOSING POOL CONSTRUCTION MATERIALS

POLYTHENE LINER
Only useful for larger excavations if sandwiched between two layers of soil; low burst resistance; difficult to install, has no elasticity; perishes easily if exposed to sunlight; not easily repaired.

PVC LINER
Flexible and easily installed; often available in a range of colours; economical to buy; said to have a useful life of 10-15 years; can be repaired.

LDPE LINER
Flexible and easily installed; economical to buy; has a long life; can be repaired.

BUTYL RUBBER LINER
Flexible and very durable with a pleasing unobtrusive finish; expensive, but easily repaired.

POLYTHENE PRE-FORMED POOL
Considerable resistance to sunlight degradation; little choice of shape; often poor accommodation for plants

PLASTIC PRE-FORMED POOL
Cheap and resistant to sunlight degradation; more difficult to install than most other pre-formed pools; little choice of shape; often poor accommodation for plants.

FIBREGLASS PRE-FORMED POOL
Resistant to sunlight degradation; the most expensive pre-formed pool, but very durable; little choice of shape; often poor accommodation for plants.

CONCRETE
Versatile; can be used to create a wide variety of water features; needs skilled installation; often difficult to repair successfully, but if properly installed, very durable.

CLAY (INCLUDING BENTONITE)
Difficult to install; demands skill to maintain successfully.

BENTONITE (CLAY) BLANKET
Excellent for natural ponds, especially large water features; demands skilled installation; self-healing if punctured.

POOL LINERS

The pool liner offers a greater degree of flexibility than any other pool construction method, but there is a potential for making mistakes at the marking out stage. Indeed, defining the area to be excavated, and ensuring that it meets all practical and aesthetic requirements, is a task that should be carefully undertaken before the liner is purchased. This will ensure that it will adequately line the excavation without necessitating short cuts, which may have undesirable long-term consequences.

DEFINING THE POOL

Before a definite decision is taken about a pool's configuration, an approximate shape should be laid out on the ground and adjusted until it satisfies the eye. Even a formal pool with fixed angles and curves should be treated in this manner, so that you are perfectly happy about its proportions in relation to the rest of the garden.

Use pegs and string to outline a formal pool, or a length of rope for an informal pool. A hosepipe is often recommended for this purpose, but many modern plastic types seem to have a mind of their own, making it almost impossible to achieve a smooth curved shape.

When creating an outline for an informal lined pool, take into account that while it is perfectly possible to line almost any shape of excavation, there is a limit to what can be achieved without significant folds and creases appearing in the liner. However, for all practical purposes, if you make any curves or arcs no tighter than could be successfully negotiated with the domestic lawnmower, the liner will usually fit snugly. If the pool is to be set in a lawn with grass to the water's edge, this will be an obvious requirement.

Having created the shape, take a look at it from all angles. In the majority of cases, the view from the house will take priority, and of course this does not just mean from ground floor level, but from any upper floor, too. Take time to make the final decision, if necessary leaving the line or rope in place for two or three days and then making any minor adjustments as necessary.

When creating a pool, clearly define its outline so that it rests easily in the garden landscape. With an informal pool it is essential that the arcs and curves of the edges are such that they can be both constructed and maintained easily.

MARKING OUT THE POOL

Whatever the final shape of the pool, marking out should begin from a fixed point. If you have drawn the shape accurately on a scale plan of the garden, use a fixed point, such as a path or the side of a building, as a baseline. If, on the other hand, the position of the pool and its outline have been established by eye, choose a point at one end to serve as the base point and drive a small stake securely into the ground to serve as a marker.

A CIRCULAR POOL

This is the easiest pool of all to mark out successfully. From your base line or fixed point, determine the centre. Knock a strong stake securely into the ground at this point and attach a string to it, the length of which is equal to the radius of the pool. Tie a pointed stick to the other end of the string and use it to mark the ground as you walk around the centre stake, keeping the string taut. You can make the mark more legible by sprinkling sand or lime on it.

THE OVAL POOL

Again, from the baseline or fixed point, establish the centre of the pool and mark it with a garden cane. Take two more canes and mark each end of the oval in a similar way. Then place a stake between each end cane and the centre at a point two-thirds of the distance between them, working from the centre cane. Tie a loop of string around one of the stakes and the end cane furthest from it. Remove the other end cane and pull the first from the ground. Keeping the string taut, use this to scribe an oval shape on the ground around the stakes and centre cane.

IRREGULARLY-SHAPED POOLS

There are few special considerations when marking out irregularly-shaped pools, except that sweeping arcs and curves are preferable to fussy niches and contortions, which may crumple the liner when it is installed. You can use the principles described for formal shapes, when appropriate, marking out a square or rectangle that embraces the entire pool and using each side as a baseline from which to create the shape.

A RECTANGULAR POOL

A baseline must be established as one side of the pool, using either your existing baseline or a fixed marker. The baseline should be the actual length of the pool and be parallel to, or bear another precise relationship to, other garden features.

Once the baseline has been established, right angles can be created at each end, using the 3-4-5 method. First push a cane into the ground at one end of the baseline. Then mark along the line by 3 units and push another cane into the ground at this point. Next tie a length of string to the first cane with a pointed stick at the other end. Make the string 4 units long and, keeping it taut, scribe an arc on the ground at approximate right angles to the baseline. Use a second length of string (5 units long) and the pointed stick to scribe an arc from the second cane. Where this cuts through the first arc, push a third cane into the ground. A line between this and the first cane will be at right angles to the baseline and can be marked off for correct length accordingly. Repeat this procedure until all four right angles have been laid out.

MARKING OUT THE POOL PROFILE

Place a peg in the centre of the circle. Attach a piece of string the length of the radius of the pool. With a sharp stick attached to the end, inscribe a circle to mark the outline.

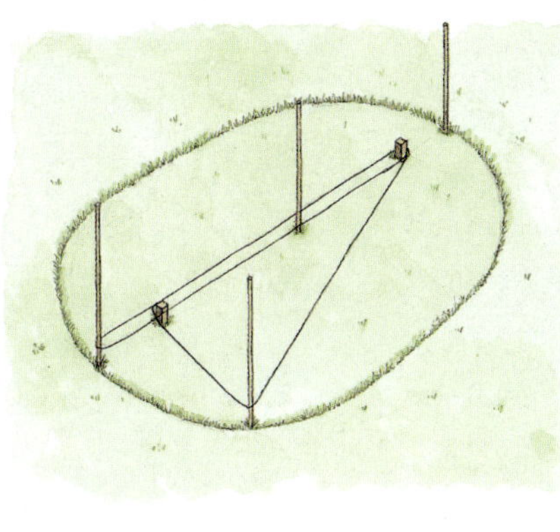

From a fixed point establish the centre of the pool and each end of the oval. Loop a piece of string around the farthest peg. Using the centre cane, tighten the string and mark out the oval.

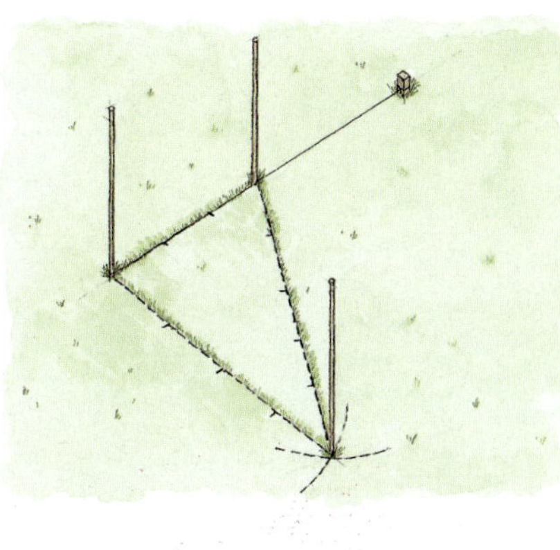

To create a right angle, mark out a baseline of 3 measures. Fasten a string to each end, one 4, the other 5 measures long. Cross each in an arc to produce the angle of the second and third sides.

CHOOSING A FLEXIBLE LINER

A pool liner is a flexible waterproof membrane that covers the sides and floor of a pool excavation. There are several different kinds to choose from, each with different properties and being suitable for a variety of purposes and budgets.

POLYTHENE

Although polythene pool liners are available for the home gardener, there is little to recommend them apart from their low cost. Often coloured bright blue, they have a very short life and are difficult to install. A polythene pool liner must be moulded to the shape of the pool before water is added, making it almost impossible to install without producing masses of wrinkles. The material is also degraded by ultraviolet light, and any unprotected parts of the liner, notably between the surface of the water and the surrounding ground, are likely to deteriorate, crack and leak.

Polythene is only useful in water garden construction as the filling of a sandwich in a naturally managed pool. In this case, the excavation is made larger than finally required, then it is lined with the polythene. Finally, the liner is covered completely with soil, which prevents any degradation by sunlight. Under such circumstances, wrinkles and creases are of no consequence.

PVC

These are traditional liners that have a similar appearance to polythene, but are much more resilient. They have a degree of elasticity that permits them to mould readily to an excavation when water is added, and they have a much greater burst resistance than polythene. This is often enhanced by a terylene web that is incorporated into the liner, giving it a rougher bumpy feel. If you are into bright blue, sea green or pebble-pattern liners, the PVC manufacturers can usually oblige. With a life that is usually guaranteed for a minimum of ten years, PVC is a good buy, but it has largely been overtaken by the more modern low-density polyethylene (LDPE).

LDPE

Low-density polyethylene liners offer an economical alternative to PVC. Invariably, they are black, but they have enormous flexibility compared with PVC, giving a much neater finish to the pool. They form to the contours of an excavation more snugly and rarely produce significant wrinkles if folded boldly at the corners.

BUTYL RUBBER

Rubber liners have long been regarded as the best method of

A pool liner is often difficult to disguise, particularly in a shallow pool. Here a generous layer of cobbles successfully covers the liner completely and deals adequately with the problem of hiding the edge and blending it into the surrounding garden.

pool construction, offering versatility with durability. However, they are quite expensive. Unlike other forms of pool liner, rubber can be welded satisfactorily into almost any size and configuration. It can also be repaired without serious difficulty.

A rubber liner exhibits the same flexibility as an LDPE type and can be installed with the minimum of creases. It is said to have a life of more than 25 years, and provided you do not accidentally push a garden fork through it, this is likely to be the case. Unlike other lining materials, rubber does not have a shiny finish, which means that it rapidly becomes covered in the pond's micro-flora and blends quickly into the background.

THE CORRECT LINER

Most pools can be constructed from most liners, but in some circumstances one will offer particular advantages over another. Otherwise, the choice is likely to depend on cost, and in most cases, it is wise to buy the best you can afford.

Where no part of the liner is exposed, polythene is perfectly adequate. It is not always necessary to employ a proprietary polythene pool liner either; ordinary builders' polythene, such as that used as a damp-proof membrane beneath concrete, is perfectly adequate.

If a much tougher material is required, a stack or truck load cover can be used. These are exceptionally tough and are ideal if they are to be covered completely with soil. They have ring eyelets around the edges, allowing them to be secured easily with pegs or large metal staples if required.

Rubber liners are better where exposure is inevitable, especially in formal water features that have limited planting because the water itself is the main attraction, perhaps as a reflecting pond or a turbulent fountain. Not all pond owners are enthusiastic gardeners; many have water for its own sake. Similarly, in formal situations where a fitted liner is desirable, it is more practical to use rubber, as this can be welded to the shape with accurate corners and curves. Indeed, with a square, oblong or circular pool, a rubber liner can be manufactured precisely to the correct shape, thus avoiding wrinkles or folds.

CALCULATING LINER SIZE

Never buy a liner and attempt to dig a hole to accommodate it; always finish the excavation first and calculate the size to fit. Irrespective of the pond's shape or configuration, calculating liner size follows a simple formula: take the length and add twice the maximum depth, then do the same with the width. This will provide a liner that will suit the excavation and have sufficient overlap at the edges for a satisfactory finish, but with the minimum of wastage.

In large formal lined pools it is best to use a material like butyl rubber, which can be welded to a specific size and does not then create disfiguring folds. Here it is completely unobtrusive and carefully disguised by the overhang of the paved edge.

INSTALLING A POOL LINER

The method of installing a pool liner is identical for all materials except polythene. This needs shaping to the excavation before water is added, as it offers little or no flexibility. All other liners are malleable and use the weight of the water to mould them to the contours of the excavation.

DIGGING THE HOLE

The excavation for a pool liner should be the same size as the final pool, with a small allowance being made for a protective fabric or sand underlay. Complete accuracy will be difficult to achieve when digging, but this is not usually necessary.

The most important requirement when digging is to ensure that the walls of the excavation remain solid. It is almost impossible to replace any soil that has been dug out in error so that it will provide solid support for the liner. The hole should be dug in the soil in almost the same manner as one might cut cheese, making very definite lines that allow solid compacted soil to remain.

The best way to do this is to excavate the whole area of the pool to the level of the marginal shelves. Mark out the shape of the deeper part on the floor of this excavation, then dig down again. If there is a further deeper level, repeat the process. This ensures that the hole is accurately produced with a solid base and walls that will remain firmly in place when the liner is installed and water added.

Another important aspect is being sure that the levels are correct. Before beginning to dig, drive a peg into the soil as a prime datum from which to work. At strategic points around the pool shape, drive in additional pegs, ensuring that their tops are level with the first. To do this, lay a wooden board on edge across their tops and set a spirit level on top of it. This will give you an idea of whether the ground itself is level and provide reference points from which to measure down to the various levels of the pool. It is important that the edge of the excavation is level all around, otherwise there is a possibility of unsightly pool liner showing when the pond has been completed.

PUTTING IN THE LINER

It is always surprising just how much liner is required for even a small hole and, irrespective of the material being used, how heavy it is. For the most part, the successful installation of a pool liner is a job for two people.

No matter how tough the material being used, all liners benefit from some cushioning to protect them from the imperfections of the hole. Builders' sand and specially manufactured protective fleece are widely used for this purpose.

Fleece makes a good cushioning layer once all sharp stones have been removed. However, it is not the easiest material to install, often taking as much effort to get right as the liner itself, and in some cases, its imperfections will show through. Builders' sand is much easier to use, for although very fine, once dampened it is extremely versatile. However, it cannot be used where the sides of the hole are vertical,

A liner is ideal for an informal-looking pool as it can be easily moulded to various shapes, is suitable for any but the largest size of pool, and its edges can be effectively masked with grass, plants or, as here, with a pebble beach.

since it will not remain in place. If sand is the option, dampen it sufficiently so that it can be applied in the same manner as plaster, using a plasterer's trowel. If you do not have such a trowel, it can be applied just as easily by hand, but make sure you wear heavy-duty gardening gloves. Smooth the sand over all the walls, the shelves and the floor, then put the liner in place while it is still damp.

Spread the liner across the excavation, weighing down the edges with rocks or bricks, then run water into the centre so that it moulds to the contours of the hole. The weights around the edge can be removed gradually as the liner forms to the shape. Take great care when lining an irregularly-shaped pool to ensure that the liner is positioned correctly before adding water. There is little more frustrating than finding an excess of liner at one end and a shortage at the other when the pool is half full of water. Once the water begins to run into the liner, it is not just a matter of sitting back and waiting for the pool to take shape. This can be a time of quite frantic activity, since all the wrinkles will need smoothing out as the weight of water increases. Do not forget that if things begin to go wrong, you can always shut off the water supply. So many people fight against the increasing weight of water without considering that they could stop the flow. Rather than create a multiplicity of folds, it is preferable to make only a few bold ones. These will be much more effective and easily disguised.

Once the pool has been filled to the required level, and you are happy that the liner is satisfactorily in place, trim off the surplus around the edges. However, remember to leave enough for securing to the ground with your chosen edging.

INSTALLING A POOL LINER

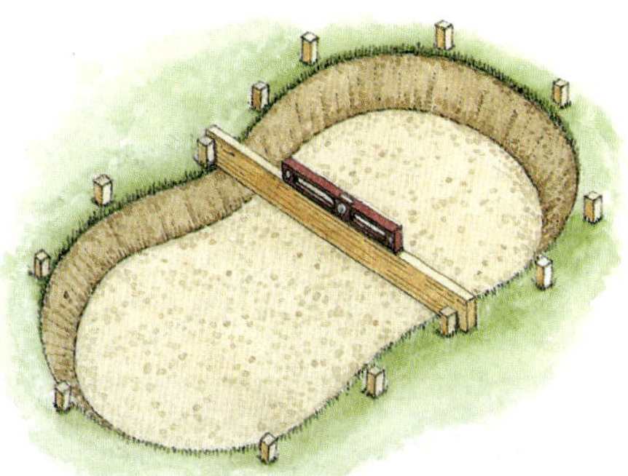

1 Mark out the desired shape of the pool using pegs, making sure their tops are level, then dig out the whole area to the depth of the marginal shelves. Check all levels with a spirit level.

2 Mark out the shape of the deeper level of the pool on this excavation and dig out. Remember to check levels. If the pool is to contain a further deeper level, you can repeat this process.

3 Builders' sand is the easiest material to use as a protective underlay for the liner. Dampen the sand slightly to make it more manageable and spread it over the base and sides of the excavation.

4 Put the liner in place while the sand underlay is still damp; you will probably need help even for a small pool. Spread it over the whole area, weighing down the edges with bricks or rocks.

5 Run the water into the centre of the pool so that the liner moulds to the contours of the hole. Wrinkles in the liner will need smoothing out as the weight of the water increases.

6 Once the pool has been filled to the required level, trim off the surplus liner around the edges. Remember to leave enough for securing to the ground with your chosen edging material.

PRE-FORMED POOLS

Pre-formed pools are usually manufactured from plastic, fibreglass, or a PVC or rubber composition material. They are of a fixed shape and have a degree of rigidity. Both formal and informal shapes are available, in a wide range of sizes.

CHOOSING A DESIGN

If you are planning a formal circular, square or oblong pond and a pre-formed shape is available in the size required, choose it in preference to any other pond construction material. The moulding will be accurate in every respect and, in most circumstances, will be the easiest material to install.

Informal pools, however, can be a different proposition, for often the design of the pre-formed pool will have been created for ease of manufacture, rather than the well-being of the plants. As pre-formed pools are sold on appearance, the way they look when out of the ground is obviously of great importance to the vendor. The gardener, however, will be more interested in the internal configuration and its suitability for plants, along with the overall surface appearance in relation to other features in the garden.

If you want an informal pre-formed pool, beware of any fussy corners that may cause difficulty with installation or maintenance. Look carefully at the marginal shelves, not only to establish that they are in the right place for your design ideas, but also sufficiently large to accept a well planted basket of marginal plants.

Many pre-formed pools have marginal shelves that are intended for direct planting, but are impractical for this purpose. Sufficient depth should be available for a waterlily, and this equates with its likely spread. Even when accommodated within the restrictions of a planting basket, most waterlilies still manage to achieve a surface spread of at least one-and-a-half times the depth at which they are growing. Only the better pre-formed pools have such a balanced width-to-depth ratio.

SECTIONAL POOLS

Some of the constraints imposed by the pre-formed pool can be relieved by using a sectional pool. The manufacturers of these offer a series of different pool sections that can be joined together to form different overall configurations. While it is possible to create a very elaborate pool with these

Although pre-formed pools often have limited accommodation for plants, they are not difficult to install and, when accompanied by paving, walling and edging, can be unobtrusively and successfully blended into the garden landscape.

sections, installing such a feature may be quite difficult. The best use for sectional pools is to lengthen a particular pool configuration, rather than to create added complexity.

TYPES OF MANUFACTURE

The traditional fibreglass pool is the best and most durable of the pre-formed types. The material is rigid and tough and, if accidentally damaged, is very easily repaired using an automotive fibreglass repair kit. However, fibreglass can be quite heavy, which limits the size to which manufacturers are prepared to work. It is rarely suitable for a large informal pool.

The cheaper end of the market is dominated by vacuum-formed plastic pools. These are very thin, light in weight and are more difficult to install than their heavyweight counterparts. Many are of a questionable shape, often not providing suitable accommodation for aquatic plants. Some come with a small central island moulded in, which is hollow beneath and difficult to support unless filled with soil or sand before installation: a difficult task.

Composition PVC or rubber pre-formed pools are similar in most respects to fibreglass pools. However, they are lighter in weight, allowing them to be readily manufactured in larger shapes and transported easily. Their designs are generally perfectly adequate for the requirements of plants and fish.

The surfaces of vacuum-formed plastic pools are normally very shiny and not conducive to the rapid establishment of micro-flora, while fibreglass pools, although apparently smooth, soon become coated. Composition types also spawn rapid growth, for these have a rough finish to which algae and similar aquatic life clings.

The only other consideration when choosing a pre-formed pool is the manner in which it is finished around the edge. Some manufacturers decorate the edge with imitation rocks that not only look hideous and never mellow, but also create enormous difficulties with installation, especially when it comes to levelling the pool.

A broad edge may be useful if the poolside is to be paved, but if planting is to be a priority, it can be a nuisance. Most of the composition material pools have lips that are narrow, functional and unobtrusive, being easily disguised by plants.

PRE-FORMED FOUNTAIN OR ROCK POOLS

Among the many pre-formed pools available are fountain or rock pools. These are not intended for planting, but as small water features in their own right or as a reservoir to serve a moving water feature. Although they are usually well made and functional, do not be led into believing that they are anything other than a supplementary feature to the main water garden, being unsuitable for housing most plant life and all the popular ornamental pond fish.

While the edges of some pre-formed pools are difficult to disguise, the problem is easily overcome when a paved sitting out area runs up to the waterside . A pool with sweeping curves is easier to construct as a pre-formed shape than with a liner.

AN OVERSIZE EXCAVATION

Although it may be rather tiresome to excavate more soil than is necessary for the final shape and size of a pool, making an oversize excavation does provide a much easier and more accurate installation for a pre-formed pool. By digging a hole that embraces the greatest dimensions of the pool and allowing sufficient space for backfilling, you will ensure complete support of the moulding, while levelling will also be greatly simplified.

MARKING OUT THE SITE

Before starting to excavate for a pre-formed pool, knock pegs into the ground at regular intervals around the edge of the site. Level their tops, using a board on edge and a spirit level. The peg that projects most from the ground indicates the lowest point, and the surface soil should be removed from the entire area so that the distance between the top of each peg and the soil is exactly the same. Only by starting the excavation with a level soil surface will you be able to accommodate the pool properly.

Having ensured a level from which to work, mark out an area with sand or lime that embraces the maximum length and width of the pool. Add an extra 15cm (6in) at each end and side to provide manoeuvring room.

DIGGING OUT THE HOLE

Unless a major part of the pool is either shallower or narrower than the rest, dig out the entire marked area to the required depth. This makes installation so much simpler than trying to create a hole that matches the shape of the pre-formed structure.

The hole should be about 2.5cm (1in) deeper than the pool to allow for a cushioning layer of sand on the bottom and for the fact that if the pool is allowed to remain empty, it will inevitably rise a little while it is being backfilled. A mechanical digger can be hired to do the job if the pool is particularly large.

In most cases, the soil that is excavated will not be suitable for backfilling once the pool is in place, nor is it likely to be of much use elsewhere in the garden, so it should be disposed of. If, however, the structure of the soil is such that it flows easily around the pool shape, it is probably too good to waste and should be saved for another gardening project.

INSTALLING THE POOL

Once the excavation is complete, spread a generous layer of builders' sand over the base of the hole on which the pool can be rested. Set the moulding in place, where appropriate

When digging the hole for a pre-formed pool, remove more soil than is necessary. In most cases this aids installation, but can also create opportunities for re-soiling and planting the surroundings. Here a sunken container is embraced by plants grown in a gritty soil.

propping it up on bricks, especially if part of the floor is higher than the rest. Loose bricks provide much better support than any backfilling mixture and can be left in situ.

The pool must be supported completely all round and underneath if it is to remain level and resist the damage that may be caused by a heavy footfall when cleaning out. The latter can cause an immediate fracture in a fibreglass pool. Sand or pea gravel are both excellent backfilling materials, pea gravel flowing beautifully to fill all the niches and providing excellent all-round support.

Add the backfill evenly, otherwise there is a risk of the pool structure tilting. Walk around the pool, systematically pouring the gravel into the space between the moulding and sides of the excavation. Keep a constant check on the levels across and along the pool structure to ensure that they remain true. Inevitably, the backfilling process will necessitate adjustments if the pool is to achieve the desired level.

If the pool is of vacuum-formed plastic, the weight of the gravel pushing against the flexible walls will cause them to buckle. In this case, the only way to guarantee a neat fit in the hole is to make sure that the edge of the pool is in the correct final position and add water at the same time as backfilling. This will balance the pressure against the sides and also prevent the pool from rising during the process.

Run water into pool, making sure that its level keeps pace with the backfilling. Too much backfilling will cause an inward buckling; too much water will result in bulging outwards. Remember that you can shut off the water flow completely if necessary. As the process continues, make sure that the pool remains level from side to side and end to end.

INSTALLING A PRE-FORMED POOL – METHOD ONE

1 Mark out an area that will embrace the maximum width and length of the pre-formed pool shape. Excavate this area to the maximum depth of the pre-formed pool.

2 Place a generous layer of builders' sand evenly over the bottom of the excavation. This provides a cushioning layer and ensures that the pool shape rests evenly in the hole.

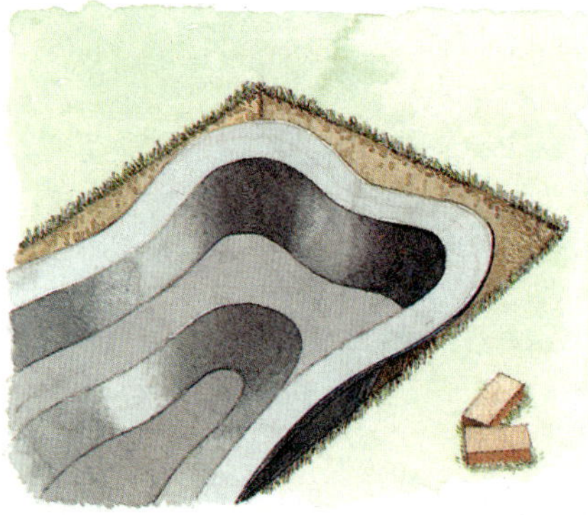

3 Place the pool in position and, where necessary, use loose bricks to provide temporary support beneath the marginal shelves before backfilling. These can remain in situ, if desired.

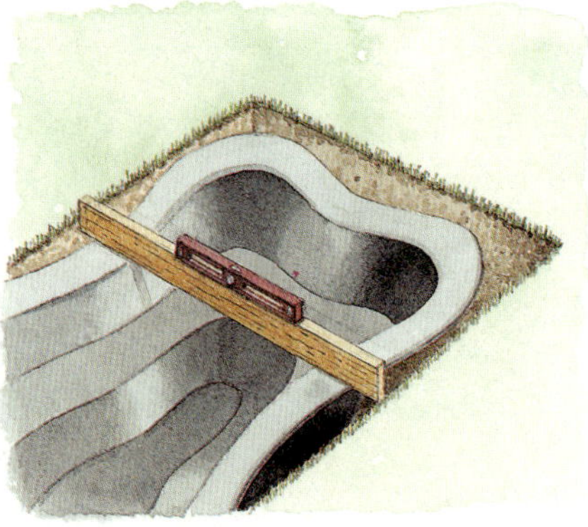

4 Make sure that the pool is level from side to side and end to end using a spirit level. It should just be resting below the surrounding ground level, as backfilling will cause it to rise slightly.

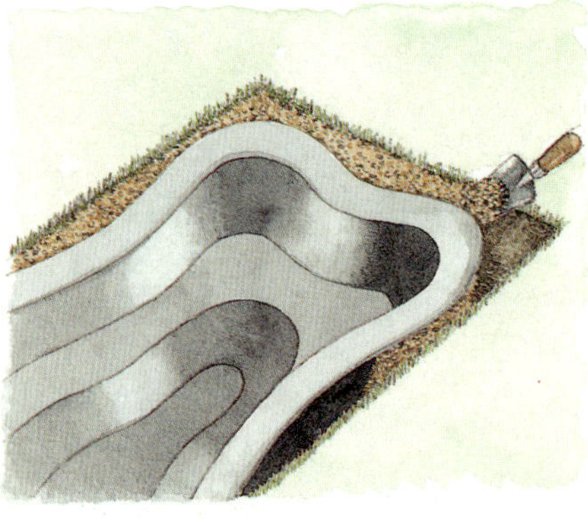

5 Backfill with sand, pea gravel or crumbly soil, taking care to eliminate any air pockets. Ensure that the pre-formed pool does not rise above the surrounding soil level.

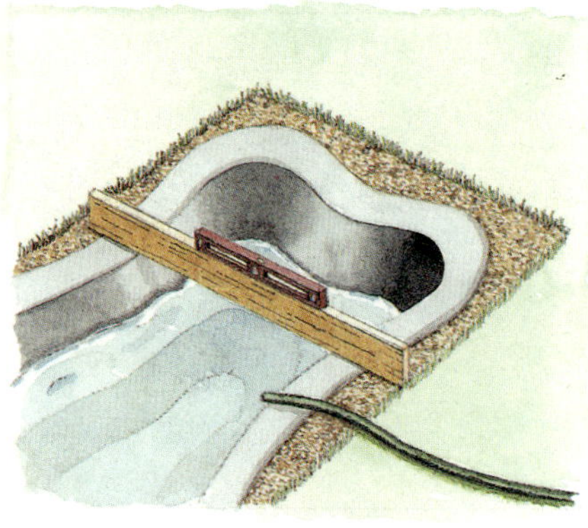

6 Add water, at the same time watching the levels carefully in order to avoid subsidence. For vacuum-formed plastic pools, water must be added from the beginning to give stability.

A TAILOR-MADE HOLE

As an alternative to making a large excavation based on the maximum length and width of the pool, it is possible to limit the amount of digging required by excavating a hole that matches the shape of the pre-formed pool. Although this demands a much greater degree of skill, it may be a preferable method of installation if the pool is being inserted into an established garden landscape or is to be linked to an existing feature such as a rock garden.

MARKING OUT THE SITE

Carefully position the pre-formed pool, supporting it approximately 8cm (3in) above the ground on bricks or pieces of wood and making sure that the rim is level in both directions. Transfer the shape of the outer edge to the ground at regular intervals by placing a spirit level vertically between the rim and the ground. Mark the points by scratching the soil with a stick, then remove the pool and scratch a line through the points to complete the outline. Once the overall shape has been marked out, the hole can be dug.

As with the previous method, it is vital to begin with a level site. This can be achieved in the same manner by driving a series of pegs into the ground at 30cm (12in) intervals around the pool's outline, levelling their tops and digging away the soil until they all project by an equal amount.

INSTALLING A PRE-FORMED POOL – METHOD TWO

1 Secure the preformed pool with bricks and mark out the exact shape, using a spirit level in a vertical plane. Mark points at short regular intervals to ensure accuracy.

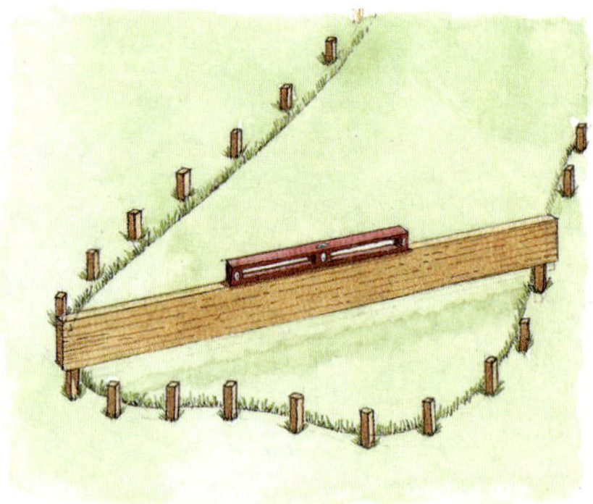

2 When marking out is complete, check that all the pegs across and for the length of the excavation are level with each other. Absolute accuracy is essential with this sort of excavation.

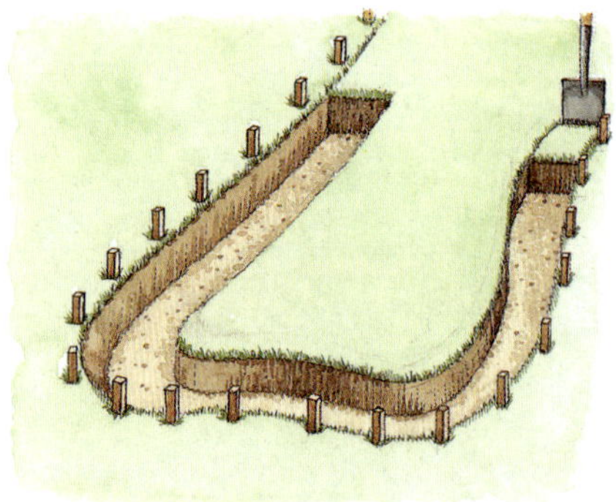

3 Take the first spit of soil out from around the marked out area in order to define it clearly, then remove the remainder of the soil to level of the marginal shelf.

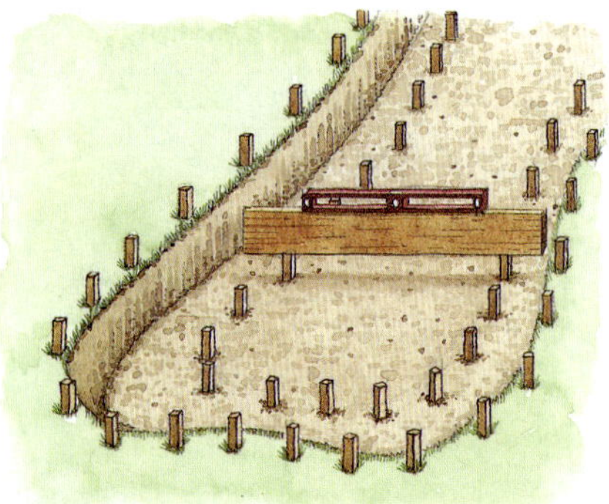

4 Mark out the area for the marginal shelves within the excavation and, using pegs, check carefully that the shelves are level before you undertake any further digging.

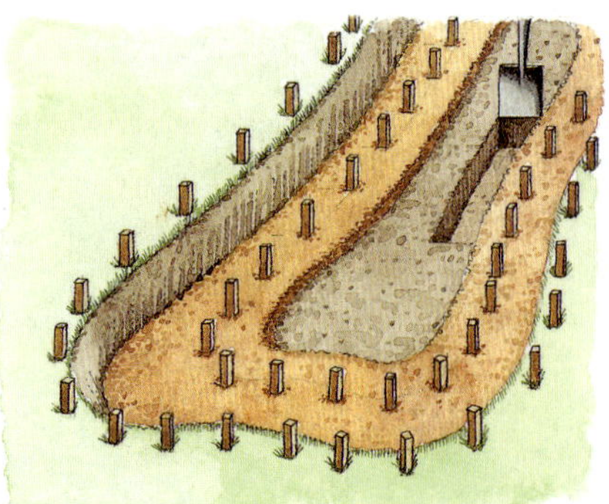

5 Excavate the deep area of the pool, once again using a spirit level at regular intervals to make sure that the excavation is even and level from side to side and end to end.

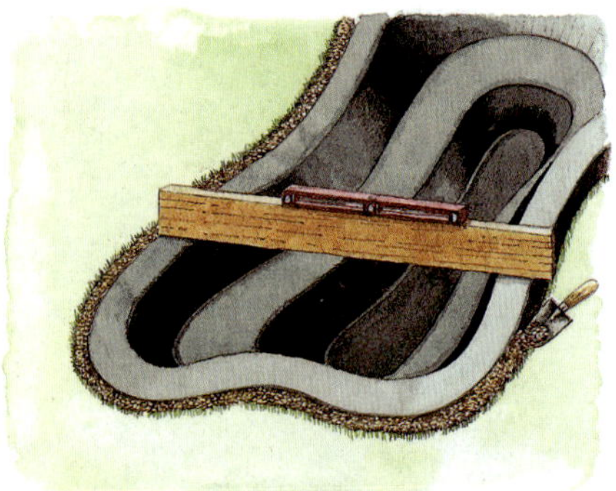

6 The pool shape can be placed into the accurately dug excavation. Continue to monitor levels, while carefully backfilling around the edges of the pool with sand or pea gravel.

DIGGING THE HOLE

For accurate excavations such as this, hand digging is the only option. Begin by digging a very accurate trench around the inside of the pool's outline. Its depth should match that of the marginal shelf in relation to the rim. Remove all the soil to the same depth across the pool, taking frequent measurements from the tops of the pegs to ensure that you never remove more soil than necessary. It is not desirable to have loose backfilling beneath the shelves or base.

Make sure that the shelf is level by knocking in pegs and levelling their tops in the same way as when originally setting out the site. It is surprising how quickly levels can go adrift if you depend solely upon your eye.

As the correct level for the shelf is reached, you can mark out the inner deeper area to be excavated, using sand or lime to indicate the digging line. To determine the size of the floor area, place the pool in position and press it down firmly. This will leave an imprint that shows the exact outline of the lower part of the pool. If the soil is not sufficiently fine for an imprint to be clearly shown, scatter a thin layer of sand over the top first. If the pool has sides that slope gently inwards, the initial hole will be slightly smaller than that ultimately required. However, it is not difficult to pare away the sides to achieve a neat fit.

FITTING THE POOL

It is much more difficult to install a pool in a tailor-made hole than in a large excavation, even if provision has been made in the upper part to allow for backfilling. The pool will have to be lifted in and out several times before an exact fit is achieved, but the support offered will be excellent.

In most cases, however, some backfilling will be necessary near the top. The pre-formed shape may not sit accurately in the hole and, therefore, levels must be checked from end to end and side to side. As the backfill is added, these will need constant monitoring, although it is possible to secure and weigh down the pool by adding some water once it has been levelled accurately.

This method of installation is not suitable for vacuum-formed plastic pools because of their tendency to buckle.

It is vitally important when constructing a pool to be aware how the water can show up discrepancies in levels, even though the land fall appears in order to the naked eye. When the surroundings are formal, it is even more essential that accurate levelling takes place.

INSTALLING A SECTIONAL POOL

Unless a sectional pool is of a simple configuration, it is better not to attempt to dig a hole that matches the slope of its sides. A much larger excavation makes for easier manipulation.

Assemble the pool according to the manufacturer's instructions, screwing the units together and sealing the joints with the specially prepared sealant provided. Once the excavation has been dug, spread a 10cm (4in) layer of damp builders' sand across the floor, levelling it carefully. Mark off the position of each joint and place a length of 10x10cm (4x4in) timber along each mark. Push these down into the sand until they reach the earth floor, then remove them to leave narrow recesses.

When the structure is lowered into the hole, the joints will fit snugly into the spaces left by the timber. Stabilize the pool by adding sufficient water to hold it in position while backfilling.

CONCRETE POOLS

Although concrete is a well tried and traditional method of pool construction, the more modern techniques, using flexible or pre-formed liners, require less skill and are likely to present fewer problems. However, concrete does offer a degree of permanence that is lacking with other construction methods. Moreover, such a structure may also blend readily with other more traditional landscape materials.

THE PROPERTIES OF CONCRETE

The successful use of concrete depends upon a very clear understanding of its properties, especially while under construction, and the limitations which may be placed upon it by the complexity of a pool's design. If the pool is to have any vertical elevations or steeply sloping sides, shuttering will be required to support the concrete while it sets. Reinforcing rods or mesh will also be needed, and a knowledge of the various stresses and strains that the pond will be expected to endure will determine the type and quantity of reinforcing material to be used.

Wet concrete also remains workable for only a short time. It can go off within a few hours and become useless. When constructing a pool, it is essential that all the concreting is completed within a day. If you intend using ready-mixed concrete, it will arrive irrespective of the weather in one con-

Concrete ponds are sturdy and permanent, but they are difficult to integrate into the garden unless sufficient prior thought is given to peripheral planting. Where suitable accommodation is provided, the hardness of the material is softened and it is scarcely noticed.

signment and will have to be dealt with quickly. If the weather is very wet, a major problem can arise in trying to prevent the mixture from being diluted and washed out. It is extremely difficult to lay concrete and protect it at the same time. Mixing concrete yourself with a hired mixer will allow you to select a suitable day to safely undertake the task. However, it will be much more difficult to ensure a uniform mix, especially if waterproofing compound is being added.

WATERPROOFING

Concrete pools demand very careful waterproofing. Even the best laid concrete can be porous and permit water to escape, and one method of preventing this is to install a polythene membrane beneath the concrete. Alternatively, you can add a waterproofing compound when mixing the concrete. This will ensure that there is no porosity, although it cannot legislate for faulty workmanship and cracks.

Problems will arise from the escape of free-lime into the water, which is harmful to fish and can cause problems to some aquatic plants if present in excessive amounts. This will not be prevented by the inclusion of a waterproofing compound at the time of mixing. However, the face of the concrete can be treated with a special product that not only traps the free-lime, but also seals the concrete by a process known as internal glazing.

Winter damage is another potential hazard for the concrete pool. It is vital to take precautions against this, for even the most professionally laid concrete can be damaged during a really severe winter. The problem is caused by the exertion of pressure by ice on the walls of the pool. If no relief is provided, this can cause fracturing of the concrete. To prevent this damage, float a rubber ball or piece of wood in the pool from the time of the first frosts, as this will absorb the pressure and protect the walls.

The construction of a concrete pond is not for the inexperienced. Not only is it hard work, but the potential for losing water if the pool is inappropriately constructed is great, especially when there is considerable water movement. For the larger pool consult a professional.

CONSTRUCTING A CONCRETE POOL

DIGGING THE HOLE

The hole for a concrete pool must be at least 15cm (6in) larger all round than its finished size to allow for the thickness of concrete required. It should be set out and dug in the same manner as an excavation for a flexible liner pool. If it is to have sides that are vertical or slope at an angle greater than 45 degrees, wooden shuttering or formwork must be created to support the concrete while it sets. This must be of sturdy construction to resist the considerable pressures produced by the weight of the concrete. Erecting this is a skill in itself, and if you have never had any experience of building formwork to create a suitable mould for concrete, it is essential to entrust this to a professional.

If you do not want to use shuttering and you intend lining the excavation with a polythene membrane, give the sides of the pool as shallow a slope as possible. This will make it less likely that the concrete will slump because of the smooth surface of the polythene.

LINING THE HOLE

Even though concrete can be laid directly onto the soil, it will be much better if laid over a polythene liner. Not only will this prevent water seeping from the pool, but it will also help to prevent the freshly laid concrete from drying out too quickly and developing hairline cracks. These often lead to unsightly surface flaking. The polythene itself need only be builders' clear material.

When laying a polythene membrane, treat the excavation in the same manner as you would when installing a flexible pool liner, for it is equally at risk of being punctured. Remove all sharp stones and roots from the hole, and spread a layer of sand over the soil to serve as a cushion before laying the polythene. Although it is neither possible nor essential to remove all the creases when putting down the polythene is should be installed carefully, much as a pool liner.

It is important to seal concrete with a waterproof sealer to prevent the escape of harmful free-lime. Take care when finishing pool edges, especially if paving is being laid on a mortar bed.

LAYING THE CONCRETE

Working outwards from the centre of the pool, spread a 10cm (4in) layer of concrete over the entire excavation. Where appropriate, use a plasterer's trowel to ensure evenness and a reasonably smooth finish. Make sure that the floor and marginal shelves are roughly level, using a short board and a spirit level. Then press a layer of wire mesh, such as that used for poultry runs, into the wet concrete as reinforcement. On top of this, spread a further layer of concrete, approximately 5cm (2in) deep. This is the final layer, so care should be taken to ensure that it is level where necessary, especially the floor and marginal shelves, and that it is polished to a neat smooth finish with a plasterer's trowel.

Damp sacking or similar material should be laid over the wet concrete to ensure that it dries out slowly. If this is impractical, water the surface of the concrete gently several times a day until it has set, using a watering can fitted with a fine rose. This is less satisfactory, but it will prevent cracking.

SEALING

Once the concrete has set, it can be treated with a sealant to prevent free-lime from escaping into the water. Not only is this harmful to fish and plants, but it also creates white cloudiness in the water, which looks unattractive and eventually settles out, coating the foliage of submerged aquatics. The sealant is supplied in crystalline form for mixing with water and painting on to the concrete. It will also assist in waterproofing the concrete.

If bright colours are more to your taste than grey concrete, excellent waterproof plastic paints are available that not only provide a smooth coloured finish, but also assist in preventing free-lime from escaping. However, to ensure that they adhere properly to the concrete, a special primer must be applied to the surface first.

MIXING CONCRETE

It is quite possible to mix concrete yourself, but unless the pool is quite small, it is likely to be uneconomical and time consuming. It is essential that all the concrete required can be mixed and laid in the same day to avoid the development of weak areas where different mixes meet. Consistency is vital, a uniform mixture of materials, especially waterproofing compound, being essential to guarantee a high-quality finish.

If mixing will be done at home, use one part of cement to two of builders' sand and four of gravel. Mix the dry materials together until they reach an even consistency and uniform greyish colour. Add water and waterproofing compound, carefully following the manufacturer's instructions. Allow the concrete to mix for a few minutes, then turn out a little into a wheelbarrow and check its consistency. The mixture should be sufficiently wet that when a shovel is placed into it and drawn across it in a series of jerks, the ridges it creates should retain their shape without slumping.

Ready-mixed concrete is much better, but you have to calculate and order the quantity in advance, specifying the day you want it delivered. If the weather is exceptionally wet, it will still arrive with all the attendant problems. However, its mix will be consistent and have the waterproofing compound evenly distributed throughout. You must be ready to use it immediately and have good access from the delivery point to the pool site.

CONSTRUCTING A CONCRETE POOL

1 Excavate a hole which is at least 15cm (6in) larger than the finished pool, to allow for the thickness of the concrete, and line with builders' polythene to prevent rapid drying out.

2 Working outwards from the centre of the pool, spread a layer of concrete evenly over the polythene to about two thirds of its finished depth (that is about 10cm/4in) and smooth it off evenly.

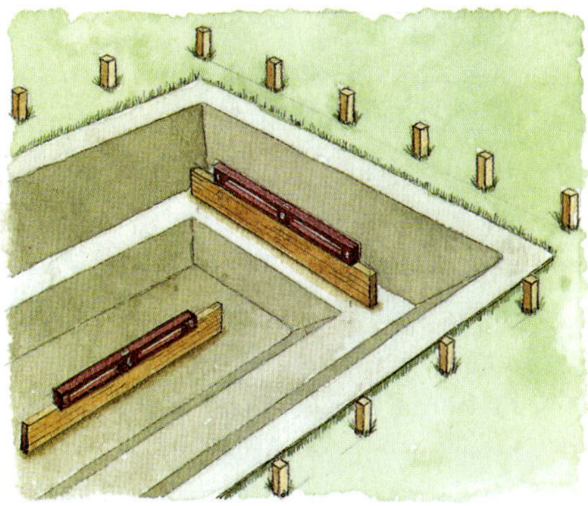

3 Tap the concrete firmly and ensure that it is reasonably level before putting the layer of reinforcing wire mesh into place. This should be done while the concrete is still wet.

4 Once the reinforcing mesh has been pressed into the wet concrete, cover it with a further layer of concrete (about 5cm/2in thick) and produce a smooth finish with a plasterers' trowel.

5 Cover the wet concrete with damp sacking or similar material and water the surface to prevent it drying out too quickly. Rapid drying out causes surface cracks to appear.

6 Once the concrete has dried out, apply a sealant to prevent free-lime from escaping into the water. If a plastic paint is to be used, the concrete should be treated with a special primer first.

CONCRETE KOI PONDS

Concrete, in solid and block form, is still the favoured material for koi ponds, since most pre-formed pools are too shallow, while a pool liner is not as easy to clean as a properly rendered concrete pool, especially when this is tiled. The last may be going to extremes, involving extra expense and effort in construction, but it is a fad that is gaining momentum among koi enthusiasts. The only minor difficulty with a solid concrete koi pond is the need to slope the sides slightly to reduce the effect of winter icing. However, most koi keepers will ensure that there is at least a small permanent vent in the ice during the winter to allow the escape of noxious gases. This will also reduce the pressure of ice on the sides. If total ice cover is unlikely to occur because of the management system, vertical sides can be built. These will be much easier to construct.

A RAISED BLOCK POND

With a raised concrete koi pond, the quantity and pressure of water must be taken into account when designing the structure. If you have any doubts about its ability to withstand that pressure of water, seek professional advice. This is essential with concrete block pools which, if built to 1.5m (5ft) above the ground, are very vulnerable to bursting.

There are several remedies for this situation, the most obvious being to sink part of the pool into the ground, which will absorb some of the pressure. However, if the entire pool is to be above ground, some sort of reinforcement will be necessary. Tying a double-skinned block wall together with wall ties does offer some security, but this arrangement is not ideal. A double-skinned wall with a reinforced cavity, filled with concrete, will be much safer.

For this kind of construction, steel reinforcing mesh should be incorporated in the floor of the pool and continued vertically into the cavity between the walls, which should be built either on top of the floor or on a foundation set into the floor. In this way, the floor and concrete wall infill will be tied together as almost one structure. The cavity itself should be 10cm (4in) wide and filled to the top with concrete, the blocks acting in the same manner as shuttering. Although it will be difficult to tie the walls to each other, ties can still be inserted between the courses and allowed to project into the cavity, where they will become set in the concrete infill.

Such a structure will need careful rendering with sand and cement on the inside, and given some form of decorative treatment on the outside if it is to remain clean, be easy to manage and fit into the garden landscape.

SOLID CONCRETE CONSTRUCTION

Of course, erecting shuttering and casting the pool in solid concrete is another option. This is a more traditional method and, in some ways, it is easier to undertake, provided the shuttering is prepared properly. The weight of the concrete will be substantial and may cause the shuttering to move, even though it may appear to be secure.

With this kind of construction, it is essential to prepare everything so that all the walls can be cast at the same time. They may be constructed first and the floor concreted afterwards, or the floor laid and the shuttering for the walls erected on it. There is no satisfactory means of casting the floor and walls from the same concrete mix so that they form a continuous barrier, unless the pool is in the ground and the shuttering hung and braced. While this is possible, it is very

A koi pond can be enjoyed to the full if raised. This is easy to achieve by the use of a concrete block construction which is then lined or rendered and waterproofed. The edges of the pool can be disguised with decorative stone or paving.

CONSTRUCTING A CONCRETE KOI POOL WITH SHUTTERING

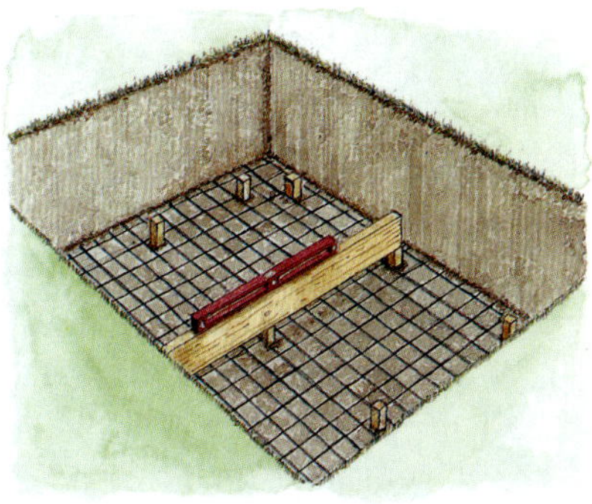

1 Excavate a hole which is at least 15cm (6in) larger than the finished pool to allow for the thickness of the concrete. Put in half the depth of concrete and add the reinforcing mesh.

2 Cover the reinforcing mesh with a further layer of concrete and tamp down firmly. Ensure that the surfaces are level using a board, spirit level and a series of pegs.

3 While the concrete is still wet, insert metal reinforcing rods at regular intervals where the centre of the walls will be. It is essential that these rods continue to the top of the excavation.

4 Once the concrete is set, construct wooden shuttering to leave the desired width of the walls, ensuring that it is well braced. The timber used should be straight and strong.

5 When the shuttering is constructed soak the timbers with water to prevent the concrete sticking . Pour the concrete behind the boards and tamp firmly but carefully to exclude air.

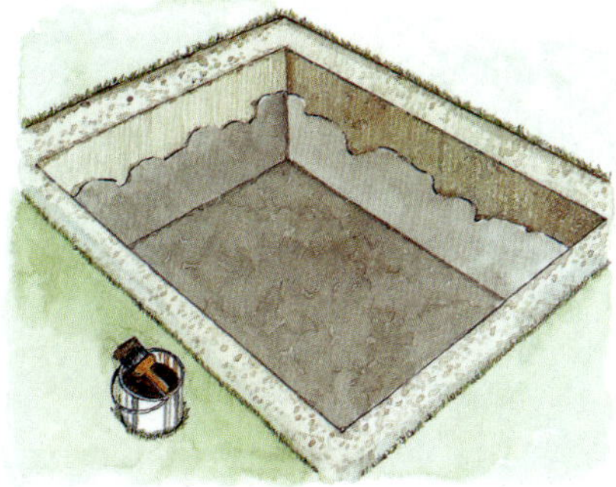

6 It is usually safe to remove the shuttering after three or four days. After a few more days, treat the set concrete with a sealant, and finally coat with a primer and plastic pool paint.

hazardous, especially for the do-it-yourself enthusiast because it can easily go wrong.

When constructing walls on a pre-concreted floor, which has been reinforced with mesh, it is essential that the reinforcement be continued to the top of the walls. Insert the vertical rods into the wet concrete and allow this to harden before you erect the wall shuttering. For a square or rectangular pool, the shuttering will consist of four inner and four outer panels, which should enclose the einforcing rods. The timber should be straight and strong, and strengthened on the outside at regular intervals to prevent buckling.

Once in position, the boards should be soaked thoroughly with water. Alternatively, if practical, the faces that will come into contact with the concrete should be painted with a wash of garden lime and water. This will prevent the concrete from sticking to the boards when the shuttering is 'struck', or removed. Use a standard mixture and consistency of concrete, pouring it between the boards and tamping it down carefully to exclude air. However, do not be too vigorous, or you may distort the shuttering. The boards and top of the walls should be kept damp while the concrete hardens.

It is usually quite safe to remove the shuttering after three or four days, provided the weather allows. Although the concrete will not be cured completely, after a few more days, it will be ready for treating with a sealant.

It is quite a simple matter to install a drain during the construction of the floor in a concrete koi pool, and worth sloping the floor towards it. Remember to lay the pipes underground first, and make all the appropriate preparations for disposing of the water before casting the floor.

RAISED POOLS

The major advantage of a raised pool is that it brings the water garden closer, allowing its inhabitants to be more readily observed and enjoyed. It is fascinating to watch the hustle and bustle of aquatic life at close quarters and in relative comfort, for if proper arrangements are made, it is possible to sit on the pool's edge and dabble your fingers in the water.

From a practical point of view, a raised pool will be easier to maintain because it is closer to the gardener, a tremendous advantage for anyone who is less able or of advancing years. Indeed, the construction can be arranged even to accommodate the requirements of the wheelchair gardener provided that you carefully consider this from the outset.

The major disadvantage, however, is that during severe winter weather, there is a greater danger of it freezing solid. Cold can penetrate from all sides; the temperature and conditions within a raised pool can be startlingly different from those in a pool set in the ground. Both plants and fish may suffer and, in some circumstances, the structure, too, unless precautions are taken.

A raised pool allows the owner to enjoy the aquatic plants and inhabitants at closer quarters. A suitable edging that can serve as a seat will enhance both pleasure and ease of maintenance.

CHOOSING A STRUCTURE

A concrete raised pool can be simple to construct if it is built from ready-made, hollow concrete blocks, rather than solid concrete poured into prepared formwork or shuttering. If you want a fancy shape, of course, poured concrete is essential, but the complexities of construction are so great that you are advised to leave this job to a skilled professional.

A blockwork pool is a different proposition, although you will be restricted to a rectangular and formal style. Construction involves creating a foundation upon which to build the blocks in the same manner as a double-skinned wall (but with no gap between the skins), the inner floor area also being concreted. The inner faces of the walls are rendered with a mortar mix incorporating a waterproofing compound, while complete waterproofing is ensured by building a polythene membrane into the floor and between the inner and outer skins of the pond walls.

Ideally, the outer skin of the walls would be of brick, but this could also be of concrete blocks finished with a decorative render. A generous coping would finish off the structure and provide a pleasant place to sit. With this type of construction, shelving for marginal plants can easily be installed by building up small platforms with concrete blocks.

Of course, bricks could be employed instead of concrete blocks to build a raised pool, although they are likely to be more expensive. If you use them, make sure they are frost resistant. In fact, winter damage is more likely to occur to a concrete or brick pool than one made from any other mate-

A SOLID FOUNDATION

Regardless of whether you are using concrete blocks or bricks to build your raised pool, it will be necessary to excavate an area of ground for the floor and foundations of the walls. This should be about 10cm (4in) deep and 10cm larger all round than the external dimensions of the pool. Surround the excavation by wooden boards nailed to pegs driven into the ground. The boards should be levelled with the aid of a spirit level and you should ensure that they are flush with the surrounding ground.

Line the excavation with a polythene sheet, which must be large enough that once the floor and foundation have been laid, it can be lifted on all four sides to the height of the walls. Then fill the hole with concrete, levelling it with the formwork using a long wooden board with a sawing motion. Cover the concrete with sacking or polythene to protect it from frost and leave for two or three days to harden fully. The concrete mix should be the same as that used for a concrete pool set in the ground.

A pool of this kind is relatively simple to construct, provides an important feature in a small space and is very easy to maintain. It is of a simple blockwork construction faced with stone.

rial. If the pool freezes, the pressure exerted by the ice on such a structure can lead to fracturing, so it is essential to prevent this by floating pieces of timber or rubber balls on the water throughout the winter.

Constructing a concrete or brick wall to surround a preformed pool is another option. This has the great advantage that the pool will be watertight from the beginning, but it can be constraining in size and configuration.

A flexible pool liner could also be used inside a brick or concrete structure. The advantage of having a liner that you can see and reach is that if seepage occurs, it can easily be dealt with, even to the extent of replacing the liner.

This versatility is offset somewhat by the fact that it is not easy to install a liner in a raised structure without creases or wrinkles showing, and they will be more obvious because the liner is closer to the eye. In this case, it is worth considering a welded rubber liner, made specifically for the shape and size of the structure. In fact, using a fitted liner is one of the neatest raised pool construction methods.

Liners also allow other materials to be used for the structure, such as wood, and special kits are available that provide everything you require. Remember that a raised pool does not have to be constructed specifically as a pool; if you exercise your imagination, you may find all manner of containers that can be adapted to this use with the aid of a flexible liner.

The pool wall greatly enhances the structure of this corner of the garden, forming a division which is pleasing to the eye and plays host to a different range of plant life. Even the small unlit lanterns enhance the clear cut lines of this design.

CONSTRUCTING A RAISED POOL

A BLOCK OR BRICK STRUCTURE

Once the concrete has set, you can construct the walls, trapping the polythene membrane between the inner and outer skins as they are built. Although laying concrete blocks and bricks requires skill, it is not beyond the capabilities of the amateur, provided care is taken. Use a simple running bond, each block or brick being overlapped by half of the one above. Build up the corners first, using a spirit level and a set square to ensure that they are vertical and true right angles.

All block- and brickwork must be laid so that the faces of the walls are vertical and the individual courses truly horizontal with uniform mortar joints. This may not be particularly easy for the newcomer to achieve, but constant use of the spirit level will help. Moreover, strings can be stretched between the corners to indicate the top of each course. Another easily made aid is a gauge rod, a wooden batten marked off to indicate several courses with an allowance made for mortar joints between them. Generally speaking, the joints should be about 1cm (3/8in) thick.

After rendering the inner face of the walls, the coping should be put in place to finish the structure. The result will be a neat and watertight construction for a permanent raised pool. A waterproof sealant should be applied to the walls in order to prevent the escape of free-lime into the water.

USING A PRE-FORMED POOL

When incorporating a pre-formed pool in a brick surround, it is only necessary to construct concrete strip foundations for the walls. These should be about 20cm (8in) wider overall than the thickness of the walls and about 10cm (4in) deep. When the concrete has set, the pool should be placed in position and its outline marked on the foundations in a similar manner to that used when setting a pool in the ground. Using the marks as a guide, you can build the walls, leaving enough room around the pool to permit it to be backfilled. Again, use sand or pea gravel for this purpose, as you would with a pool in the ground. Then the edge can be finished and capped.

The disadvantage of this method is that the wall and capping create a rather broad edge at the top. While this may be perfectly acceptable with a large pool, this is often not the case with a small structure. In this case, it is better to secure the pool in position, then build the walls closely around it. This secures the pre-formed pool within the walls and makes the edging a relatively simple brick overhang.

LINED RAISED POOLS

If a liner is to be used within a brick or block enclosure, proceed in the same manner as when using a waterproof render and polythene membrane, but omit these from the structure.

The beautifully proportional and neatly cut stone of this circular pond are as much of an attraction and a feature as the plants and water. The peripheral planting is an attempt to soften the stone and tie the feature to its surroundings.

BUILDING A RAISED BRICKWORK POOL WITH LINER

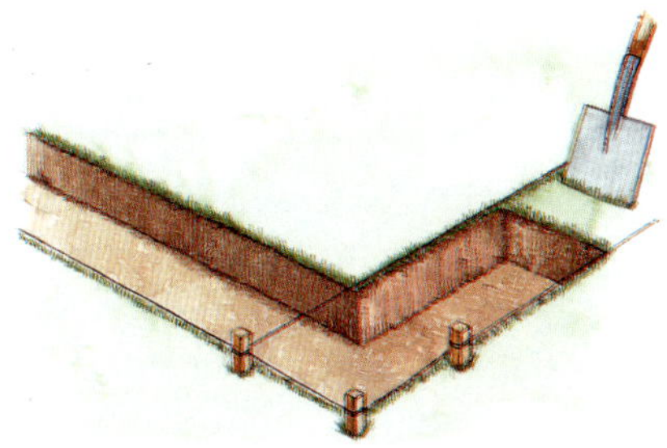

1 Mark out the area of the pool with pegs and excavate a foundation for the retaining wall about 10cm (4in) deep and 10cm larger all round than the external dimensions of the pool.

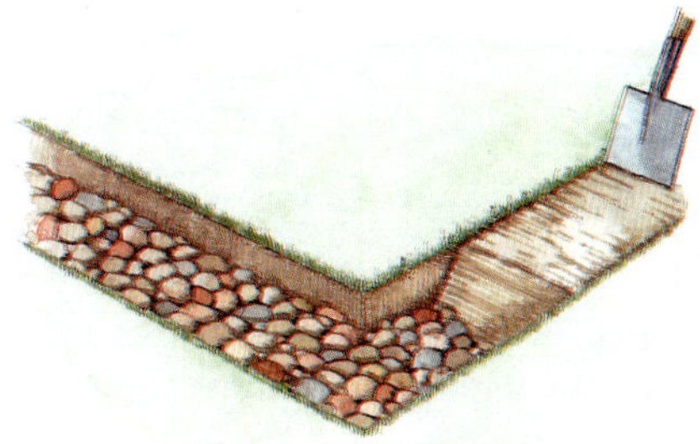

2 Place some crushed hardcore into the base of the foundation trench. Finish off with a level layer of concrete of the same mix as that used for a concrete pool set in the ground.

3 Build up the walls starting from a corner and use a traditional English bond. The wall must be both level and upright. Check levels regularly with a spirit-level.

4 To prevent liner damage from abrasive brickwork, secure fleece, geotextile matting or polystyrene sheets to the surface of the brickwork, using an industrial adhesive..

5 Install the liner, taking care to fit it neatly to the corners. A welded rubber liner is the best option.Turn the liner over the top edge of the brickwork so that it can be secured.

6 Finish the top of the wall with coping stones, or with a final row of bricks, bedded on mortar. The top edge of the liner will be trapped beneath this, just above the proposed water level.

Once the wall is nearing completion, the liner can be installed, its edge being trapped beneath the coping stones or a final row of bricks. To prevent any abrasive damage between the liner and the rough masonry, secure fleece or geotextile matting to the surface of the brickwork, using an industrial adhesive.

As an alternative, an attractive raised liner pool can be constructed using timber. This requires a level base slightly larger than the pool's overall dimensions. Although the timber must be treated with preservative and can be laid directly onto the ground, if the base is concreted this will further reduce the likelihood of the timber rotting.

Such a raised pool can be made from old railway sleepers, although any clean timber with a minimum cross-section of 10x15cm (4x6in) can be used. Cut the timber to size, carefully notching the ends to form halving joints. Use a set square to ensure that the corners of the structure are at right angles, then fasten them together using dowels or rustproof screws. Make sure that each length of timber is level before positioning the next. Build the timbers up until the desired height is achieved.

The interior of the wooden structure can be lined with fleece to prevent any damage to the liner. Simply tack this to the timber. Then lay the pool liner in place, making substantial folds in the corners if the liner has not been welded to the required shape. Rubber liners are unquestionably the best, but both PVC and LDPE can be used to good effect. Secure the liner either by trapping it beneath the uppermost timbers, or by nailing narrow wooden laths around the top, just above the proposed water level.

NATURAL WATER FEATURES

In gardening, modern thinking is that all that is natural must be the best. The whole concept of being environmentally conscious has spread throughout the garden, and has even extended to the area of water gardening. The logical outcome of this is that many gardeners have become interested in constructing pools wholly from natural materials; in this case, puddled clay.

THE PUDDLED CLAY POOL

Using puddled clay is the traditional method of creating a pool. However, it must be realized that clay-puddling is a labour-intensive task fraught with problems. Moreover, the finished pool will require constant maintenance to ensure that it remains watertight.

Obtaining the right kind of clay is the first requirement. This need not be from any particular source, but is should have specific qualities of malleability. To test whether a clay is likely to be suitable for lining a pool, take a sample, remove any extraneous material, and roll it in the palm of your hand. If the clay is usable, it will be pliable and rather like modelling clay. If it is dry and crumbly, or shows definite cracks when rolled around in your hand, even when damp, it will be unlikely to form a watertight seal.

The excavation for a puddled clay pool is prepared in much the same way as one that will be lined with concrete. Thus, it must be 15cm (6in) larger all round than the finished pool size, this thickness of clay being necessary to guarantee a good seal. The pool can be of any configuration, but it will be easier to construct if any curves are gentle and sweeping, acute angles being avoided. The sides of the pool should slope at an angle no greater than 45 degrees, otherwise the clay may slump.

CHOOSING A CLAY

For the most part, a local clay that conforms to the simple rolling test is likely to be the most satisfactory for the home gardener. However, there are bentonite clays that have been especially prepared for puddling water features. They are not commonly available to the amateur gardener because their application is somewhat specialized, but if you intend employing a contractor, rather than constructing the pool yourself, they are certainly worth discussing.

There are both sodium and calcium forms of bentonite clay. These are available as a powder and, when mixed with an existing heavy soil or clay base, swell to produce an impermeable material. The sodium version swells to approximately 15 times its volume, the calcium type to eight times. If it dries out, sodium bentonite clay will swell up again when wet, but the calcium form will not.

Such clays should only be used for a large pool. Anything smaller than 1.8x2.4m (6x8ft), with a maximum depth of less than 1.2m (4ft), can create difficulties, although not in the actual application process. Problems occur because chemicals seep from the clays and can prove toxic to fish in a small volume of water. To minimize this, even in a larger excavation, spread soil over the pool floor and marginal shelves.

When using this traditional method, calculating the quantity of clay you require can be difficult. Up to a third of the volume of clay delivered will be air, which will disperse once water is added. Therefore, to estimate the amount of clay that you will need for puddling, multiply the thickness you intend using by the area to be covered, then increase the result by a third.

PUDDLING

Once the excavation has been prepared, dampen it with water, then spread it with a generous layer of soot, ash or lime. This will act as a deterrent to earthworms, which have the irritating habit of puncturing the clay lining and drowning themselves in the water beyond.

Prepare the clay by adding sufficient water to make it sticky. Place a board on the floor of the excavation from which to work and, moving backwards from one side of the pool to the other, begin applying the puddle. The simplest method is to press it on to the soil by hand, wearing a pair of strong rubber gloves.

While you work, make sure that the clay already placed is kept moist. Use a watering can fitted with a fine rose to apply a gentle spray and, if available, spread damp sacking over the puddled area to reduce evaporation. Keeping the puddle

THE BENTONITE BLANKET

Although generally only used for large pools and installed by experienced contractors, the bentonite blanket is a fairly recent innovation that creates the benefits of puddling without some of the heartache. It comprises a specially-manufactured form of natural sodium bentonite, which is supplied in a pre-hydrated impermeable state as part of a geotextile blanket. This is installed rather like a pool liner, but swells on contact with water to become an impermeable barrier. It is also self-healing, so if you happen to push a garden fork through it, it will seal itself.

damp is absolutely vital, so choose a dull day on which to undertake the task, as this will also minimize evaporation.

Apply the clay in two or three layers, rather than attempting to lay the whole lot at once. It is much more difficult to obtain a consistent lining with a single application. The disadvantage when applying several layers is that you have to work from a fairly constrained position on a board placed on your previous work. Successful puddling is not an easy task.

Once the puddling process has been completed, spread soil over the floor and marginal shelves. Water can then be added carefully. To prevent the puddle from being disturbed, lay the end of the hosepipe on to a plastic bag on the floor of the pool. When the pool is full, look carefully for any streams of air bubbles that may indicate an incomplete seal. Initially, there may be many, as pockets of air will have been trapped in the soil and the surface layer of clay. If bubbles persist in any spot for more than 24 hours, it is likely that there is a problem, which should be investigated immediately.

Throughout the life of a puddled pond, it is vital to maintain the water level at the top of the puddle. Any exposure of the clay to the air is likely to result in cracking and leakage. The ill-thought out establishment of plants that may crack or pierce the puddle is also a potential problem, particularly in a situation where an informal wildlife pool is proposed and more invasive species of aquatic plant may be grown. In such circumstances it is sometimes possible to isolate them within profiled features by creating lined sections filled with soil from which they cannot easily escape. If these are associated with adjacent deep areas into which the plants cannot establish, then control is reasonably complete.

BUILDING A CLAY-PUDDLED POND

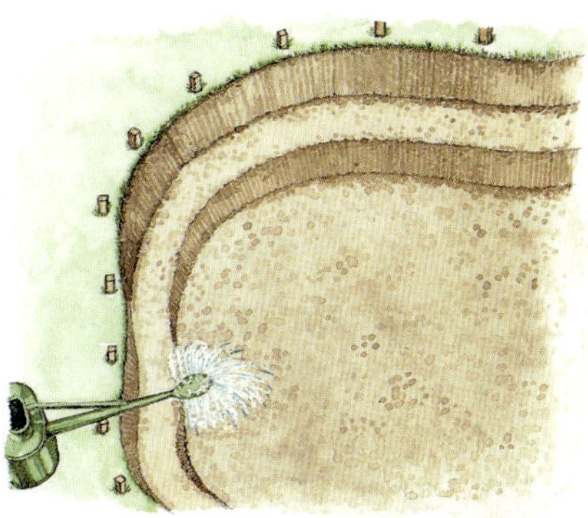

1 Mark out the area for the pool with pegs, then excavate to the finished size of the pool, remembering to allow for any marginal shelves. Dampen the soil with water.

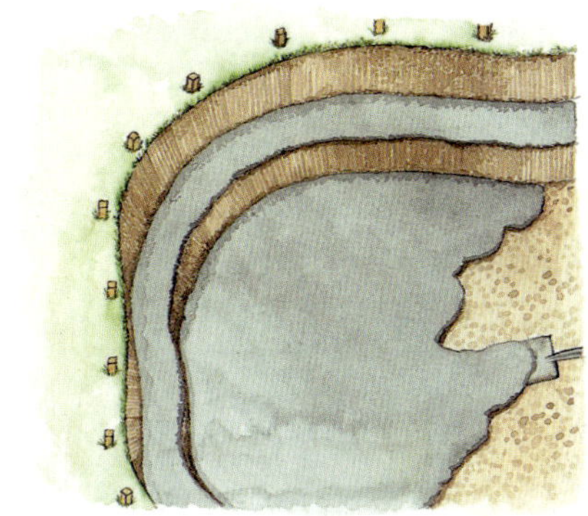

2 To prevent earthworms from puncturing the clay puddle (and drowning themselves in the water), dress the surface of the excavation with soot, ash or lime.

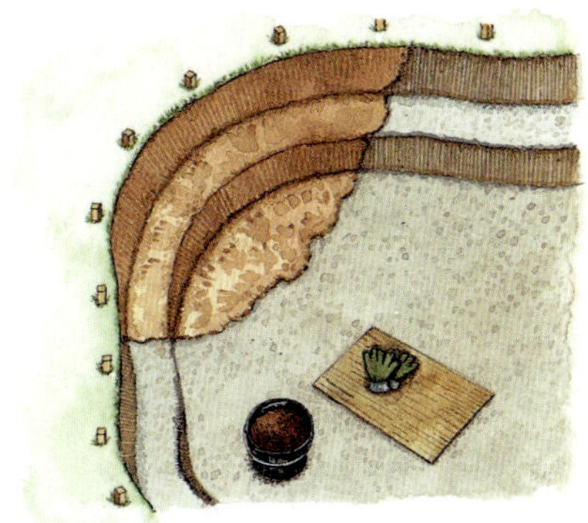

3 Prepare the clay by adding sufficient water to make it sticky and, working backwards from a board, apply the puddle. Press it on to the soil by hand while wearing strong gloves.

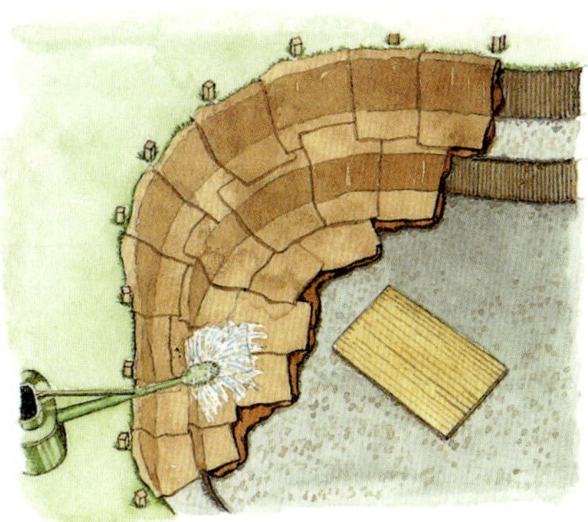

4 As work progresses, cover the puddled areas with damp sacks and moisten them regularly, using a watering can fitted with a fine rose, to prevent the clay from cracking.

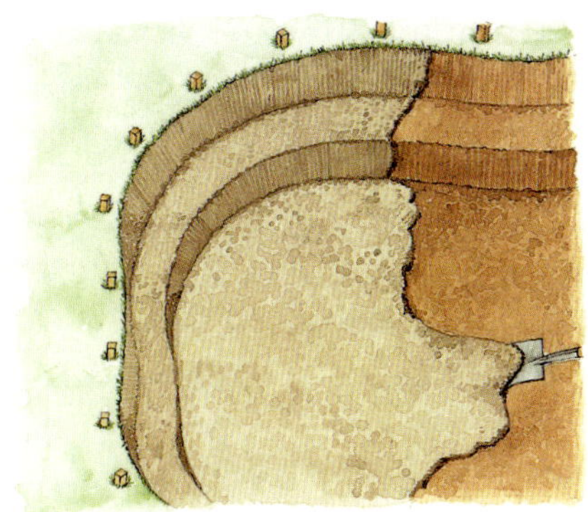

5 Apply the puddle in two or three layers for the best result. Make sure that the clay is kept damp throughout. Once puddling is complete, spread soil over the floor and marginal shelves.

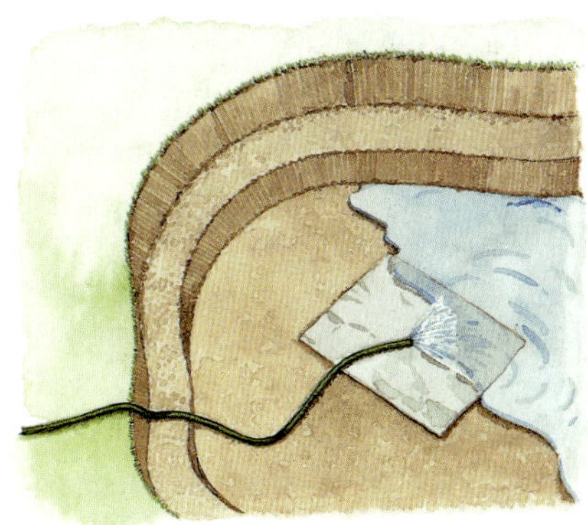

6 Finally, fill the pond with water by placing the end of the hose on a polythene bag placed on the floor of the pool to ensure that the flow of water does not disturb the puddle.

POOL EDGINGS

The edges of a pool are among the most difficult aspects of the construction to finish off effectively. The treatment applied can either make or mar the whole feature aesthetically, and the manner in which it is achieved can have a considerable effect on the longevity of the pool structure. An ill-conceived edge, especially around a lined pool, can create all manner of problems.

There are almost as many forms of edging as there are types of water garden. A variety of traditional edgings is available, but there are other innovative kinds, too, which provide further opportunities for developing interesting waterside features.

There are many edgings which can be used to finish off a pool. Paving is the most widely used and offers the opportunity for both access and recreation. Bricks and stones are also suitable.

COMPATIBLE EDGING

Visually, the edging must fit in with the overall style of the feature. A formal pool is normally easier to cope with, as it can be surrounded by paving or coping stones. Provided that the edge of the pool is level, there should be no serious impediment to achieving a neat formal finish.

However, paving stones often look out of place if used around an informal pool. You may be able get away with this if they are used at the front of the pool, while the remainder is surrounded by vegetation. Indeed, there is a practical purpose in using paving, provided that it is tastefully laid, as it will reduce wear on the lawn at the most natural point for anyone to stand and observe the pool or feed any fish. A couple of well placed paving slabs will be much more satisfactory than soggy worn turf.

Wildlife pools look ill at ease when any hard landscape materials are used around them. Instead, a planted or grassed edge should be employed, although this will be very difficult to make convincing and, in the case of grass, the most difficult to maintain.

PAVING

Irrespective of the pool construction method used, paving can be successfully installed as an edging. It is essential that the pool is level from side to side and end to end, and that sufficient surrounding ground has also been levelled to accommodate the paving.

The slabs should be laid on a mortar bed, about 2.5cm (1in) thick, using a mixture comprising five parts by volume of builders' sand and one part of cement. Combine these thoroughly in their dry state, then gradually mix in water until you achieve a stiff, but wet, consistency. Spread enough mortar along the edge of the pool to bed two or three slabs at a time, taking it out to the width of the slabs. Trowel it off roughly level. Do not lay all the mortar in one go, as it is likely to dry out before you finish bedding the slabs.

Each paving slab should be firmly bedded on the mortar and overhang the pool edge by about 5cm (2in). This will help disguise the construction material and, in the case of a pool liner, provide some protection from the possibility of bleaching by the sun.

Make sure that each slab is level in both plains with a spirit level. Once all the slabs have been laid, the gaps between them can be pointed with mortar, but take care not to let any fall into the water and seal them to prevent lime from leaching into the pool.

A GRASS EDGE

Some pool designs only work well where there is a natural turf edge. For the most part, these are constructed for the beauty that still water can offer, rather than for myriad colourful aquatic plants. They act as focal points in a landscape and are natural forms of art. In practical terms, however, a pool with turf running right to the water's edge can produce maintenance difficulties. Not only is there the constant problem of grass mowings falling into the water, but also the possibility that applications of lawn feed and weed-killing preparations will seep into the pool.

The important consideration with a turf edge is the depth of soil required over the edge of the pool construction. To ensure that this does not dry out, a minimum depth of 5cm

PAVED EDGING

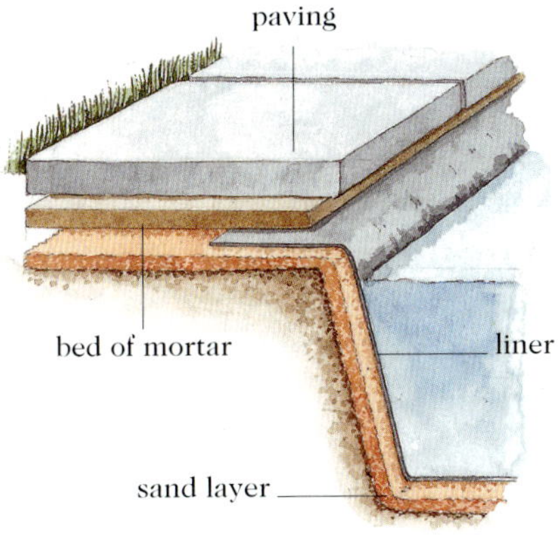

A neat formal edge for a lined pool can be made with paving laid on a bed of mortar. The liner is securely trapped between the soil and the paving, above the water level of the pool.

GRASS EDGING

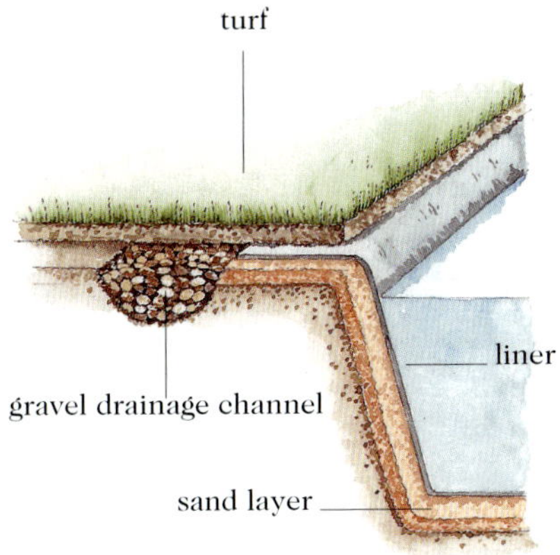

Turf laid up to the edge of the pool forms a most natural edge. A drainage channel filled with gravel just behind the liner will prevent ground water from muddying the pool.

PLANTED EDGING

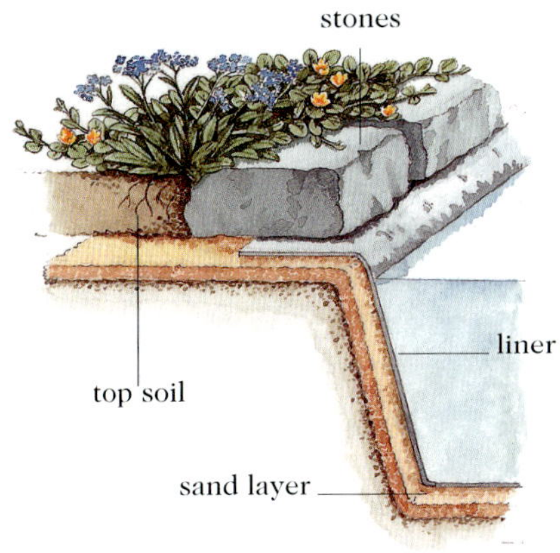

The use of plants behind a stone or brick edging softens the harshness of the pool side and is ideal for an informal pool. The plants will eventually spill over edge of the stones and disguise the liner.

(2in) is required, although 10cm (4in) would be much better. There is nothing worse than a verdant summer lawn spreading towards a pool surrounded by a yellowish border, indicating a lack of moisture.

Of course, if the edge is carefully contrived and the grass laid as turf, which is in contact with the water, provided the pool is kept topped up, water will seep up through the turf by capillary action and the grass will remain healthy. It will soak up quite a lot of water during hot summer weather, and as the pool will also lose some of its contents through evaporation at this time of year, diligence will be required to ensure a consistent water level.

A PLANTED EDGE

A planted edge is by far the best solution for an informal pool. This can be achieved with the aid of strategically placed rocks and soil pockets, but great care must be taken. Use the rocks to form a barrier around the edge of the pool and,

Random paving provides an interesting edge and sitting out area beside this modest pool. There is sufficient hard landscaping for practical purposes, but more than would suit such a small pool if it were not for the softening effect of surrounding planting.

TIMBER EDGING

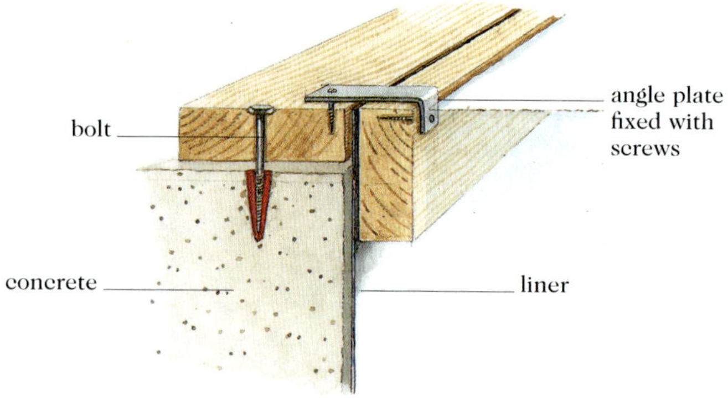

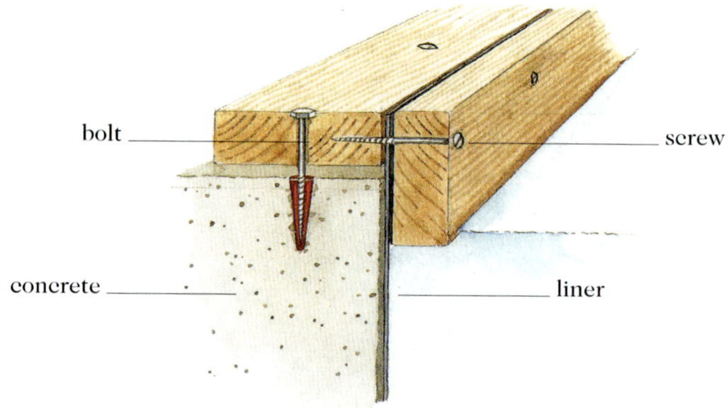

If you want the surface of the water in the pool to come right up to the top of the wooden edging, level with the surrounding ground, you will need to use timber plating joints to secure the two pieces of timber and trap the liner. This avoids puncturing the liner and so eliminates risk of seepage.

When the water level is below the timber, ordinary wood screws can be used to secure the wood and trap the liner. In either case, you will need to construct a concrete surround, into which to bolt the solid timber edge. Use heavy-duty brass or zinc screws to avoid rusting.

where a liner has been used, to secure this, too. Placing the rocks so that they overhang the water will also help to conceal the pool construction.

Unless the edging is to be a link between a rock garden and the pool, use rocks of modest size. Narrow flat rocks are ideal. These will form a retaining edge for the soil and should be largely disguised by the tumbling foliage of the plants established behind them.

Good soil preparation is vital to the success of such a venture, while sufficient depth must be available to establish the plants successfully. Often the depth of soil will be limited, and although the plants will be in close proximity to the water, they are unlikely to be aquatics, for in the summer the soil conditions could be quite dry. Consequently, some of the more boisterous rock garden plants would be appropriate.

Place the rocks in position and fill behind them with a good soil mixture incorporating a generous quantity of organic matter to help retain moisture. Plant behind the rocks and, where appropriate, add a second layer, either immediately behind or above. If you feel that rocks would be too large or intrusive, a similar edging can be contrived by laying paving slabs with pockets of soil between them. Once the plants are established, they will tumble over the slabs, softening their harsh angular lines. If the slabs are likely to be walked upon, they will need bedding on pads of mortar to ensure that they are stable and will not tilt.

USING TIMBER

Although not as permanent as traditional rock or paved edges, timber can prove extremely useful and versatile. If the pond is being constructed in conjunction with wooden decking or a causeway, timber edging will be a natural extension of this garden feature. There are several ways of fixing it, depending upon the effect you want to achieve. If the surface of the water in the pond is to be level with the surrounding ground, a fairly elaborate system must be employed. This involves constructing a concrete surround, into which a solid timber edge is bolted and which lies flush with the surrounding soil. The liner is trapped between this section of timber and the wooden edging that will sit in the water. Timber plating joints are used to hold the two wooden sections tightly together. Their screws do not penetrate the liner and, therefore, permit the water level to come right to the top without any fear of seepage.

Wooden decking and causeways provide good access for both pleasure and pool maintenance. Although a natural material, timber planking generally works best in fairly formal settings.

The edge of this pool has been developed into an extensive and very attractive beach feature. Pockets of soil have been created to allow clumps of contrasting plants to grow lustily.

If most of the timber edging is to be exposed, a similar system can be used, but instead of plating joints, screws are driven through the face of one section into the other. Since these will be above the final water level, it does not matter if they pass through the liner. Indeed, with this arrangement, the water should barely reach the bottom of the timber.

BRICKS

While paving slabs are the traditional edging for a formal pool, a properly executed brick edging can look superb. It is vital to use only engineering bricks or decorative bricks that are intended for outdoor use. These will not flake or shatter if exposed to frost when soaked with water.

The decision to employ a brick edging must be made early in the planning stage so that a rim to accommodate them can be formed when the pool is excavated. They should be bedded on mortar in the same manner as paving slabs, the face of each brick being 'buttered' with more mortar before placing it alongside its neighbour. Keep the joints between the bricks uniform, about 1cm (3/8in) wide, and carefully remove any mortar that squeezes from between them. Make sure none falls into the water. When all the bricks are in place, point the joints with more mortar.

THE BEACH

Beaches have become very fashionable features, especially for water gardens where wildlife is the major interest. Attractive, as well as simple to make, a beach will provide birds with an opportunity to bathe and give errant hedgehogs an escape route from the pool if they tumble in.

The simplest method of making a beach is to trap the edge of the liner between two rows of bricks or stones. This arrangement will allow it to be pulled tight and kept at a consistent level. The area in front, behind and over the bricks should be covered with cobbles and pebbles. This type of edging is very economical to install and looks good, but it will not produce a beach that will withstand constant wear.

If you intend regularly walking or standing on the beach, a more robust foundation will be necessary. Lay a shallow concrete footing on top of the liner, having allowed in the excavation for the depth of two bricks before reaching the surface of the beach. Lay the bricks as a low wall, pull the liner up behind them, then bank concrete up against it. Finally, add the cobbles or pebbles, covering the entire area.

PEBBLE BEACHES

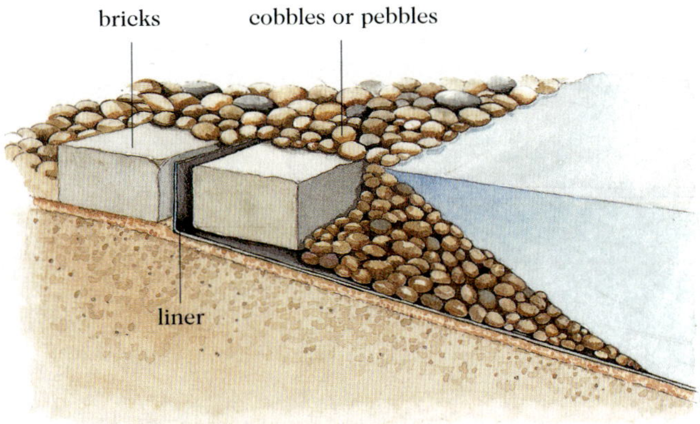

For a simple pebble beach in an inexposed area, the edge of the liner can be trapped beneath and between two rows of bricks or stones. These are then covered with cobbles or pebbles. This is an economical and simple edging for an informal pool, but it will not withstand constant wear.

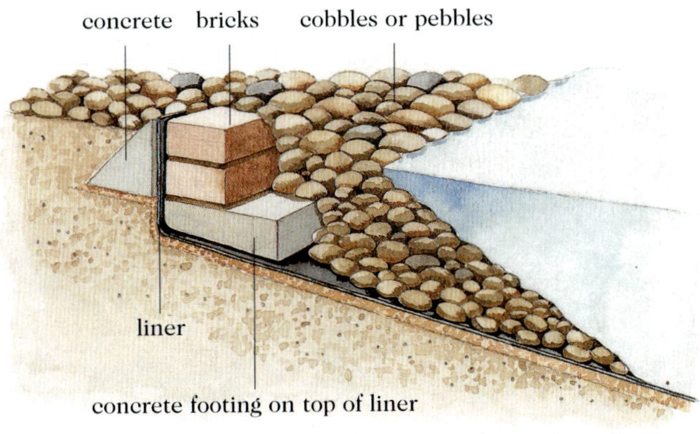

When heavy foot traffic is likely to be experienced at the pool side, a more substantial foundation will be necessary. Lay a shallow concrete footing on top of the liner and build a small wall, trapping the liner in place behind it. Bank concrete up against this, then cover the whole area with cobbles or pebbles.

BOG GARDENS

A bog garden can make the most wonderful adjunct to a pool or streamside, not only being pleasing to the eye, but also providing an opportunity to grow a wide range of fascinating plants. Some plants that often struggle in the herbaceous border flourish when provided with a constant supply of moisture, for example astilbes, hostas and ligularias.

THE NATURAL BOG GARDEN

If you have a naturally boggy area in the garden, you may be keen to turn it into a bog garden. However, do not begin work upon such a project until you are absolutely certain that it is boggy all year round. Many areas that are damp through autumn and spring, and wet during winter, dry out completely in the summer months. Often, such wet areas are the result of poor or disrupted land drainage, which creates a wet patch. Sometimes wet areas are fed by a spring, in which case they may well be permanent, but subject to change if the ground is cultivated too deeply, so take great care .

One of the major difficulties with a natural boggy area is ridding it of pernicious weeds. These normally comprise reeds and rushes of inelegant growth with a tremendous ability to seed freely, or spread by means of underground rootstocks. They also have waxy foliage that repels herbicides, leading to more frequent applications. Hand weeding will be tedious and, because of the boggy nature of the soil, it will often be impossible to completely remove invasive species like couch grass. Disturbing boggy ground also causes seed that has been lying dormant to germinate freely. So the natural boggy area is not the easiest to bring under control.

However, by the persistent use of a systemic herbicide in which glyphosate is the active ingredient, weed cover can be cleared up. For the best effect, the chemical should be applied when the weeds are growing actively with plenty of leaf to accept the spray. This will be absorbed and taken right down through the sap stream to the roots, killing the plants completely. Several applications will be needed, not only to ensure proper absorption by established plants, but also to cope with dormant seeds, which inevitably sprout when competing weed cover is removed.

Systemic herbicides do not act quickly, so if nothing much happens during the first couple of weeks, do not be concerned, especially if the weather is cool. Resist the temptation to seek a rapid result by burning off the foliage with a contact weedkiller. This will reduce the effectiveness of the systemic herbicide and may result in incomplete destruction, particularly of extensive underground root systems. Once heavy weed cover has been killed off, remove it by raking vigorously with a spring-tined rake. Then cultivate the ground prior to planting by digging it over with a garden fork, adding plenty of organic material at the same time.

CONSTRUCTING A BOG GARDEN

If you do not have a natural boggy area in your garden, it is a relatively simple task to construct one as an extension to a

Bog garden plants are available in great diversity. They only succeed in really damp areas and look happiest at the stream or poolside. Special provisions need to be made for them if the waterproof nature of the pool membrane creates dry conditions at the waterside.

CONSTRUCTING A BOG GARDEN AT THE POOL EDGE

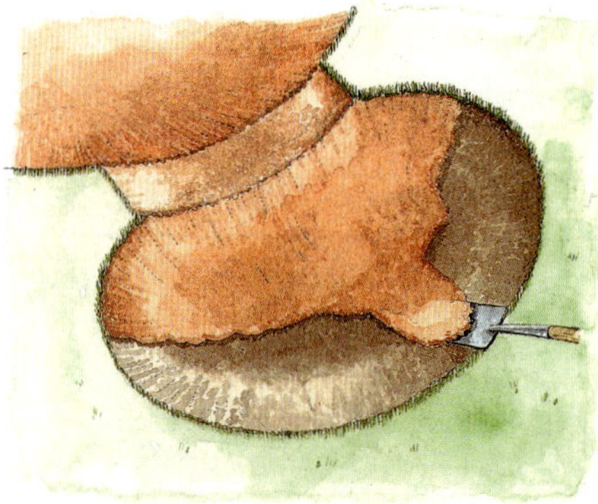

1 Excavate the area for the bog garden adjacent to the pool, ensuring a barrier between the two. Scour the excavation for sharp stones that could puncture the liner, then spread it with builders' sand.

2 Pull the pool liner over the edge in order to line the bog garden excavation, securing it in the same fashion as with the pool. Wrinkles in the liner are not important as they will not be seen.

3 Place a layer of stones between the pool and the bog garden to retain the soil. You will need to make sure that these are higher than the intended water level of the pool.

4 To prevent soil spillage into the pool, place fine rigid netting on the inside of the stones. This is particularly important if the stones are irregularly shaped. This will be secured by the soil.

5 Fill the bog garden with a friable organic rich soil, taking care not to damage the liner. This should be level with the top of the stones and at least 5cm (2in) above water level.

6 Fill the pool with water and allow it to seep through until the bog area is saturated and ready for planting. Some sinking may occur and further soil may be required.

pool when it is being built. Not only will bog garden plants look appropriate in this setting, but they will also provide a link with the surrounding garden and a more natural means of disguising the harsh edge of the pool.

The inclusion of a bog garden as an integral part of a pool must be planned well in advance if it is to be a success, for it needs to be part of the pool's actual construction. The most effective method of construction is to use a flexible liner. The excavation should form a shallow 'pool', with a uniform depth of between 30 and 45cm (12 and 18in), alongside the main water feature, being dug out at the same time. Scour the area of the bog garden for sharp stones and sticks that may puncture the liner and spread a layer of damp bricklayers' sand over the soil in the same manner as the pool itself. Although there will be no standing water in the boggy area, as in the pool, preventing leaks is just as important, as they might allow the soil to dry out.

Once the liner has been installed, the area between the pool and the bog garden should be clearly defined by a loose-laid retaining wall of bricks or stones. This will keep the soil out of the pool while allowing water to percolate through to the soil and create boggy conditions. Ideally, the soil in the bog garden should be at least 5cm (2in) above water level. It should be a heavy mixture incorporating a generous amount of well rotted organic matter.

If irregularly shaped stones are used to provide a barrier between the pool and bog garden, there is a chance that soil may spill through into the former. To prevent this, stretch fine garden netting across the inner face of the stones. This should be barely discernible when in place.

THE INDEPENDENT BOG GARDEN

Adding a bog garden to an existing pool is more difficult without having an adverse effect on the structure. The only time that this is really practical is when a pre-formed pool has been installed and a similar pre-formed shape is used as a bog garden, the two being linked by discreetly adding a short length of piping. Where a liner has been used, a much better job can be achieved if the old liner is removed, the excavation enlarged to encompass the boggy area, and a new larger liner purchased. In all other cases, it is preferable to build an independent bog garden. For all practical purposes, this will be self-contained, but to the uninformed observer, it may appear to be an integral part of the pool feature.

When creating an independent bog garden, the general rules that apply to building a normal pool should be observed. A pool liner is the easiest and most versatile form of construction, although both concrete and pre-formed pools can be used successfully.

The most important practical aspect of the boggy area's construction is achieving the correct depth. Unlike a bog garden that forms part of a pool complex and is kept damp by the pool water, an independent feature must retain its own moisture as much as possible. Since it will be isolated from the surrounding ground, it will not benefit from the natural percolation of moisture through the soil and may dry out rapidly. In view of this, a minimum depth of 60cm (24in) is recommended. An extensive boggy area could probably be a little shallower, but for the most part, the deeper it is, the better. The depth should be the same across the entire site.

The size of the excavation will depend upon the material being used in its construction. Despite the fact that only wet soil is involved, it would still be prudent to allow for up to 15cm (6in) of concrete if this material is to be employed.

Water provides a background to this marvellous bog garden, a wonderful contrast of flower and foliage, showing what can be achieved by extending the pool liner into the surrounding garden.

When a pre-formed pool is used as a bog garden, it is just as important to be able to support the weight of someone walking in it and, as such, it must be supported as completely underneath as a conventional pool.

A pool liner is installed in exactly the same way for an independent bog garden as for a pool, taking the same precautions to prevent puncturing. However, it need not be of

CONSTRUCTING AN INDEPENDENT BOG GARDEN

1 The excavation for an independent bog garden should be large enough to retain sufficient dampness. It should have a minimum depth of 60cm (24in) across the site.

2 Line carefully with polythene and fill with a good quality organic-rich soil. The liner finishes close to ground level to prevent moisture seepage and allow enough margin to secure with.

3 After planting ensure that the bog garden is kept constantly moist. It is also possible to install a hosepipe beneath the soil to the bog garden so that it can be watered discreetly.

PVC or rubber; polythene sheeting is perfectly adequate. When completely covered by soil, it does not suffer from exposure to ultraviolet light and subsequent degradation, as it would do in a pool. Also, as the liner does not show, any wrinkles or creases in it will not be evident. It will not be quite as easy to mould to the excavation as the other types of liner, but it is important to fill it properly, ideally with a little slack. If stretched too much in the corners, it may burst under the weight of soil.

A sufficient margin of liner should be allowed around the edges so that it can be secured satisfactorily. If you intend growing grass around the bog garden, you can cover the edge of the liner with soil and lay turf over the top. Make sure that the liner is not buried so deeply that moisture can escape from the upper layer of soil in the bog garden, effectively creating a leak. Remember that an independent bog garden acts very much like a pond and will require constantly moistening with water. Any escape of moisture may actually have an adverse effect on nearby plants.

If the bog garden is adjacent to other cultivated areas, the edge of the liner must be secured in a different manner. Where it has a straightforward formal outline, lengths of timber can be used, the liner being wrapped around these and secured by nailing on wooden laths. The wood and liner can then be buried just beneath the surface of the surrounding garden. The liner will protect the wood from rotting, while the whole arrangement makes finding and securing the edge of the liner a simple matter if major maintenance tasks or alterations are required.

Where a more informal outline is desired, the same effect can be achieved with bricks. This is a little more time consuming, since each brick must be wrapped under the edge of the liner and positioned against its neighbour, the entire edge then being buried, but it does allow great flexibility in shape.

A MINIATURE BOG GARDEN

Since many of the most popular bog garden plants are quite large, there is a common misconception that you can only have a bog garden if you have plenty of space. This is not so, for a very acceptable bog garden arrangement can be created in a wooden tub or sink buried in the ground. Indeed, there is an advantage to this kind of feature, as such containers are much easier to keep permanently wet. When planting a miniature bog garden, use plants of smaller scale, such as the lovely little *Primula rosea* and the bog asphodel (*Narthecium ossifragum*). Alternatively, you could devote the container to an individual vigorous species like *Primula florindae*, using it as a focal point or feature.

A bog garden can be free-standing and need not be associated with open water. Often such a feature is on the edge of the manicured garden and can be allowed to develop into a wildlife haven, garden plants mingling with colourful natives.

WATER MEADOWS

A water meadow is an area that is kept constantly moist by the close proximity of a river, rather than a pond, and often becomes a flood plain or wash during the winter, being periodically inundated as the river rises. Obviously, in a garden, this situation would not be desirable and, in any event, would be difficult to arrange. However, it is still possible to create the impression of a water meadow by careful planting and preparation of the soil. A water meadow should be planned as an extension to a water feature that is intended to appear natural, being a lush grassy area that is home to colonies of interesting moisture loving plants, which enjoy such conditions rather than the clinical manicured cleanliness of the formal bog garden.

In many respects, a water meadow is very similar to an alpine meadow. However, alpine meadows recreated in gardens are normally only reliably damp during the spring, often becoming quite dry in the warmer summer months. With a water meadow this must not be permitted to happen; constant moisture is the key to success.

CREATING SUITABLE SOIL CONDITIONS

In nature, a water meadow consists largely of silt, which is continually deposited by flooding, yet it drains freely after inundation. It also has a relatively heavy covering of grass. Therefore, the soil excavated when creating a pool or stream is unlikely to be suitable for spreading around the feature if a water meadow is contemplated. Heavy clay soil or any soil containing a large proportion of stones should be disposed of elsewhere. Good average garden soil, particularly a medium loam, is a much better proposition. Indeed, any garden soil that is neither extremely light nor heavy can be prepared to allow the successful establishment of water meadow plants. However, the first requirement is good drainage, which can be achieved by laying a system of pipes below ground.

The drainage system should be installed at least 45cm (18in) below the surface of the soil. this will allow water to percolate through the soil and into the pipes, rather than rush away freely and create rapidly drying surface conditions. The prevention of standing water for any lengthy period is the main requirement.

Any standard land drainage pipes are suitable. They should be installed in a simple herring-bone pattern that leads with a gentle fall to either a main drain or ditch. If neither is available, the water can be directed into a soakaway. For the most part, a soakaway filled with broken bricks will adequately remove excess water.

The success of a water meadow depends upon a happy relationship between the grasses and the desirable plants. Although a water meadow is a damp feature, neither grasses nor other plants will enjoy sitting in prolonged wet conditions during the winter.

The water meadow needs to be carefully managed to ensure that stronger species do not crowd out the weak. This can be contolled by a cutting regime that allows seeds of the less vigorous kinds to mature while those of invasive plants are removed before ripening.

Once the drainage system is in place, the soil should be prepared by digging in plenty of well rotted garden compost or similar organic material. Remember that a genuine water meadow is likely to be rich in both nutrients and organic material owing to regular winter flooding. The plants that prosper under such conditions demand much richer soil than one might suppose, especially since they will be competing with vigorous grasses.

SOWING THE GRASS SEED

The soil preparation should be sufficiently thorough that it can be raked out smoothly, allowing grass seed to be sown. Although water meadow plant seed mixtures are available, sometimes incorporated with an appropriate grass mixture, it is much more satisfactory to establish the grass first, then plant the water meadow plants through it. For the best effect, use a fine-leaved grass such as fescue. While this is not a species that would tolerate the kind of inundation to which a natural water meadow might be subjected, it will provide a satisfactory background for water meadow plants and permit them to prosper with minimal competition.

Once the soil has been raked out, firm it down by shuffling across the area with your feet, then rake out the surface again. While it need not be level from one end to the other, it should be free from unnecessary undulations. Mark out the area to be sown in metre or yard squares, depending on the coverage specified on the seed packet. You can either use the edge of a hoe to mark a grid in the freshly prepared tilth, or stretch strings between pegs set around the edge of the site. Measure out the required amount of grass seed for each square in a cup and spread this evenly over the soil. Gently rake over to provide a smooth finish.

Germination will take place within a week or ten days, depending upon the weather. It is best to sow the grass in spring or autumn when the weather is not too cold and the soil moisture content is good. While you can sow grass seed during the summer, regular watering will be essential if it is to grow away strongly.

Any weeds that appear among the grass seedlings should be removed by hand, as at present there is no satisfactory selective weedkiller that can be used freely on seedling grass. Once the turf has knitted together, it is vital to spray it with a selective broad-leaf weedkiller. This will kill all potential competition before your chosen water meadow plants are introduced. Once the latter have been planted, it will be almost impossible to spray, as most of the desirable water meadow plants are broad-leaved types.

ADDING THE PLANTS

Having ensured a clean established turf, you can then plant the water meadow species. These are best raised in plugs and planted out with a small rootball. Establishing the grass in spring and allowing it to come through the summer is ideal, as the flowering water meadow plants can be planted during the autumn and will become well established by the following spring and summer flowering season.

PROBLEM-SOLVING

INHERITING A POOL

I have just moved into a house with an overgrown concrete garden pond. Can you please advise me of the best way of dealing with the problem? I would like to start the whole thing again.

An overgrown pool can only be cleaned out satisfactorily, and some of the plants salvaged for replanting, during spring or early summer. If you are not concerned about saving any of the plants, the work can be undertaken at any time. The first task is to reduce the water level sufficiently so that you can work comfortably in the pool. Normally, using a hosepipe to syphon out the water is the best way of doing this. Do not remove too much water, as fish may be lurking among the plants, and you may not come across them until some of the plants are removed. Indeed, throughout this process, the fish will be at risk of being damaged. However, little can be done to protect them, except to take great care when lifting the plants and to be aware of their possible presence.

Once the plants have been removed, drain the pool completely. Any remaining fish will be found in the muddy mess that always settles on the bottom. Remove them carefully, placing them in buckets of clean water in a cool place, well out of the sun. Exposing them to warmth is likely to cause stress and even death. To make them feel at home, and provide a little cover, add a handful of submerged aquatic plants to each bucket.

The plants that have been removed should be left as they are until you are ready to replant them. Marginal aquatics are best placed in clumps on a piece of thick

An inherited pool that is overgrown needs very careful handling. Remove all the plants individually and ensure that they do not dry out. Although an unsightly tangle, a pool like this can often yield some interesting plants. Fish are often flourishing too.

polythene and put in a corner of the shed or garage. Waterlilies can have all their leaves cut off and the rootstocks submerged in buckets of water. Submerged aquatics can be gathered together and placed in a polythene bag with the top securely fastenedand left for several days without coming to any harm.

Having removed the plants and fish from the pond, scrub it thoroughly to remove algae and any other extraneous matter. Leave it to dry out, and check that it is intact and there are no signs of leaks or fractures, before refilling with water.

When replanting, choose only the best plants from the collection that has been removed. It may be better to discard the more invasive species. In any event, take only the vigorous outer shoots from a group, and do not attempt to plant large clumps back into the pool. These rarely grow away as quickly as young growths. Moreover, by using such small pieces, it will be possible to wash them completely clean, removing the possibility of re-introducing troublesome pests like the great pond snail.

Irrespective of how the pond was planted previously, it is wise to use aquatic planting containers. These may not necessarily provide complete control of invasive species, but with a little careful management, they will contain the plants and can prevent the sort of mess that you inherited from occurring again. If the plants have started to grow vigorously, cut them back hard at planting time. This will encourage vigorous stable growth.

Leave the plants to establish for four or five weeks before re-introducing the fish. If you put them back sooner, they will disturb the plants and cloud the water. While they are out of the pool, ensure that they are kept cool and in clean water, and fed regularly with a good-quality fish food.

Trees create enormous problems for the pool owner. Not only do they reduce light drastically, but they also pollute the water with their fallen decomposing leaves. Such a severely affected pool should be abandoned.

I have inherited a pool that is in an unsatisfactory position, being partially shaded by trees. It is made from a strong pool liner, which looks to be in good condition. I would like to empty the pond and re-install the liner in another part of the garden, but I am not sure how to do this.

It is not impossible to move a pool liner successfully, but it can be quite difficult, and you should be aware of the potential problems before you attempt the task. First, you need to be fairly certain that the pool liner is intact. If the pool is holding water and the liner is made from rubber or low-density polyethylene, there is a chance of success. If it is of another, cheaper, material, attempting removal is likely to be a waste of time.

Assuming that all the plants are growing in containers, it will be a simple matter to remove them and pump out the water, along with the accumulated silt on the floor of the pool. Be sure to remove all the fish and ramshorn snails first. If the liner is covered with soil, removing it without causing damage will be almost impossible. In this situation, the only satisfactory method is to agitate the soil until it becomes a slurry, then to pump this out with a sludge pump. However, the expense of hiring the pump is likely to outweigh the cost of buying a new liner in the first place, which will almost certainly be the better alternative.

If you are able to remove the liner successfully, remember that it will restrict the size and configuration of the new pool. It is always easier to create an excavation that fits into the garden landscape, then purchase a liner to fit, rather than try to make a pool of pleasing configuration from a liner that limits its size, shape and depth.

CHAPTER THREE

WATERFALLS AND STREAMS

Moving water is a wonderful asset in the garden, and never more so than when incorporated as a natural feature. There can be few sounds more romantic and soothing than water tumbling over rocks, and with modern technology it is relatively simple to add this magical aspect to your garden. In the past, the greatest deterrent to the use of moving water in domestic gardens was the mechanism needed to make it work; it could be quite complicated to achieve constant flowing water easily, cheaply and without a considerable amount of pipework. Modern submersible pumps have rid us of all the paraphernalia of plumbing, and in recent years have become very efficient and extremely reliable. Indeed, unless you contemplate an extensive scheme, the submersible pump is likely to do the job well. The introduction of sectional streams has also made practical stream construction more reliable for the amateur, although the lined stream is still the least intrusive, even if it is the most demanding to make. The same applies to the waterfall, although with the careful use of stone, it can be impossible to detect the presence of a liner. Apart from streams and waterfalls, other moving water features can also be constructed. For inspiration, look to the wonderful creations that our forebears made. We do not have to rely upon gravity as they often did, and we can be much more inventive, putting small pumps into all sorts of places to create moving water that is surprising yet reliable. While moving water does have an adverse effect upon some aquatic plants, particularly waterlilies, which are naturally plants of quiet backwaters, stream banks provide extensive opportunities for growing marginal and bog garden plants. A waterfall will confer more restrictions on planting, but few can deny the benefits it can bring to the most modest of schemes, the water itself becoming the primary attraction.

A natural-looking waterfall not only adds sounds and movement, but also provides an opportunity for imaginative planting. Sadly, waterlilies will not tolerate turbulent water.

WATERFALLS

Few gardens are blessed with natural waterfalls, although some with natural streams have what amount to small rapids. These are best left undisturbed, especially if well worn by the water and coated with algae.

In most cases, a waterfall must be constructed, but this must be done with care and sympathy for its surroundings. It is not aesthetically desirable simply to create a mound of rocks or soil to provide sufficient height for a cascade; a waterfall must flow naturally from adjacent garden and landscape features if it is to be completely effective.

A SUITABLE BACKDROP

The normal method of integrating a waterfall is by building a rock garden as a backdrop to the pool. When done tastefully, this can be very successful, but it must be a true rock garden, not a heap of rocks with stones protruding from it. If you intend constructing this type of feature, do not use the spoil from the pool's excavation for the mound, as this subsoil will not be suitable for growing alpine plants. The structure of a rock garden should be formed by placing the rocks carefully in layers so that they look like natural rocky outcrops. You will then need to backfill them with a suitable free-draining growing medium.

Of course, the soil removed from the main excavation can be used to support a waterfall if the backdrop is not to be a rock garden. A planted mound can be quite effective if the soil is contoured in such a way that the mound appears to grow out of the ground, rather than being placed upon it. This is not always easy to achieve by soil profiling alone; often, thoughtful planting to obscure or enhance views is the most effective way of coping with the problem.

Provided a waterfall is considered during the planning and construction stages of a pool, there should be no undue difficulty in fitting it into the garden landscape. Only when the water garden already exists, and the feature is considered as an addition, will any significant difficulties arise.

A combination of controlled water flow and the careful placement of weathered rock has produced an outstanding natural looking feature. Waterside niches have been thoughtfully created for marginal aquatics and rock dwelling shrubs.

A LINED CASCADE

While pre-formed waterfall units are doubtless the easiest and most secure method of construction, they can be inflexible and difficult to integrate naturally into the garden landscape. Heavy planting and liberal use of rocks is the only way to disguise them. If you want to have an unobstructed view of water movement, or to create a completely natural effect, you will need to consider alternative forms of construction.

Using a pool liner to create a waterfall or cascade provides great opportunities for the skilled designer, for it is possible to produce all manner of tumbling and splashing effects by careful manipulation of the structure. In some cases, the liner may simply be concealed with a layer of pebbles, but using it as a waterproof barrier behind an arrangement of rocks and gravel is preferable. With careful construction, there need be no visual evidence of the liner at all.

DIGGING OUT

The excavation for a lined waterfall should begin adjacent to the pool. If the finished feature is to comprise the liner alone, perhaps covered with a layer of washed pebbles and a rock edging, it is important to dig out the soil to the final shape, but with an allowance for a bedding layer of sand. As far as possible, the excavation must be cut from compacted soil; a little slippage is not as critical with a lined waterfall as with a pre-formed unit, but it can destroy the entire effect and make reconstruction necessary. If the falls will be of rock with the liner forming a waterproof barrier behind, provision must be made when digging to accommodate the rocks, though of course adjustments can be made in the excavation as the rocks are installed.

One of the most critical points to remember is that each area at the base of a drop must tilt backwards. Water should be able to cascade into it, then by sheer volume overflow into the next section. If the base of a fall is flat, or slopes forward, it will dry out when the pump is switched off.

The edge of a fall can also be designed to provide interesting water movements. A continual curtain of water will result from a uniform edge, but violent tumbles can be arranged by pinching the water and forcing it through narrow gaps. This can be achieved with a plain liner, but it rarely looks natural. Placing suitable rocks along the edge of the drop, in a manner that gives the desired water effect, will look much better and be easier to arrange.

ADDING THE LINER

As with lining a pool, remove any sharp objects from the excavation and spread a layer of sand over the base and sides to cushion the liner. (Fleece and similar materials are difficult to install without creating lumps and creases.)

Ideally, a single sheet of liner should be used, but in many cases this will be impractical. Where two or more pieces are necessary, work from the pool upwards and ensure that each has a generous overlap in the direction of water flow. If there are any awkward corners in the shape of the waterfall, make bold folds and pleats, rather than trying to spread the irregularities, which will only introduce unsightly wrinkles.

The edge of the liner must be buried or covered with stone, but make sure it is above the highest intended water level of the waterfall, otherwise extensive seepage will occur into the surrounding soil.

MAKING A LINED CASCADE

1 Excavate the shape of the cascade feature, ensuring that the back part of each bowl is deeper than the front so that when the pump is switched of some still water remains for pleasing effect.

2 Line carefully with pool liner, ensuring a generous overlap where necessary. Smooth out the liner so that any folds are large and deliberate. These will be much easier to disguise.

3 Trim back the surplus liner and place rocks in position to hide the edge. For the best effect, the rocks should be from the same source so that they are of similar colour and strata.

INSTALLING A PRE-FORMED WATERFALL

There is a wide range of pre-formed waterfall and cascade units that can be used as an addition to a pool. Some are quite attractive, but others are awful. The worst are made from plastic or fibreglass and have an artificial rock edging. Not only are these ugly, but the fake rocky edge also makes them extremely difficult to install so that they look natural.

Some pre-formed waterfall units are single structures, while others comprise a series of separate sections with varying shapes that provide some flexibility in the final design. None is easy to install so that the finished appearance is convincing, unless they are liberally planted or disguised by carefully positioned rocks. However, they do have the virtue of being watertight, something that is often difficult to achieve with other forms of construction.

PREPARING THE SITE

A waterfall must be installed on a slope, so some form of mound or soil profiling will be essential. This should be tall enough to permit the installation of the pre-formed units and broad enough to accommodate their length. The soil should have been allowed to settle for some months before installation takes place, since the waterfall must have a sound base that will not sink. To obtain the right effect, and to ensure that water both remains and flows in all the right places, accurate levelling of the units, in both planes, is critical.

MARKING OUT AND EXCAVATING

Place the units in position and mark around them. Start with the lower unit, for it is essential that the position of the final drop is directly over the pool. Carefully excavate an area that matches the outline and contours of the unit, allowing enough extra room for a layer of sand. Repeat the process for the remaining units until you reach the top of the waterfall.

INSTALLING THE UNITS

Spread a generous layer of sand in and around the excavation for each unit so that it can be firmly bedded. This will be much better than using the soil, as the sand is finer and permits much greater accuracy when levelling. Soil can be used to finish off around the unit.

Position the lower moulding first, making sure that it is secure. The second and any subsequent units can be added

A waterfall can be a wonderful focal point in the garden, but rarely is its structure elegant. Here beautifully arranged planting enhances the appearance of tumbling water and completely disguises the structure.

INSTALLING PRE-FORMED CASCADE UNITS

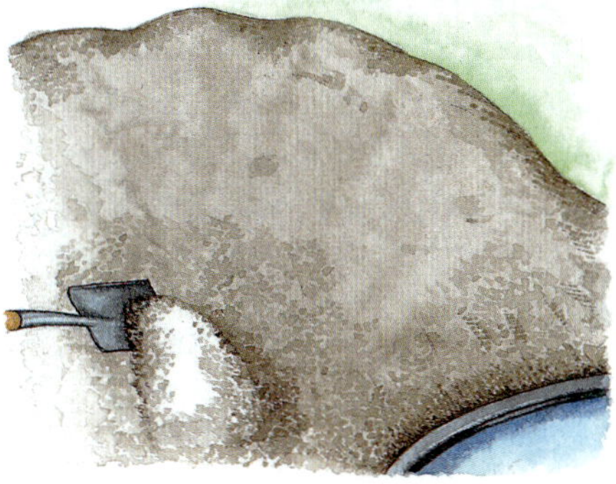

1 Pre-formed waterfall units should be installed on a slope. If artificially created, this should be tall and broad enough to permit their comfortable accommodation and the soil allowed to settle first.

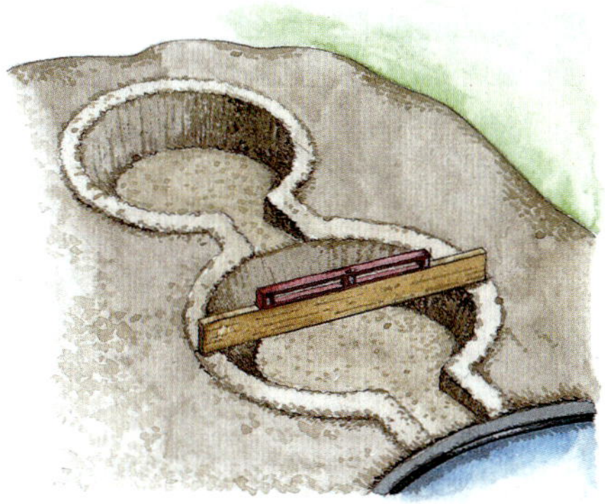

2 Place units in position and mark around them. Start with the lower unit to ensure that the drop is directly over the pool. Excavations should be slightly larger than each unit and the base level.

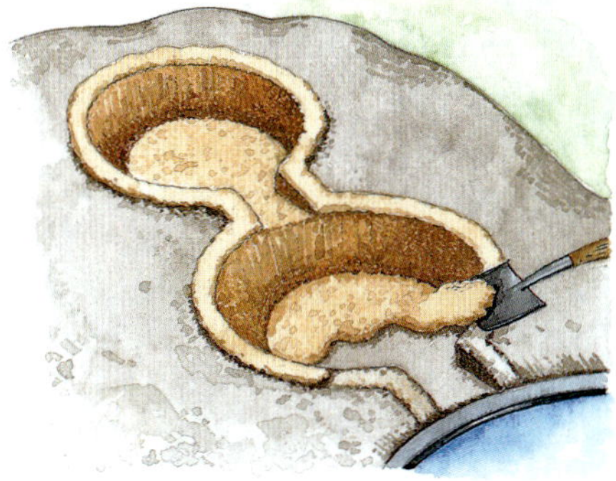

3 Spread a generous layer of sand around the excavation so that each unit can be firmly bedded. Sand is much more satisfactory than soil, permitting much greater accuracy of installation.

4 Position the lower unit first, making sure that it is securely bedded. Then position subsequent units with the lip of each directly over the moulding below, or else splashing and seepage will occur.

5 Once units are securely in place, the edges can be disguised with stone, which should be from a single source. If soil is to be retained by the stones, cement them to prevent seepage into the units.

6 Pre-formed pools can look harsh and unnatural if full advantage is not taken of the opportunity to plant around them. Remember that the soil in these areas will not be dampened by the waterfall.

next, taking care to position the lip of each directly over the moulding below, otherwise splashes and seepage will occur.

Given the unsightly appearance of most pre-formed waterfall units, it is worth trying to disguise the edges. Those of very simple form are easier to deal with, for soil can be brought up to the edge and rocks placed strategically around the rim, pockets of soil being incorporated to allow planting.

It is also possible to disguise the floor of each unit by covering it with well washed pebbles. The flow created by a standard submersible pump is unlikely to cause any disruption to this layer, and the effect of water tumbling over the stones will be very pleasing.

Pre-formed waterfall units can also be very effective if the ground is terraced. This offers a splendid opportunity for creating a cascade.

As an alternative to an irregular land form or a rock garden, build a simple low rock wall at the edge of the pool. This can be constructed with pointed mortar joints or simply laid dry. Either way, pockets can be incorporated to allow for planting, which will soften some of the harshness of the raw stone immediately after construction.

Backfill behind the wall with soil and, if desired, create a further wall and water drop. However, if you do this, something rather larger than the traditional cascade unit will have to be used beneath the lip of the upper unit. Otherwise, water will splash everywhere.

Take great care when positioning the unit that its lip projects just beyond the face of the wall. This will prevent any possibility of the water splashing and scouring any of the planting pockets created.

CONCRETE WATERFALLS

While their successful construction demands considerable skill, concrete waterfalls make permanent features that have much to commend them. When used in conjunction with rocks and stones, they can be the most effective and natural looking of all moving water features.

BUILDING A CONCRETE WATERFALL

When a traditional waterfall is constructed from concrete, its excavation must be 10cm (4in) larger all round than the finished feature. If the waterfall will be built on a mound of soil, it is essential that this be allowed to settle or be compacted before work begins. Shrinkage or slippage of the soil beneath the concrete can cause serious fractures. If you have doubts about the soil base, it may be wiser to use a liner or preformed unit instead. Of course, a concrete waterfall may be constructed as an integral part of a rock garden which, if soundly built, will provide a suitably solid foundation.

As with concrete pool construction, it is preferable to line the excavation with builders' polythene, not only to act as a waterproof membrane, but also to prevent rapid dying out of the concrete, which can lead to cracking. If the weather is very warm, protect the surface with damp sacking or a similar material. When the surface has tightened up, sprinkle it regularly using a watering can fitted with a fine rose.

MAKING A CONCRETE WATERFALL

1 Excavate the cascade feature, removing sufficient soil to comfortably accommodate thd edging stones. If the excavation is being made on disturbed soil, this should be well compacted.

2 Install the polythene liner, ensuring sufficient overlap along the sides. This will not only act as a waterproof membrane, but will also prevent rapid drying out and cracking of the concrete.

3 Put a layer of concrete down to about two thirds of the required finished depth and place the wire mesh reinforcement over the top. Push this firmly and evenly into the concrete.

4 Add a further layer of concrete over the mesh and tamp down firmly to provide an even finish. Position the edging stones carefully while the concrete is still wet.

5 Dress the floor of the cascade with decorative pebbles set into the final concrete layer. To obtain the best effect, carefully place each one, taking care not to splash them with wet concrete.

6 Cover with damp sacks and keep watered to prevent the concrete drying out too quickly, which often leads to hair cracks appearing, later resulting in larger cracks or flaking of the surface.

The concrete mixture and construction method are the same as described for a concrete pool (see pages 84-9), but any rocks or stones must be added while the concrete is still wet so that they become an integral part of the structure. Adding them once the concrete has set will be very difficult, and they will look unconvincing. Therefore, before you begin concreting, you must know exactly what you are going to do and how you are going to place the rocks so that the basins of the waterfall appear like natural stone structures, rather than concrete. Pebbles can be set into each basin, and rocks arranged at the lip to provide suitable water flow.

Concrete waterfalls do not have to take a traditional form, however; the construction method lends itself to a number of variations. One of the most interesting is the grotto, where a pool is constructed with a background that is similar in appearance to a rock garden. At the summit of this, a small cavern is constructed to house a pump outlet set in a sunken container filled with well washed pebbles or stones. The stones extend down a concrete watercourse, into which they are embedded. Water is pumped into the grotto where it emerges from among the stones and wends its way down the pebble-strewn watercourse, which should be planted with ferns and moisture loving plants, to the pool below.

WATER STAIRCASES

The water staircase makes a complete contrast to the normal waterfall. Widely constructed by the French and Italians throughout the last two centuries, this fascinating water feature can be easily incorporated into the modern suburban garden. As the name implies, the feature comprises a number of steps, which are transformed by sparkling silvery water that tumbles down them. The water staircases of European gardens were very grand affairs, and part of their appeal was their scale. However, an impression of this romantic era can be created in the small garden using concrete drainage pipes. These should be set horizontally, one behind the other, into a bed of concrete laid over a waterproof membrane, each pipe being slightly higher than the one before. This produces a staircase with rounded steps.

The end of each pipe should be filled with concrete or soil, and a suitable arrangement of rocks and planting put into place to disguise the ends. It is advisable to treat the pipes with a sealant to prevent the escape of free-lime into the pool below. The feature will look a little stark to begin with, but once the pipes begin to be tarnished by algae, they will soon look well established. Make sure that the pump is powerful enough to produce a vigorous splashing cover.

A gentle flowing staircase with shallow steps creates an attractive rippling effect. The water catches the sunlight and changes mood as it dances on downwards.

MAKING A SIMPLE WATER STAIRCASE

1 Prepare a slope to accommodate the pipes. If it is artificially created permit it to settle. Spread over a layer of builder's polythene to act as a waterproof membrane before laying concrete.

2 A stiff mix of concrete should be made and placed over the polythene. Starting from the bottom, set each pipe firmly in the concrete, placing the next evenly behind it.

3 When all the pipes are in position, the ends can be disguised with concrete, soil or stones. A slight upstand of stones at the cemented in edges will ensure that water does not seep from the edges.

STREAMS

Some gardeners are fortunate enough to have natural streams running through their gardens. Even a ditch can be transformed into a stream-like feature, so if you already have such an asset, take the opportunity to exploit it to the full.

The major problem with a natural stream is a constant supply of water. In dry summer weather, you need to be sure that it will not dry up if you are planning to use traditional waterside plants. With a ditch this may often be the case, water only flowing freely during winter and spring. Seasonal stream features, such as this, need careful handling and should only be planted with bog garden subjects that are tolerant of periodic drying out. It is no use fighting such a feature; accept the situation and contrive your planting to produce as natural a waterside look as possible.

If a stream flows freely all year, it will merely need decorating with appropriate planting and perhaps a stone or shingle bed. Small adjustments may also be necessary to improve the way in which it flows.

Remember, however, that only part of the stream is yours; it will belong to someone else at the points where it flows into and out of your garden. This is a very important consideration, especially if you anticipate making alterations to its flow rate, which can have an effect both upstream and downstream. Not only should you consult the owners of neighbouring properties, but also any local or rivers authorities. This also applies if you wish to take a backwater or pond off the stream, although once filled and settled, this is unlikely to alter the flow rate at all.

THE ARTIFICIAL STREAM

Most gardeners who want a stream, however, have to create it themselves, using the same methods as when constructing a pool. The main virtue of an artificial stream is that you have complete control over the flow of water. The disadvantage is visual, since it has to begin and end somewhere. Naturally, an artificial stream will be a recirculating feature, but it must be laid out so that it appears to have a purpose. Apart from the careful plotting of its route, skilled planting must be employed if you are to integrate it satisfactorily in the garden landscape.

Unlike a natural stream, an artificial stream can flow where you want, and specific planting niches can be created. Water levels can be planned, and the ideal conditions for a variety of aquatic species guaranteed. Make sure that you consider all the possibilities, and plan the construction of the feature very carefully in advance.

A natural stream needs careful treatment, planted areas being protected from erosion. The simple removable bridge enables the floral display to be readily viewed from the opposite bank and provides access for mowing the grass.

A LINED STREAM

A liner is easy to disguise and offers a flexible method of construction. Accurate excavation will be necessary if the liner is to be left exposed, but if rocks are to be incorporated into the edge and pebbles used to cover the stream bed, this will not be quite so critical. However, a fall is vital in both cases, and this should not exceed 30 degrees if the stream is to be effective. This can be achieved in the same manner as when installing pre-formed units.

As with any feature that relies on a liner, all sharp objects that might puncture the material must be removed from the excavation. Then spread the normal layer of damp builders' sand along the stream bed and up the sides. A fleece underlay can also be employed for a stream, as it will be quite easy to put in place.

If the stream is short, it may be possible to obtain a suitable single length of liner, but where there are to be variations in level or elaborate curves and arcs, it will be easier, if not essential, to use several separate sheets. These must always be laid from the pool back to the stream source, ensuring that there are generous overlaps in the direction of flow. Where possible, these should be arranged to coincide with shallow drops or cascades so that the end of the downstream section of liner will be above the water level for that part of the stream.

The liner must be secured at the edges with either soil or rocks, and it must always remain higher than the stream's maximum water level, otherwise seepage into the surrounding ground will occur. Another form of edging can be made by filling hessian bags with soil, rather like sand bags, then planting them. The plants will soon colonize the bags, producing an attractive, natural-looking marginal or boggy edge.

There are great opportunities for establishing colonies of marginal aquatics like marsh marigold and skunk cabbage in the permanently wet areas beside a natural stream.

A lined stream offers wonderful opportunities for creative designs with rocks. If positioned carefully, these can be used to modify the flow of water, producing a variety of effects.

MAKING A LINED STREAM

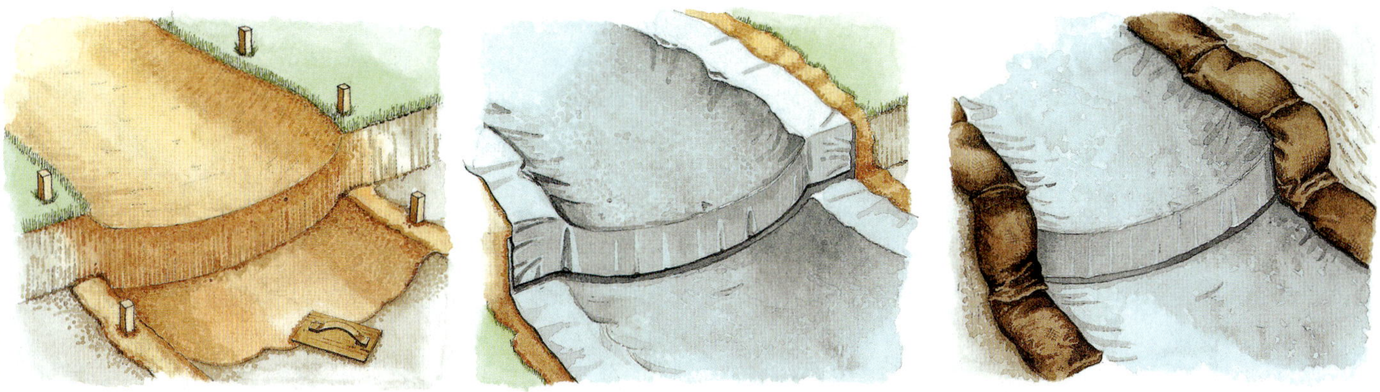

1 Excavate the stream bed to the finished size and line with builder's sand, having removed any sharp stones, sticks or other objects that may puncture the liner.

2 Position the liner carefully, ensuring that there is sufficient overlap at the joints and the edge. It is important to smooth out any wrinkles and to ensure that any folds are significant.

3 The edges of a natural looking lined stream can be disguised with bags of soil, which can be planted with trailing plants to link the surrounding garden with the water.

INSTALLING A PRE-FORMED STREAM

Another option for creating an artificial stream is to use pre-formed stream units. These are similar to waterfall and cascade units and can be linked together in various configurations to suit your particular needs. As with pre-formed waterfalls and cascades, careful thought must be given to their positioning, as they are not easy to disguise or make appear natural. However, if correctly installed, they will be completely watertight.

CREATING A LAYOUT

Before marking out the position of the stream, lay out the units to achieve the desired effect. A stream should start somewhere logical, and not race and cascade down the garden. It will be most effective if it appears to start as a bubbling spring, an effect that is quite easily contrived.

Use a container such as an old plastic dustbin, sinking it into the ground and disguising it with rocks and plants; this will form the head of the stream. The hose from the pump can be led into the container, which should be filled with large stones. The water should be allowed to bubble through these as if from an underground spring. Alternatively, construct a header pool at the top of the stream, into which the pump outlet can be discreetly placed. The hose can be concealed among surrounding plants and rocks.

The only problem that arises with such an arrangement occurs when the head of the stream is a long distance from the pump. In that case, a powerful surface pump and permanent piping must be installed, for a stream will logically be recirculated from a pool in most domestic gardens. If you wish to employ a standard submersible pump, try to arrange for the head of the stream to be within easy reach of the pool. This may not look convincing if both can be seen from the same point, so shrubby planting may be necessary to separate the features. When a rock garden abuts the pool, the header may be simply arranged at the rear and form an integral part of that aspect of the rock garden. Of course, there is no reason why a stream cannot begin with a cascade, the water tumbling down another face of the rocky outcrop.

Moisture loving perennials throng the banks of this streamside. The bold magenta Primula pulverulenta *is softened by the ostrich feather fern and contrasts with the hosta opposite.*

DIGGING OUT

Having decided upon the precise position of the stream, mark out its run by driving pegs into the ground. Then excavate the entire stream bed, allowing for a fall towards the pump. Make provision for any pools and similar features at the same time. Ensure that the excavation is level from side to side by placing pegs at appropriate intervals and levelling them with the aid of a short board on edge and a spirit level. The excavation should be about 15cm (6in) longer and wider than the finished units, and 7.5cm (3in) deeper. This allows for the bedding layer of sand and for any necessary adjustments during installation.

ACHIEVING THE CORRECT GRADIENT

For the best effect, a stream should be laid to a gradient of between 10 and 30 degrees. You can allow the water to run directly from the stream head to the pool, or slow its progress by running it through a series of shallow waterfalls and small pools. In such cases, the sections of stream between the pools must be almost flat so that the water flows smoothly. If you want to make the flow of water appear to speed up in places, position rocks in the stream to narrow it once construction has been completed.

When marking out the run of the stream with pegs, in the first instance, knock them in so that all their tops are level, checking this with the aid of a wooden board placed on edge and a spirit level. This will give you a clear indication of the existing soil levels. Each successive peg should then be knocked down to provide the desired angle of fall. A simple wooden set square can be tacked together to give the angle and will ensure accuracy.

Once the pegs are at the correct depth, the areas where soil needs removing or adding will become obvious, the aim being to have each peg protrude by an equal amount above the soil. Making these adjustments to the lie of the land will simplify the process of excavation for the stream itself.

INSTALLING STREAM UNITS

A stream should be constructed from the pool backwards. Do not start with the header in the hope that the last unit will meet the pool neatly and at the correct angle. However accurate you may be with a tape measure and spirit level, it is unlikely that everything will fit together satisfactorily.

Remove stones and roots from the excavated stream bed and spread a generous layer of builders' sand evenly over the floor and sides. If damp, this will mould easily to the shape of the excavation. When using more than one unit, take care to ensure watertight overlaps. Check units are level from side to side and firmly bedded, then fill in around them with soil.

The edges of most pre-formed stream units are rather ugly, so great care will be necessary in disguising them with rocks and plants. The bed of the stream can also look stark, but can be effectively transformed if liberally covered with a layer of washed stones. There is no need for any of the plastic or fibreglass to be exposed.

USING SECTIONAL UNITS

Some pre-formed stream units are sectional in nature, rather than being prefabricated in specific shapes. Like sectional pools, these connect together and are made watertight with a sealant. Sectional stream units come with special height adjustment panels that are invaluable when dealing with a sloping site. These ensure that the water level is maintained in each stream component, even when the pump is switched off. The other main advantage of using sectional stream units is that they make it easy to create more natural-looking sweeping arcs and curves.

INSTALLING PRE-FORMED STREAM UNITS

1 Measure out the dimensions of the stream using a series of pegs and excavate carefully. The excavation should be 15cm (6in) longer and 7.5cm (3in) deeper than the finished unit.

2 Ensure that the stream is level from side to side and the bottom has a gentle slope. If care is taken at this time to ensure the correct configuration of excavation, installation will be simplified.

3 Line the excavation with builder's sand as bedding so that the stream sections will rest in neatly. Some stream units come with special height adjustment panels.

4 Position the sections carefully, ensuring that each side is level and firmly embedded in the sand base. It may take several attempts to position them correctly.

5 Disguise the edges with stones and cover the stream bed with decorative pebbles. Cement edging stones in place for extra security, especially if they are intended to retain a bed or border.

6 Finish by planting the streamside with decorative moisture-loving plants. Remember that the stream is waterproof and will not supply dampness to the surrounding soil.

CONCRETE STREAMS

If you want a more permanent stream than that provided by pre-formed units or a liner, a concrete watercourse is the only answer. Although more skill will be required than when installing either of the latter, it will not be as great as when constructing a concrete pool, and with care the work should be well within the abilities of the amateur. The concrete mix should be the same as that for a pool.

The method of constructing a stream with concrete does not differ too radically from that of one with a liner. Obviously, the excavation must be 10cm (4in) larger all round than the finished feature to accommodate the thickness of the concrete, and to achieve a watertight construction it is essential to try to lay all the concrete on the same day; even a 24-hour lapse between laying successive mixes will leave a potential point of weakness.

The excavation should be lined with polythene membrane before the concrete is laid. Once concrete laying begins, keep in mind an overall idea of the final stream so that rocks can be placed in appropriate positions to help soften the edges and produce flow patterns within the stream.

Use a fairly stiff concrete mix to prevent it from slumping, and spread it over the contours of the excavation with a trowel. As with a pool, apply about half the thickness of the concrete required and bed wire mesh in it to act as reinforcement. Then add the final layer.

With a concrete construction, it is also vital to consider marginal planting, as the soil immediately beyond the concrete edge of the stream will often be dry. To overcome this problem, create pockets in the concrete that can be filled with soil, which will be kept damp by the passing stream.

A stream uncluttered by planting can be used to entice visitors to other parts of the garden. Grass and water together have a simple beauty, but require very careful management.

CREATING FLOW PATTERNS

The careful positioning of rocks in the bed of a stream can create interesting flow patterns. For example, a barrier of rocks with a gap in the middle will produce fast-moving water, while stones of varying sizes placed across the stream to form a gentle dip will produce a less strident effect. Flat stones tend to produce much smoother water.

MAKING A CONCRETE STREAM

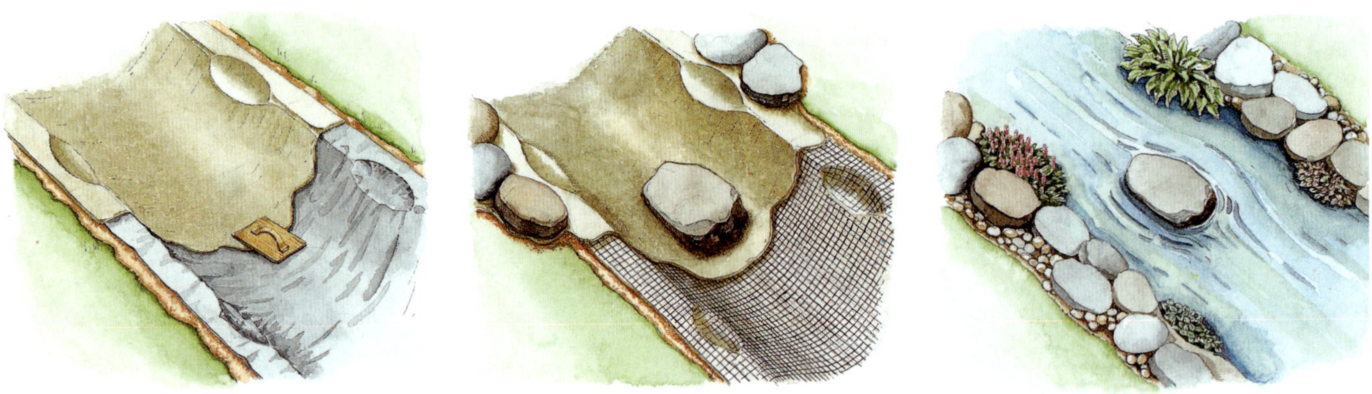

1 Having lined the stream bed with polythene, add a layer of concrete. The polythene provides a waterproof barrier and prevents the concrete from drying out too quickly and the surface cracking.

2 Lay the reinforcing mesh and cover with a further layer of concrete, positioning edging stones to provide a neat finish. To obtain a pleasing effect, they should be from the same source.

3 Stones in a stream bed alter the flow of water. The depth of the stone affects the way in which water speed is reduced, those appearing above the water having the greatest impact.

PROBLEM-SOLVING

MOVING WATER

I have a natural stream that has wildly varying water levels. After a thaw during the winter, it can become a raging torrent and cause considerable damage to my waterside planting. What is the best way of controlling this erosion?

There are several options that can be adopted when planting is not sufficient to prevent erosion, but wood is the easiest and most tasteful to use. With a little ingenuity, it is often possible to drive in stakes and erect boards in the water, close to the muddy banks. This will allow you to reclaim an area of nutrient-rich soil, which is ideal for growing moisture-loving perennials.

Take strong stakes, which have been treated with a non-toxic wood preservative, and hammer them into the stream bed along the desired line of the bank. Then place preservative-treated wooden boards between the stakes and the eroded bank, building them up to the level of the surrounding ground. Backfill the eroded area between the boards and the bank with soil. This area can then be planted, and the wooden boards disguised with scrambling plants.

I do not have enough room for a proper stream in my garden, but in some old gardens I have seen a series of channels that link to a water feature. How would I go about constructing such channels?

A popular feature in many old gardens was a wall mask spouting into a small pool, which was connected to a number of channels that flowed through the garden into a lower pool. Usually, these had quite a steep slope and the water raced down them. Their finished size was rarely more than 30cm (12in) deep and 30cm (12in) wide.

To create such a feature, dig out a trench 15cm (6in) wider and 10cm (4in) deeper than the finished structure. Construct simple shuttering boards to form a mould within the trench. Concrete the floor of the trench and press wire netting into the wet concrete as reinforcement. Position the shuttering and fill behind it to create the walls, ensuring that the concrete is tamped down firmly. As the concrete dries, periodically sprinkle it with water from a watering can fitted with a fine rose. This will prevent the drying process from being too rapid, which could lead to the formation of hairline cracks in the surface of the concrete.

A natural stream can be greatly enhanced by the addition of choice moisture loving plants.

I have a spring in my garden; how can I turn it into a moving water feature?

This rather depends on how permanent the spring is, and how constant its flow. If the latter is irregular or inconsistent in any way, it is best to allow the spring to feed directly into a pool, which is allowed to overflow into a small watercourse. The resulting feature could provide a useful habitat for bog garden plants.

If you are satisfied that the spring flows freely all year round, treat it rather like a permanent water supply and direct it into a stream or waterfall. Of course, it will need an outlet and must be permitted to run into a land drain, which should be contrived in a discreet manner.

The problem with using spring water, even if there is a consistent flow, is coping with the inevitable wealth of nutrients that it will bring with it. A constant fresh supply of plant foods will encourage the rapid development and continuous growth of algae, especially the green water-discolouring types. This will not manifest itself in the stream or waterfall so much as in any permanent pond feature. Therefore, it is best to treat a spring as a purely decorative moving water feature, which should be separated completely from any water garden development.

PUMPS

A suitable pump is fundamental to the success of any moving water feature. Particularly important is the flow rate it produces, for upon this depends the visual effect produced by the water's movement. Whatever the type of pump you select, always choose a model that produces a flow rate that is greater than your present needs require; spare capacity will be invaluable if you want to modify the feature in the future.

THE SUBMERSIBLE PUMP

Modern domestic water gardens depend almost totally upon submersible pumps. These are excellent investments, being reliable, easily maintained and simple to install. They are placed on the floor of the pool and either fitted with a fountain spray outlet or a hose that feeds a waterfall or stream. Some larger-capacity pumps can be equipped with an adaptor that allows both fountain and waterfall to be supplied simultaneously.

Modern submersible pumps are efficient, safe, and completely self-contained, providing endless opportunities for creating imaginative moving water features.

The submersible pump is a self-contained sealed unit that draws in water through a filter and pushes it into the outlet pipe. The filter unit must be removed regularly so that the element can be washed to remove any debris it collects; a clogged filter will impair the pump's operation.

The pump will be fitted with a waterproof cable, which will be long enough to reach well outside the pool. An armoured cable will be required to carry electricity from the house to the pool, the connection between this and the pump cable being made beneath a paving slab at the pool's edge. This will not only protect the connection from the weather and accidental damage, but will also provide you with easy access.

Only when the pool is deeper than 90cm (36in), and a significant lift is needed for a fountain or waterfall, will problems arise with a submersible pump. In this situation, if a suitable pump cannot be obtained, it will have to be raised within the pool to reduce the depth of water above it.

THE SURFACE PUMP

Few domestic pool owners will want to use a surface pump. However, such a pump will be necessary for a fountain that shoots high jets of water, and for streams or waterfalls with large outputs. They are also used by fish keepers who operate powerful filtration systems. A surface pump must be housed in a separate chamber constructed alongside the pool.

Ideally, the chamber should be situated below water level; if it is above water level, a foot valve and strainer must be fitted to the suction tube so that the pump remains primed when not running. In this situation, the vertical distance between the pump inlet and the water level must not exceed

SELECTING PUMP OUTPUT

Most modern submersible pumps have a small discharge, so it is important to have a clear idea of the quantity of water that you wish to move, then to shop around for a suitable pump. The majority will produce a satisfactory fountain, but a surprising amount of water is required for an effective waterfall. Most ready-made cascade units require an output of at least 1140 litres (250 gallons) per hour to put a thin sheet of water across their width, while 1365 litres (300 gallons) per hour are required to make a continuous filmy flow 15cm (6in) wide.

If you have any doubts about the required flow, a simple test can be employed to calculate the necessary capacity. Run water into the upper unit of the waterfall or stream from a hosepipe, and adjust the flow to produce the desired effect. Then collect the water that passes over the entire feature for a period of one minute. Measure the quantity collected, convert it into litres or gallons and multiply that figure by 60. This will give you the amount of water that your pump will have to move in an hour. Check the flow rate chart for your chosen pump, making sure that the desired rate corresponds with the amount of lift that it will be required to achieve.

the suction lift capacity. If the chamber is constructed below water level, only an inlet strainer will be needed, as gravity will keep the pump primed.

The pump chamber must be dry. It need only be a modest brick structure, but an air brick should be incorporated to ensure ventilation, while a removable paving slab can be used for the roof.

CONNECTING A PUMP

The armoured cable that carries power to the pump must be controlled by a switch inside the house. The circuit must incorporate a residual current device, which will cut off the power automatically if the cable is damaged or a short circuit occurs. Since water and electricity do not mix, it is essential to seek the help of a qualified electrician.

The cable should be laid in a trench, at least 60cm (24in) deep, and buried in sand. Lay a warning tape over the cable before backfilling the trench with soil, to indicate the potential danger if someone digs in the area in the future (see also page 151). A simple map indicating the route of the cable should also be kept in a safe place. Connections to the pump cable must be made using weatherproof outdoor fittings.

LOW-VOLTAGE PUMPS

Some small pumps operate on low-voltage power, provided by a transformer plugged into the domestic electricity supply. Unlike mains electricity, the current flow in a low-voltage system is not harmful, so the cable can be run on the surface, provided it is kept out of the way. It can be disguised by passing it among plants, but plastic conduit should be used to carry it under paths and other vulnerable areas. However, if any substantial water movement is required, a low-voltage pump is unlikely to have the necessary capacity, and a mains powered unit will be required.

The selective placement of rocks of different shapes and sizes, together with careful water flow control, can produce a very natural looking waterfall. Strategic planting can be used to soften the rock work along the edges of the feature, as here.

CHAPTER FOUR

SPECIAL FEATURES

While many gardeners establish water features for the cultivation of plants and the enjoyment of fish, there is much more to aquatic gardening than these activities alone. Moving water and lighting are aspects of the art of gardening, rather than the science of working with nature, but each has a role to play in the overall scheme of things and the enjoyment of a garden.

Modern pumps are compact and reliable, requiring minimal attention to ensure successful operation. They provide opportunities for producing spray patterns of a size and diversity that almost defies the imagination, and which can be changed automatically every few seconds if desired. There are lights that float in the water and create spectacular effects, while others can be incorporated to illuminate fountains in a kaleidoscope of colour. You can even arrange for your beautifully lit fountain to dance to the tune of piped music. This is may be taking things a little too far, but it does demonstrate the enormous strides that have been made in the domestic use of moving water.

There are other special features that, at first, may not seem relevant to your water garden if you have a modest plot. Bridges may only seem suitable for large gardens, but they can be equally useful and decorative in the small garden. A clapper bridge is a natural feature where water garden and rock garden meet, while a simple plank causeway may provide easy access to another part of the garden, and will give a different perspective to the tiniest stretch of water. When planning your water garden, consider the many features that could be included. You cannot incorporate them all, but it is worth knowing what would be desirable, so that provisions can be made during construction. Although most can be introduced later on, the disruption may be considerable and, in many cases, the end result not as co-ordinated as if properly planned from the beginning.

A variety of small water features like these can create a wonderful opportunity for introducing interesting hardy ferns and waterside plants to the smaller garden.

FOUNTAINS

One of the great pleasures of the decorative water garden is the fountain. True, the turbulence that it creates in the pool below prevents the successful growth of a number of aquatic plants, including waterlilies, but the qualities that it can bring are immeasurable. The sound of moving water is equally as desirable as the twisting and glinting of fountain spray. The whole experience is magical.

A fountain is very important and should be the focal point of the water feature, which is why many gardeners choose a naked pool in which to place it prominently. To some extent, a fountain should be regarded as an aquatic sculpture, the spray jet arrangements that are available being capable of producing all manner of fanciful shapes. Of course, the fountain itself is often part of an ornament, which may be a sculpture in its own right.

Water movement and fountain ornament should be in harmony, the jet producing a spray which is appropriate for the figure and which can be safely contained in the pool below.

Using a fountain in this manner will simplify its maintenance requirements, the water being treated chemically to control algae and filtered to ensure that it remains clean and fresh. There is no need to consider fish or plants.

CHOOSING A FOUNTAIN

The simplest fountain is a single jet of water, produced by a basic spray unit, which is attached to a submersible pump and appears just above water level. Alternatively, it may be part of a figure or artificially contrived feature, which may be served by either a submersible or surface pump. These are very simple to install and for many gardeners they are perfectly adequate.

If you wish to be a little more adventurous, fancy spray patterns can be created by adding an adaptor that will vary both the height and shape. The bell fountain is one such innovation, which creates a globular spray pattern almost like a glass bell in appearance. Single bells are wonderfully simple and effective, but triple bells are quite outstanding. A tubular fountain ring, incorporating five or more adjustable jets, can be attached to a pump jet outlet to provide a variety of spray patterns, which will create a similar effect to the bell fountain.

Where a fountain is to be the focal point of the water feature, and the pool in which it stands is simply a reservoir for the water, a hemispherical fountain is worth serious consideration. This looks rather like an over-elaborate sputnik, each arm carrying a small fountain jet. The effect is a twinkling, turbulent semi-globe of watery spray. It makes a wonderful fountain for a well lit sunny position, where it will appear as a crystal dome, with an ever changing spectrum of colours.

Other possibilities include conventional spray jets that are embraced by a globe of water and, of course, gushing geysers, which give a white-water effect. In warm weather, this kind of fountain is extremely useful, for it cools and oxygenates the water for the fish, although few aquatic plants will like the conditions it produces.

USING ORNAMENTS

While the water movement and patterns are the main attractions of a fountain, the ornaments from which the water is often expelled can also add to the overall enjoyment of the feature. There are innumerable classical figures, such as dolphins, cherubs and water carriers, but some of the more elaborate and esoteric modern tubular structures should not be overlooked.

When selecting a fountain ornament, be sure that it will provide the effect that you expect. Some very attractive ornaments may leave a lot to be desired as fountains. An ornament that produces a dribble, rather than a strong flow, will be a great disappointment. Before you buy, ask to see it demonstrated and find out which pump it requires to achieve the desired result.

ILLUMINATED FOUNTAINS

A water garden is at its loveliest in the summer months when you are more likely to be outside enjoying the garden, often until quite late in the day. At this time of year, there will be many occasions when an illuminated fountain can be enjoyed in darkness or twilight. Most are self-contained units that can provide a night-time spectacular, but during the daytime revert to an normal fountain.

A simple underwater spotlight can also be added to the ordinary fountain. This type of fitting is sealed in a waterproof body and available with a choice of coloured lenses to give a single-colour fountain. For the more ambitious, a colour changer can be used. This revolving disc incorporates a variety of coloured segments that automatically change the colour of the fountain. The rate at which the changes are made can be adjusted at will.

Automatically changing spray patterns are also possible. Often, as many as 18 spray patterns are obtainable in a set sequence, each lasting for around 16 seconds. Such a fitting can be used with both submersible and surface pumps, but the more powerful the pump, the higher and wider the spray patterns that will be produced.

TYPES OF FOUNTAIN JET

A conventional spray pattern for a pool or fountain bowl. The height can be easily adjusted to accommodate the vagaries of weather and the size of the bowl or pool beneath.

The careful placement and variation in the size of holes of the spray jet permits an illusion of three tiers of water. This type of arrangement best used with a simple bowl or pool.

The combination of air and water produces the white water effect of a foaming spray. In some pools the turbulent effect of this jet will need arresting in the water below.

A tulip jet produces one of the best spray configurations for uplighting in the pool. A simple underwater spotlight, sealed in a waterproof body, can often be attached to the pump unit itself.

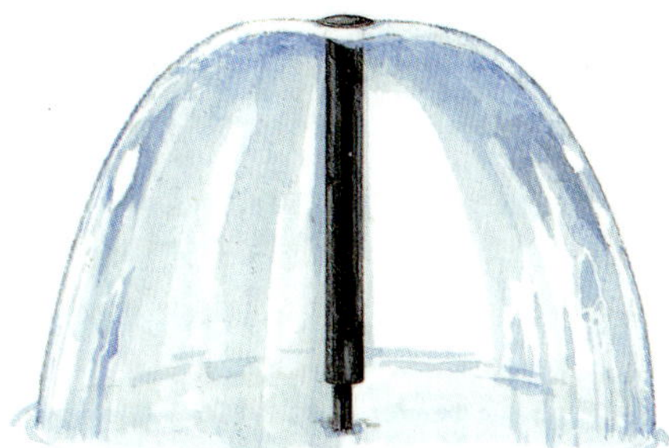

The symmetrical curtain of water created by a bell jet catches sunlight and produces rainbow patterns. This is best used in a sheltered area where it is undisturbed by the wind.

The hemispherical spray pattern is one of the most elaborate with its contrasting configurations. An interesting spray pattern for uplighting with coloured lights.

INSTALLING A FOUNTAIN

The installation of a ready-made fountain will not be too difficult. Make sure you take into account the spray jets and the manner in which they will eject water when deciding on the position. It is all very well to enjoy an attractive spray pattern on a still day, but jets of water, especially tall jets, will be blown around by the wind. Choose a site for the fountain where a playful breeze will not drench the surrounding ground or passers-by. On very windy days, a fountain should not be switched on.

Remember that the pump will require periodic servicing – at least the regular cleaning of the inlet filter – so you will need relatively easy access. If it is placed in the centre of the pond, you may need to wade into the water to reach it. For this reason, you may prefer to position the pump at the edge of the pool and invest in a longer delivery pipe. However, this will have a detrimental effect upon flow and will demand a more powerful pump to achieve the same result as a more modest model placed directly beneath the fountain outlet, or indeed where the outlet is attached directly to it. Alternatively, the fountain plinth can be arranged to provide support for a wooden board that will span the water from the bank. Such a feature can only be made in concrete, lined or natural pools, and is only necessary for a large deep body of water.

Classical fountains are simple to install but provide an impressive focal point irrespective of the size of garden. They usually look best in a pool of formal design.

THE PLINTH AND PUMP

Most fountain arrangements in domestic garden pools require a plinth on which to stand the pump or ornament. In the simplest case, this is a sound structure that lifts a submersible pump to a point just below the surface of the water, which allows the fountain head to appear at water level. With this arrangement, the head can be changed, if required, to give different spray patterns, and the filter easily reached for cleaning. The disadvantage is that the pump is close to the surface and not easy to hide. It will be obscured by turbulent water when the fountain is working, but when it is switched off, it can tend to look like a metallic basking shark.

If an ornament is to be incorporated as part of the fountain, it will be very much easier to hide the pump. The ornament need not be an elaborate sculpture, attractive though these are. A prepared rock or cast symmetrical shape, through which the fountain outlet can be supplied, will be perfectly adequate. Indeed, any method will be suitable if it permits the delivery hose to be secured with the fountain head at a distance from the pump. When this can be arranged, it is quite a simple matter to hide the pump beneath the plinth. However, given the extra length of outlet hose required, it would be wise to check the capacity of the pump to ensure that it will deliver the required spray with the increased lift.

Although a simple structure, a plinth must be built soundly, especially if it is to support the end of a board that will provide access to the pump for maintenance. It must have a very solid foundation which, ideally, should be allowed for when the pool is being built. In the case of a liner pool, for example, a concrete pad can be incorporated into the floor of the excavation before the liner is installed. Provided that a piece of geo-textile or fleece is laid between the liner and the concrete, and also between the liner and the base of the plinth, no damage will be caused to the liner.

Use a section of paving slab for the foot of the plinth. This will be unobtrusive and spread the load. Construct two simple brick piers on the slab, leaving a gap between them to accommodate the pump if you want to separate it from the fountain head and conceal it. Ensure that the piers are level, then place another section of slab across the top. This should only be large enough to support the head, pump or fountain ornament or, in the case of a large pool, the end of the access

METHODS OF INSTALLING A FOUNTAIN

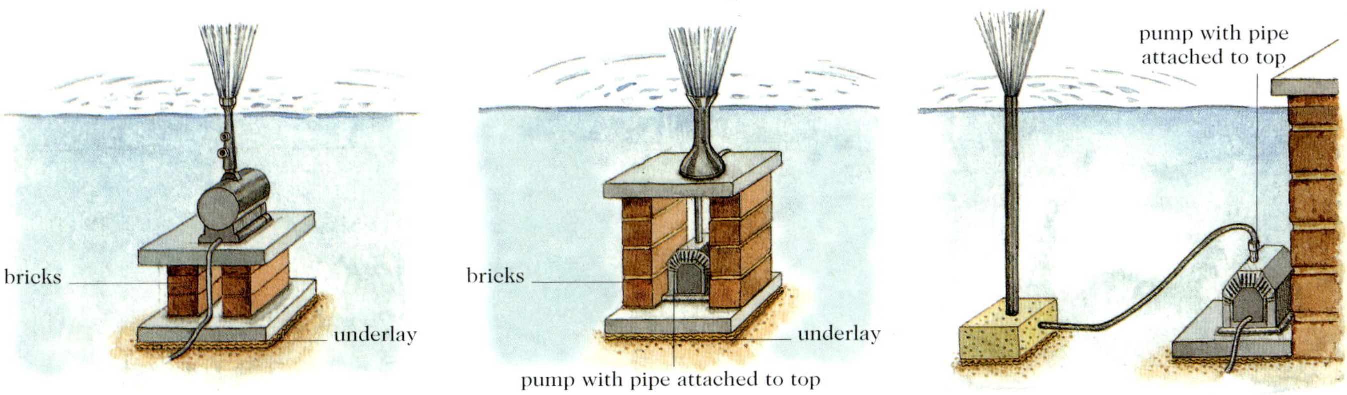

A conventional arrangement, where the submersible pump is placed on an adjustable plinth. This must be level and stable. Such an arrangement will also provide fish with a hiding place.

Where an ornament is used, a purpose built plinth can hide the pump. Depending on the strength of the pump, it may be necessary to raise it in order to reduce the water lift required.

Creating a simple fountain away from the pump demands careful calculation with distance and lift. Generally a much stronger pump will be necessary than if it were placed just beneath the fountain.

board. It should be set in place with mortar before the fountain unit is added. If the latter is an elaborate ornament, such as a sculpture, it should also be secured with mortar. Apart from ensuring stability, this will provide added security, for such ornaments are often stolen. If attached to a substantial plinth, it will be more difficult to remove. Finally, place the pump in position, connecting its outlet hose as necessary.

If you want to position the pump close to the pool's edge, or the fountain unit requires no more than a simple slab plinth on the floor of the pool, you can create a safe haven using a couple of pieces of paving slab. Stand the pump on top of one, then raise the other to hide it, either by building into the wall of the pool, where appropriate, or constructing two small brick piers for support.

MAKING YOUR OWN FOUNTAIN FEATURE

In addition to using a standard, ready-made fountain which, with one of the various specially produced ornaments, is simply installed rather like a do-it-yourself kit, you can make your own fountain feature. One of the most adventurous fountain arrangements comprises a series of bowls and a conventional fountain spray. Water is pumped up through a tall central stem into a bowl. Beneath this are several other bowls of the same construction, but with progressively greater diameters. When the top bowl has been filled, the water spills over and falls like a curtain into the second, and so on until it reaches the pool below. The rim of each bowl must be set level so that the curtain of water falls evenly around it. The only problem with this arrangement is that it creates excessive turbulence in the pool below, which restricts the cultivation of plants. However, if plants are required towards the edge of the pool, it is possible to confine the water movement with a large metal ring, which is greater than the diameter of the lowest bowl. The ring should be about 5cm (2in) deep and held at the water's surface by three braces attached to the central stem. Then marginal plants can be grown in the relative calm water outside the ring.

WALL FOUNTAINS

Wall fountains, particularly those disguised as masks and gargoyles, have a long tradition of use throughout the gardens of Europe, and modern versions abound in garden centres. All produce a jet of water from a wall, which flows into a raised or sunken basal pool, bowl or dish and is recirculated back to the spout. They are extremely versatile features, often allowing moving water to be introduced to a tiny or enclosed garden in a grander fashion than is possible with a conventional pool and fountain.

Masks and gargoyles are available in a wide range of shapes and sizes, being made from such diverse materials as real or imitation stone, lead, terracotta, fibreglass or plastic. In many cases, the more artificial materials are quite convincing in their appearance and, additionally, are often much easier to install.

REQUIREMENTS FOR A WALL FOUNTAIN

Careful thought must be given to the manner in which a wall fountain will function. It will be operated by a submersible pump, but installing the pump in a shallow pool or bowl at the base of the wall may be undesirable, or even impractical.

WALL FOUNTAIN

A wall fountain arrangement should be carefully thought through before you begin construction. The basal pool is the last part of the whole feature to be incorporated.

The magic of moving water in a cool secluded corner. The sound of water brings an added dimension to the garden. The adaptation of the old pump is inspirational.

FIXING A WALL FOUNTAIN

1 Use a plumb line to accurately relate the inflow pipe to the outlet and drill a hole through the wall. Accuracy at this stage will ensure that installation of the pump hose is straightforward.

2 Feed string through the upper and lower holes in the wall. Attach the pump hose and gently pull. Do not detach the string until the hose has been firmly secured to the wall.

3 Connect the hose outlet to the wall fountain and then securely screw the unit to the wall, using wall plugs and rustproof (brass or zinc) screws to ensure stability.

The water level may be too low, or the pump too obtrusive. Therefore, it is better to make other arrangements, which must be carefully thought out before construction or fixing the wall fountain begins.

Placing the pump in a sump outside the pool is the best option. This must be as close to the wall fountain as possible to prevent the output from being reduced by excessive lift or length of delivery hose. It must be accessible for maintenance and can often be concealed beneath a removable slab in the paving around the pool.

A special watertight chamber can be constructed to accommodate the submersible pump, or alternatively a large container, such as a dustbin, can be sunk into the ground. Whichever method is used, the water it contains must be deep enough to cover the pump entirely. It must be connected directly to the basal pool so that the water drains continuously into the sump, from where it will be pumped back up to the wall fountain spout.

This arrangement, although a little more elaborate to construct, makes a much finer job than simply placing the pump in the pool for all to see. Furthermore, the discharge pipework and the armoured cable supplying electricity to the pump can be readily concealed beneath the ground.

The wall to which the fountain is fixed can also present problems. If it is of old brick, water constantly splashing on to it, which is inevitable with even the most carefully contrived water jet, may cause deterioration or unpleasant staining. In this situation, it would be worth making a splashback, which, in most cases, need be no more elaborate than a neatly rendered area that can be designed to enhance the feature.

FIXING A WALL FOUNTAIN

Regardless of type, installing a wall fountain is always a matter of innovation, the method being dependent upon individual circumstances. If a wall is to be constructed for the feature, make sure that it is of the cavity type. This will solve many of the difficulties, since the cables and pipes can be neatly concealed in the cavity.

If a cavity wall already exists, installation should be relatively simple. Knock a hole through the face of the wall at the point where the pump delivery hose will be attached to the spout. Then knock a second hole into the wall, just above the edge of the pool, using a plumb line to ensure that it is directly below the first. Feed a stout length of cord into the wall through the top hole and pull its end from the lower hole. Tie the string to the pump delivery hose and pull it up through the cavity until it can be extracted at the top.

Connect the hose to the spout and fasten it to the wall, using rustproof screws and wall plugs. Then reinstate the lower hole in the wall, hiding the inlet hose and pump with a small plinth structure surrounded by suitable plants. In such circumstances, semi-evergreen and evergreen submerged aquatics will fit the bill.

A solid wall will create difficulties in disguising the discharge pipe from the pump. The pipe will either have to be threaded through to the rear, or run in a channel cut into the face of the wall, which should be made good with mortar. However, the latter option will only be effective if the wall is rendered and painted, otherwise the work will leave an ugly scar on the wall.

Although many spouts are designed to be mounted to the face of the wall, others have to be built into it. Obviously, this should ideally be done at the time the wall is constructed, although with care, it may be possible to create an opening, set the spout in place, then fill in around it with bricks or stones. Considerable skill will be needed to achieve a neat finish, and if you are not a confident bricklayer, this work is best left to a professional, for it is absolutely vital to ensure that it sits vertically within the wall.

THE BASAL POOL

The shape and size of the basal pool or bowl will be determined by a number of factors. Of prime importance is that it should be large enough to catch as much of the falling water as possible, for even a modest spout, fixed waist-high, will create considerable splashing. One of the regular maintenance requirements of a wall fountain is the constant topping up with water to compensate for loss through splashing and evaporation. Keeping the falling water within the pool is also important aesthetically and practically, especially if the pool is adjacent to a path. Other considerations that affect the pool's shape and size are the space available and the role the fountain is to play within the overall garden scheme.

The pool can be raised or sunken, the former being the best practical option for management. It also has the advantage that if you construct the surrounding wall wide enough, you will be able to sit on the coping and enjoy the water feature at close quarters.

The methods of construction described in Chapter 2 can be adapted to provide an appropriate pool for a wall fountain.

The pleasure of moving water can be enjoyed without the requirement for an elaborate pool or plumbing. Here an ancient gargoyle gently spills water into a cool leafy corner uncluttered by the paraphernalia of a traditional water garden. A wall fountain feature like this one is ideal for a small, and quite possibly shady, city garden.

However, it is possible to buy sectional basal pools of reconstituted stone, which are simple to install and good looking. They usually require simply connecting together and sealing, although some incorporate a custom made internal liner.

THE PRE-FORMED WALL FOUNTAIN

A variety of pre-formed wall fountains are available that are self-contained, incorporating a pump and reservoir. Some are very simple and merely need hanging on the wall, connecting to an electricity supply and filling with water. They produce the most modest of water flows, and may take the form of wall plinths, decorated with characters such as nymphs with water jars, or mythical masks. The smaller kinds should be regarded with caution, for where the dish or basin into which the water flows acts as a reservoir, evaporation problems can be considerable, especially if the fountain is to function continuously. If you can only accommodate this kind of self-contained feature, regular maintenance is vital, the basin requiring constant topping up with water. Unless there are people present to enjoy the feature, the pump should be switched off. If the reservoir of water is depleted and the pump continues to run, there is a danger of it burning out.

Some wall fountain assemblies are self-contained, in that the circulation of water is linked in an almost closed system, but the amount of water available makes them more practical, albeit more complex to install. The water source is provided by a small cistern, which must be readily accessible, but disguised. It is best hidden at the base of the wall, in a hole in the ground beneath a paving slab, or behind the wall where it may be obscured by planting. The last is preferable, especially if it can be placed in a box attached to the wall, for this will allow it to be positioned opposite the fountain outlet, removing any problems that might occur with a high lift.

Although functional, the self-contained wall fountain is not as satisfactory as a proper wall mask and basal pool, and should not be countenanced when sufficient space is available for such a feature. However, in confined areas and modest outdoor living spaces, where room is at a premium, it can be an invaluable investment.

Simple moving water features are often the best, especially where space and budget are limited. Only the sound of gently flowing water leads one to this modern wall fountain.

This simple but elegant self-contained wall fountain brings the pleasure of moving water to a confined space. Its modern design would be perfect for a city garden.

CONTAINED WATER FEATURES

Constraints placed by lack of space need not preclude the enjoyment of water gardening, for acceptable water features can be established and effectively maintained in tubs or half-barrels. The secret of success lies in not attempting to create a miniature balanced aquatic environment, but to accept that the container is a separate kind of water gardening opportunity, which has different requirements.

One of the most satisfying uses for a water-filled tub is to grow pygmy waterlilies as individual plants. They are quite resilient and, after the summer season, should be dried off and stored in frost-free conditions. That is the container should be drained, and the rootstock allowed to remain dormant in the mud at the bottom. This means that the feature can be displayed for the summer only; there is no need to spend the other six months of the year looking at an apparently lifeless container of water.

A tub or half-barrel also provides an opportunity for experimenting with a tropical waterlily or lotus. The plant can be started off under glass, then moved outdoors. Alternatively, it can remain as a greenhouse feature. Both tropical waterlilies and lotus can be lifted and stored during the autumn and winter, then replanted in spring.

TUB FOUNTAINS

Apart from using a tub or barrel for cultivating aquatic plants, you can also make one into an unplanted water fea-

The most effective tub gardens use only two or three types of planting arranged tastefully. Here dwarf rushes, parrot's feather and pygmy waterlilies live comfortably together.

An effective use of moving water complemented by tasteful planting. Water spills over the edge of the pot and creates permanently damp conditions at its base for bog garden subjects.

PREPARING A TUB OR BARREL

Garden centres offer a range of tubs and half-barrels that are suitable for use as small contained water features once treated. Scrub any tub or barrel thoroughly with clear water. Never use a detergent, as it may contaminate the water later. If the tub is sound, but you are unhappy about its cleanliness, consider lining it. This is quite a good idea anyway, for most tubs and barrels will have been allowed to dry out, and there is no guarantee that they will tighten up and be waterproof when soaked again.

If you use a black liner, this will scarcely be noticeable. Carefully calculate the size of liner required and insert it into the tub, making as few bold creases as possible. Pour in water to within 7.5cm (3in) of the top of the container to hold it firmly in place. Using small pieces of timber batten, firmly screw the liner to the tub, just above the final water level. Alternatively, use flexible carpet edging strips.

A number of pre-shaped rubber liner inserts, which fit precisely into standard tubs and barrels, are available and worth investigating as an alternative to a plain liner. Although relatively expensive, they do make a very neat, crease-free job.

If a liner is not used, take steps to preserve the timber. Most tubs and barrels have a long life, but this can be greatly enhanced by charring. Turn the tub on its side and run a blow torch over the interior to produce a hard blackened surface. This will be very resistant to decay.

ture incorporating a fountain. This can be most attractive. It is also a very safe method of introducing water to the garden if you have young children.

The most effective moving water feature for a tub is the pebble fountain. This is constructed using internal wooden supports, a simple submersible pump and some well washed pebbles. The tub, of course, should be waterproofed and the pump placed inside on the bottom. The side of the tub should be marked about 5cm (2in) above the top of the pump body, and pieces of timber wedged across the tub at this point to form a level surface, effectively creating a grille. Alternatively, cut a piece of marine-grade plywood to fit the tub at the marked point, drilling a series of holes through it and making provision for the pump outlet and cable.

Cover the grid or plywood with large pebbles, in the latter case providing additional supports below to bear the weight. In some cases, cobbles rather than pebbles may be preferred.

A tub fountain like this can be most attractive. Moreover, the maintenance requirement will be reduced to keeping a check on the water level. It is surprising how much water can be lost through splashing and evaporation, so regular topping up, to keep the pump submerged, is essential. While the simple bubbling of water through the pebbles or cobbles is most attractive, using an outlet fitting that gives a more gushing effect, or produces a bell-like rounded curtain of water, will provide additional interest. The opportunities for innovation are considerable.

It is common to think of tub water gardens as movable features that can be placed on a terrace or patio, but they are equally at home sunk into the garden as miniature pool features. In fact, they are often easier to manage like this during the hot summer weather, as the cool conditions provided by the surrounding soil reduces the rapid development of green algae that will discolour the water.

TUB FOUNTAINS

1 Place the pump in the tub and mark the level of the plywood insert around the edge, allowing for a layer of cobbles. At the same time make provision for access for the pump cable.

2 Fit the plywood insert into the tub and drill holes evenly around the central fountain outlet. Marine plywood is the best type to use as it is much more tolerant of wet conditions.

3 Place a generous layer of well washed cobbles or pebbles on the top and fill the tub with water. Tub fountains are equally successful free-standing or sunk into the ground.

MINIATURE WATERSCAPES

Apart from the conventional tub or half-barrel, other small contained water features can be created, often from unconventional vessels. One of the most interesting and potentially attractive is the old kitchen sink, which can be transformed from a utilitarian object into a miniature waterscape.

This type of scaled-down water feature will need regular care if it is to maintain its character. The reason for this is that although the plants used should be of dwarf stature and modest growth, they will quickly overwhelm the waterscape if not rigorously controlled.

CREATING A MINIATURE WATERSCAPE

A sink is not normally the most attractive of objects, unless you are fortunate enough to find an old stone type. A glazed sink will need rendering if it is to be acceptable visually. This is not difficult provided that you use the correct mixture to produce a hypertufa finish, which will mellow naturally.

To produce hypertufa, mix two parts by volume of moss peat, one part of sand and one part of cement in their dry state. When thoroughly combined, add water until the mixture is stiff and capable of being applied to the sink like plaster. To ensure that it adheres well, spread a liberal amount of PVA adhesive over the exterior of the sink to act as a bonding agent. After approximately 15 minutes, the adhesive will become tacky, at which point the hypertufa mixture can be applied with a small pointing trowel. Coat the outside of the sink with about 1.25cm (½in) of hypertufa mixture, taking it down inside approximately 7.5cm (3in) so that when water is added, the level will be above the rendered finish.

The surface is best left slightly rough and uneven for a natural look, but if you want to produce a replica of a stone sink, very careful smoothing will be required if the result is not to look contrived. Once dry, the hypertufa will produce a tough and weather-resistant coating. Its appearance can be 'aged' artificially by painting the surface with a mixture of milk and cow dung, then standing the sink under cover until it has dried. This unsavoury concoction is a traditional and very effective method of encouraging development of moss and algal growth, which also mellows the colour of the coating. Live yoghurt or a manure solution could also be used.

The waterscape within the sink should be simple if it is to be effective. One or two pieces of rock, positioned strategically so that they just appear above water, will be ideal. The gaps between the edge of the sink and the rocks should be filled with aquatic planting compost to allow a degree of planting. When choosing rocks for a miniature waterscape, avoid sandstone and limestone, for they often crumble when kept immersed in water.

Restrained planting is the keynote for success in this miniature waterscape. Rather than detract from the overall feature, the plain white of the container enhances the scene, contrasting happily with peripheral planting.

SELF-CONTAINED FOUNTAIN FEATURES

In some cases, particularly where space is at a premium, it may be desirable to install a moving water feature without all the paraphernalia of pool construction. In such a situation, the flexibility of a self-contained fountain unit can prove very useful.

FOUNTAIN BOWLS

The self-contained fountain bowl is a simple unit that incorporates a submersible pump and merely requires the addition of a suitable fountain outlet to provide the required effect. Fountain bowls are usually available as fully portable kits that can be used on their own indoors, or turned into something much more elaborate outdoors. The great advantage of this type of water feature, apart from its attractiveness and modest scale, is the fact that it is equally useful in sun or shade. Neither plants nor fish are required, so you can position it anywhere.

Apart from the reservoir and pump, the kit usually includes a small liner that is large enough to line an excavation up to 1.2m (4ft) in diameter. This creates a waterproof surround into which the pump and reservoir unit are installed. Well washed pebbles or cobbles are used to fill in around the reservoir and up to the level of the pump outlet. With a suitable bell-shaped or gushing fountain outlet fitted, the water will appear to bubble and rush up from between the stones. The water simply drains back through the cobbles and is recirculated.

When making such a feature, it is important to have a clearly defined edge, which can be simply provided by paving slabs, or more elaborately by concrete or stone edgings. These are available as self-assembly units to create pond surrounds and are invaluable in enabling the cobbles and the water to be lifted to a more suitable height for enjoyment.

The most traditional use of moving water is with a fountain that has bowls of increasing size. The water flow can be controlled to create either a gentle trickle or a curtain of water.

ORIENTAL-STYLE WATER FEATURES

Oriental gardens are a rich source of inspiration for fountain ideas. The simple, stone Oriental-style fountain – a variation on the millstone fountain – is very versatile and useful in the modern garden. While it might not be easy to drill a stone yourself to accommodate the outlet pipe and fountain spray connector of a submersible pump, this can be undertaken successfully by a stone mason. Then all that is required is the creation of a simple lined sump, or reservoir, which will take the pump unit itself and a protective structure of bricks that will partly enclose the pump. The remainder of the sump should be filled with cobble stones. The main stone, with pump outlet and fountain jet attached, is positioned, the pump switched on, and the water will begin to bubble out. For the most impressive effect, use a fountain jet that mixes air with water and produces a low, throbbing geyser-like plume.

Although not strictly fountains, bamboo water chutes and pipes have similar origins and give a charming tranquil feel to the garden. The bamboo chute normally delivers water to a strategically placed stone bowl on a cobbled or pebbled base. The Japanese create various complexities with dripping water and chutes that rock to unload their contents at regular intervals, but the simple chute pouring water continuously through a hollow bamboo cane is also very attractive. The pump's outlet is connected to the cane, while the water eventually percolates through the cobbles or pebbles into the reservoir below.

To make a bamboo chute, take two standard garden canes, about 90cm (36in) long, and push them into the ground to form an X shape. Where they meet, bind them tightly together to make the stand upon which the chute will

An oriental ambience can be created by connecting two lengths of bamboo of different diameters and using a simple submersible pump to circulate the water through them.

be placed. A thicker cane is required for the chute itself. This should be hollowed out and cut to a length of 45-60cm (18-24in), one end being shaped at an angle.

MILLSTONE FOUNTAINS

Of all the contained moving water features, the millstone fountain is one of the most effective and popular. You may not be fortunate enough to find a real millstone, but very creditable fibreglass replicas are available from fountain manufacturers. Once their rough surface has developed a coating of algae, they can look remarkably like the real thing.

A millstone should be fitted over a lined excavation or a suitable container, such as a fountain bowl or sunken dustbin. This will act as a reservoir and house the submersible pump. For a lined excavation, mark out an area that is slightly larger than the diameter of the millstone. When using a dustbin, excavate so that the lip of the dustbin is flush with the ground or sunk to the depth at which the millstone will rest. For the most effective installation, prepare a margin around the hole that will support the millstone and can be lined before covering with pebbles. To make the installation as waterproof as possible, ensure that the excavation has a distinct fall towards the reservoir.

A genuine millstone should be supported by a circle of concrete building blocks, or even three or four piers, set in the ground before the lining is added. This will prevent the stone from twisting under its own weight.

Once the excavation has been lined, place the submersible pump in position and tie a string to the outlet hose.

Water bubbling over rocks and cobbles is both a safe and attractive way of introducing water to the garden. The pink-flowered polygonums will soon spread and soften the edge of the stones with their soft green leaves.

MAKING A MILLSTONE FOUNTAIN

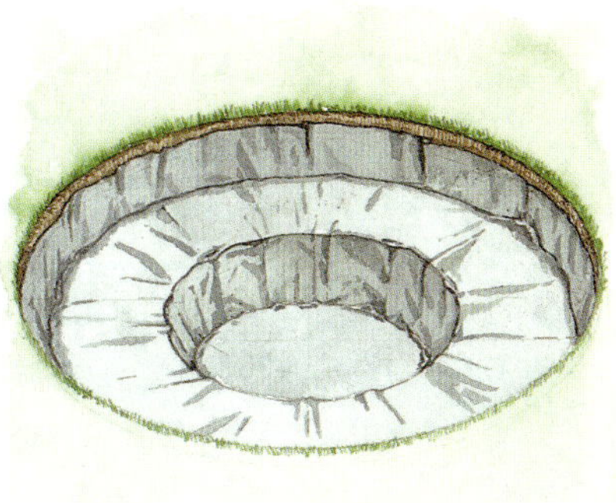

1 Excavate the hole accurately, but slightly larger than required and insert a pool liner. It is advisable to protect the liner from possible damage with an underlay of fleece.

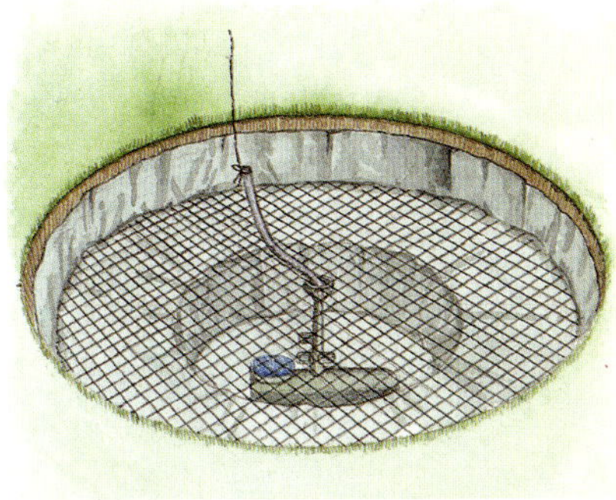

2 Position the pump and attach a string to the outlet hose, drawing it through the metal grid. Place the metal grid in position and carefully draw the pump hose through the centre.

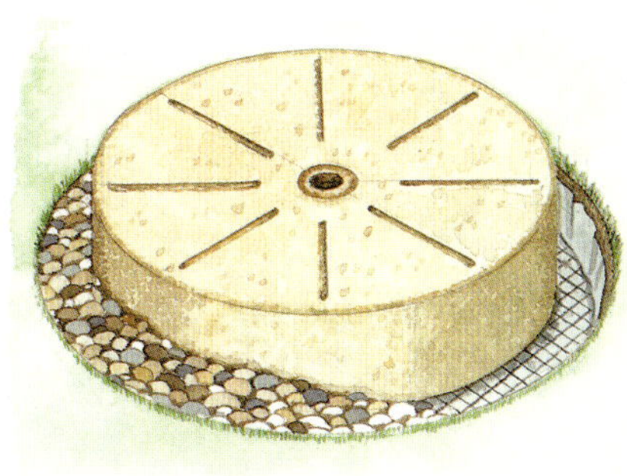

3 Position the millstone, drawing the pipe through the centre. Ensure that it is sitting evenly in the centre of the hole and then surround with well washed cobbles or pebbles.

To provide additional support for the millstone, lay either steel reinforcing rods or reinforcing mesh over the hole to create a grid with gaps no more than 10cm (4in) square. Draw the string and outlet pipe through the grid, then through the stone prior to positioning it and fitting a simple fountain outlet. Finally, fill the margin around the stone with pebbles or cobbles.

When the fountain is operating, water will cascade over the stone and seep back into the reservoir through the margin of pebbles or cobbles. Top-up water will need adding regularly to this margin, for a millstone fountain, like a fountain bowl, suffers considerable water loss through evaporation. Pay particular attention to this as a drastically reduced water level can damage the pump.

Millstones, whether genuine or of reconstituted stone, are most attractive additions to the garden. The water is recirculated from a chamber beneath the cobbles, through the centre of the stone and spills gently and evenly over the edge.

WALKWAYS

BRIDGES AND CAUSEWAYS

Being able to cross the water, on a bridge or causeway, will allow you to see the water garden from another viewpoint. You can make the most of this by arranging the planting to provide focal points that are not visible from the edge. In some circumstances, a bridge may be a focal point itself, its role as a means of crossing the water being secondary. Occasionally, in Japanese-style water gardens for example, it may be the primary focal point.

CHOOSING A BRIDGE

There are many different kinds of bridge, but for the average garden there are three principle types that can be used as the basis for a wide variety of structures. The simplest comprises a single flat slab or rock that will span a narrow stream or watercourse and may be equipped with a handrail. A traditional wooden bridge can be of almost any design imaginable, usually being constructed in one piece or from several sections bolted together. The third type is the stone clapper bridge, which is best suited to a water feature associated with a rock garden.

A clapper bridge is a very simple structure that normally consists of a pair of spans, two slabs being supported by a flat stone at each end and a strong central pier, which comprises two or three stones laid lengthways. Water passes under each span of the bridge, which should be higher than the surrounding ground. Traditional clapper bridges are often mounted by steps, but in the garden, a simple link from one bank to the other is sufficient. This in no way detracts from the attractiveness of a well built clapper bridge.

A simple board bridge is both functional and appealing in this natural setting. Although of modest appearance, sturdy foundations are still essential.

CONSTRUCTION PRINCIPLES

Irrespective of the method of construction used, a bridge requires firm foundations. These will not only ensure the safe passage of people across the bridge, but also provide stability. Even a modest bridge can be of considerable weight, and settlement may occur if it is built without sufficiently strong foundations.

To be safe, dig the footings for each pier to a depth of 60cm (24in). Piers can be precast, but for most domestic gardens, it is simpler to cast them in position. Indeed, for most bridge structures, excavating a hole and filling it with concrete is adequate. On clay soils, where shrinkage may occur, some form of reinforcement should be incorporated into the concrete.

If precast piers are being used, dig the footings so that they are 15cm (6in) larger all round than the piers. Stand each pier in its hole, then pour some concrete around it. Check that the pier is level in both directions and also in relationship to its neighbours. Finally, backfill the hole with more concrete to secure the pier.

If the bridge is a wooden structure, it is usually bolted to the piers. The simplest method of doing this is to use expansion bolts. Drill countersunk holes for the bolts and their nuts through the wooden bridge bearers, then lay these in place on the piers. Using the holes in the bearers as guides, drill holes in the piers with a masonry bit. Finally, insert expansion bolts and tighten their nuts with a box spanner or socket. This will cause the bolts to expand in the holes, providing a firm fixing.

Where a pier needs constructing in the pond itself, it

MAKING A SIMPLE TIMBER BRIDGE

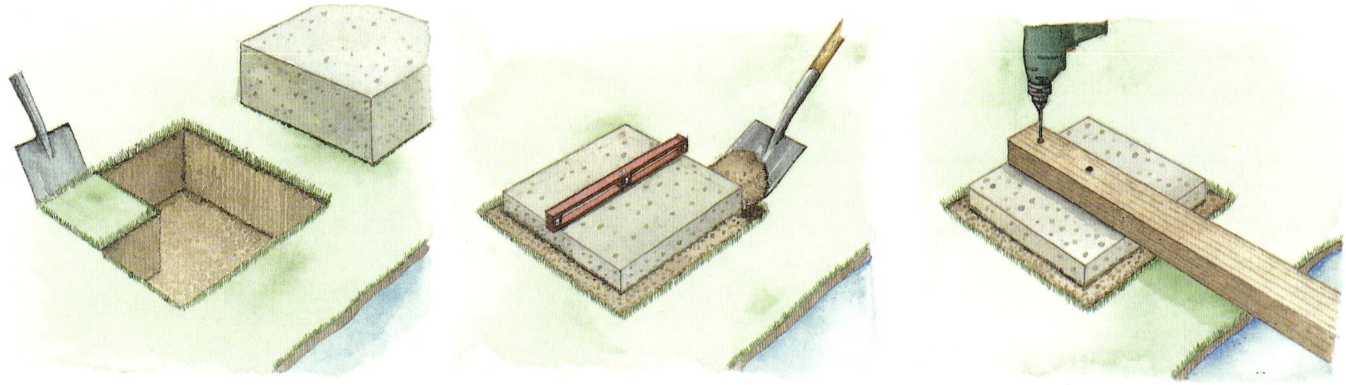

1 Accurately measure and mark the position of each pier. Excavate a hole slightly larger than necessary to allow for adjustment; 15cm (6in) larger all round is ideal.

2 Ensure that the pier is level in both directions and backfill with concrete. It is essential that it is absolutely stable. Allow the concrete to set before fixing the timber bearers.

3 Use expansion bolts to secure wooden bearers accurately to the concrete piers. The timber should be tanalized and you should allow at least two (rustproof) screws for each fixing.

should have a solid concrete footing. If a liner is being used, it is better to plan for such footings before construction begins so that a proper concrete base, of the correct dimensions, can be laid in the bottom of the excavation. The liner is then laid over the top of this, and the pier built on top of the liner. Laying a footing directly on top of a liner is hazardous, unless the liner is taken down into an additional shallow excavation below the footing, as it is likely to be unstable. Within a lined pond, the only footing that will be secure is a substantial raft of concrete, or a large block, into which the piers are embedded.

When the bridge is a simple slab crossing, or being constructed in the clapper style, the stones should be fixed securely to the piers with mortar. When doing this, check that the bridge is approximately level and, if necessary, make minor adjustments with mortar.

CAUSEWAYS

A causeway is generally an extension of the bridge idea, carrying the visitor across a larger body of water, not necessarily by the most direct route. One of the attractions of the causeway is the range of experiences it can provide by zig-zagging from one part of the pool to another, often creating an opportunity for the visitor to walk dry shod among reeds and rushes planted in the pool.

The piers that are used to support a causeway consist of short lengths of pipe set into concrete slabs, the wooden uprights of the causeway being dropped into them. Horizontal bearers are bolted to these uprights, and a board walkway screwed to the bearers. Garden designers believe that the way in which the boards are arranged affects your behaviour when using a causeway. When they are placed lengthways, it is said that they encourage you to cross; if they are fastened crossways, you are more likely to linger. Irrespective of the manner in which the boards are fastened, once the causeway has been constructed, they should be covered with fine mesh wire netting to prevent the formation of a slippery surface due to the growth of algae.

To preserve the timber, it should be tanalized. If this is done properly, it will not only give the structure a life of many years, but also will not cause any pollution problems in the pool. Once the preservative has dried, it is safe in water, causing no oily scum or damage to ornamental fish or aquatic plants. Untreated timber has a very short lifespan.

THE CAUSEWAY

Ensure a secure foundation with pipes set in concrete. Use preserved timber and take great care to see that all levels are accurate. Allow the concrete to set before adding timber.

DECKING

Decking is a convenient means of hiding a pool edge or providing a landing platform. When built well, it can be most attractive and very functional. With a large pool, it can be extended over the water to provide a place to relax among the aquatic life.

CONSTRUCTION OF DECKING

When decking extends over the water, it must be arranged tastefully and not detract from the overall beauty of the water garden. For most garden pools, it need not project much beyond the edge, its supports being set into the surrounding ground rather than the pool itself. However you decide to construct it, decking will be most effective if it is just above the surface of the water. In such circumstances, its reflection in the water will be less obvious and will not dominate the scene. At the same time, the appearance of water running back below it will produce a much more attractive effect than if dry land is revealed.

For most water garden features, decking is likely to run along the edge of the pool in a fairly narrow strip, rather like an expanded causeway, but much closer to the water. It can

DECKING

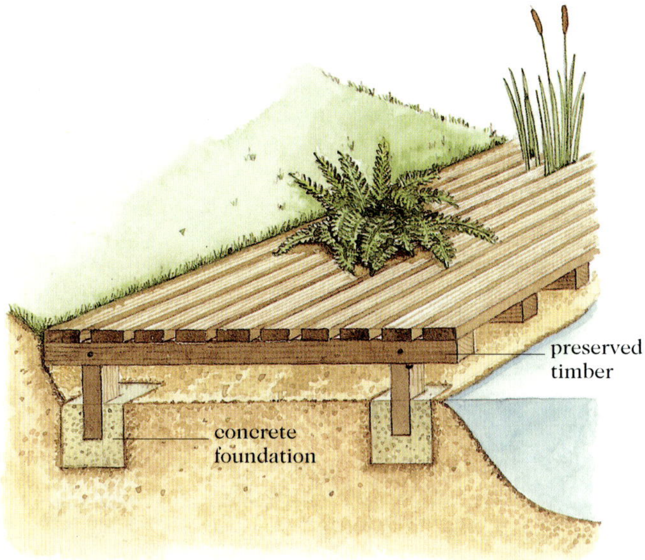

Accuracy is essential in the satisfactory construction of decking. Be sure that the levels are correct and that the structure is in proportion. Make provisions for any plants from the outset.

Decking should be constructed so that it does not dominate the water garden, however, it should offer opportunities for recreation, both for strolling and for sitting out. Provided that it is carefully designed, decking can produce a neat edge for the pool.

be used more imaginatively with formal pools and can be integrated much more effectively as an element of the formal landscape. All manner of shapes can be devised, including octagons, rectangles, triangles and squares. Hardwood is the best material to use, not only being very tough and weather resistant, but also mellowing to a pleasant silvery brown. Narrow boards, about 10cm (4in) wide, will be ideal.

As part of the decking will be over dry land, it will be possible to incorporate one or two neat openings to allow plants to grow through. This will help link it with the surrounding landscape. Use hardy plants to ensure their survival.

If the decking is to extend into the pool, proper foundations should be provided. The same technique described for bridges should be employed. When timber uprights are used, they should be at least 10cm (4in) square and can either be set in large blocks of concrete, or dropped into pipes set into concrete in the same manner as for a causeway. Strong wooden posts should also be used to support the landward side of the decking. Whether timber uprights or piers are used, they must all be vertical and their tops level. The horizontal deck bearers can then be bolted to them, and the boards screwed to the bearers. The boards should be laid with gaps of about 1cm (3/8in) between them, which will not only look attractive, but also allow surface water to drain off.

FINISHING TOUCHES

Decking that extends out into the water often ends with a feature, such as a circular or octagonal platform that can be used for sitting out. It is not desirable to install extensive safety rails along the edges of decking, for this will detract from the beauty of the feature. However, if you have young children, you will have no option, even if the decking is constructed in shallow water. When the children are old enough to understand the dangers of the water, you can remove the rails.

Where children will not be involved, the only concession to safety need be a low kick-board, which can be accommodated without causing any visual distraction. This will be particularly useful if a wheelchair is likely to be taken on to the decking. An upright, which may be an extension of one of the posts at the landward end of the decking, should also be provided as a hand hold for the less agile. If a small boat is part of the watery scene, the upright can serve as a mooring post.

The clever use of brick and timber provides a neat and pleasing edge to the pool, the channel linking the water feature to the surrounding garden. The bog garden plants are neatly contained but the planting still appears loose and informal.

STEPPING STONES

The provision of stepping stones in a water feature is an invitation to enjoy it from a totally different angle: from the water. They are also a useful alternative to a bridge, which may be overbearing and intrusive. In addition, stepping stones can be used as a decorative feature and a means of altering the flow of moving water.

For safety reasons, it is unwise to install stepping stones in pools or streams that are more than 30cm (12in) deep. Moreover, they should protrude at least 5cm (2in) above the maximum water level to ensure that their top surfaces remain dry. Obviously, it would be unwise to consider stepping stones for prefabricated streams or pre-formed pools, as their weight combined with that of a person using them is likely to cause fracturing.

If stepping stones are to be used in a lined water feature, it is essential to plan ahead and create concrete pads in the excavation before the liner is installed. The positions of these need to be marked out accurately from a fixed point so that when the stepping stones are placed in position, they will rest exactly on top of the concrete pads. Each concrete pad need only be 10cm (4in) deep, the surface being flush with the floor of the pool or stream bed. Before pulling the liner over the concrete, place a piece of fleece or geo-textile material on each pad to cushion the liner.

NATURAL STONES

Natural stones are the best choice for stepping stones, but it may be difficult to find enough of suitable shape and quality. Ideally, each should be of much the same depth with flat, roughly parallel top and bottom faces so that they sit safely in the water. They should also be of sufficient size to take a large foot comfortably.

The type of stone that is used is very important. Limestone and sandstone are unsatisfactory, as they either shale or disintegrate during very frosty winters. Granite and millstone grit are among the toughest and best stones. The latter, in particular, is both very practical and attractive. Westmorland slate is very resilient, too, but it can become quite slippery and dangerous during wet weather.

ARTIFICIAL STONES

Garden centres often sell artificial stepping stones, which are made either from concrete or reconstituted stone. They are frequently used in wide borders, rather than water, to provide easy access to plants and shrubs. Most are perfectly suitable for water features, but it would be wise to check with the vendor that they will survive the winter when partially, but permanently, immersed in water. Although most look manmade, they will mellow after a couple of years and begin to look quite natural. Almost invariably, they have non-slip surfaces, which is a positive advantage.

The do-it-yourself enthusiast can make stepping stones quite easily, using a technique that often produces better end results than those manufactured en masse. To begin with, it is not essential for them all to be of the same shape or size. In fact, a variety of shapes will look more natural, although from a practical point of view, they should all be of the same depth and have flat top and bottom faces.

The best stones are made by pouring concrete into holes dug in the ground, in a spare part of the garden. Make sure

STEPPING STONES

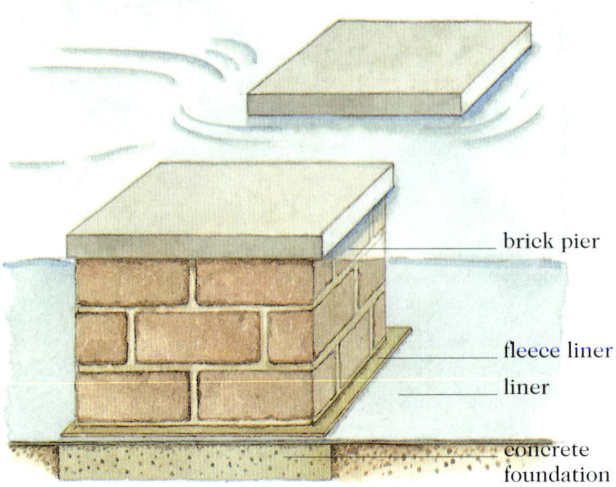

Stepping stones need a secure foundation to safely cope with the weight of foot traffic and the vagaries of water flow. Use a slightly larger slab than the foundation to hide the latter neatly.

Although placed for their visual appeal, these stepping stones are large enough to be functional. Close placement is alright in a pond, but would restrict water flow in a stream.

The cobbles in this stream neatly disguise the liner. The formal stepping stones provide a striking contrast, but they must be well supported beneath the liner.

that the holes are of the same depth, but different shapes and sizes to match the requirements of your water garden scheme. If you want to produce several stones of the same size and shape, perhaps for a very formal setting, use the same hole as a mould for all of them, but set narrow wooden battens around the edge to act as shuttering and ensure a consistently-neat edge.

Use a concrete mix comprising 1 part cement, $1^1/_2$ parts sand and $2^1/_2$ parts aggregate. Pour it into each hole, taking great care to smooth off the surface. This will actually become the base when the stone is lifted from the ground and set on the bottom of the pool. Allow the concrete to harden for about a week, sprinkling it with water from a watering can fitted with a fine rose. This will prevent it from drying out too quickly in the early stages, which can lead to hairline cracks in the surface and flaking. Then dig up the stones and brush off all the soil. It is amazing how good they will look. Use a concrete sealant to prevent the escape of free-lime, mixing it with water and painting it over the entire surface of each stone.

Lining the excavations with polythene, before pouring the concrete, has the merit of preventing rapid drying out if the soil is very dry. However, the polythene will often stick to the concrete, and so it is particularly important to ensure that there are no creases in it, which could become trapped in the concrete or create unsightly marks in the moulded stones. Provided that you are careful, however, polythene can be used with little disadvantage for very formal stones.

POSITIONING THE STONES

The exact positions of the stones should be decided very early during the construction, especially if concrete pads have to be made before the water feature is lined. The spacing between the stones must not only produce an aesthetically pleasing effect, but also be such that people can use them without any risk. It is worth measuring the stride of the shortest person who is likely to use the stones regularly and place the stones accordingly.

Wherever possible, the stones should be bedded in concrete, but if this is impossible (as with a lined water feature), you must take steps to ensure their stability. If there is any doubt about this, set each stone on a larger piece of paving slab, bedding it in mortar. The result will be an extremely stable construction.

These stepping stones have been imaginatively used to form an architectural feature, but at the same time are clearly functional. The contrast between the informality of the plants and the stark symmetry of the stepping stones is striking against the cool glassy stillness of the surrounding water. An excellent example of how, occasionally, informal and formal styles can mix harmoniously.

PROBLEM-SOLVING

BRIDGING WATER

I have a naturally very wet area in the garden that floods at certain times of the year. I intend planting it as a bog garden, but I need some means of access to get the most enjoyment from the feature and for essential maintenance. Is there any way of creating a suitable duckboard or boardwalk arrangement?

Duckboards are an excellent way of bridging broad stretches of still water or boggy areas. They should be supported on wooden crossmembers attached to posts set in the ground.

The supporting posts should be driven into the ground to a depth of at least 45cm (18in), and at intervals of about 2m (6ft) across the site. Ideally, the timber should be tanalized to ensure a long life. They can be rounded or square, and the crossmembers can be attached to them by means of cross halving joints and bolts, or simply bolted flat against them. Crossmembers should be set below the tops of the posts so that the latter extend slightly above the boards.

The boards themselves should be sturdy and similar in size to scaffold boards. As with the supports, they are best tanalized, and they should be secured with rustproof screws.

Although duckboards will produce a very straight and formal feature, variation and interest can be created by setting the boards at right angles to one another at intervals across the bog garden. The boards need not all be of the same length either. However, they should always be installed level, for sloping duckboards can be dangerous, even if covered with fine-mesh wire netting to improve grip on the slippery wood.

Normally, a handrail will spoil the effect of a duckboard walk and, for the most part, will be unnecessary. However, when such a feature runs out into an open body of water, terminating in a viewing area, a simple rail is worth adding for safety's sake.

An alternative to conventional duckboards is the rustic log walkway, which also fits in well with a bog garden area. It requires similar supports to the duckboard walk, but instead of running lengthways, the logs are placed across two strong supporting rails. These should be tanalized and bolted to the posts, the log sections being bolted to the rails. Rounded logs will be difficult to fix, even if quite small, so they must be sawn through lengthways to produce a flat surface to rest on the supporting rails. The log sections should be pushed together to create an almost corrugated effect.

A simple board walk constructed of plain timber provides access and gives structure to the tangled informality of this water garden.

Tanalizing is also important for the logs, which as far as possible should retain their bark. Pine is the best timber for this purpose, since the bark is not only attractive, but also it usually remains on the timber, despite the passage of feet. Normally, wire netting is not necessary on such a walkway, as the bark provides grip. However, it must be inspected regularly, for despite the best preservative treatment, logs will not last as long as more conventional planed planking.

I have seen a natural turf bridge, which I think would be ideal for my garden, providing a continuous link from one lawn to another across a stream. How do I set about creating such a feature?

Almost any form of construction can be used to provide support for a turf bridge, including brick and stone. However, sufficient depth of soil and good drainage are both essential if the grass is to succeed. For this reason, slab and concrete supports are undesirable, since the turf will either dry out or become very wet and soggy.

Although unconventional, the best supports for such a bridge are substantial logs, such as poplar or elm. These will last for many years before they need replacing. Ideally, the logs should be 30cm (12in) or more in diameter. Lay them across the stream, pushing them together and sinking their ends into the banks, but make sure that there is sufficient clearance beneath the logs to allow the passage of winter water. Push the logs together and create a small upstand along each side of the bridge, using smaller diameter lengths of the same timber. If desired, hand rails can be fixed to the sides at the same time.

The upstands retain a layer of soil and the turf, and should be large enough to ensure that the depth of soil and turf combined is at least 10cm (4in). Spread a layer of polythene, pierced with drainage holes, over the logs first to prevent the soil from falling through the gaps between them. The turf is laid on the soil in conventional fashion and should be kept well watered for the first season. It will establish quickly, and once it has knitted to the lawn on each side, a certain amount of natural moisture transfer will take place, and unless you experience unseasonably hot weather, it should remain green.

If the grass turns brown and struggles in the summer, top-dress with peat in the spring, aerating the turf to break up compaction and admit air. Dust sharp sand into the holes, adding some of the moisture-retentive gel crystals used for hanging baskets. This ensures the retention of moisture in the turf and a continuous green sward all summer long. Do not neglect to feed the turf either; a liquid lawn fertiliser applied twice during the summer will be beneficial.

I would love to have a small arched stone bridge, but I cannot find anyone who can make one. Is there any alternative for a similar effect?

It is very difficult to find a stone worker who can construct an arched garden bridge. A similar effect can be achieved using concrete and suitably cut stones.

The base of the bridge can be constructed of concrete with metal reinforcing, using well supported marine plywood shuttering to create a suitable curve. Providing that the stones that you use are cut to look as if they curve, they can be bedded into the concrete. For extra security drill each stone, insert a short length of metal rod and set this into the concrete. Once the first layer of stones is in position, a parapet can be constructed and the second stone layer can be tied into the concrete base of the bridge, which will further secure the curved bottom layer. Once the concrete has set firmly, the plywood shuttering can be removed.

The natural mossy covering seen on this traditional stone bridge can be encouraged by painting the stonework with a mixture of cow dung and milk.

ISLANDS

An island is rarely suitable for a small pool. Not only will it look out of keeping, but also, given the diminutive scale on which it will need constructing, it will not be of any significant use. With a small body of water, the only justification for constructing an island is to provide a predator-free haven in a wildlife pool. Even then, if the pool less than about 4.5m (15ft) square, it will not serve much useful purpose.

CREATING AN ISLAND

How you create an island will depend upon the type of pond you intend constructing. The scale of the excavation will help you decide whether to dig out the pond entirely, seal it, then build an island, or dig out the pool to leave an island. In the latter case, unless you intend sealing the pool with a bentonite blanket, or lining it with concrete, making the pool watertight may be quite difficult. A liner can be used, but its shape is likely to be rather awkward, unless you choose a rubber example and have it cut and welded to suit. The major benefit of creating an island in this way, however, is that it can be formed around an existing large shrub or tree to give an instant sense of maturity.

If an island is to be created after the pond has been excavated and lined, or sealed, there are several methods of construction to choose from. The simplest and most natural-looking is to build the island while the pool is empty, using hessian sacks filled with soil. These can be arranged to form a hollow square, or similar shape, which can be filled with soil. To ensure that the pool does not receive excessive quantities of nutrients, all but the top 30cm (12in) of soil, in which plants will be grown, should be of poor quality, preferably subsoil. As an alternative, a substantial amount of the space in the centre of the island can be filled with hardcore, provided it does not include any limey material, which may pollute the water. Once the pool has been filled with water and the soil is well soaked, you can begin to plant up the island.

This island creates a striking focal point in an uncluttered water garden. It is important that the edges are protected against erosion and that any trees used will tolerate the soil conditions and not disrupt island or pool with their roots or heavy leaf fall.

In a concrete pool, an excellent stable island can be constructed from blockwork, which should be built to within 10cm (4in) of the normal water level. Marine plywood boards should be fastened around the top of the blockwork, with brass screws and wall plugs, so that they just break the surface of the water and act as a timber edging. Then the centre of the island should be filled with soil, or with a combination of hardcore and soil, to create the island above the water level.

An island does not have to be covered completely with vegetation; it can be a rocky outcrop with pockets of soil, in which small plants can grow. The rocks should be concreted to the floor of the pool and gradually built up to form the island shape, the centre being filled with more concrete to ensure stability. If you use rocks in this way, make sure that you use only good-quality material, and that the strata all lie in the same direction once they have emerged from the water. Sandstone and limestone rocks should be avoided, as they will crumble and flake during freezing winter conditions.

METHODS FOR CREATING AN ISLAND IN A POOL

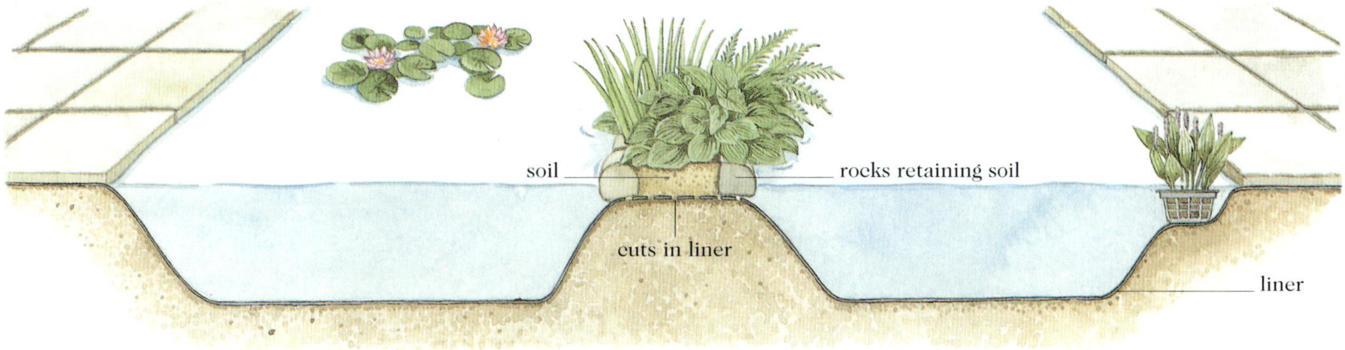

It is possible to create an island by contouring the excavation when the water garden is constructed. This demands a high degree of accuracy with levelling from the outset.

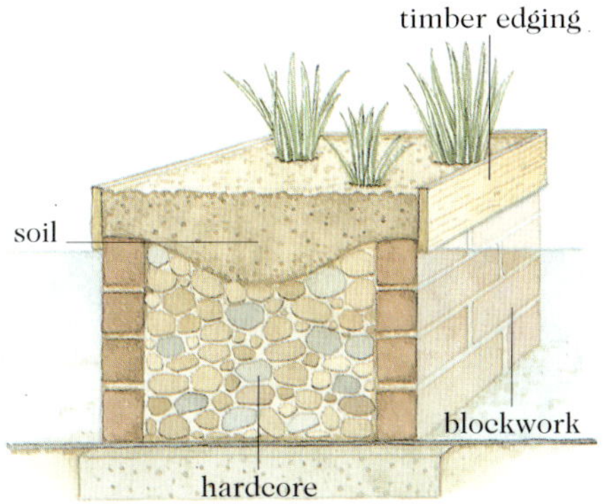

A simple island can be constructed with bricks or blockwork and finished naturally with wood at water level. This edging disguises the structure beneath and appears more natural.

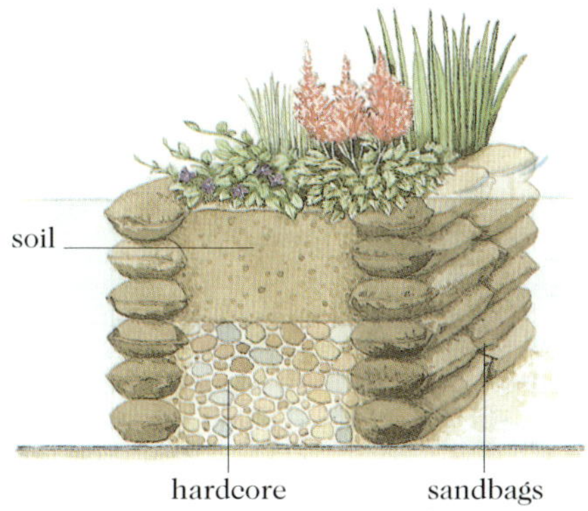

A soil or sand bag construction gives greater flexibility with the shape and size of the island. It soon mellows into its surroundings and plants and algae also establish on it freely.

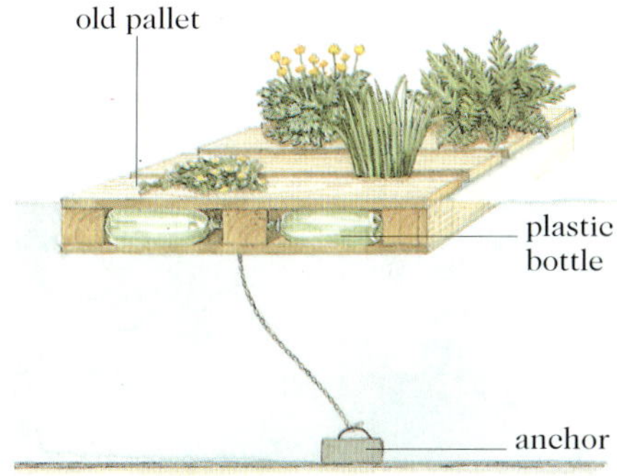

A wooden pallet secured to the pool floor is an economical form of construction for a floating island. The discreetly hidden plastic bottles provide added buoyancy.

Apart from the simple islands described here, if you become really enthusiastic about wildlife, you can create duck huts and similar island accommodation for breeding and sheltering wildfowl. However, these are very specialized, and advice on their construction is best sought from a local nature conservation group or similar organization.

THE FLOATING ISLAND

Creating the elaborate structure needed for a permanent island will not suit everyone. However, an inexpensive alternative is to make a floating island (see 3 above). The basis for this can be an old wooden pallet or a construction similar to a section of decking. This should float quite successfully, but depending upon the timber used, and the scale of the island, you may need to add some extra buoyancy. Old plastic soft-drink bottles and similar containers are ideal for this and can often be concealed within the island raft. The island should be secured by a nylon cord to a suitable anchor, such as a piece of concrete with a large metal staple embedded in the top. The length of the cord will determine the amount by which the island is allowed to move around on the surface of the water; if the cord's length is equal to the depth of the pool, the island will remain in a fixed position.

With a little care, it should be possible to accommodate some plant life on the floating island. This can be planted in small growing bags made from old tights. Fill the tights with good garden soil, soak them thoroughly until the soil is sloppy and malleable, then plant small rooted cuttings of water mint or brooklime through slits cut in the tights. You could also add a small rush or water forget-me-not. Push the growing bags into the gaps between the wooden boards of the island. The plants will establish quickly and, provided that you add only a few, the weight will not be excessive.

When the use of soil is impractical and may cause the island to sink, jam cut willow stems into the gaps between the boards. They will root into the water and produce a seasonal small bush, which will have to be discarded at the approach of winter.

LIGHTING

Whether water is still or moving, it can be greatly enhanced by lighting, which can create a magical atmosphere as darkness closes in. You may think that lighting your water feature will be a rather sophisticated and expensive undertaking, but modern garden lighting systems are easily installed, inexpensive to buy, and economical to run. So this added dimension to the water garden should be considered from the earliest planning stages. If conduit for cabling can be incorporated during construction, this will prove a distinct advantage, but if you already have a pool, or decide to add lighting once construction is under way, it will still be relatively simple to light your pool tastefully.

Picking out important structural features, as well as the moving water, and lighting them alone provides garden entertainment not unlike that offered by a firework display.

CHOOSING LIGHTS

There are several different types of light, each of which serves a slightly different purpose. The simplest is the spotlight, which will enhance a specific area with a single beam. Multiple units, comprising two or three lights, are also available and are perfect for illuminating large fountain features. White light is most effective in the garden, but sometimes spotlights with coloured lenses, which give amber and warm red glows, may be incorporated to advantage. Such spotlights can be positioned anywhere around the pool.

Underwater lighting is provided by special sealed units. These are usually placed directly beneath a fountain or waterfall, or positioned around the edge of the pool, pointing in towards the centre. However, exactly where you position this form of lighting will depend on the elements of your particular water feature, and you may need to work by trial and error until you achieve the best visual effect.

This is where the floating light can sometimes be used to great advantage. This functions in the same way as a static underwater light, but it is more readily adjusted to suit the prevailing conditions. Along with the other lighting systems, this benefits from being con-

A well lit garden can be a delight. All the structures, major plantings and focal points are bathed in light, but the water remains dark and mysterious, reflecting the surroundings in its mirror-like surface.

sidered early in the planning stages of water garden construction, so that there is a connection point for an electrical supply close at hand.

Finally, there are illuminated fountains, which have integral lights. These provide a wonderful spectacle when it is dark, but become a normal fountain during the day. Such fountains are usually sold as kits, comprising a submersible pump with fountain attachment and a sealed underwater lamp, which is secured to the pump. Some kits also come with a colour changing unit. This is a simple disc, fitted with different coloured lenses, that revolves as the pump functions, changing the colour of the light in a slow sequence.

INSTALLING LIGHTS

Water and electricity are poor companions, so it is essential that only purpose designed underwater or outdoor lighting systems are used, and the manufacturer's instructions followed implicitly. The majority of garden lighting systems, whether designed for use in the pool or around its edges, operate from a transformer that is linked to the normal domestic electricity supply. The transformer reduces the voltage to a safe level, which means that cables can be run on the surface if required, being concealed among plants. This is particularly useful, as it allows adjustments to be made to the system without a lot of disruption. No underground wiring is required, unless the transformer is installed in a building away from the house. The lamps can be fitted anywhere along the cable and are completely portable.

If a mains powered lighting system is chosen, great care will be needed in providing suitable cabling to the connection point. Armoured cable should be used as a matter of course. It must be installed underground, being buried in a trench at least 90cm (36in) deep to avoid the likelihood of any disturbance during normal gardening work, and run as close to the pool as is convenient. As a precaution, when burying the cable, cover it with a row of roofing tiles before backfilling the trench. This will prevent any accidental contact when digging in later years. A further warning of the cable's presence can be given by laying brightly coloured tape along the tops of the tiles for the entire length of the cable run. In addition to these precautions, any connection to the mains power should be through a circuit-breaker known as a residual current device.

USING LIGHTING

For the most part, water gardeners who install lighting use it only during the hours of darkness when they may be relaxing beside the pool. There is no reason why the lights cannot be run continuously, but consider the fish; it is rather unfair to bathe them in bright light for nights on end.

INDOOR POOL LIGHTING

The same criteria can be applied to lighting the indoor pool, except that some of the lamps may be too powerful for the kind of indoor feature that most domestic gardeners could afford. In most cases, smaller and simpler light units will be more suitable, multiple units being inappropriate.

As with outdoor features, it is possible to buy illuminated fountains for indoor use. Some are not really comparable to traditional water features, but act more as room humidifiers. They are totally self-contained, being filled with water and connected to the electrical supply, after which they will run continually. They have no facility for plants or fish, and neither would be desirable.

LAYING ELECTRICAL CABLE

1 Excavate a trench at least 90cm (36in) deep to ensure that the cable is not accidentally disturbed during gardening operations and mark it on a simple plan for future reference.

2 Lay the cable carefully in the bottom of the trench and cover it with a row of roofing tiles to provide added protection. Armoured cable should be used as a matter of course.

3 Lay a brightly coloured tape over the tiles for the entire length as an additional warning and backfill the trench. It may take some weeks for the soil to settle again.

CHAPTER FIVE

STOCKING THE POOL

Once you have constructed the pool, you can begin to paint the water garden picture, that is to choose and establish the plants, and introduce the fish, bearing in mind the requirements of the pool as an independent ecosystem. For most gardeners, this is a time of great excitement, as the majority of plants that are grown in a water garden will be completely new, and the fish a wondrous mystery. The manner in which aquatic plants grow and their seasonal behaviour in a watery environment are fascinating. The aquatic world is totally dependent upon plants to ensure its well-being; clarity of water will only result from the proper balance of plants, and the gardener has to assemble these in both scientific and artistic arrangements. Fish and other livestock add extra spice, for with few exceptions, all the creatures that inhabit the pool will be desirable or interesting. Many will arrive of their own accord, but by carefully selecting plants, you can entice others to set up home. The garden pool can become a haven for wildlife of all forms; whether they be lovely dragonflies, ugly toads or slinky newts, there is room for them all to live in harmony. The pool surrounds are also very important, for although they may not play an important part in developing a sustainable balance within the water garden, they do frame the picture and in many cases provide a unique opportunity to grow a range of plants which are tricky to establish elsewhere in the garden.

The boggy area beside the water also contributes to the life of the pool in that it is the home for many attractive creatures which utilise the water but are not sustained by it. In may cases of course the area beside a pool is dry and this too can have its advantages. The chance to grow plants of a character associated with dry conditions next to water is a garden designer's delight, for artistic license can be invoked and the laws of nature theoretically flouted.

A well balanced water garden is not only a floral delight, but a complete miniature underwater world where plants, fish and snails depend upon one another for their continued existence.

CREATING A BALANCE

To ensure a trouble-free pool, it is essential to achieve the correct ecological balance. This not only guarantees water clarity, but also that all the inhabitants co-exist in harmony. Once the correct ingredients are in place, a balance will usually be maintained, provided that all aspects of the pool flourish; if one element fails, the ecological balance will collapse.

ACHIEVING THE CORRECT BALANCE

It is essential that all the elements involved achieve a reasonable harmony from the beginning. There are no hard-and-fast rules about what should be used when stocking a pool initially, for no two pools will be the same. There is likely to be great diversity in all aspects, from situation to water chemistry and nutrient levels. However, experienced water gardeners have developed rough-and-ready formulas which, although crude in scientific terms, tend to work well for most circumstances.

If we look at the principles of natural balance, we find that there are very distinct key areas that need attention. Submerged plants are the crucial element in achieving suc-

In order to create a natural and harmonious balance there must be liberal planting of submerged aquatics, together with plants with floating foliage to provide a degree of surface shade. The marginal plants make little contribution, but frame the watery picture.

cess, for they perform an invaluable and often diverse role. Their main task is to mop up nutrients in the water, and to provide oxygen during the daytime for fish and other aquatic creatures. However, they are also a food source themselves, a habit for aquatic fauna (which is another food source) and, in many cases, a nursery for young fish. Thus, their value in the pool's ecosystem is incalculable.

Their most important role of removing excess nutrients reduces the incidence of algae, which is the bane of the pondkeeper's life. Suspended single-celled algae turn the water green, obscuring the fish and many plants from view. If enough submerged plants are established, by virtue of being higher forms of plant life, they will starve out the algae in the pool by utilizing all the mineral salts upon which the algae would normally feed.

Submerged plants also oxygenate the water freely during the day, although at night the process is reversed and carbon dioxide produced. This will not be a serious problem unless there is an over-abundance of submerged growth, an over-population of fish and very warm night-time temperatures. In such circumstances, some of the plants may need removing. However, for most of the time, the more submerged plants there are, the better the pond balance will be.

Green water is also regulated by the amount of light available. Algae, like most other aquatic plants, enjoy full uninterrupted sunlight, so you can control it with shade. However, planting trees and shrubs to shade the pond is not a good idea, as this will prevent the desirable higher aquatics, like waterlilies, from growing well. The answer is to provide shade on the surface of the water itself, using floating plants and waterlily foliage, which will also add interest to the pool. These should not cover the entire pool, for complete shading will kill the submerged plants as well. No more than one third of the surface area should be covered if green suspended algae is to be controlled successfully and the submerged aquatics permitted to continue in healthy growth.

Fish are also essential elements when it comes to achieving a natural balance in the pond. They are invaluable for keeping pests under control, not only troublesome creatures like caddis fly larvae, which chew the leaves of aquatic plants, but also mosquito larvae which, if allowed to continue unchecked, will become adults and ultimately the scourge of the gardener. The waste matter they produce is of benefit to the plants, too. Other useful creatures are ramshorn snails, since they graze on filamentous algae, which is difficult to control in any other way.

Within this broad outline, there are places for many other creatures and plants, all of which have their parts to play in ensuring an ecological balance, which is easily upset if one aspect is ignored in favour of another.

The appearance of green water can be regulated by controlling the amount of light falling into the water, along with restricting the availability of dissolved plant nutrients. Waterlilies provide shade and submerged plants mop up the mineral salts.

A FORMULA FOR BALANCE

When stocking a pool, the principles outlined previously must be considered carefully, and a formula for initial planting developed. Unless the plants have been chosen to produce a very definite visual effect, you may have to modify the formula slightly to achieve the desired balance. Categorize the plants by their mode of life, then choose sufficient to fill the requirements of the formula.

Calculate the surface area of the pool, excluding the marginal shelves in square metres or yards and, for every square metre or yard, plant nine or ten bunches of submerged plants. These can be grouped in clusters of containers, rather than being spread evenly around the base of the pool.

A similar calculation must be made before the quantity of waterlilies and floating aquatics can be decided upon. Remember that no more than a third of the pond's surface area may be occupied by foliage at any one time. Any excess should be regularly removed to ensure that the submerged plants receive plenty of light.

The margins of the pool are important from the decorative point of view, but make little contribution to the overall balance of the water garden. For the best visual effect, plant them in groups.

If you want your fish to be happy, to grow and, ultimately, to breed, do not stock at a rate that exceeds 45cm/sq m (18in/sq yd). When calculating the length of a fish, include its tail. Ramshorn snails can be introduced freely, as the fish will control the population if it begins to get out of hand.

Once the formula for ensuring water clarity has been settled, specific varieties and species can be selected, within the limited constraints that the formula places upon you. As can be seen, the quantities of waterlilies, floating plants and submerged aquatics are all subject to restrictions, but marginal and bog garden plants can be introduced without constraint.

THE MARGINS

The marginal areas around the pool are very important, too. How you treat them will have a marked effect upon the overall visual quality of your water garden. In a very formal pool, their use is best restricted to three or four good basketfuls of quality architectural plants, like irises and rushes, which should be positioned with care. This will leave plenty of open water for creating reflections – a vital element in presenting a pleasing picture with a formal pool.

An informal pool can support massed marginal plantings, provided that you can reach the water's edge at some point. For all water gardens, except the most unruly wildlife pool, container cultivation is essential. It is the only way to keep the pool under control. Never be tempted to plant directly into soil or the marginal shelf, for the plants will spread into each other and you will face a constant battle to keep the feature looking attractive. Tall plants in containers, such as the poker-headed typhas, must also be positioned carefully so that they will not be blown over.

WATERLILIES

Waterlilies are unquestionably the queens of the water garden. Indeed, for many gardeners, they are the main reason for establishing a pool. While they can form part of the cluttered picture of an informal cottage-garden-style pond, they will be seen at their best when planted in isolation in open water. Select varieties that are compatible with the depth of water and surface area available, ensuring that they are lifted and divided regularly according to their requirements. In that way, you will ensure that there will always be spreading flat lily pads and beautiful starry blossoms. If you choose the wrong variety for the prevailing conditions, or neglect to divide them frequently enough, the plants may climb partially out of the water in an untidy bunch and be sparsely flowered, or they may struggle to push vigorous leaves to the surface.

SUBMERGED AQUATICS

The least favoured of all plants are the submerged aquatics. They are not very appealing to look at, but are essential nev-

A bog garden can be created as an extension of the pool or as a stand-alone feature. The benefits of an extended flowering season and the wealth of attractive foliage plants available makes this a tremendous asset for any water garden.

ertheless. Almost all flower, but the majority of blooms are insignificant. Only the water crowfoot (*Ranunculus aquatilis*) and the water violet (*Hottonia palustris*) produce blossoms of any quality. These should be used where flowers are required and where floating foliage will present no problem. They are not suitable for a reflecting pool, where submerged plants are essential to preserve clarity, but should appear as no more than dark masses on the bottom. Here, totally submerged species like the Canadian pond weed (*Elodea canadensis*), willow moss (*Fontinalis antipyretica*) and hair grass (*Eleocharis acicularis*) can be utilized.

OPEN WATER

The danger faced by the enthusiastic gardener is over-populating the pool with plants, thereby excluding much of what is essentially water gardening's most useful element: open water. While a certain number of plants will be necessary to ensure a balanced pool and clear water, the benefits of open water, and especially its reflective qualities, should not be underestimated. Moving water is also vital to many gardeners, for creating both fascinating visual effects and magical sounds. Its presence will have an impact upon planting ideas, as many aquatics do not enjoy growing in moving water. Consequently, how you will use the water is very important when considering which plants should be grown.

FLOATING PLANTS

To some extent, floating plants are an acquired taste. They can be both useful and invasive, but of all the aquatics, they are the most difficult to control, for even a modest breeze can transport them across a pool. Because of this, they are best used in an informal situation. In a formal water feature, the essential surface shade should be provided by waterlilies or other deep-water aquatics with floating foliage. The latter will root strongly into containers on the pool floor and will thus remain in position.

BOG PLANTS

A bog garden is not an essential extension of a pool, but it does make a significant difference to the overall appearance of the feature. Bog garden plants can extend the flowering season at both ends, for they flower long before any other plants in the pool, and continue after the waterlilies have faded. However, their greatest virtue is their diversity of foliage, which not only offers amazing shapes and sizes, but colours and contrasts, too, especially as autumn approaches.

PLANTING IDEAS

INFORMAL PLANTING

The arrangement of plants in a pool is a very personal matter: what appeals to one gardener, may not hold any attraction for another. The visual qualities of water must also be considered, for they can be as important as the plants.

With an informal style of gardening, it is tempting to think that, as the plants do not appear to conform to any set arrangement, it will be easy to make a pleasing display. Nothing could be further from the truth. Creating a successful, well balanced scheme, which can also be managed efficiently, is extremely difficult. The plants have to look cared for, but with no evidence to that effect.

This problem can be eased to some extent by the use of planting baskets, which allow plants that might invade one another's territory to be placed cheek by jowl in the knowledge that they will remain more or less where you put them. The disadvantage is that containers can create rigid formal blocks of plants, so some ingenuity must be used when positioning them, with perhaps occasional underplanting to soften the edges.

When using stiff upright plants, like *Schoenoplectus lacustris* and *S. l. tabernaemontani* 'Zebrinus', there should be no difficulty in accommodating a low growing marginal aquatic in the same basket. Use only one upright and one lower plant per basket. The brooklime (*Veronica beccabunga*) and water forget-me-not (*Myosotis scorpioides*) are two of the best for this kind of arrangement. Neither has a root system that is too invasive, so they will not cause any difficulty for the main plant. Take care not to repeat such plantings throughout the pool margin, otherwise the effect will appear very formal.

An informal planting can be more difficult to achieve than a formal one. The plants should appear to have colonised the area naturally, must look well cared for, but with no evidence to that effect. A subtle, tangled informality needs careful planning.

A SUMMER FEATURE

One of the first points to accept is that the water garden is predominantly a summer feature in terms of flowering and interesting foliage. The informal arrangement depends heavily on planting. The placid stillness of the water during winter is rarely as effective, or important, as in a formal pool, where it may be contrived as a major garden focal point. Therefore, when creating your scheme, you should take into account the fact that, while there are a few early flowering species of aquatic plant, for the most part it will be mid-summer before you see anything resembling a good show.

Arrange the plants to account for their differences in flowering period so that adjoining groups blossom at the same time. Cotton grass (*Eriophorum angustifolium*) makes a pleasing picture when planted alongside the pretty water forget-me-not (*Myosotis scorpioides*), while the pickerel (*Pontederia cordata*) is a natural companion for the flowering rush (*Butomus umbellatus*). In the spring, place the bog bean (*Menyanthes trifoliata*) with the common marsh marigold (*Caltha palustris*), and allow the bright, gold and green, sword-like foliage of Iris pseudacorus 'Variegata' to contrast with the glossy evergreen leaves and white sail-like spathes of the bog arum (*Calla palustris*).

A water garden is essentially a summer feature. During the winter most plants die back completely, the open water then becoming a placid mirror which can reflect all around it.

CREATING A THEME

To most water gardeners, an informal planting suggests a cottage-garden look, where foliage and flowers mix in a tangled, but controlled, manner. The marginal shelves of the pool appear rather like a small version of a herbaceous border, which may run into the larger herbaceous bed of the bog garden. In a cottage-garden setting, this is obviously the correct thing to do, for this form of gardening is very much about growing a wide range of plants in visual harmony. However, if your garden is not of this tradition, being simply informal, consider theming your planting arrangements.

One of the most pleasing themes is based on the use of pinks and white. Select a bright red waterlily, such as 'Firecrest', as a centre-piece and complement it in the deeper part of the pool with the vanilla-scented, long flowering white water hawthorn (*Aponogeton distachyos*). In fact, you can use two or three groups of aponogeton around the waterlily in a large pool. Clear water around these deep-water aquatics is essential for the best effect, so do not be tempted to introduce any floating plants.

For the margins use *Houttuynia cordata* with its purplish foliage and white flowers, the plum-coloured *Iris versicolor* 'Kermesina', silvery-white *Caltha leptosepala* and pink-flowered *Butomus umbellatus*. These can all be supplemented with leafy reeds and rushes.

The marginal plantings can be extended into the bog garden, taking the colour theme with them. Deep carmine *Primula pulverulenta* and selected pink-flowered forms of candelabra primulas, along with the stately *P. japonica* 'Postford White', make lovely combinations, all flowering at the same time. They will look a little untidy later on, so distract the eye, perhaps with *Aruncus sylvestris* and *Astilbe* 'White Gloria', both of which have splendid feathery creamy or white blossoms in spires above handsome deeply cut foliage.

Apart from the obvious contrasts and complements that any skilled gardener makes when choosing plants, in a water garden an additional consideration is finding a means of disguising the structure of the feature. The edges will demand particular attention, so any arrangement must include plants that will conceal the pond materials and any containers.

If done sensitively, this can improve the whole display, but if done without care, the planting may detract considerably from it. Where associated plantings seem to be either inappropriate or impractical in the same container, make liberal use of creeping Jenny (*Lysimachia nummularia*), pushing short stem cuttings into the tops of the containers and allowing the bright green foliage to cascade all around. This adaptable plant is equally at home when used to form a carpet among plants in the bog garden. Its very modest rooting system and abundant, well behaved foliage are perfect.

The apparent rough and tumble of what most gardeners perceive as being the typical domestic garden pond does not suit everybody, especially if the garden is laid out in a formal style. In consequence, fewer plants may be used because open water, or a moving water feature, is a more important element in the design. In this situation, the correct selection and positioning of the plants are often even more critical than in a loose, tangled informal gathering.

FORMAL PLANTING

A formal water feature tends to depend upon rather rigid, or mathematical, principles to which the planting must conform. Although there are few aquatic plants that really lend themselves to such order, either in appearance or habit, the combination of careful plant selection and tightly controlled planting can produce the desired effect.

To provide height and focal points within a pool, choose from the various schoenoplectus. The common bulrush (*Schoenoplectus lacustris*) is first class, but do not select the type that produces large, brown poker-like heads, which is really a reedmace. *S. lacustris* has slender dark green stems, which are like large knitting needles. Often used in the wildlife garden, and a poor relation of the zebra rush (*S. l. tabernaemontani* 'Zebrinus') and *S. l. tabernaemontani* 'Albescens', which it closely resembles, it can provide sombre structure where others fail. It is not a plant for general decoration, but in such circumstances, or the wilderness of a wildlife pool, it has its uses.

If the pool is to look really sophisticated, *S. l. tabernaemontani* 'Zebrinus' and 'Albescens' are naturals, providing bold upright structural foliage of high quality, which can only be equalled for effectiveness by some of the cultivars of *Iris laevigata*. The variegated foliage of *I. l.* 'Variegata' is extremely effective. Forget the blue flowers, although these are a bonus during early summer, and plant for the effect of the handsome sword-like leaves.

Variegated sweet flag (*Acorus calamus* 'Variegatus') does not produce significant flowers, but really high-quality,

Formal gardens demand formal planting, the major groups of plants being arranged at even spacings with a balance of clear water between. With a formal pool, the areas of open water are as visually important as the plants themselves.

Where the pool occupies a flat site it is important to provide height and structure. The evenly spaced groups of rushes do this admirably without dominating the pool.

ORIENTAL PLANTING IDEAS

Not all formal pools will follow traditional Western ideas. With the increased interest in keeping koi carp, Oriental themes have become very popular. These depend for their success upon the combination of landscape materials, such as cobbles, paving and gravel, and very specific planting. Although the plants chosen do not have to originate from the Orient, they must conform with the overall theme and, in most cases, should be able to stand alone.

The dwarf reedmace (*Typha minima*) is a classic Oriental plant, while the zebra rush (*Schoenoplectus lacustris tabernaemontani* 'Zebrinus') has all the desired qualities. All the *Iris laevigata* cultivars are true Orientals and, for the bog garden, *Iris ensata* fits the bill. Hostas, especially the variegated kinds and the large-leaved *H. sieboldiana* var. *elegans*, are perfect for the moist edge of an Oriental water feature, particularly when backed by the bold leaves of *Darmera peltata*.

cream, green and rose-tinted leaves. Although not evergreen, its foliage will be in evidence for much of the year and has a very pleasant tangerine fragrance.

Bold plants like these should be used as focal points within the pool or as a means of providing height to the scheme. When matching plants that will grow side by side, select material of similar age and condition, planting it in a uniform compost in containers of the same size. This is vital when trying to achieve a symmetrical display. The same applies to waterlilies, especially when attempting to match pairs in a still open stretch of water.

CHOOSING A THEME

As with informal plantings, a formal pool can be themed to a particular colour or colour combination. Fewer plants will be required, but you will need more than one example of each. In a simple square or rectangle of water, with provision for marginal plantings in each corner, select the lovely upright foliage and greenish spathes of *Peltandra virginica* to mix with the oval or spade-like leaves of the water plantain (*Alisma plantago-aquatica*), which has spreading panicles of pinkish-white blossoms. For the open water, choose a simple white-flowered waterlily such as 'Hermine'. If desired, the water chestnut (*Trapa natans*) can be added, but this floating plant will not necessarily remain in the same place and may detract from the overall symmetry of the arrangement.

If a pink and white theme does not appeal, look to a yellow and white combination. Fill a container with early flowering, bright yellow marsh marigold (*Caltha palustris*) and the low growing, summer blooming brass buttons (*Cotula coronopifolia*). Alternatively, plant baskets solid with *Mimulus luteus*. As a centre-piece, use either a bright yellow waterlily like 'Marliacea Chromatella' or a very classy white, such as a 'Virginalis' or 'Gonnère'.

Consider fragrance as part of your planting scheme, especially if the pool is in an enclosed area, such as a courtyard. Scents will tend to linger in the warm still atmosphere and make a significant contribution to the pleasure of the poolside experience, especially if accompanied by splashing water. Choose a fragrant waterlily like 'Rose Arey'. This is very free flowering and has a rich aniseed fragrance. It should be grown in isolation from other scents so that its cloying richness can be enjoyed to the full. Treat the water hawthorn (*Aponogeton distachyos*) in a similar fashion. Its heady vanilla fragrance is best enjoyed alone.

With raised pools, scented foliage can be enjoyed more readily because the leaves will be easier to touch. It is not advisable to grow scented plants in close proximity to one another, as might be expected in a herb patch, for the smell of each may be overwhelmed by its neighbours. In most cases, it is preferable to grow them individually and to enjoy their fragrance in isolation. Choose from water mint (*Mentha aquatica*), the sweet flag (*Acorus calamus*) and the unusual, but spicily aromatic, *Mentha cervina*. All have leaves that release pungent aromas when touched on warm days.

CHOOSING PLANTS

Selecting plants for a water feature is a very personal matter, but there are many aesthetic and cultural aspects to consider when making a choice. It is important to make an early decision about the cultural methods to be used. If you grow your plants within the pool in aquatic planting baskets, the options for successful cultivation will be increased, even if it will be marginally more difficult to make the arrangement look natural. Planting baskets will make it much easier to control the development of your plants. Where necessary, such as with the acid loving cotton grass (*Eriophorum angustifolium*), they also make it possible to create special soil conditions in isolation from the other plants.

SELECTING FOR EASY MANAGEMENT

As with most garden features, the management of a water garden can be made simple or complex, depending upon the plants that are grown. By carefully selecting plants that do not creep about or seed themselves freely, caring for the water garden can be greatly simplified.

The most amenable plants are those that remain in orderly clumps, like marsh marigolds, the pendulous pond sedge (*Carex pendula*) and the more modest growing irises, such as *Iris laevigata*, *I. versicolor* and their varieties. None of these creates undue difficulties with self seeding either. The pickerel (*Pontederia cordata*) is well behaved, so too is the flowering rush (*Butomus umbellatus*). Indeed, both are so easy-going and restrained that they are among the few marginal plants that could be tried together in the same basket. They have contrasting habits, but flower in harmony, the pickerel with a blue flower spike and the flowering rush a rose-pink umbel. In general, joint planting is not to be recommended, except where upright spiky rushes would look better with some basal softening, using a creeping aquatic like the brooklime.

Staking is not practical in most pools, so it is essential to assess the exposure of the plants to strong winds. Resist growing tall subjects if they are likely to suffer from wind damage. In draughty places, tall marginal plants growing in containers may be blown over into the water, unless secured, and constantly look drab. They will often pick up algae and debris from the water and will need careful regular manicuring. Shorter, more stable, plants are the practical answer, although in some situations, this may cause the aesthetics of the feature to suffer through a lack of height.

Pests and diseases are relatively few and far between. Waterlily aphids are probably the worst and are quite indiscriminate, feeding on any succulent plants that take their fancy. Waterlilies are the obvious target, but *Butomus*

By selecting restrained but colourful plants like the pickerel, Pontederia cordata, *water garden management can be simplified. Not only is it not invasive, but it only requires lifting and dividing every three years, whereas some marginals benefit from annual division.*

Among the earliest flowering aquatic plants are the marsh marigolds and the yellow skunk cabbages. These are in their glory before most of the other marginal plants have appeared.

umbellatus and the arrowheads, or sagittaria, are also great attractions. Where this pest is a constant nuisance, do not grow butomus or sagittaria, although you may still find it on other aquatics. For the most part, selecting plants upon their susceptibility, or otherwise, to predators is not necessary, as in a well ordered pond, natural controls will be maintained.

SELECTING FOR FLOWERING PERIOD

During the winter, the pool will be dead, and the only chance of creating any interest at all will rest with the skeletal remains of the flower heads of plants like the water plantain. These can be most attractive, especially after a snowfall, but their durability cannot be depended upon.

The first flowers in the water garden are usually provided by the marsh marigolds, especially the common *Caltha palustris* and its double-flowered variety 'Flore Pleno'. In the adjacent bog area, *Primula rosea* produces its bright pink flowers alongside the bold white or lilac-blue drumstick heads of *P. denticulata*. These are followed by the brilliant mixed colours of the *Iris ensata* hybrids and, in the margin of the pool, the *Iris laevigata* varieties.

At about this time, the waterlilies start to blossom, becoming the focal point for the pool and remaining until late summer. Alongside them, the various reeds and rushes push up their brownish flowers, while the yellow musk and brass buttons add splashes of gold. Pontederia and butomus bring up the rear, the water dock (*Rumex hydrolapathum*) taking the water garden into autumn with its bright red and coppery foliage tints.

FOLIAGE EFFECTS

Apart from the water dock with its bright autumn colours, very few aquatics create a leafy spectacle, although among the great diversity of marginal and bog garden plants there are myriad handsome foliage plants. A number of these are quite exotic-looking, while others are more comfortably natural. Consequently, they may require careful selection if you are to achieve the desired effect.

Darmera peltata is one of the best examples. It is a super plant for a water garden where hostas abound, but a square peg in a round hole when it comes to the wildlife pool. Here, the graceful pendulus sedge, Joe-pye-weed (*Eupatorium purpureum*) and meadow sweet are more appropriate.

If the pool is small and well manicured, it will never look completely natural. It will always be a garden pool, so you will be able to get away with mixing and matching foliage contrasts, and also use them effectively to disguise the fading remains of early plants. The great shuttlecock-like crowns of the ostrich feather fern (*Matteuccia struthiopteris*) are perfect for hiding the fading blossoms of marsh marigolds and early primulas, then creating a beautiful soft green foliage effect themselves. They have the added advantage of not only being excellent bog garden plants, but also being tolerant of living in shallow standing water.

Some of the finest architectural plants are among those that prosper in the bog or margins of the water garden.

BUYING PLANTS

Although aquatic plants grow very quickly and a weedy specimen can often be transformed into a lusty grower, it is far more sensible to look for good-quality plants from the outset. The best way to ensure good quality is to visit a specialist aquatic plant supplier or a garden centre where there is an aquatics department with dedicated staff. Aquatics are a mystery to many general garden retailers, and a lot of heartache can be bought if you are unlucky enough to patronize one where the stock is questionable and the staff know little.

THE PLANTING SEASON

The planting season for aquatics extends from spring until late summer, the second half of the season being less satisfactory than the early part. Later plantings do not establish quite as quickly as those planted during the spring, the plants usually being of poorer quality, especially if they have been in a sales tank since the beginning of the season. Here, they will quite possibly have been mauled by potential buyers, tipped over and generally abused, their growth being stunted by the constraints of a sales container. Of course, this scenario is by no means universal, but it is fairly typical of many non-specialist aquatic suppliers.

The flowering rush, Butomus umbellatus, *is a slow starter in the spring and is often forced into early growth. It is best to wait until early summer to plant a naturally grown specimen.*

Wholesale plant suppliers often force some of the slower growing varieties by placing them in polythene tunnels. The plants sprout vigorously and look excellent in the sales tanks in the nursery or garden centre, but once taken home to your pond, they will soon become sad and jaded. The shock of the change of climate, from warm tunnel to outdoors, will cause them to be badly checked. Rarely will they die, but often it will be the regrowth that provides a summer display, rather than the soft sappy foliage produced by forcing. There is really no advantage to purchasing plants that have been treated in this manner.

It is not always easy to identify plants that have been forced, but there is one group of aquatics that cannot possibly be leafy saleable specimens at the beginning of the season. It is their nature to be late developers. The group includes both the rushes *Schoenoplectus lacustris tabernaemontani* 'Albescens' and *S. l. tabernaemontani 'Zebrinus'*, all the arrowheads, frogbit (*Hydrocharis morsus-ranae*), flowering rush (*Butomus umbellatus*) and water chestnut (*Trapa natans*). You will have to wait until early summer for all of these species if you wish to produce naturally developed plants.

RECOGNIZING A GOOD PLANT

It is more difficult to recognize a good aquatic plant than a tree or shrub. Unlike woody plants, aquatics have no structure until well developed during the summer, and then it is not permanent. However, you should be able to tell whether a plant is a good one by its vigour and general aspect.

The main criteria when choosing aquatics are health and vigour, plus an ability to recognize that you have been sold the correct plant. The last can be a major problem, for general retailers are often unfamiliar with aquatics, and common, sometimes misleading, names are rife.

One of the most critical areas of confusion is between pondlilies and waterlilies. The former are the vigorous and often, in their juvenile stage, more attractive nuphars. These are not suitable, except for the bleakest and shadiest of ponds. They produce rampant leaves and small yellow flowers, and are not at all what the gardener expects of a waterlily. To obtain the true waterlily, nymphaea must be purchased. Nymphaeas are often slow to start into growth and rarely look as appealing as a nuphar, but they come up trumps in the end.

When choosing a waterlily, make sure that it will suit the depth of water in your pool and be of compatible spread. It is always difficult to be certain that you are obtaining the correct variety, but if you are paying a fair price for a plant, there is a very good chance that it will be true to type. Be very suspicious of cheap waterlilies; there is no such thing. For the most part, you get what you pay for.

All aquatic plants should look bright and lively when you buy them. There should be no evidence of the black clustering waterlily aphid or the small grubs of the waterlily beetle. Thin cigar-like cylinders of jelly, which may be found attached to all manner of waterlily plants, are not fish spawn, but the eggs of the troublesome greater pond snail (see page 286). This will eat waterlilies and other floating foliage in preference to algae. It is safe to buy plants that bear these snail eggs, but you must remove them before you put the plants in your pond.

If you buy plants bare-rooted, rather than those that are growing in a container, make sure the rootstock is solid. This is very important with waterlilies. A soft waterlily rootstock is not only likely to die, but also may spread infection throughout your pond. Submerged aquatic plants should always be fresh. Avoid any that have remained in a tank and become heated and faded.

When choosing a waterlily be sure that it will grow satisfactorily in the depth of water that is being provided and that the potential spread is compatible with the space available. Be suspicious of cheap unnamed waterlilies; they are unlikely to be a bargain.

PLANTING

Fortunately, the planting season for aquatics coincides with the active growing period, which makes handling the plants much easier than if they were dormant. In addition, you can see the prospects for growth. Plants should also be lifted and divided at the same time, there being a clear indication of what will be good and what should be discarded.

USING CONTAINERS

The use of planting containers is essential in the modern domestic garden pool. Without containing the plants in some way, the whole thing can rapidly get out of hand. Even the most desirable of aquatics, the waterlilies, will overwhelm everything else when planted in an earth-bottomed pond. It is true that containers produce some constraint upon growth, but if the plants are fed and maintained properly, any potentially adverse effects will be minimized.

A wide range of containers has been used for planting aquatics in the past. Before the advent of plastic planting baskets, plants were grown in wooden crates and wicker baskets, although in larger pools specially built planting pits were prepared. Today, the plastic planting basket, in its many different shapes and with micro-mesh holes, is the most popular container for aquatics. Like its predecessors, it is more expensive than a conventional plant pot, and the question posed by many newcomers to water gardening is why aquatics must be grown in this type of container, rather than a normal pot.

In fact, some aquatic plants will grow tolerably well in pots for some time. A number of submerged plants, which use their roots mainly for anchorage and derive nourishment through the foliage, will be perfectly happy under such conditions. Some vigorous marginal plants also grow well in pots, but because of their height and the tapered shape of the pots, become unstable and will regularly tumble into the water. There is little more unsavoury than a reed or rush that has spent half its life being blown over into the pond by the wind,

The use of planting containers for growing marginal subjects like the water forget-me-not is essential for easy management. Although containers place some constraint upon the growth of aquatic plants, they equally prevent their unchecked spread.

then reinstated having gained a coating of filamentous algae. Pots are not stable when growing emergent aquatics, which is why planting baskets are designed with wide bases.

For most aquatics, especially waterlilies and other deep-water subjects, an open latticework container is vital. They require freedom for gaseous exchange, which is restricted by a solid pot. The latter leads to offensive conditions within the compost, which becomes blue-black in colour, anaerobic and foul smelling. This causes the roots to begin to die, and the plant rapidly diminishes in size. While waterlilies suffer the worst effects from closed containers, the majority of other plants also suffer to some degree from this type of constraint.

PLANTING TECHNIQUE

Planting aquatics is very simple, provided you follow a few simple rules. Each container should be lined with a square of hessian to prevent any soil from escaping into the water, although this is said to be unnecessary with modern micro-mesh baskets. Loosely fill the container to the top with soil or compost, then plant the aquatic.

Using a watering can with a fine rose, thoroughly soak the container. This will drive out all the air and the compost will sink. Add further compost and water again until it has settled solidly, about 1cm (3/8in) below the rim of the basket. Then add a layer of pea gravel and water thoroughly once more. This will ensure that the plant remains securely planted when the container is eventually placed in the pool. The gravel will help to prevent soil from escaping from the top of the container and, in the longer term, stop fish from stirring up the compost and clouding the water. Aquatic planting baskets become the home for all manner of aquatic insect life and their larvae, which are a valuable source of food for fish. The latter will delve into the compost in search of such delicacies, but if they have to probe through the pea gravel, they are less likely to cloud the water.

At the beginning of the planting season, aquatics can be planted almost in the condition in which they are received from the nursery; later on, they will require cutting back. Do not be frightened to remove the foliage from any rooted aquatic plant. Provided the crown is sound, it will grow away quickly. Of all garden plants, the aquatics are among the most rapid growers.

Waterlilies that have excess foliage when planted, especially if bare-rooted, will rarely remain planted securely. The floating foliage acts as a buoyancy aid, lifting the plant out of the basket. This is a common occurrence when attempts are made to stand waterlilies on heaps of bricks so that they are at the same depth as in their previous home and their existing foliage floats on the surface. Doing so is a waste of time. Cut the leaves back to the crown, plant properly and place the waterlily on the floor of the pool in its permanent position. The fresh foliage will reach the top in a matter of days and will not linger, looking sickly and yellow, as it does when plants are moved and their leaves preserved.

Do not be concerned about cutting back very tall marginals in the same way. Often, by mid-season, a new marginal subject will have grown completely out of proportion with its surroundings. Shortening the foliage will encourage rapid rooting and speedy regrowth. It will merely look a little less pleasing than a plant established in early spring and allowed to grow away freely. Bunched submerged plants should be planted exactly as they are received, with the lead intact. Plant so that the weight is covered completely by compost. If it is left exposed, the stems will rot through at that point and the tops will break away. Then the plants will need re-bunching and re-establishing.

PLANTING IN CONTAINERS

1 Although said to be unnecessary with the newer micromesh aquatic planting baskets, it is probably best to line all planting containers with hessian to prevent soil spillage into the pool.

2 Fill the planting basket with a good clean heavy soil or an aquatic planting compost. Using a watering can fitted with a fine rose, thoroughly soak the soil to drive out the air before planting.

3 Press the plant firmly into the compost, water again and then cover the surface of the compost with a layer of fine pea gravel. This will prevent the fish from disturbing the soil.

SOILS, COMPOSTS AND FERTILIZERS

As with all plants, aquatics will directly reflect the quality of the medium in which they are growing. Special aquatic planting composts are available, but in most cases carefully prepared garden soil will be quite satisfactory. The only consideration that must be given, over and above the well-being of the plants, is the ecology of the pool. The constituents of the growing medium can have a direct influence upon the water clarity and chemistry of the pool, so it is often better to begin by looking at this aspect, then move towards the plants' particular nutritional requirements.

A BALANCED GROWING MEDIUM

As far as the ecology of the garden pond is concerned, a growing medium should have a heavy structure, ideally a clay or very heavy loam, which will not disperse readily into the water and will cause problems of clouding. Although particles of clay and loam are quite small, they tend to stick together better than the irregular particles of sandy light soil, which can escape from planting containers and swirl around like aquatic dust.

Organic matter is undesirable, as this will decompose in the same way as an accumulation of fallen leaves, causing a build-up of noxious gases. These will escape freely and harmlessly into the air during the summer, but if the pond freezes in the winter, they will be trapped beneath the ice and will be a danger to the fish. Not only are the gaseous results of decomposition undesirable, but also the unpleasant contamination that can cause the water to turn deep amber or cloudy. If the organic matter is rich in nutrients, it will lead to abundant algal growth.

This is a major difficulty when selecting any growing medium for aquatic plants. You must be sure that sufficient nutrients are available for the plants that will grow in it, but there should not be an excess that will leach into the water and cause a serious algae problem to develop. Simply looking at a growing medium, or even analysing it scientifically, will not indicate accurately whether it contains an excess of nutrients. All that can be done is to choose the soil carefully and apply slow release fertilizers adjacent to the plants, where there will be little chance of leaching occurring.

While there are specific aquatic planting composts available for waterlilies, there is no reason why good clean garden soil, which has not recently been dressed with fertiliser, should not be used.

Proprietary brands of aquatic planting compost vary in quality, but those from leading manufacturers will be composed scientifically and, although comparatively expensive, will produce healthy plant growth with a minimum of nutrients escaping into the water. If you are a newcomer to water gardening and have little understanding of plant nutrition, or your garden soil is of questionable quality for satisfactory aquatic plant growth, buying prepared aquatic plant compost will be a good investment.

PREPARING YOUR OWN COMPOST

Aquatic plants benefit from a heavy growing medium, so if your garden contains a clay, or a medium-to-heavy loam soil, there is no reason at all why you should not prepare your own growing medium. If you are uncertain about the nature of the soil, you can carry out a very simple structural test, which will also indicate the amount of organic matter that is present.

Take a small sample of soil from the area that you intend using for making the compost. This should be a part of the garden that has not been dressed recently with artificial fertilizer, as it will escape into the water. What is required is an area where the soil is clean, but preferably impoverished, or at least that has not been treated with fertilizer or animal manure for the past two seasons.

Having removed a good trowelful of typical soil, dry it out until it can be powdered. This can be hastened by putting it in the oven. Place the finely powdered dry soil in an old coffee jar. Add water and shake the jar vigorously until the contents have the appearance of thick muddy water. Then stand the jar somewhere safe where it should remain undisturbed for three or four days.

Provided that the soil sample was dried and pulverized properly, then mixed completely with the water, when it settles out, the various constituents will be clearly visible. Sand particles, being large and heavy, will settle out within a very short space of time. Clay particles may take several days, while organic material will float. The result will be a series of layers in the jar. The bottom layer will be the sand, on top of which will be the clay. Above the clay will be water, and any organic material will float on the surface. Based upon your observations, a decision can be made as to the suitability of the soil: if at least 75 per cent of its content is clay, it should be a satisfactory growing medium for aquatic plants.

When digging up the soil, remove any obvious weeds, old pieces of turf and anything else that is likely to decompose and pollute the water. Discard large stones and pass the soil through a garden sieve placed over a wheelbarrow. This will retain any undesirable debris, like sticks or pieces of glass or pottery, leaving a neat heap of finely graded soil.

The soil should be used in this form without adding any fertilizer, although traditionalists may feel happier if some bonemeal is mixed in. This will do no harm to the water, but it takes such a long time to break down that it is difficult to imagine what value it can have to the plants. A much better idea is to plant aquatics directly into the soil, then administer a balanced, slow release fertilizer. This may be obtained in tablet form or as a small perforated sachet. Both should be pushed into the soil, immediately beside the plant, in the centre of the container. In this way, the plant will benefit from the fertilizer, while there will be virtually no prospect of it seeping into the water.

The majority of bog garden plants are happy in any soil that is kept constantly moist, although they do prefer an organic-rich growing medium. Take care to ensure that this is not rich in plant nutrients, which may leach into the pool and cause an algal bloom.

PLANTING A BOG GARDEN

A bog garden is similar to other water garden environments, but it does demand slightly different cultural practices. The plants should be allowed to grow freely in the soil, unrestrained by planting containers. This ensures a very natural appearance and lusty growth, but also creates its own management problems.

PREPARING THE SOIL

Most bog garden plants will grow in the majority of soils if they are kept constantly moist. However, in their natural environment, the growing medium is rich in organic material. Therefore, incorporating organic matter into the soil is desirable, although this can be hazardous if it is in direct contact with the water of an adjacent pool. Nutrients can leach out into the water and create an algal bloom in the pool, which will be uncontrollable because of the huge nutrient reserve in the bog garden.

Mix only well rotted organic material with the soil, preferably not from animal manure. A friable decomposed leaf mould is ideal, since it will add humus to the soil without over-burdening it with nutrients. Not that the bog garden soil should be impoverished. On the contrary, it needs to be fertilized to sustain the substantial leafy growth that most bog garden plants produce. Initially, a good general garden soil, of

The majority of bog garden plants are happy in any soil which is kept constantly moist, although they do prefer an organic-rich growing medium. Great care should be taken to ensure that nutrients do not leach out freely into the adjacent pool.

medium-to-heavy structure, should be adequate, although within 18 months some feeding will be required. Use slow release capsules or pellets, distributed close to the plants, and apply an annual spring mulch of well rotted organic matter. The purpose of the latter is not to conserve moisture, but to top up the organic content of the soil, which will dissipate rapidly under the very wet conditions.

When planting a new bog garden, it is preferable for the soil not to be saturated; heavy sticky soil is extremely difficult to plant into properly. Planting will be easier under the drier conditions normally found elsewhere in the garden, then the bog garden can be subjected to inundation. However, if soil preparation is undertaken before a winter, it will be difficult to achieve this ideal.

Dig the area thoroughly in the autumn, turning up the soil in large lumps, which should be left exposed to the weather. The rain and frost will break them down into a fine tilth for the spring. This also helps rid the soil of many undesirable pests. When digging, mix the organic matter into the bottom of the trench and cover it over. If you can make preparations like this in the autumn, spring planting will be much easier and more successful.

PLANTING

The manner in which bog garden plants are arranged largely depends upon the feature's scale. The commonest mistake is to plant only one example of each plant; even if you only have a modest patch, planting fewer varieties in small groups of three will produce a much better effect. Although the keen gardener will want to use the opportunity offered by these special conditions to try as wide a range of plants as possible, the overall appearance of the bog garden must be considered.

Treat a bog garden in much the same way as an herbaceous border arrangement, grouping the plants in relation to their heights and colours, in a manner that appeals. Be aware of their vigour, for a number can be quite rampant in good boggy conditions. In fact, on occasion, there may be a case for eliminating a plant from your scheme because it may rampage and upset the whole effect, creating maintenance problems. The fast creeping bog and marginal *Houttuynia cordata* is one of the worst culprits.

Within a large bog garden, it is possible to isolate some of the more vigorous plants by dividing the area into sections where they can be accommodated and left to grow freely. Use fine-mesh plastic garden netting, burying it in the soil. This will effectively restrain the plants while permitting moisture to pass through, ensuring a consistent moisture level throughout the bog garden.

Most bog garden plants are sold in containers. Plant them carefully in a hole that is larger than the pot ball and add a generous quantity of peat or well composted bark to the soil as the hole is backfilled. As with all plants, this friable organic matter in the immediate vicinity of the roots will encourage the rapid development of root hairs and speedy establishment of the plants.

BARE-ROOTED PLANTS

Many bog garden plants are available in bare-rooted form. Those purchased from the nurseryman should be healthy and vigorous young stock, which has been produced as a result of regular lifting and dividing. If planted during the dormant season, they will establish quickly.

If you intend using bog garden plants that have been growing elsewhere in the garden, or that may have been given to you by a friend, be sure that you only use the vigorous outer portions from large clumps. The hardy woody inner parts of plants like Siberian iris and astilbe rarely develop quickly into attractive and presentable plants. Unless there is no other stock available, these should be discarded.

The best effects are created by planting several plants in a group. Treat a boggy area rather like an herbaceous border and group the plants in relation to their heights and colours.

If the pot-ball is solid and the plant appears to be pot-bound, it is wise to disrupt the root-ball a little without causing a check in growth. Simply run a knife gently down the side of the pot-ball in two or three places, then insert your fingers and tease the roots out a little. This will allow them to penetrate the surrounding soil much sooner. A tight pot-ball can be quite constraining, the plant remaining isolated and producing stunted growth for a season or more, merely because it is growing in a different medium to that in which its roots have become tightly entangled

PLANTING A STREAMSIDE

A streamside is a very different prospect from any other aspect of a water feature, for not only must the planting be tasteful and properly executed, but it must also tolerate occasional inundation and periodic drying out. Erosion should be uppermost in the gardener's mind, when thinking about when and how the streamside is to be planted, especially if the stream is uncontrollable with a flow rate that is subject to the whim of nature. An artificial stream is an altogether different proposition, and much of the advice given for planting a bog garden is applicable.

PREPARING THE BANK

With an artificially constructed stream, the method of preparing the soil will be similar to that required by a bog garden, although if the banks are steep, some account must be taken of the fact that soil may slip into the water following heavy rain. Prevention of this erosion does not differ from the treatment advocated for the natural stream.

With a natural streamside, it is an advantage to have a covering of vegetation, even if this is of weeds. Plants of any kind, which have become established on the banks, will hold them together and prevent erosion. This factor must be taken seriously, even with a tiny stream or ditch if it has uncontrollable water levels. The substantial cultivation of a streamside can lead to rapid erosion, so allowing the roots of any vegetation to remain and bind the soil together is a sensible move. Modern herbicides, in which the active ingredient is glyphosate, are marvellous. Not only are they completely harmless to aquatic life, but they also ensure the positive destruction of any weeds treated. Glyphosate works on contact with green leaves, being absorbed into the plant's sap stream and translocated throughout, preventing the weed from producing essential protein and killing it from within. The great advantage of this, apart from a total lack of contamination of the soil, is the fact that, while the tops of the plants die away completely, the root systems remain intact

It is essential to appreciate the potential for erosion on a stream bank when plants are first being established. Often the plants have to be planted into soil which has had the minimum of disturbance.

THE GRASSY BANK

Although many may wish to see the streamside as a riot of colour, in some cases, it will be very effective if grass banks extend to the water. Achieving this may not be as simple as one might imagine, however.

Whether you use turf or seed, the banks must be cultivated, and a light forking is the minimum requirement. Ideally, any existing weed cover should be killed off with a glyphosate based weedkiller to minimize the prospect of serious erosion taking place. As an additional precaution, protect the most vulnerable areas with fine-mesh garden netting. Professional landscapers use custom made erosion matting, which is pegged down to the soil, but this is difficult for the amateur to obtain and garden netting is the next best thing.

Peg the netting to the ground, covering the bank from below the minimum water level to above the maximum expected level. Then lay turf on top, or spread fine soil over it and sow grass seed. Most grass seed mixtures are suitable for a streamside, but one containing a proportion of rye grass is preferable.

Once well established, streamside planting will successfully bind the bank together, but take care that plants are not too invasive.

as a fibrous web throughout the soil. This effectively prevents serious erosion of the stream banks.

The temptation to cultivate and prepare the soil, once the green herbage has died back, should be resisted. This would be fatal, as disturbing the fibrous mat of roots would undo the benefit of the decomposing weeds' presence. A generous mulch of well rotted organic matter would be beneficial, however. Not only will this improve the humus level in the soil, but it will also smother any emerging weed seedlings. These are almost certain to appear once the existing weed cover has been removed.

The ideal time to kill off the weed cover is during late summer. Then the mulch can be applied and the streamside remain unplanted for the winter. Occasionally, the mulch may be scoured out at high water level, particularly in the turbulence following a snow melt, but the soil bank below should remain firm. Any loss of mulch can be redressed in the early spring and planting commenced. The weed root network will remain effective for about nine months after spraying, so planting young plants in the spring is ideal. They will grow away strongly, their root systems replacing the slowly decaying roots of the weeds by mid-summer.

Do not plant a natural streamside during the winter months. Although periodic flooding may not wash away the plants completely, it can cause disruption. Even during the spring, it is preferable to use pot grown plants, as these will be more stable if unexpected inundation occurs. If you have a river bank to plant, rather than a stream, pushing a large wire staple through the pot-ball of each plant and into the soil below will provide extra security.

The arrangement of plants on a streamside is very much a matter of taste. Be conscious of plants that will seed freely and may make themselves a nuisance, keeping them away from the water's edge. Water is a fine distributor of seeds, and a streamside can quickly become engulfed in water forget-me-not or mimulus if the plants are allowed to seed unrestrained by the water's edge, especially when planted upstream. Care should also be taken not to introduce any plants that might be transported to places further downstream, where they could become a nuisance and affect the native flora. Seeds and pieces of plant like *Mimulus ringens*, which root easily as cuttings, should be used responsibly.

PLANTING FOR WILDLIFE

A wildlife pool must be more carefully planned and planted than any other water feature. This may seem surprising, since the most successful examples look as if they have occurred naturally, growing in a seemingly unruly, but controlled, manner. Achieving this completely natural look demands an understanding of the plants and their behaviour, as well as their overall appearance. While attracting wildlife is a priority, it should not be the overriding factor when choosing plants. The majority of plants that are normally recommended will provide a haven for most wildlife, and if there is a particular insect or butterfly that you wish to attract, you can include specific plants at strategic points.

PLANTING ARRANGEMENTS

To some extent, the method of planting will determine the type of planting arrangements that you can make. Using baskets may not be the most natural way of growing wild plants, but it provides the best option for efficient management of the feature. If you insist upon growing plants directly in soil on the floor of the pool and along the marginal shelves, then no matter what planting combinations you begin with, by the end of the year, they are likely to bear little resemblance to your original scheme and may simply be a tangled mass. In some circumstances, especially with large water features, this may be acceptable, but it is difficult to live with in the domestic wildlife pool.

Visually, it does not matter which plants are arranged next to one another, provided their growth rates are compatible, for most wildlife plants are of less striking appearance than their cultivated cousins. Thus, the possibility of strident colour clashes is remote. The arrangement of the plants is also of little importance to the wildlife that will inhabit them, for insects and other creatures will home in on their favourite host plants wherever they are.

It is important to contain fast growing rhizomatous plants as much as possible, although with some of the taller kinds, like the reedmaces, baskets are less than ideal. These plants grow quite tall, and it is common for individual examples in baskets to be blown over by the slightest breeze. When reedmace is considered desirable, plant a bold stand, rather than a single container. Place three baskets in a group and allow the plants to grow through the lattice sides into each other to create a solid mass. This will not only look better, but also produce a very stable arrangement.

The same can be done with phragmites and the bur-reeds, or sparganium. Grown more conventionally, they are not

While it is essential to create a natural visual effect, account must be taken of maintenance. It is sometimes possible to isolate plants like purple loosestrife in discreetly hidden containers so that they do not become too dominant in the overall picture.

easily controlled. Although phragmites and reedmaces are often excluded from wildlife pools because of their stature and invasive tendencies, they should be carefully considered for their winter value. Few other aquatics, except perhaps the water plantain (*Alisma plantago-aquatica*) can create winter interest in the water garden with their dried seeding heads or wind dried foliage. There is much that is stark and beautiful about the brown heads of reedmace, delicate tiered filigree of water plantain, and the rustling bustling foliage of phragmites on a bright winter's day after a modest snowfall.

Spring and summer pleasure is the priority, however, for it is then that insect life is at its most active. Intersperse plants that provide colour with the more mundane reeds and rushes. Select flowering highlights that extend across the season so that a range of blossoms is available to insects for much of the time. Marsh marigold (*Caltha palustris*) starts the parade, followed by yellow flag (*Iris pseudacorus*) and the flowering rush (*Butomus umbellatus*). All can be grown successfully in containers.

In any adjacent boggy area, begin with primulas. Although native to Asia, *Primula rosea* and *P. denticulata* are early nectar plants that make attractive and colourful additions to the spring garden. Other primulas follow, including *P. japonica* and *P. pulverulenta*, all much loved by bees and a variety of insects. To conclude, there is *P. florindae*, which often flowers into the early autumn. There are primulas for everyone, but if you do not like the brightly-coloured examples, select the more subtle shades. *Primula bulleyana*, *P. japonica* 'Postford White' and *P. florindae* all blend nicely with other wild looking bog garden foliage.

Associate primulas with moisture loving ferns for good effect, allowing the creeping sensitive fern (*Onoclea sensibilis*) to scramble in and around them and create an apple-green foil. As each primula comes to the end of its flowering time, it can quietly slip back among the sensitive fern's foliage. The same kind of planting arrangement can be created by combining the yellow musk (*Mimulus luteus*) with the sensitive fern.

The purple loosestrife (*Lythrum salicaria*) makes an interesting combination with meadow-sweet (*Filipendula ulmaria*) and its double form, 'Flore Pleno'. The meadow-sweet usually starts flowering ahead of the loosestrife, but when they come together, they are most effective, producing contrasting flower colour, stature and foliage. As meadow-sweet declines, the loosestrife continues, extending the season of colour and providing ongoing sustenance for the local insect population.

Autumn is a dull time in the water garden, but it can be greatly enhanced by the water dock (*Rumex hydrolapathum*), the foliage of which turns crimson or rusty red with the shortening days. Its seed spikes are beautiful in their starkness, making this a plant that should hold centre stage at that time of the year. Plant it where its autumn colour will be reflected in the water, surrounding it earlier in the year with scrambling mounds of water forget-me-not.

Primulas, in their rich diversity, can provide colour from early spring until autumn. The hybrid candelabra types are extremely versatile and easily increased from seed or division.

Extensive shallows and marginal plantings are beneficial to wildlife, but deeper areas of open water are equally important. The spread of plants can be easily controlled by pond profiling.

ATTRACTING WILD CREATURES

Apart from its appearance as a gem of the countryside, the wildlife pool should become a focal point for all manner of creatures. In addition to the aquatic life and those creatures that depend upon the plants and associated fauna as a food source, mammals will come to the pool to drink. Birds will also enjoy bathing in the margins, although whether this should be encouraged is questionable, as they sometimes carry pesticides on their plumage, especially in country areas. Even a small quantity of such chemicals can cause devastation to fish if it gets into the water. On balance, while it may be pleasing to watch birds enjoying themselves in the pool, if you live in a rural area, it would be a safer option to plant the pool margins heavily and place a bird bath somewhere else in the garden.

PLANTS FOR FISH

While fish dine predominantly on aquatic insect life, they do benefit from some green matter in their diet. Several species enjoy grazing on filamentous algae and the foliage of certain submerged aquatics. The starworts, or callitriches, are savoured, along with the softer-leaved pond weeds like *Potamogeton crispus*. At one time, *Crassula helmsii* was thought of as a good food plant, but in recent years, it has become unfashionable, as it has escaped into the wild and colonized many open areas of water, choking out native species. If you can be sure of keeping it in your pond, there is no doubt that, as a food plant for fish, it will be difficult to surpass. It is also good for ensuring water clarity.

Fish enjoy a number of the submerged aquatics with finely divided foliage as well. These provide a suitable place for depositing spawn and act as a nursery for fish fry. The milfoils, or myriophyllums are the most favoured, but the bristly-leaved hornwort is also much appreciated.

OTHER AQUATIC FAUNA

Apart from fish, there are myriad other aquatic creatures that enjoy living among submerged plants. Many of the water snails deposit their eggs in the tangled foliage, and tiny aquatic insects find sanctuary among the masses of leaves. If these become enmeshed with filamentous algae, aquatic insects will be well protected from even the most ardent of preying fish. While excessive algae should not be encouraged, a small quantity is not objectionable and will create an even more refined habitat.

Floating foliage is important for many creatures. With the exception of ramshorn snails, all the pond snails enjoy eating fresh waterlily pads. The more vigorous nymphaeas are rarely troubled by this, for although they may look rather unsightly with their chewed leaves, they should be strong enough to cope. China mark moths take pieces of floating foliage as well, their caterpillars pupating in little shelters constructed from pieces of waterlily pad. Caddis flies do similar damage, although they do not take such large pieces of leaf. They also gather little stones and other pond debris, sticking it together to create little, mobile tube-like shelters in which the larvae live. Mining midges chew a tracery of lines across floating leaves, which eventually rot and crumble, then fall to the pool floor where other life intervenes.

The foliage, flowers and seed of marginal plants make the major contribution to life outside the immediate aquatic environment. However, their spreading roots, like the long dangling roots of some of the larger floating plants, provide cover for insect life and sometimes a place for fish to deposit their spawn. The submerged parts of the stems also provide useful perches for dragonfly larvae.

Most marginal plants are suitable habitats for invertebrates, the various crowfoots, or ranunculus, and spearworts being acknowledged as among the best. Amphibious bistort (*Persicaria amphibia*) is ideal as an insect habitat, but also produces good wildfowl food in its seeds. The rushes, or

Not the most elegant decorative planting, but a paradise for wildlife, from the tiny roots of the floating duckweed to the fern-laden wall, there are opportunities for different native species.

This garden pond provides a wonderfully rich and well established environment for wildlife. Such a corner should remain undisturbed except for the occasional manicuring of plants and the removal of weeds that will be necessary.

When maintaining a sustainable feature it is important to realise that minor adjustments may have to be made on practical grounds in order to retain harmony.

schoenoplectus, are also good sources of wildfowl food, along with the bur reeds and lesser reedmace.

Nesting birds appreciate the Norfolk reed, or phragmites, as well as the greater reedmace (*Typha latifolia*). The latter provides fluffy down from its crumbling, thick brown poker heads in the spring, after winter storms have battered them into submission. The reeds offer a wonderfully secure place in which to build a nest.

The blossoms of almost all popular aquatic wildflowers attract insect pollinators, bees being particularly fond of water mint (*Mentha aquatica*) and scrambling freely among the pouting flowers of yellow musk. Inspect any open blossoms around the wildlife pool and you will find a menagerie of insects, all intent upon finding succour. Ultimately, their activities lead to fertilization and the production of seeds: miracles of regeneration and food for other wildlife.

MAKING COMPROMISES

Choosing plants to suit the requirements of wildlife and to present a pleasing picture is the primary aim when creating a wildlife pool, but it is important to realize that, on occasion, minor adjustments may have to be made for practical reasons. Unlike manicured pond plants, many native aquatics do not respect boundaries and may take on an unexpected dominant role, or they may become regressive because of some quirk of water or compost. For most of the popular varieties, even when planted into an unrestricted earth-bottomed pond, management can be assisted by the arrangement of plants.

PRACTICAL PLANTING CONSIDERATIONS

For the planting scheme of a wildlife pond to be successful and manageable, the nature of the individual species must be recognized and appropriate conditions provided to accommodate their growth habit, yet ensure containment. The most problematical plants are the rhizomatous species. A rhizome is a creeping stem, which can vary from a thin stringy growth to a chunky pointed rootstock. It will have buds at intervals along its length, and these are capable of producing fresh plants.

Sometimes, if the water is cool and covers them comfortably, rhizomes will only branch occasionally, the main terminal growth expanding quickly. However, if grown in conditions where the water level varies, or drying out occurs, many of the buds may burst into growth in an effort to ensure the rhizome's survival. Initially, the plants will be quite puny, but following inundation by water, they will become a forest of growth.

Fortunately, many rhizomatous species are very sensitive to water depth. Therefore, they can be effectively contained and root pruned by the profile of the pool floor. A sudden drop, for example from 30cm (12in) to 90cm (36in), will be sufficient to prevent even the most ambitious reedmace from spreading. A sloping margin into the pool can create the correct conditions for a variety of species. Those that demand shallow water will only advance to a certain depth, beyond which they will not be comfortable. Others will grow better in deeper water and so on. By selective planting and careful positioning, you should be able to maintain effective control over the spread of all the plants.

Rhizomatous species tend to develop as close-knit stands in nature, so it is sensible to plant several examples together so that they form a tough blanket that chokes out other species. The stand will tend to advance outwards until it meets another species, or some form of physical barrier. As with cushion forming rock garden plants, which tend to die out in the centre if not regularly given a pinch of slow release fertilizer, the centre of a vigorous stand of rhizomatous aquatics will deteriorate, too. Applying a slow release fertilizer, of the kind given to waterlilies, will sustain lusty growth.

If your wildlife pond is arranged like a conventional garden pool, using planting baskets, some of the more vigorous rhizomatous aquatics, like the reedmace and bur-reed, will be unsuitable. They will certainly grow in such containers, but they will rapidly fill them with rootstock, distort them and possibly even burst them unless very regularly maintained. In addition, taller species like the reedmaces become very unstable if confined to a container, and will topple over in the wind unless weighted or fastened down in some way.

This well established group of yellow water iris forms a natural colony which is constrained by the depth of the water. With such water features maintenance is minimal as the plants obtain liberal quantities of nutrients from the water and rarely need dividing.

NON-INVASIVE PLANTS

Fibrous-rooted marginal aquatics adapt well to container life, however, so if your pool will be planted exclusively using baskets, choose well behaved plants like the flowering rush (*Butomus umbellatus*) and the clump forming cotton grass (*Eriophorum angustifolium*). A perfectly acceptable wildlife pool can be created with non-invasive plants such as these.

Submerged aquatics, in the wildlife pool, can be grown either directly on the floor or in containers. Direct planting into soil is certainly the most natural and attractive method, but the number of species you will be able to plant together will be determined by their relative vigour. Few species can compete with Canadian pond weed (*Elodea canadensis*), for example, while the starworts, or callitriches, will curl up and disappear if planted with a boisterous neighbour. If you want to grow a diversity of submerged plants, basket cultivation is the answer; if a generous forest of underwater foliage is the main requirement, one or two equally vigorous species, allowed free rein, will produce a satisfactory result.

Floating plants need equally careful appraisal. Those that form mats or carpets of foliage on the water surface, like the myriad duckweeds and fairy moss, are perfectly acceptable, but they do need very careful restraining. They are ideal for controlling the development of green suspended algae, by reducing the amount of light falling into the water, but they can cut out too much light, damaging submerged oxygenating plants as well. If you are prepared to spend time on the regular maintenance of your pond, these carpeting floating plants are quite acceptable. However, if the pool is to become an independent balanced ecological entity, they would be better omitted and replaced by less intrusive kinds, such as the frogbit and water soldier.

Waterlilies and pondlilies should be treated in much the same way as in a conventional garden pool. Despite the fact that they will grow well on an earth-bottomed pond, they will be much easier to control, cultivate and manicure if grown in a large container. A plastic laundry basket, lined with hessian and filled with soil, is ideal.

Fibrous rooted plants rarely have invasive root systems, however, they can spread freely from seed. Sometimes a compromise has to be sought between the potential problems self-seeding can produce and the usefulness of the seeds as food for wildlife.

PROBLEM-SOLVING

PLANTING THE WATER GARDEN

I have quite a large natural pond that is at least 90cm (36in) deep in the centre, and I would like to plant it with waterlilies. What varieties should I use and how should I plant them? The ordinary aquatic planting baskets are inadequate, and would seem to be pointless, given that the floor of the pond is earth.

When reed-mace takes over it can be quite difficult to control by hand. Weedkiller in which glyphosate is the active ingredient is safe with water and very effective.

It is important to choose waterlilies that will enjoy the depth of water in your pond, and which can be readily identified, for in an earth-bottomed pond, they may grow into one another. Select varieties such as *Nymphaea* 'Gladstoneana' for the very deep areas, and the likes of *N.* 'Marliacea Chromatella' for the shallower parts. Each of these varieties has very distinct foliage, so if they grow into one another, they can be separated easily.

The easiest method of planting natural areas is to carefully place the waterlilies by hand or, if the water is too deep, gently lower them from a boat. Cut all the foliage from each bare-rooted waterlily, leaving a tuft of submerged leaves on the nose. Wrap the plant in a 30cm (12in) square of hessian, with a generous quantity of soil, and tie around the plant. Then place into the water. Eventually, the hessian wrapping will rot, but in the meantime, the roots will grow out and invade the surrounding soil, leading to the formation of large waterlily colonies.

Nymphaea 'Marliacea Chromatella' *is a particularly useful variety where waterlilies are being grown in close proximity as it has distinctive mottled foliage.*

I have substantial groups of reedmace growing along the banks of my pool. They are most attractive and wonderful for wildlife, but they are also very invasive and grow into adjacent plants. Unfortunately, the pool is lined, and although there is a good depth of soil over the liner, I am reluctant to use a spade to dig them out, as I may damage it.

There are two possible solutions to your problem. The first is to cut the reedmace to below water level during late summer in those areas where it is a nuisance. The hollow stems will fill with water and, in most cases, the plant will rot away. Sometimes, the main terminal growth beneath the water may continue to develop, but usually very weakly.

You could also use a herbicide, in which glyphosate is the active ingredient. This is a systemic weedkiller that is absorbed by green foliage and taken into the sap stream, killing the plant from within. Thus, it is harmless to everything except green living plants. Even fish and aquatic insect life are completely unharmed by glyphosate.

The problem with applying a herbicide to a plant like the reedmace is that the extensive rhizome system will carry it to parts of the plant that you may wish to keep. So take a sharp knife and cut through the rhizome at the point where you wish to restrict the plant's spread. The rhizome will be just beneath the surface of the mud, so it should be possible to severe it without damaging the liner. Then the unwanted detached portion can be treated with the herbicide. Once this has died back, it must be removed, otherwise the decaying foliage will pollute the water. Normally, the rhizome will decay beneath the mud and will cause no contamination unless it is disturbed in the pool.

I have been told that waterlilies should be planted in old turf and rotted cow manure, but surely this will cause the pond to turn green?

It is a widespread belief that waterlilies will only grow well if they are given a very friable soil and plenty of cow manure. Traditional gardening books, published during the first half of the 20th century, almost always stated that this was how waterlilies should be grown. It is true that they flourished, but always in a pool that was green, especially immediately after planting. Of course, the algae that caused the green colour would slowly disappear as the nutrients provided by the turf and manure were exhausted, but at the same time, the waterlilies would also be running low on food. This was a most unsatisfactory situation for the pool ecology and for the waterlilies themselves, since their nutritional requirements were not provided for.

Waterlilies and all other aquatic plants grow best, and yield a better pond ecology, when grown in properly prepared aquatic planting compost or good clean garden soil, which has not been dressed with artificial fertilizer and contains relatively little organic matter. Slow release fertilizer should be added in sachet or tablet form, next to the plants, so that they can utilize it before it leaches out into the water and creates a green algal bloom.

The hardy maidenhair fern is perfect for growing in close proximity to a waterfall. It enjoys damp conditions and is not resentful of regular splashing on its foliage.

Can you suggest any rock garden plants that would tolerate the splashing from my waterfall?

The majority of rock garden plants dislike constant dampness. Only a selection of alpine ferns really enjoy such conditions. These are beautiful little plants and include the maidenhair spleenwort (*Asplenium trichomanes*), the wall rue (*Asplenium ruta-muraria*) and the hardy maidenhair fern (*Adiantum pedatum*). The polypodies, including *Polypodium vulgare* and its fancy fronded forms, also prosper, especially where a little organic-rich soil is incorporated into their planting pockets.

Many of the musks will also adapt well to life among damp rocks, especially the little ones, such as 'Highland Pink', 'Highland Red' and the vivid 'Whitecroft Scarlet'. Not all of these plants are winter-hardy, but they are easily raised from seed each year. Although too large for some situations, the yellow *Mimulus luteus* is also a fine addition to the rock garden watercourse.

Nymphaea 'Aurora'

Depth: 30-45cm (12-18in)
Spread: 30-60cm (12-24in)
Situation: Full sun
Flowering time: Summer
Propagation: By division of established crowns during the growing season, these being replanted immediately in their permanent positions. Alternatively, by removal of young 'eyes' from the creeping rootstocks, which are potted individually in a heavy, soil-based potting compost and placed in an aquarium with water just above the pot rims.

'Aurora' is ideal for a tub garden, offering attractive, purplish and green leaves and fine blooms. Known as a chameleon or changeable waterlily, the plant bears cream buds that open to yellow flowers, then pass through orange to blood-red. This occurs over several days, so a number of different colours may be seen at the same time.

Nymphaea 'Graziella'

Depth: 30-60cm (12-24in)
Spread: 30-75cm (12-30in)
Situation: Full sun
Flowering time: Summer
Propagation: By division of established crowns during the growing season, these being replanted immediately in their permanent positions. Alternatively, by the removal of young 'eyes' from the creeping rootstocks, which are potted individually in a heavy, soil-based potting compost and placed in an aquarium with water just above the pot rims.

This is an ideal waterlily for a sink or tub garden. Orange-red flowers, little more than 5cm (2in) across, have deep orange stamens and are produced freely throughout the summer. Olive-green leaves are liberally spotted with brown and purple. This cultivar benefits from division of the crown every three or four years when growing lustily.

Nymphaea 'Odorata Minor'
Mill Pond Lily

Depth: 30cm (12in)
Spread: 30-45cm (12-18in)
Situation: Full sun
Flowering time: Summer
Propagation: By division of established crowns during the growing season, these being replanted immediately in their permanent positions. Alternatively, by the removal of young 'eyes' from the creeping rootstocks, which are potted individually in a heavy, soil-based potting compost and placed in an aquarium with water just above the pot rims.

A lovely wild form from the bogs of New Jersey in the USA. This is undoubtedly one of the finest waterlilies for tubs and shallow pools. Its fragrant, star shaped white blossoms are about 8cm (3in) in diameter with pale green or olive sepals and mahogany stalks. The soft green leaves are 8-10cm (3-4in) across and have dark red undersides.

Nymphaea 'Pygmaea Alba'
Pygmy White Waterlily

Depth: 10-30cm (4-12in)
Spread: 20-40cm (8-16in)
Situation: Full sun
Flowering time: Summer
Propagation: Of all the hardy waterlilies, this is the only example that can be raised successfully from seed. Sow the seed in trays of heavy, soil-based compost as soon as it ripens and place in a bowl or aquarium. Prick out the seedlings, moving them to individual pots for growing on.

Botanically, few can agree about the status of this waterlily, which is also believed to belong to the *Nymphaea tetragona* group. This does not affect its beauty and usefulness. It is ideal for growing in a tub or sink, or in the margins of a large pool. Tiny, papery white flowers, no more than 2.5cm (1in) across, are produced among small, more or less oval, dark green leaves, which have purple reverses.

Nymphaea 'Pygmaea Helvola'

Depth: 10-30cm (4-12in)
Spread: 20-60cm (8-24in)
Situation: Full sun
Flowering time: Summer
Propagation: By division of established crowns during the growing season, these being replanted immediately in their permanent positions. Alternatively, by the removal of young 'eyes' from the creeping rootstocks, which are potted individually in a heavy, soil-based potting compost and placed in an aquarium with water just above the pot rims.

This is the easiest and most free flowering of the pygmy waterlilies. Beautiful canary-yellow blossoms with orange stamens are produced among olive-green leaves, which are heavily splashed and stained with purple and brown.

Nymphaea 'Pygmaea Rubra'

Depth: 10-30cm (4-12in)
Spread: 20-60cm (8-24in)
Situation: Full sun
Flowering time: Summer
Propagation: Remove young 'eyes' from the rootstock and pot individually in a heavy, soil-based potting compost. Place in an aquarium with water just above the rims of the pots. This cultivar rarely divides successfully and also produces few 'eyes'. Thus, it is quite expensive.

Tiny, blood-red blossoms with orange-red stamens are produced among purplish-green leaves, which have distinctive reddish undersides. Ideal for the tub garden, this waterlily can even be grown successfully in a large bucket.

Nymphaea 'Froebelii'

Depth: 45-60cm (18-24in)
Spread: 45-75cm (18-30in)
Situation: Full sun
Flowering time: Summer
Propagation: By division of established crowns during the growing season, these being replanted immediately in their permanent positions. Alternatively, by the removal of young 'eyes' from the creeping rootstocks, which are potted individually in a heavy, soil-based potting compost and placed in an aquarium with water just above the pot rims.

One of the most popular free flowering waterlilies for the small pool. Deep blood-red blossoms with orange stamens are produced between dull, purplish-green leaves. Among the finest red waterlilies once well established.

Nymphaea 'Hermine'

Depth: 45-75cm (18-30in)
Spread: 45-90cm (18-36in)
Situation: Full sun
Flowering time: Summer
Propagation: By division of established crowns during the growing season, these being replanted immediately in their permanent positions. Alternatively, by the removal of young 'eyes' from the creeping rootstocks, which are potted individually in a heavy, soil-based potting compost and placed in an aquarium with water just above the pot rims.

This interesting white-flowered waterlily has blossoms that are almost tulip shaped and have yellow stamens. Possibly a horticultural selection from the wild white waterlily, *Nymphaea alba*, nevertheless, is very lovely. It produces dark green oval leaves.

Nymphaea 'Laydekeri Fulgens'

Depth: 30-60cm (12-24in)
Spread: 45-75cm (18-30in)
Situation: Full sun
Flowering time: Summer
Propagation: By division of established crowns during the growing season, these being replanted immediately in their permanent positions. Alternatively, by the removal of young 'eyes' from the creeping rootstocks, which are potted individually in a heavy, soil-based potting compost and placed in an aquarium with water just above the pot rims.

Fragrant, bright crimson flowers have reddish stamens and dark green sepals with rose-blush interiors. The dark green leaves have purplish undersides. A distinctive brown speckling around the leaf stalk is a unique characteristic of this waterlily, which is among the easiest of reds to grow for the small pool.

Nymphaea 'Laydekeri Purpurata'

Depth: 30-60cm (12-24in)
Spread: 45-75cm (18-30in)
Situation: Full sun
Flowering time: Summer
Propagation: By division of established crowns during the growing season, these being replanted immediately in their permanent positions. Alternatively, by the removal of young 'eyes' from the creeping rootstocks, which are potted individually in a heavy, soil-based potting compost and placed in an aquarium with water just above the pot rims.

Rich vinous-red flowers have bright orange stamens. The leaves are small, numerous and purple beneath, commonly being marked on the surface with black or maroon splashes. This cultivar will often begin to flower a little earlier than its companions.

Nymphaea 'Moorei'

Depth: 45-75cm (18-30in)
Spread: 75-90cm (30-36in)
Situation: Full sun
Flowering time: Summer
Propagation: By division of established crowns during the growing season, these being replanted immediately in their permanent positions. Alternatively, by the removal of young 'eyes' from the creeping rootstocks, which are potted individually in a heavy, soil-based potting compost and placed in an aquarium with water just above the pot rims.

A beautiful, soft yellow variety with pale green leaves, sprinkled with purple spots. It is excellent for a small pool, but more vigorous cultivars, such as *N.* 'Marliacea Chromatella', may be mistaken for 'Moorei'. These would swamp a small pond. 'Moorei' has plain green flower and leaf stems; those of other cultivars are striped with red.

Nymphaea 'William Falconer'

Depth: 45-75cm (18-30in)
Spread: 45-90cm (18-36in)
Situation: Full sun
Flowering time: Summer
Propagation: By division of established crowns during the growing season, these being replanted immediately in their permanent positions. Alternatively, by the removal of young 'eyes' from the creeping rootstocks, which are potted individually in a heavy, soil-based potting compost and placed in an aquarium with water just above the pot rims.

Medium-sized, blood-red flowers have yellow stamens. The young foliage is purplish when it first appears, but steadily ages to a deep olive-green. Once well established, this waterlily is very free-flowering.

Nymphaea 'Albatros'

Depth: 30-60cm (12-24in)
Spread: 60-120cm (24-48in)
Situation: Full sun
Flowering time: Summer
Propagation: By division of established crowns during the growing season, these being replanted immediately in their permanent positions. Alternatively, by the removal of young 'eyes' from the creeping rootstocks, which are potted individually in a heavy, soil-based potting compost and placed in an aquarium with water just above the pot rims.

Large, pure white blossoms have central clusters of bright yellow stamens. The rounded leaves are purplish when young, but become deep green when fully expanded. An easily grown, free flowering cultivar.

Nymphaea 'Arc-en-ciel'

Depth: 60-90cm (24-36in)
Spread: 90-120cm (36-48in)
Situation: Full sun
Flowering time: Summer
Propagation: By division of established crowns during the growing season, these being replanted immediately in their permanent positions. Alternatively, by the removal of young 'eyes' from the creeping rootstocks, which are potted individually in a heavy, soil-based potting compost and placed in an aquarium with water just above the pot rims.

This waterlily is grown for its beautiful variegated leaves, rather than its soft blush-pink, papery flowers, which are only produced occasionally. The olive-green foliage is liberally splashed with purple, rose, white and bronze. This coloration also extends to the sepals. An interesting waterlily for summer-long colour.

Nymphaea 'Gloire du Temple-sur-Lot'

Depth: 45-90cm (18-36in)
Spread: 90-120cm (36-48in)
Situation: Full sun
Flowering time: Summer
Propagation: By division of established crowns during the growing season, these being replanted immediately in their permanent positions. Alternatively, by the removal of young 'eyes' from the creeping rootstocks, which are potted individually in a heavy, soil-based potting compost and placed in an aquarium with water just above the pot rims.

A most remarkable waterlily with fully-double, rose-pink flowers having upwards of a hundred incurving petals and bright yellow stamens. The petal colour fades as each bloom ages. It takes one or two seasons to become established well enough to flower freely, but the wait is worthwhile. Large, fresh green leaves complete the picture.

Nymphaea 'Gonnère'
(Syn. *Nymphaea* 'Crystal White')

Depth: 45-75cm (18-30in)
Spread: 75-90cm (30-36in)
Situation: Full sun
Flowering time: Summer
Propagation: By division of established crowns during the growing season, these being replanted immediately in their permanent positions. Alternatively, by the removal of young 'eyes' from the creeping rootstocks, which are potted individually in a heavy, soil-based potting compost and placed in an aquarium with water just above the pot rims.

This waterlily has multi-petalled globular blossoms of the purest white, which look rather like floating snowballs, but with conspicuous pea-green stamens. The plant grows in a well disciplined manner and has attractive, very rounded, bright green leaves. It is a very classy waterlily that flowers easily.

Nymphaea 'James Brydon'

Depth: 45-90cm (18-36in)
Spread: 75-120cm (30-48in)
Situation: Full sun
Flowering time: Summer
Propagation: By division of established crowns during the growing season, these being replanted immediately in their permanent positions. Alternatively, by the removal of young 'eyes' from the creeping rootstocks, which are potted individually in a heavy, soil-based potting compost and placed in an aquarium with water just above the pot rims.

A lovely cultivar that bears rich crimson, paeony-shaped blooms with a mild, pleasant fragrance. The stamens are deep orange, tipped with bright yellow, while the dark purplish-green leaves are often flecked with maroon. 'James Brydon' does not yield 'eyes' for propagation very freely, so this cultivar is usually quite expensive.

Nymphaea 'Marliacea Albida'

Depth: 45-90cm (18-36in)
Spread: 75-120cm (30-48in)
Situation: Full sun
Flowering time: Summer
Propagation: By division of established crowns during the growing season, these being replanted immediately in their permanent positions. Alternatively, by the removal of young 'eyes' from the creeping rootstocks, which are potted individually in a heavy, soil-based potting compost and placed in an aquarium with water just above the pot rims.

A very easily grown, free flowering waterlily with large, pure white, fragrant blooms held just out of the water. The stamens are yellow, while the sepals and backs of the petals are often flushed with soft pink. The large, deep green leaves have red or purplish undersides. New growth often has a strong purplish caste as well.

Nymphaea 'Marliacea Chromatella'

Depth: 45-75cm (18-30in)
Spread: 90-120cm (36-48in)
Situation: Full sun
Flowering time: Summer
Propagation: By division of established crowns during the growing season, these being replanted immediately in their permanent positions. Alternatively, by the removal of young 'eyes' from the creeping rootstocks, which are potted individually in a heavy, soil-based potting compost and placed in an aquarium with water just above the pot rims.

An old, very popular cultivar that flowers abundantly. Its slightly fragrant blossoms may reach 15cm (6in) across, with broad, incurved, canary-yellow petals surrounding a boss of golden-yellow stamens. The pale yellow sepals are flushed with pink, while the fine, rounded, olive-green leaves are splashed with maroon and bronze.

Nymphaea 'Marliacea Flammea'

Depth: 45-75cm (18-30in)
Spread: 90-120cm (36-48in)
Situation: Full sun
Flowering time: Summer
Propagation: By division of established crowns during the growing season, these being replanted immediately in their permanent positions. Alternatively, by the removal of young 'eyes' from the creeping rootstocks, which are potted individually in a heavy, soil-based potting compost and placed in an aquarium with water just above the pot rims.

Another Victorian waterlily that has stood the test of time and is still very popular. Its fiery red flowers are flecked with white, the outer petals being deep pink and the stamens bright orange. The dark olive-green leaves are heavily mottled with chocolate and maroon.

Nymphaea 'Odorata Sulphurea Grandiflora'

Depth: 45-60cm (18-24in)
Spread: 60-120cm (24-48in)
Situation: Full sun
Flowering time: Summer
Propagation: By division of established crowns during the growing season, these being replanted immediately in their permanent positions. Alternatively, by the removal of young 'eyes' from the creeping rootstocks, which are potted individually in a heavy, soil-based potting compost and placed in an aquarium with water just above the pot rims.

This free flowering yellow waterlily has dark green foliage with a heavy maroon mottling. Its star shaped blossoms have many petals and sulphur-yellow stamens. They are moderately fragrant. The flower buds are tall and pointed, rather than broad and chunky, as with most other waterlilies. A reliable cultivar for the average garden pool.

Nymphaea 'Pink Sensation'

Depth: 45-75cm (18-30in)
Spread: 60-120cm (24-48in)
Situation: Full sun
Flowering time: Summer
Propagation: By division of established crowns during the growing season, these being replanted immediately in their permanent positions. Alternatively, by the removal of young 'eyes' from the creeping rootstocks, which are potted individually in a heavy, soil-based potting compost and placed in an aquarium with water just above the pot rims.

A fragrant, free flowering pink waterlily with star-like blossoms that are reputed to remain open longer than those of most hardy types. Blooms may reach 20cm (8in) across and have oval petals up to 10cm (4in) long. The deep green rounded leaves have reddish undersides. One of the finest introductions of the past 50 years.

Nymphaea 'Rose Arey'

Depth: 45-75cm (18-30in)
Spread: 60-120cm (24-48in)
Situation: Full sun
Flowering time: Summer
Propagation: By division of established crowns during the growing season, these being replanted immediately in their permanent positions. Alternatively, by the removal of young 'eyes' from the creeping rootstocks, which are potted individually in a heavy, soil-based potting compost and placed in an aquarium with water just above the pot rims.

This popular pink waterlily has large, open, star-like flowers with golden stamens and an overpowering aniseed fragrance. The green leaves are tinged with red, young foliage being crimson until breaking the surface of the water. 'Rose Arey' may self seed, and any seed pods should be removed to prevent the growth of inferior seedlings.

Nymphaea 'Virginalis'

Depth: 45-75cm (18-30in)
Spread: 60-120cm (24-48in)
Situation: Full sun
Flowering time: Summer
Propagation: By division of established crowns during the growing season, these being replanted immediately in their permanent positions. Alternatively, by the removal of young 'eyes' from the creeping rootstocks, which are potted individually in a heavy, soil-based potting compost and placed in an aquarium with water just above the pot rims.

This is an outstanding white-flowered waterlily for the medium-sized pond. Its semi-double flowers have bright yellow stamens and sepals, which are rose tinged towards the base. The leaves are green with a purple flush. It may take a season to settle down before flowering freely, but otherwise is an excellent cultivar.

Nymphaea 'Attraction'

Depth: 60-120cm (24-48in)
Spread: 90-180cm (36-72in)
Situation: Full sun
Flowering time: Summer
Propagation: By division of established crowns during the growing season, these being replanted immediately in their permanent positions. Alternatively, by the removal of young 'eyes' from the creeping rootstocks, which are potted individually in a heavy, soil-based potting compost and placed in an aquarium with water just above the pot rims.

Large garnet-red flowers are flaked with white, and may be as much as 25cm (10in) across on well established plants growing in deep water. Rich mahogany coloured stamens are tipped with yellow, while the sepals are off-white infused with rose-pink. Leaves are large, rounded and plain green. A very vigorous plant.

Nymphaea 'Charles de Meurville'

Depth: 60-120cm (24-48in)
Spread: 90-180cm (36-72in)
Situation: Full sun
Flowering time: Summer
Propagation: By division of established crowns during the growing season, these being replanted immediately in their permanent positions. Alternatively, by the removal of young 'eyes' from the creeping rootstocks, which are potted individually in a heavy, soil-based potting compost and placed in an aquarium with water just above the pot rims.

Immense, plum-red blooms are tipped and streaked with white, but become deep wine with age. A vigorous plant with abundant olive-green foliage. It is a good alternative to 'Attraction', which has introduced the devastating crown rot disease from Japan. 'Charles de Meurville' is not produced commercially in Japan, so normally it is safe.

Nymphaea 'Escarboucle'
(Syn. *Nymphaea* 'Aflame')

Depth: 60-180cm (24-72in)
Spread: 90-270cm (36-108in)
Situation: Full sun
Flowering time: Summer
Propagation: By division of established crowns during the growing season, these being replanted immediately in their permanent positions. Alternatively, by the removal of young 'eyes' from the creeping rootstocks, which are potted individually in a heavy, soil-based potting compost and placed in an aquarium with water just above the pot rims.

When grown properly in deep water with plenty of room to spread, this is the finest red waterlily. A well established plant may produce blooms up to 30cm (12in) across. These will be deep crimson, fragrant and have a boss of bright yellow stamens. The leaves are very large, rounded and plain green.

Nymphaea 'Gladstoneana'

Depth: 60-240cm (24-96in)
Spread: 120-300cm (48-120in)
Situation: Full sun
Flowering time: Summer
Propagation: By division of established crowns during the growing season, these being replanted immediately in their permanent positions. Alternatively, by the removal of young 'eyes' from the creeping rootstocks, which are potted individually in a heavy, soil-based potting compost and placed in an aquarium with water just above the pot rims.

This waterlily becomes truly enormous when grown in deep water. Its very large flowers have high-quality, waxy white petals and distinctive central clusters of yellow stamens. They are slightly fragrant. The large, dark green circular leaves have thick stalks, which are distinctively marked with brown.

Nymphaea 'Marliacea Carnea'

Depth: 45-150cm (18-60in)
Spread: 75-180cm (30-72in)
Situation: Full sun
Flowering time: Summer
Propagation: By division of established crowns during the growing season, these being replanted immediately in their permanent positions. Alternatively, by the removal of young 'eyes' from the creeping rootstocks, which are potted individually in a heavy, soil-based potting compost and placed in an aquarium with water just above the pot rims.

Large flesh-pink blossoms with bright yellow stamens have a distinctive vanilla fragrance. On newly established plants, they are often white for the first season, taking on their normal hue in the second year. Leaves are large, rounded and purplish when young, but deep green on maturity. The blooms can be used as cut flowers.

Nymphaea tuberosa 'Richardsonii'

Depth: 75-150cm (30-60in)
Spread: 90-270cm (36-108in)
Situation: Full sun
Flowering time: Summer
Propagation: By division of established crowns during the growing season, these being replanted immediately in their permanent positions. Alternatively, by the removal of young 'eyes' from the creeping rootstocks, which are potted individually in a heavy, soil-based potting compost and placed in an aquarium with water just above the pot rims.

A quick growing, very beautiful, white-flowered waterlily. It is free flowering, having globular blossoms with waxy petals, conspicuous pea-green sepals and golden stamens. The large, green orbicular leaves are green beneath, unlike most waterlilies, which display a purplish caste. Its brittle rootstock is difficult to contain in a planting basket.

Aponogeton distachyos
Water Hawthorn

Depth: 30-90cm (12-36in)
Situation: Full sun
Flowering time: Summer
Propagation: By division of established plants during early spring. Easily raised from seed if sown when fresh and green.

Blossoms with a strong vanilla fragrance float on the water, or are held just above it. They are forked and consist of two white, bract-like organs with black stamens. The floating leaves are rectangular in outline, but have rounded ends. They are dark olive-green, but occasionally may be splashed with maroon or deep purple.

Nuphar advena
American Spatterdock

Depth: 45-150cm (18-60in)
Situation: Full sun
Flowering time: Summer
Propagation: By division of established plants during the early spring.

This pondlily has thick, green leathery floating leaves rather like those of a waterlily, but they are more vigorous. The globular yellow blossoms, some 8cm (3in) across, have a distinctive purplish caste and conspicuous coppery-red stamens. Because of its vigorous nature, this is not a plant to choose for a small pool.

Nuphar lutea
Yellow Pondlily, Brandy Bottle

Depth: 30-240cm (12-96in)
Situation: Full sun
Flowering time: Summer
Propagation: By division of established plants during the early spring.

This is the commonest of the pondlilies and is widely grown in wildlife features. However, it is too vigorous for the average modern garden pool. Bright green, leathery, waterlily-like pads are produced in abundance, while the flowers are small, bottle shaped and yellow. They have a distinctive alcoholic aroma.

Nuphar minimum
Dwarf Pondlily

Depth: 30-45cm (12-18in)
Situation: Full sun
Flowering time: Summer
Propagation: By division of established plants during the early spring.

This more restrained, dwarf growing pondlily has bright green, almost heart shaped, leathery floating pads. It produces tiny, rounded yellow blossoms. The plant can be accommodated in a tub or very small pond, and is particularly useful where a lily-pad effect is required alongside a fountain. Pondlilies tolerate moving water; waterlilies do not.

Nymphoides peltata
(Syn. *Villarsia nymphoides*)

Depth: 30-75cm (12-30in)
Situation: Full sun
Flowering time: Summer
Propagation: Easily increased by separating some of the tangle of runners and detaching them as individual plants, each with a portion of root.

This plant is rather like a small waterlily in appearance. Heart shaped, fresh green leaves, occasionally blotched with brown or maroon, float in spreading masses on the surface of the water. Its flowers are bright yellow and attractively fringed. *N. peltata* is suitable for both the decorative pool and the wildlife water garden.

Orontium aquaticum
Golden Club

Depth: 45cm (18in)
Situation: Full sun
Flowering time: Spring
Propagation: By sowing fresh seed, immediately it ripens, in trays of mud.

This relative of the arum lily has bright gold and white, pencil-like flower spikes, which are held well above the surface of the water among floating masses of glaucous, lance shaped leaves. It is very adaptable and can also be treated as a marginal plant, but then its foliage becomes upright and much less attractive in appearance.

Acorus calamus
Sweet Flag

Depth: Moist soil to 5cm (2in)
Height: 90-120cm (36-48in)
Situation: Full sun or partial shade
Flowering time: Mid-summer
Propagation: By division of the fleshy rhizomes during the active growing season.

Acorus calamus has foliage that looks rather like an iris, although surprisingly it is a member of the arum family. The leaves are long, bright green and sword-like with a fragrance of tangerines if bruised. They arise from fat fleshy rhizomes. The insignificant, yellowish-green, horn-like flowers appear among the foliage during summer.

Acorus calamus 'Variegatus' has handsome foliage that is boldly variegated with cream, green and rose. The first shoots of spring take on a strong crimson hue. This plant is one of the most startling of the marginal aquatics.

Alisma plantago-aquatica
Water Plantain

Depth: Moist soil to 15cm (6in)
Height: 60-90cm (24-36in)
Situation: Full sun
Flowering time: Mid-summer
Propagation: By sowing fresh seed, immediately it ripens, in trays of mud, or by division during the growing season.

This adaptable marginal plant can be used in both decorative and wildlife pools. Bright green ovate leaves are carried upright through the water, while pink and white flowers are borne in loose pyramidal panicles. These become woody after flowering and can be gathered for indoor use. This should be done before the seed ripens, otherwise masses of young plants will clog the pool next season.

Alisma plantago aquatica var. *parviflorum* has more rounded leaf blades on stouter stalks. The neat heads of white, or rarely pinkish, blossoms are also shorter (30-75cm/12-30in).

Baldellia ranunculoides
Lesser Water Plaintain

Depth: Moist soil to 5cm (2in)
Height: 8-45cm (3-18in)
Situation: Full sun
Flowering time: Mid-summer
Propagation: By sowing seed, immediately it ripens, in trays of mud, or by division during the growing season.

Baldellia is a rapidly spreading marginal most widely used in the wildlife garden. Elegant, slim, lance shaped green leaves are produced in clumps, from which arise small umbels of blush or pink blossoms. If allowed to develop unhindered, the plant will quickly form spreading colonies. Remove the old flower heads to prevent prolific seeding.

Butomus umbellatus
Flowering Rush

Depth: Moist soil to 23cm (9in)
Height: 60-90cm (24-36in)
Situation: Full sun
Flowering time: Mid- to late summer
Propagation: By removing bulbils from the base of mature plants in early spring, or by division of established clumps during the growing season.

Although of rush-like appearance, technically butomus is not a reed or rush. It produces handsome, succulent, bright green triquetrous foliage and spreading umbels of showy pink flowers, which are an excellent complement to the bright blue of *Pontederia cordata*. A white-flowered form, *B.u. alba*, is sometimes available from specialized nurseries.

Calla palustris
Bog Arum

Depth: Moist soil to 5cm (2in)
Height: 15-30cm (6-12in)
Situation: Full sun
Flowering time: Late spring to early summer
Propagation: By cutting the creeping stems into small sections, each with a bud, and planting in trays of mud in spring. Also by sowing seed immediately it ripens.

The bog arum is an excellent scrambling plant for disguising the edge of a pool. Its strong creeping stems are densely clothed with bright, glossy green, heart shaped leaves. From among these, small white blossoms, rather like those of the peace lily (spathiphyllum), are produced. They are followed by spikes of succulent, orange-red fruits, which remain until the autumn.

Caltha leptosepala
Mountain Marigold

Depth: Moist soil to 5cm (2in)
Height: 15-45cm (6-18in)
Situation: Full sun
Flowering time: Late spring
Propagation: By division during the growing season, or by sowing seed, immediately it ripens, in trays of mud.

This is a lovely marginal, especially for the small pool. Its broad, white, saucer shaped blossoms are borne among dark green scalloped leaves. The plant forms a neat hummock of foliage that makes an attractive feature even outside the flowering season.

Caltha palustris
Marsh Marigold

Depth: Moist soil to 30cm (12in)
Height: 30-60cm (12-24in)
Situation: Full sun
Flowering time: Spring
Propagation: By division during the growing season, or by sowing seed, immediately it ripens, in trays of mud.

Apart from being one of the most beautiful marginal plants, the common marsh marigold flowers at a time when there is virtually no other sign of life in the water garden. Its dark green mounds of scalloped foliage are smothered with bright, golden-yellow waxy flowers. As the leaves tend to look unsightly later in the season, it is worth planting marsh marigolds with vigorous summer flowering marigolds that will disguise some of the fading foliage. There is a white-flowered variety, *Caltha palustris* var. *alba*, which is interesting, but not particularly inspiring.

Caltha palustris 'Flore Pleno'
Double Marsh Marigold

Depth: Moist soil to 5cm (2in)
Height: 15-30cm (6-12in)
Situation: Full sun
Flowering time: Spring
Propagation: By division of established plants during the growing season.

This is one of the finest spring flowering marginal plants. It is excellent for a small pool. The fully-double, bright golden-yellow blossoms are not unlike pom-pon chrysanthemums, but their petals have a waxy texture. These are borne over compact mounds of bright green glossy foliage. Unlike other marsh marigolds, the double form does not set seed.

Caltha palustris var. *palustris*
Himalayan Marsh Marigold

Depth: Moist soil to 30cm (12in)
Height: 60-105cm (24-42in)
Situation: Full sun
Flowering time: Spring and early summer
Propagation: By division during the growing season, or by sowing seed, immediately it ripens, in trays of mud.

This is a large and free flowering species, which is only suitable for a large pool or streamside. Large trusses of bright golden-yellow flowers are borne above big bold hummocks of dark green foliage. The handsome scalloped leaves may be as much as 25cm (10in) across. Although now correctly known as *Caltha palustris* var. *palustris*, this plant is still commonly found in catalogues and nurseries as *C. polypetala*.

Carex pendula
Pendulous Sedge

Depth: Moist soil to 5cm (2in)
Height: 90-120cm (36-48in)
Situation: Full sun or partial shade
Flowering time: Summer
Propagation: By careful division of established plants during early spring, or by sowing seed, immediately it ripens, in trays of mud.

Very few sedges are worthy of a place at the poolside, and even fewer can be grown as marginal aquatics. The majority, including the pendulous sedge, much prefer wet soil. This tall handsome plant has broad, green, strap-like leaves and long, pendulous, brownish-green, catkin-like flowers. In mild winters, the foliage remains more or less evergreen.

Carex riparia
Great Pond Sedge

Depth: Moist soil to 15cm (6in)
Height: 60-90cm (24-36in)
Situation: Full sun or partial shade
Flowering time: Summer, but the foliage is more important
Propagation: By careful division of coloured-foliage cultivars in the spring. By sowing seed of the common species, as soon as it ripens, in trays of mud.

The great pond sedge is rarely grown, except in wildlife pools, as it is invasive. It has thick, grass-like, bluish-green or mid-green foliage and dark brown flower spikes. The coloured-foliage cultivars are best.

Carex riparia 'Aurea' is a tufted grassy plant with bright golden foliage interspersed with narrow, brownish flower spikes. This prefers wet soil to standing water. *Carex riparia* 'Variegata' has similar requirements and produces tight clumps of green and white variegated foliage.

Cotula coronopifolia
Brass Buttons

Depth: Moist soil to 5cm (2in)
Height: 15cm (6in)
Situation: Full sun
Flowering time: Summer
Propagation: By sowing seed during early spring, in trays in a cold frame.

This is a monocarpic plant that dies after flowering, although usually plenty of self sown seedlings remain. Gardeners who have rock gardens will be familiar with the dwarf cotulas, which make such a fine show in spring and summer. *Cotula coronopifolia* is a truly aquatic relative with masses of bright yellow, button-like flowers above dense, light green foliage throughout the summer. Regular dead-heading is essential if self sown seedlings are not to become a nuisance.

Cyperus longus
Sweet Galingale

Depth: Moist soil to 15cm (6in)
Height: 90-120cm (24-48in)
Situation: Sun or light shade
Flowering time: Summer, although the flowers are not significant; essentially, this is a foliage plant.
Propagation: By sowing seed, immediately it ripens, in trays of mud, or by careful division during spring.

This grassy plant is related to the indoor umbrella plant, *Cyperus alternifolius*. It has fresh green spiky leaves that radiate from the stems rather like the ribs of an umbrella. The small, brownish flower heads are sprinkled among the upper leaves and are of little consequence. It is a strong growing plant with a creeping, mat-like rootstock that is ideal for stabilizing any eroded waterside areas.

Eriophorum angustifolium
Cotton Grass

Depth: Moist soil to 5cm (2in)
Height: 30-45cm (12-18in)
Situation: Full sun
Flowering time: Early summer
Propagation: By division of established plants in spring. Freshly gathered seed can be sown, but germination is always unpredictable.

This plant produces fine, grassy, almost evergreen foliage, among which cotton-wool-like flower heads are borne. It must have very acid conditions, ideally being planted into a container of acid soil mixed with liberal quantities of peat. *Eriophorum latifolium* is sometimes offered for garden pool cultivation, and is much the same as the common cotton grass, except that it has broader leaves.

Glyceria aquatica variegata
Variegated Water Grass

Depth: Moist soil to 30cm (12in)
Height: 60-120cm (24-48in)
Situation: Full sun
Flowering time: Summer, but this is not important, as the plant is grown for its foliage.
Propagation: By division of established plants during the early spring.

This handsome and vigorous perennial grass is equally happy growing in mud or relatively deep flowing water. It is a marvellous plant for stabilizing stream banks that are subject to erosion, but requires careful use in the domestic pool. The green and cream, strongly-variegated foliage has a distinct rose-pink tinge during early spring. Spires of dull fawn or off-white flower heads appear during summer. Removing these when first seen helps to maintain the quality of the variegated foliage.

Houttuynia cordata

Depth: Moist soil to 5cm (2in)
Height: 15-30cm (6-12in)
Situation: Full sun
Flowering time: Summer
Propagation: By division of the creeping rootstocks in spring.

A creeping plant for the shallows of a pool, where it can be extremely useful for disguising a harsh or unpleasant edge. Its bluish-green, heart shaped leaves have a maroon or purplish caste and give off a strong unpleasant smell if crushed. The flowers are creamy-white and four-petalled with hard, cone-like centres. *Houttuynia cordata* 'Plena' is similar, but with a showy, dense ruff of petals. *H.c.* 'Variegata' produces few flowers, but has brightly coloured foliage. The leaves are dark purple-green with bright red, yellow and cream splashes. The foliage of all houttuynias is very vulnerable to late frosts.

Iris laevigata
Asiatic Water Iris

Depth: 5-10cm (2-4in)
Height: 50-90cm (20-36in)
Situation: Full sun
Flowering time: Early or mid-summer
Propagation: By division of established plants immediately after flowering. *Iris laevigata* itself can be raised from seed sown in trays of wet mud, in early spring. The cultivars, however, will not come true from seed and they must always be divided.

This easily grown plant forms clumps of sword shaped smooth leaves. The typical plant has blue flowers, but there is considerable variation among plants, especially those raised from seed. Among the finest of the named varieties are 'Atropurpurea' (purple-blue), 'Rose Queen' (soft pink) and 'Snowdrift' (white).

Iris laevigata 'Variegata'

Depth: 5-10cm (2-4in)
Height: 50-70cm (20-28in)
Situation: Full sun
Flowering time: Early or mid-summer
Propagation: By division of established plants immediately after flowering.

Iris laevigata 'Variegata' produces clumps of sword shaped leaves, which are strongly variegated in green and cream. During summer, blue flowers appear among the foliage. This lovely plant is often sold under the name *Iris laevigata* 'Elegantissima'.

Iris pseudacorus
Yellow Flag

Depth: Moist soil to 30cm (12in)
Height: 75-120cm (30-48in)
Situation: Full sun
Flowering time: Early summer
Propagation: By division of established plants immediately after flowering. The species can also be raised from seed sown in trays of mud, in the spring.

A very vigorous plant that is unsuitable for a small garden pool, but quite at home in a wildlife water garden or at the streamside. It has tall, green, strap-like leaves and bright yellow flowers with conspicuous black markings. *Iris pseudacorus* var. *bastardii* is less vigorous and has flowers of a more creamy-yellow colour. *Iris pseudacorus* 'Flore Pleno' is a double-flowered cultivar, while 'Golden Queen' produces bright yellow blooms.

Iris pseudacorus 'Variegata'

Depth: Moist soil to 15cm (6in)
Height: 60-90cm (24-36in)
Situation: Full sun
Flowering time: Early summer
Propagation: By division of established plants immediately after flowering.

Among the finest of all variegated plants, this iris produces handsome, green and cream variegated, sword shaped leaves that are stunningly effective during spring and early summer. As the season progresses, these begin to fade to pale green. The flowers are bright golden-yellow. This is a slower growing plant than the other cultivars of *Iris pseudacorus*.

Iris versicolor

Depth: Moist soil to 15cm (6in)
Height: 60-75cm (24-30in)
Situation: Full sun
Flowering time: Early to mid-summer
Propagation: By sowing seed in trays of mud, in spring, or by division of established plants immediately after flowering. This is the only method of propagation for cultivars.

A modest grower of great value to the small pool. Violet-blue and purple blossoms are conspicuously marked with creamy-yellow. The leaves are plain green and sword shaped. *Iris versicolor alba* is a pure white selection, while 'Claret Cup' is a deep claret-purple, and 'Kermesina' has rich plum coloured blossoms.

***Juncus effusus* 'Spiralis'**
Corkscrew Rush

Depth: Moist soil to 5cm (2in)
Height: 30-45cm (12-18in)
Situation: Full sun
Flowering time: Summer, but the flowers are inconspicuous and the plant is grown primarily for its foliage.
Propagation: By division of established plants in early spring. Only propagate from material that is true to type.

This is one of the most unusual marginal aquatics for the small pond. The soft, dark green, needle-like leaves are twisted and contorted like a corkscrew. It is essential to remove any portions of the plant that do not remain true to type. A straight-leaved, gold and green variegated version, *Juncus effusus* 'Vittatus', may be encountered occasionally.

Mentha aquatica
Water Mint

Depth: Moist soil to 15cm (6in)
Height: 30-45cm (12-18in)
Situation: Full sun
Flowering time: Summer
Propagation: From stem cuttings rooted in trays of mud during summer, or by division of the creeping stems and rootstocks in early spring.

A much loved, easily grown, but often rampant, marginal plant. It is commonly used to disguise the edges of water features and to hold the soil together where erosion is a problem, for it will cover the ground, rooting at almost every leaf joint.

This strongly aromatic plant has somewhat downy, typical mint foliage on slender purple or reddish stems. Soft lilac-pink whorls of flowers are borne in summer. It is a variable plant, so selecting a good leafy, free flowering form is essential.

Mentha cervina

Depth: Moist soil to 5cm (2in)
Height: 30cm (12in)
Situation: Full sun
Flowering time: Summer
Propagation: From short stem cuttings taken during summer and rooted in trays of mud.

Mentha cervina is an interesting aromatic plant that forms spreading clumps of slender erect stems, densely clotted with small, lance shaped leaves. Whorls of dainty lilac or ultramarine blossoms appear in the summer. This is a useful plant for disguising the edges of a pool.

Menyanthes trifoliata
Bog Bean

Depth: Moist soil to 15cm (6in)
Height: 20-30cm (8-12in)
Situation: Full sun
Flowering time: Spring
Propagation: By cutting the sprawling stem into small sections, each with a bud, during early spring. then planting these in trays of mud.

This is a handsome, distinctive scrambling plant for shallow water. Showy, white-fringed flowers are produced among dark green foliage, which looks rather like that of a broad bean plant. A useful plant for disguising the harsh edge of a pool, or for planting on a natural streamside bank to help prevent soil erosion.

Mimulus luteus
Yellow Musk

Depth: Moist soil to 15cm (6in)
Height: 20-30cm (8-12in)
Situation: Full sun
Flowering time: Summer
Propagation: By sowing seed during early spring, in a frame or unheated greenhouse, or by division of the overwintered foliage rosettes in early spring.

Soft green rounded foliage is freely produced on vigorous, spreading plants. Striking spires of bright yellow flowers, which are similar to those of an antirrhinum, produce a dazzling show for much of the summer. A free seeding and spreading plant that can become a nuisance in the manicured garden if not carefully controlled, but perfect for the wildlife pool.

Mimulus ringens

Depth: Moist soil to 15cm (6in)
Height: 30-45cm (12-18in)
Situation: Full sun
Flowering time: Summer
Propagation: By sowing seed during early spring, in trays of mud in a cold frame, or by rooting summer stem cuttings in mud. Mature plants can also be carefully divided in the spring.

Although delicate in appearance, this plant is usually quite tough. Its multi-branched slender stems carry narrow, handsome, bright green leaflets. The almost tubular flowers vary in colour between soft lavender and blue, and are produced freely along a spiky stem. It is the most useful mimulus for the small pool.

Myosotis scorpioides
(Syn. *Myosotis palustris*) Water Forget-me-not

Depth: Moist soil to 15cm (6in)
Height: 15-20cm (6-8in)
Situation: Full sun
Flowering time: Summer
Propagation: By division of old plants in the early spring, retaining only the young outer portions, or by sowing seed during spring, in the protection of a cold frame.

Although having a similar appearance to the traditional bedding forget-me-not, the water forget-me-not is a reliable perennial that will continue from year to year.

This is a useful waterside plant, producing generous clumps of bright green foliage, liberally sprinkled with light blue flowers. There is a white form, 'Alba', and a vigorous seed-raised strain called 'Semperflorens', which is of neater habit and very free-flowering.

Narthecium ossifragum
Bog Asphodel

Depth: Moist soil to 5cm (2in)
Height: 20-30cm (8-12in)
Situation: Full sun
Flowering time: Mid- to late summer
Propagation: By division of established plants during the early spring.

Although not a spectacular plant, the bog asphodel is very useful in the small pool and much loved for the wildlife garden. It is short growing with wiry stems and fans of small, iris-like foliage. Short stout heads of yellow flowers appear in summer. It will prosper in standing water during the growing season, but will be much happier in wet soil for the winter months.

Peltandra alba
Arrow Arum

Depth: Moist soil to 15cm (6in)
Height: 45cm (18in)
Situation: Full sun
Flowering time: Summer
Propagation: By division of established plants during the early spring.

An interesting member of the arum family with handsome, dark green glossy leaves. The flowers consist of narrow, whitish spathes, rather like those of an arum lily, and sometimes are followed by reddish fruits. *Peltandra virginica* is almost identical, but it produces greenish spathes.

Phragmites australis 'Variegatus'
Variegated Spire Reed

Depth: Moist soil to 15cm (6in)
Height: 90-120cm (36-48in)
Situation: Full sun
Flowering time: Late summer, although this is of little significance, as the plant is grown for its variegated foliage.
Propagation: By division during spring, taking care to retain only those portions of plant that have distinct variegations.

This is the cream and green variegated form of the common spire reed, which is so despised by most water gardeners except, of course, those who want to attract wildlife. Unlike its unpopular parent, which spreads very rapidly, the variegated form is well behaved and is a desirable addition to any pool, large or small.

Pontederia cordata
Pickerel Weed

Depth: Moist soil to 15cm (6in)
Height: 60-90cm (24-36in)
Situation: Full sun
Flowering time: Mid- to late summer
Propagation: By division of established plants once they start actively growing in the spring. By sowing seed in trays of mud, when still green during late summer.

This splendid plant produces glossy green, lance shaped leaves and strong spikes of soft blue flowers. White and pink forms are also becoming available, but these are not yet widely cultivated. *Pontederia lanceolata* is a less commonly grown species, which is of similar appearance, but very much larger in every respect (90-100cm/36-40in).

Ranunculus lingua
Greater Spearwort

Depth: Moist soil to 15cm (6in)
Height: 60-90cm (24-36in)
Situation: Full sun
Propagation: By division of established plants during the early spring.

This tall growing relative of the buttercup produces bright yellow, saucer-like flowers. Its dark green foliage is carried on erect stems, which are strongly flushed with rose, especially as the shoots emerge during early spring. The most usual form available from nurseries is the much improved *Ranunculus lingua* 'Grandiflorus', although this finds less favour with those who have wildlife ponds.

Rumex hydrolapathum
Water Dock

Depth: Moist soil to 30cm (12in)
Height: 120-300cm (48-120in)
Situation: Sun or partial shade
Flowering time: Summer
Propagation: By division of established plants in early spring, or by sowing seed in trays of mud, in spring.

A much desired plant for the wildlife pond with bold, dark green, broadly lance shaped leaves on strong, cane-like stems. The foliage turns bronze and crimson at the approach of autumn. The flower spikes, which are narrow, greenish and not particularly attractive, are followed by dense clusters of dark brown papery seeds. Fruiting heads should be removed before the seeds ripen to prevent them from self sowing indiscriminately.

Sagittaria japonica
Japanese Arrowhead

Depth: Moist soil to 15cm (6in)
Height: 45-60cm (18-24in)
Situation: Full sun
Flowering time: Summer
Propagation: By division of growing clumps during the summer, or by redistribution of the winter buds, or turions.

A neat growing plant that produces clumps of glossy, mid-green, arrow shaped leaves and strong spikes of papery, white single flowers with yellow centres. Although often planted in garden pools, where it is perfectly well behaved, this is a valuable addition to any wildlife feature, especially during the winter. Water-fowl regard the fleshy, overwintering buds, or turions, as a delicacy.

Sagittaria sagittifolia 'Flore Pleno'
Double Arrowhead

Depth: Moist soil to 15cm (6in)
Height: 30-45cm (12-18in)
Situation: Full sun
Flowering time: Summer
Propagation: By division of growing clumps during the summer, or by redistribution of the winter buds, or turions.

This is an orderly and very choice plant for the serious water gardener. It produces beautiful, fully-double white flowers on strong spikes from among clumps of arrow shaped leaves. Protect the overwintering buds, or turions, from the predations of water-fowl.

Schoenoplectus lacustris tabernaemontani **'Albescens'**
(Syn. Scirpus albescens)

Depth: Moist soil to 15cm (6in)
Height: 90-120cm (36-48in)
Flowering time: Summer, although this is of little significance, as the plant is grown principally for its foliage.
Propagation: By division of growing clumps during the summer.

This is one of the finest rushes, having stout, upright, needle-like stems of glowing sulphurous-white, conspicuously marked with thin longitudinal stripes of green. Brownish flowers are produced in occasional small groups or tassels. In very cold districts, this plant benefits from a little frost protection.

Schoenoplectus lacustris tabernaemontani **'Zebrinus'**
(Syn. Scirpus zebrinus) Zebra Rush

Depth: Moist soil to 15cm (6in)
Height: 90cm (36in)
Situation: Full sun
Flowering time: Summer, although this is of little significance, as the plant is grown principally for its foliage.
Propagation: By division of growing clumps during the summer.

A short growing rush, having very distinctive, needle-like leaves that are marked with alternate bars of green and white. As this is a mutation from a plain green-leaved rush, green shoots will often appear. These should be removed immediately before they swamp the desirable variegated part.

Sparganium erectum
Branched Bur-reed

Depth: Moist soil to 15cm (6in)
Height: 45-90cm (18-36in)
Situation: Full sun or partial shade
Flowering time: Summer
Propagation: By sowing seed, immediately it ripens, in trays of mud. Established plants can be lifted and divided carefully during early spring.

This robust, rush-like marginal is widely planted in wildlife water features, but it is only a moderately inspiring addition to a decorative pool. It has narrow, bright green, strap-like foliage and produces branched, greenish flower heads, which are followed by green burrs. The variety *S.e.* var. *neglectum* has a reddish stem.

Typha angustifolia
Narrow-leaved Reedmace

Depth: Moist soil to 30cm (12in)
Height: 90-180cm (36-72in)
Situation: Full sun
Flowering: Summer, although the main interest lies in the fruiting heads of early autumn.
Propagation: By division of established plants during the early spring.

Typha angustifolia is often referred to as a bulrush, although it is a reedmace. It has tall, slender, grey-green foliage and bold, brown, poker-like seed heads, but is only suitable for a large or wildlife pool.

The fruiting heads of this and the great reedmace (*Typha latifolia*) are often used for dried indoor decoration. *T. latifolia* is too vigorous for the ordinary garden pool, but the shorter growing, cream and green variegated *T.l.* 'Variegata' is more restrained (90cm/36in) and eminently suited to the smaller feature.

Typha minima
Dwarf Reedmace

Depth: Moist soil to 5cm (2in)
Height: 45cm (18in)
Situation: Full sun
Flowering time: Summer, but the main attraction lies in the fruiting heads of early autumn.
Propagation: By division of mature plants during the early spring.

This is a beautiful miniature reedmace for the small garden pool, tub or sink. It is a complete dwarf replica, having dark green grassy foliage and chunky, rounded, dark brown seed heads. The plant is in no way invasive.

Veronica beccabunga
Brooklime

Depth: Moist soil to 15cm (6in)
Height: 15-20 cm (6-8in)
Situation: Full sun
Flowering time: Summer
Propagation: From short stem cuttings, rooted in pans of mud, at any time during the summer. It roots naturally and freely along its creeping stems, and pieces can be easily detached.

A semi-evergreen marginal with procumbent stems that are ideal for disguising the edges of a pool. The leaves are dark green and rounded, being produced in abundance. Dark blue flowers, each with a white eye, smother the plant throughout much of the summer.

Callitriche hermaphroditica
Autumnal Starwort

Depth: To 45cm (18in)
Situation: Full sun
Propagation: By division of actively growing plants. Alternatively, by taking stem cuttings during the summer, bunching them with lead strips and planting them in their permanent positions.

This plant is occasionally sold under the name *Callitriche autumnalis*. It is a completely submerged species with bright green, cress-like evergreen foliage, which is regarded as a salad delicacy by fish. The plant grows freely when water conditions are good, but often struggles in a newly made pool. Where autumnal starwort prospers, you can be sure that the pond water quality is good.

Ceratophyllum demersum
Hornwort, Coontail

Depth: Any, as it rarely roots, spending most of its life suspended in the water
Situation: Full sun or partial shade
Propagation: By separation of the scrambling growths. For commercial purposes, the plant is usually sold in bunches with a lead weight, although the latter is not necessary.

A dark green, totally submerged plant that has dense whorls of bristly foliage on brittle stems. In early spring, these will often spend a while rooted to the pool floor, but for most of the time, the plant floats just below the surface of the water. In winter, it retreats into turions, making it difficult to contain in one area of the pool. This is a very versatile plant that is excellent for difficult, deep or partly shaded pools.

Eleocharis acicularis
Hair Grass

Depth: To 60cm (24in)
Situation: Full sun
Propagation: By division of the clumps of plants during the active growing season. This plant is always sold in small clumps and never weighted bunches. Cuttings will not root.

A restrained, evergreen submerged aquatic which, when well established, looks rather like a carpet of seedling grass spreading across the pool floor or the bottom of a container. It is a tiny relative of the rush family and is particularly suited to cultivation in a tub or container water garden.

Elodea canadensis
Canadian Pondweed

Depth: To 120cm (48in)
Situation: Full sun
Propagation: By taking cuttings during the active spring and summer growing season, fastening them together in bunches with narrow lead strips and planting them in their permanent positions.

This is a handsome, almost evergreen aquatic that remains totally submerged and is much loved by fish. It has small, dark green leaves arranged in very dense whorls along extensive branching stems. Some gardeners are reluctant to introduce this plant to their ponds because of its vigorous growth rate, but if confined to a planting basket, it is easily controlled.

Fontinalis antipyretica
Willow Moss

Depth: To 60cm (24in)
Situation: Full sun or partial shade
Propagation: By separation of clumps during the growing season and replanting in their permanent positions. Vigorous young growth can be removed as cuttings during the summer months, bunched with lead strips, then planted.

An evergreen, totally submerged aquatic plant with olive-green, moss-like foliage. It flourishes in moving water, and in the wild can often be discovered clinging to stones or gravel on the bed of a fast moving stream. However, the plant is quite happy in the still water of a pool and provides wonderful cover for goldfish spawning. A smaller species of similar appearance and habit, *Fontinalis gracilis*, is sometimes offered for sale.

Hottonia palustris
Water Violet

Depth: To 60cm (24in)
Situation: Full sun
Flowering time: Summer
Propagation: By taking summer cuttings and fastening them together in bunches with narrow lead strips. Alternatively, by redistribution of emerging winter turions in spring.

The loveliest submerged aquatic, this plant produces handsome spikes of off-white or lilac blossoms, which are held well above the water. The submerged foliage is bright green, finely divided and carried on stout stems. Towards the end of the season, the stems tend to break away from one another, and much of the plant can be observed floating free. This is natural and leads to the formation of winter turions.

Lagarosiphon major
(Syn. *Elodea crispa*) Fish Weed

Depth: To 120cm (48in)
Situation: Full sun
Propagation: By taking cuttings during the active spring and summer growing season, fastening them together in bunches with narrow lead strips and planting them in their permanent positions.

This totally submerged aquatic plant has long, dark green succulent stems, densely clothed in dark green crispy foliage. It is one of the best and most versatile of submerged plants, working very effectively to control green water and being much loved by decorative fish.

Lobelia dortmanna

Depth: To 25cm (10in)
Situation: Full sun
Flowering time: Summer
Propagation: By careful division of established clumps during late spring or early summer, these being planted immediately in their permanent positions.

Surprisingly, this is a close relative of the popular bedding lobelia, but it is a hardy perennial submerged aquatic that produces short spikes of lavender coloured blossoms, which are carried above the water. It forms dense carpets of somewhat blunted, dark green foliage. This is a useful plant for shallow water, especially in tub and sink gardens.

Myriophyllum proserpinacoides
Parrot's Feather

Depth: To 60cm (24in)
Situation: Full sun
Propagation: Cuttings taken during the growing season root readily. Three or four stems should be fastened together with a lead strip and planted in their permanent position. Sometimes, the plant will layer itself and simply require detachment.

The feathery foliage of this aquatic may be totally or partially submerged. Handsome, blue-green, finely cut leaves are carried on scrambling stems, which may escape from the pool and root into the marginal shelf. Here, they will survive and grow rather like an emergent aquatic, but with foliage that turns red at the approach of autumn. In very cold areas, it is worth removing a few shoots in late summer and rooting them in a pot of mud, in the greenhouse, as an insurance against loss. The plant is frost-tolerant rather than frost-hardy.

Myriophyllum spicatum
Spiked Milfoil

Depth: To 90cm (36in)
Situation: Full sun
Flowering time: Summer, but the flowers are insignificant.
Propagation: By taking cuttings during the active spring and summer growing season, fastening them together in bunches with narrow lead strips and planting them in their permanent positions.

A totally submerged aquatic which, during summer, produces small, red and yellowish flower spikes above the surface of the water. The foliage is bronze-green and consists of masses of tiny leaflets on strong succulent stems. This vigorous growing plant is much loved by fish as a spawning ground.

Potamogeton crispus
Curled Pondweed

Depth: To 90cm (36in)
Situation: Full sun
Flowering time: Summer, but the flowers are insignificant.
Propagation: By taking cuttings during the active spring and summer growing season, fastening them together in bunches with narrow lead strips and planting them in their permanent positions.

This handsome submerged aquatic produces bronze translucent foliage rather like that of a seaweed. The leaves are crisped and crimped, being borne on extensive succulent stems. Small crimson and yellow flower spikes appear just above the surface of the water, but are of little importance.

Ranunculus aquatilis
Water Crowfoot

Depth: To 90cm (36in)
Situation: Full sun
Flowering time: Summer
Propagation: By taking cuttings during the active spring and summer growing season, fastening them together in bunches with narrow lead strips and planting them in their permanent positions.

A beautiful plant with deeply dissected submerged foliage that gives it an apt common name. Just before flowering, the plant produces floating leaves that are reminiscent of clover. The blossoms are glistening, papery, white and gold chalices, rather like very refined buttercup flowers, but infinitely more delicate. No water garden should be without this plant.

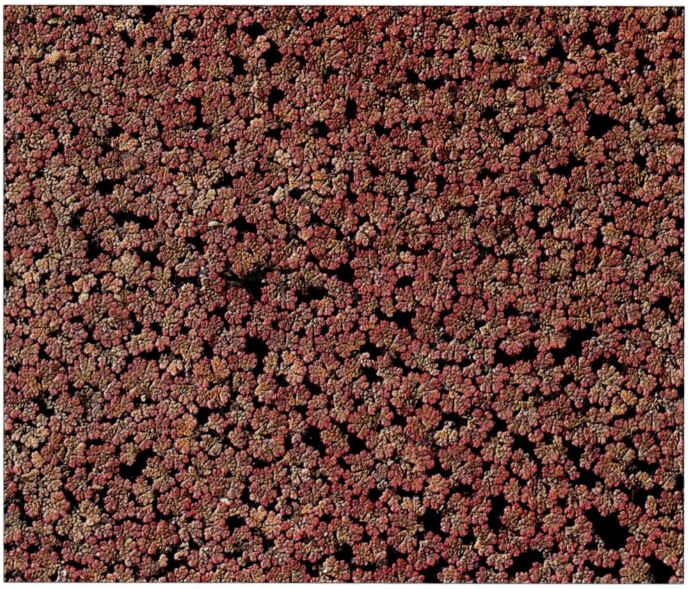

Azolla caroliniana
Fairy Moss

Situation: Full sun
Propagation: By separation and redistribution of groups of floating foliage.

This dense floating fern has beautiful, bluish-green or purplish-tinted, lacy foliage. Although regarded as frost-hardy, it will not survive severe weather. As a precaution, remove a portion towards the end of the growing season and place it in a bowl of water with a little soil on the bottom. Stand the bowl in a light, frost-free place. The portion saved in this manner can be used to start a new colony in the late spring.

Hydrocharis morsus-ranae
Frogbit

Situation: Full sun
Flowering time: Summer
Propagation: By separating individual plantlets during the growing season.

This lovely little floating plant looks rather like a tiny waterlily. It has small, bright green, kidney shaped leaves that are produced in neat rosettes. The papery, three-petalled flowers are white with conspicuous yellow centres. At the approach of winter, the frogbit produces turions, or winter buds, which fall to the bottom of the pool where they overwinter.

Lemna trisulca
Ivy-leaved Duckweed

Situation: Full sun
Propagation: By separating and redistributing groups of the floating foliage.

Most of the duckweeds are invasive and may only find a place in the wildlife pool, although even there, they can become a menace. *Lemna trisulca* is a pretty little plant with dark green crispy foliage that floats just beneath the surface of the water. Occasionally, it produces tiny greenish flowers, but these are not noticeable, the plant being grown purely for its foliage.

Stratiotes aloides
Water Soldier

Situation: Full sun
Flowering time: Summer
Propagation: By separating and detaching young plants from runners, which are produced during the growing season.

One of the most extraordinary aquatic plants that the gardener can grow outdoors, *Stratiotes aloides* resembles a floating pineapple top. It produces creamy-white papery flowers in its leaf axils. The female flowers are solitary, while the male flowers appear in clusters in a pinkish spathe. Usually, the plant overwinters as a dormant winter bud or a small plantlet.

Trapa natans
Water Chestnut

Situation: Full sun
Flowering time: Summer
Propagation: By gathering the nuts produced towards the end of the growing season and placing them in a bowl of water with some soil on the bottom. During the winter, this should be left in a cool, frost-free place. Start into growth in the spring.

A handsome plant with rosettes of dark green rhomboidal leaves and pretty, white axillary flowers. Although technically an annual, the water chestnut seeds itself freely. Even if you do not gather the nuts, sufficient are usually deposited on the floor of the pool to ensure that the plant continues.

Utricularia vulgaris
Greater Bladderwort

Situation: Full sun
Flowering time: Summer
Propagation: By redistribution of the tangled mass of foliage during the summer months.

Spikes of showy, bright yellow flowers, not unlike those of an antirrhinum, but rather smaller, arise from a tangle of dainty, dull green filigree foliage. Tiny bladders are distributed throughout the foliage and capture aquatic insect life, which the plant digests as an additional source of nutrients. At the approach of winter, the plant forms turions, or winter buds, which fall to the bottom of the pool.

Aruncus dioicus
(Syn. *Aruncus sylvestris*) Goat's Beard

Height: 90-150cm (36-60in)
Situation: Full sun or partial shade
Flowering time: Summer
Propagation: By division of established plants during the winter dormant period. Only replant the young vigorous growths from the outer portion of each clump.

A tall handsome plant with bold plumes of feathery, creamy-white flowers. The foliage is pale green, deeply cut and lobed, and produced on very stout stems. There is a much shorter (90cm/36in) cultivar, *A.d.* 'Kneiffii', which has smaller, creamy-white plumes and much more deeply divided foliage.

Astilbe x *arendsii* cultivars

Height: 30-90cm (12-36in)
Situation: Full sun or partial shade
Flowering time: Summer
Propagation: By division of established plants during the winter dormant period. Only replant the young vigorous growths from the outer portion of each clump.

A group of very fine astilbes, all of which have a neat habit with dark green, deeply divided foliage and handsome plumes of blossom. 'Fanal' (30-40cm/12-18in) is the finest of the reds, while 'White Gloria' (60-75cm/24-30in) is probably the nicest white. All are completely reliable and form the backbone of the summer flowering display.

Cardamine pratensis
Cuckoo Flower

Height: 30-45cm (12-18in)
Situation: Full sun or partial shade
Flowering time: Spring
Propagation: Division during the winter dormant period is the only satisfactory method of increasing the double form; it also works well for the common kind. The latter can also be increased by sowing seed in trays of damp, soil-based seed compost, in a cold frame, during the spring.

This charming, early flowering, bog garden plant can also be naturalized in the water meadow. Single, rosy-lilac flowers are produced freely above mounds of pale green ferny foliage. The double form, *C.p.* 'Flore Pleno', is slightly shorter and more compact with beautiful, fully-double lilac blossoms. It is particularly good for a small bog garden.

Darmera peltata
(Syn. *Peltiphyllum peltatum*) Umbrella Plant

Height: 45-90cm (18-36in)
Situation: Full sun or partial shade
Flowering time: Spring
Propagation: By division of the creeping rootstocks during the winter dormant period, these being replanted in their permanent positions immediately. It is also possible to raise plants from seed sown during spring, in a tray or pan of good soil-based seed compost in a cold frame.

This interesting early spring flowering plant is related to the saxifrages. It produces globular heads of rose-pink flowers on stout stems up to 45cm (18in) high. These are followed by handsome, glossy rounded leaves that are held aloft on strong central stems, hence the allusion to umbrellas in the common name. A very hardy plant and one of the first to flower in the bog garden.

Eupatorium purpureum
Joe Pye Weed

Height: 120cm (48in)
Situation: Full sun or partial shade
Flowering time: Late summer and early autumn
Propagation: Easily increased by division of established plants during the early spring. Discard older portions, replanting vigorous young growths from the outer part of each clump.

A rather coarse, but very useful, bog plant for large features.

Crowded heads of small purple flowers are produced on very strong stems, which are clothed in rough, oval, plain green leaves. This plant can usually be accommodated satisfactorily in a wildlife water feature.

Euphorbia palustris

Height: 45-90cm (18-36in)
Situation: Full sun
Flowering time: Spring
Propagation: Although this plant can be divided successfully at any time during the winter dormant period, it responds best to being carefully split up during early spring, just as it is beginning to sprout.

This is the bog garden member of the popular herbaceous spurge family. It produces lush mounds of soft green foliage, which become completely covered by typical, yellow-green, euphorbia flower heads. During late summer and early autumn, the foliage often takes on a reddish or bronze hue. Apart from being an invaluable addition to a manicured bog garden, it also makes a welcome addition to a wildlife feature.

Filipendula ulmaria 'Flore Pleno'
Double Meadow-sweet

Height: 90cm (36in)
Situation: Full sun or partial shade
Flowering time: Summer
Propagation: By division of established plants during the winter dormant period. Small divisions of young material always establish themselves better than old woody pieces.

This is the fully-double-flowered form of the common meadow-sweet. Dense feathery spires of sweetly scented, creamy-white blossoms are produced above handsome, deeply cut, mid-green foliage. A lovely plant that is equally at home in the bog garden and wildlife feature.

Gunnera manicata
Giant Brazilian Rhubarb

Height: 150-180cm (60-72in)
Situation: Full sun or partial shade
Flowering time: Summer
Propagation: Divide established plants in early spring, using a strong knife or spade to separate the creeping rootstocks cleanly; each terminal bud with a piece of rootstock is capable of producing a new plant. Seed can also be sown in trays, in a cold frame, but this must be done as soon as it ripens.

This immense plant looks like a huge rhubarb, but has much coarser leaves and stems, which are liberally sprinkled with unpleasant bristly hairs. In summer, an enormous flower spike is produced. This is curious rather than beautiful. Although frost-hardy, in some districts the emerging leaves are regularly caught by frost. Where this is a problem, provide protection by covering with the previous season's dried foliage.

Hosta crispula

Height: 60-75cm (24-30in)
Situation: Sun or partial shade
Flowering time: Summer
Propagation: By division of established plants in early spring as soon as the shoots begin to show through the soil, when they can easily be pulled apart. (In the autumn, a sharp knife may be needed to cut the crowns into pieces.)

A wonderful foliage plant with oval or lance shaped green leaves banded with white. The tubular blossoms are lavender and borne freely on slender stems. Hostas are much loved by slugs, which should be taken into account if selecting them for a bog garden. Even where slugs are not perceived to be too much of a problem, precautions should be taken.

Hosta sieboldiana var. *elegans*

Height: 60-85cm (24-34in)
Situation: Sun or partial shade
Flowering time: Summer
Propagation: By division of established plants during early spring, just as the new shoots begin to appear through the soil. If carefully lifted with a fork, the clump should separate easily.

This high-class plant has beautiful, steely-blue oval leaves with a ribbed and corrugated surface. It makes an impressive mound of consistent colour in the bog garden during summer, but eventually is punctuated with strong stems bearing handsome, pale lilac or slightly off-white tubular blossoms. The best of the plain-foliage hostas.

Hosta undulata var. *albomarginata*

Height: 30-45cm (12-18in)
Situation: Sun or partial shade
Flowering time: Summer
Propagation: By division of established plants during early spring, just as the new shoots are appearing. If carefully lifted at this time, old clumps usually pull apart easily. Plant divisions in their permanent positions immediately.

One of the most useful variegated foliage plants for the bog garden, this hosta produces consistent cream and green variegated leaves, sprinkled with slender spikes of pale lilac tubular blossoms during the summer. Unlike many other hardy variegated foliage plants, the leaves do not fade with age.

Iris ensata
(Syn. *Iris kaempferi*) Clematis-flowered Iris of Japan

Height: 60-90cm (24-36in)
Situation: Full sun
Flowering time: Summer
Propagation: Mixtures of *Iris ensata* can easily be raised from seed sown during spring, in trays of ericaceous compost in a cold frame. Named varieties and special selections must be divided in winter, or in summer immediately after flowering.

This beautiful bog iris will not tolerate alkaline soil or standing water in winter. The species has tufts of broad, grassy or narrow sword-like foliage and soft, velvety, deep purple blossoms. However, there are many named cultivars, including: 'Blue Heaven' (60-75cm/24-30in); the pale lavender 'Landscape at Dawn' (60-75cm/24-30in); and 'Variegata' (60cm/24in) with simple violet-blue flowers and striking, cream and green striped foliage. Higo Hybrids are the best of the hybrid mixtures.

Iris sibirica
Siberian Iris

Height: 60-90cm (24-36in)
Situation: Full sun
Flowering time: Summer
Propagation: The species can be raised from seed sown during early spring, in trays of soil-based seed compost in a cold frame. Named cultivars must be propagated by division during the winter, or in summer immediately after flowering.

A very versatile bog garden plant, *Iris sibirica* tolerates dry conditions quite well, together with periodic inundation with water. For this reason, it is ideal for the streamside. It produces vigorous tufts of grassy foliage, from which emerge elegant, pale blue blossoms on strong erect stems. There are many fine named kinds, including: the deep violet-purple 'Emperor' (90cm/36in); sky-blue 'Perry's Blue' (90cm/36in); and deep violet-blue 'Perry's Pygmy' (45cm/18in).

Ligularia dentata 'Golden Queen'
(Syn. *Ligularia clivorum* 'Golden Queen')

Height: 90-120cm (36-48in)
Situation: Full sun or partial shade
Flowering time: Late summer
Propagation: By division of established plants during the winter and early spring dormant period, replanting the youngest pieces. Although the plant self seeds, the seedlings are usually inferior and should be removed. There is no point in sowing seed, as the progeny will not be precisely like the parent.

Ideal for background planting, this big bold plant produces large, green, more-or-less heart shaped leaves, from among which striking mop-heads of bright, golden, daisy-like flowers appear. *Ligularia dentata* 'Orange Princess' is similar, but has vivid orange blossoms and green leaves with a strong purplish infusion.

Lobelia 'Queen Victoria'

Height: 60-90cm (24-36in)
Situation: Full sun or partial shade
Flowering time: Late summer
Propagation: By division of the overwintering rosettes in early spring. These should be potted up to establish a good root system before planting out in their permanent positions, in late spring or early summer.

This plant's tall spires of bright red flowers contrast markedly with the bold clumps of beetroot coloured foliage. It is one of the most startling bog garden plants and, therefore, in need of very thoughtful placing if it is not to appear strident. Although usually winter-hardy, in frosty areas, it is prudent to overwinter one or two plants of this lovely bog garden perennial in a cold frame or unheated greenhouse.

Lobelia vedrariensis

Height: 75-90cm (30-36in)
Situation: Full sun or partial shade
Flowering time: Late summer
Propagation: By division of overwintered clumps in spring, separating the individual shoots with roots attached and potting them up in a good soil-less compost. This will allow them to produce a decent root system before being planted out in their permanent positions, in late spring or early summer. Seed can also be sown in a tray or pan of good seed compost, in a warm propagator or on a window ledge in early spring.

An easy-going attractive plant with deep violet-purple flowers. The leaves are plain green with a strong purple caste. Unlike most perennial lobelias, this plant appears to be perfectly hardy. While it will not endure dry conditions, it will tolerate periodic inundations of water.

Lysichiton americanus
American Skunk Cabbage

Height: 60-90cm (24-36in)
Situation: Full sun or partial shade
Flowering time: Spring
Propagation: By sowing seed, immediately it ripens, in a tray of soil-based compost in a cold frame. Use a plastic tray with drainage holes, placing it in a larger, water filled tray without holes. Lysichitons must have very wet conditions, and filling the outer tray with water up to compost surface level will produce the best conditions for germination.

A relative of the arum lily, this plant produces a much larger, bright yellow spathe, which appears long before the cabbage-like foliage. There is a white-flowered skunk cabbage with smaller spathes, *L. camtschatcensis*, which comes from Asia, and also a creamy-coloured hybrid.

Lysimachia nummularia
Creeping Jenny

Height: 5cm (2in)
Situation: Sun or shade
Flowering time: Summer
Propagation: Short stem cuttings, taken during the summer growing period, will root readily in a mixture of equal parts peat and sharp sand, or peat and perlite, in pans or pots on a window ledge or in a warm greenhouse. This plant usually layers itself freely; the rooted pieces can be severed and lifted at any time.

This more-or-less evergreen carpeting plant is widely used for disguising the often awkward edge between bog garden and pool, or pool and surrounding ground. For much of the summer, it is studded with bright yellow, buttercup-like flowers. There is a golden-leaved cultivar, *L.n.* 'Aurea', which also has yellow flowers.

Lysimachia punctata

Height: 60-90cm (24-36in)
Situation: Full sun or partial shade
Flowering time: Summer
Propagation: By division of established plants during the winter dormant period. Select the younger outer portions, replanting them immediately in their permanent positions.

A very upright plant of great versatility, tolerating both moderately dry and excessively wet conditions. The bright yellow, buttercup-like flowers are borne on stout stems, which are clothed with coarse, somewhat downy foliage.

Lythrum salicaria
Purple Loosestrife

Height: 90-120cm (36-48in)
Situation: Full sun or partial shade
Flowering time: Summer
Propagation: By division of established plants during the winter dormant period, discarding the hard woody centre of each plant and retaining the more vigorous younger growths around the edge. These should be planted immediately in their permanent positions.

This is a bushy upright plant with myriad slender spires of rose-purple flowers above narrow, mid-green leaves that have a rose-pink caste. It is much loved for wildlife features as well as bog gardens. There are several named cultivars, but the rose-pink 'Lady Sackville' (90-120cm/36-48in) and soft pink 'Robert' (90-120cm/36-48in) are the most commonly cultivated.

Matteuccia struthiopteris
Ostrich Feather Fern

Height: 90cm (36in)
Situation: Sun or shade
Flowering time: Ferns do not flower, but this plant does produce a number of brown, spore bearing spikes during the late summer.
Propagation: By division of the creeping rootstock in early spring. Each piece of rhizome with a cluster of green, knuckle-like shoots is capable of growing into a mature fern. Plant in their permanent positions.

One of the loveliest hardy ferns, *Matteuccia struthiopteris* bears large 'shuttlecocks' of lacy green foliage around stout basal crowns. The fronds become interspersed with dark brown, spore bearing frond spikes to pleasing effect. At the first touch of frost, the fronds die back. This fern tolerates a variety of conditions, surviving in ordinary garden soil, but also coping with several centimetres of water.

Mimulus cardinalis
Cardinal Monkey Flower

Height: 45-60cm (18-24in)
Situation: Full sun
Flowering time: Summer
Propagation: By sowing seed during early spring, in a tray or pan of good seed compost under glass. The seedlings are not hardy and require frost protection while growing on in small pots. They should be planted in their permanent positions during early summer. Short stem cuttings, taken during summer, also root readily in a mixture of peat and sharp sand, or peat and perlite.

Mimulus cardinalis is not always reliably hardy, but it is worth growing, even if it has to be replaced annually. Its brilliant, scarlet-orange flowers are produced among soft downy foliage. This plant must always have damp conditions, but usually rots off if the soil becomes waterlogged.

Mimulus luteus
Yellow Musk

Height: 20-30cm (8-12in)
Situation: Full sun
Flowering time: Summer
Propagation: Overwintered rosettes can be separated in the spring and replanted in their permanent positions. Seed sown during the early spring, in trays of good seed compost on a window ledge or in a warm greenhouse, will produce plants for establishing in their permanent positions during the summer.

A very colourful and much loved plant, but one that requires careful control to prevent it from taking over the bog garden or poolside, as it self seeds readily. It produces hummocks of soft green rounded foliage and myriad spikes of bright yellow flowers. Immediately these fade, they should be removed to prevent the plant from making itself a nuisance.

Mimulus Monarch Strain

Height: 20-30cm (8-12in)
Situation: Full sun
Flowering time: Summer
Propagation: By sowing seed during early spring, in a tray of good seed compost in a warm greenhouse or on a window ledge. Prick out young seedlings and pot them on individually to produce sturdy plants for planting out in early summer.

These beautiful plants have multi-coloured blossoms, which are often attractively splashed and spotted with red or maroon. Soft green succulent foliage provides a perfect foil for the exotic looking flowers. Although they are technically perennials, Monarch Strain and other similar colour mixtures are best raised annually from seed. Overwintered plants do not seem to perform as well in their second year.

Onoclea sensibilis
Sensitive Fern

Height: 45-60cm (18-24in)
Situation: Full sun or partial shade
Propagation: By lifting the creeping mat of black rhizomes during spring and separating vigorous young pieces of rhizome with the fronds just emerging. Plant immediately in their permanent positions.

This is a particularly fine fern for the streamside, since it will tolerate standing in water as well as growing in average moist soil conditions. The fronds are erect and flattened, having a rose-pink flush in spring. Eventually, this fades to leave beautiful, pale green fronds. In favourable conditions, this fern will spread quite rapidly.

Osmunda regalis
Royal Fern

Height: 120-180cm (48-72in)
Situation: Full sun or partial shade
Propagation: By division during the winter dormant period, which is the most reliable method of propagation. However, it is also possible to raise osmundas from spores, although this is quite difficult for the home gardener, as the spores have a very short viability and require quite carefully controlled conditions.

A very regal fern with large leathery fronds that start off bright green in the spring, darken through the summer months, and in autumn turn a burnished bronze. Although this fern is perfectly hardy, most gardeners protect the emerging fronds from frost during early spring with a covering of faded fronds or straw. Although ferns do not produce flowers, the royal fern does have central, spike-like fruiting fronds.

Primula alpicola
Moonlight Primula

Height: 15-60cm (6-24in)
Situation: Full sun or partial shade
Flowering time: Early summer
Propagation: Occasionally, this primula can be divided successfully during early spring, if a number of clearly identifiable separate crowns are in evidence. If not, it is best left undisturbed. Seed should be sown as soon as ripe, in a good seed compost with the protection of a cold frame. Young plants should be grown on in pots until ready to be planted out in the early spring.

A charming plant with pendent, bell shaped blossoms that are typically pale yellow, although there are bright yellow, white and purple forms, too. They are carried on slender stems among bright green rounded leaves. A plant for a cool damp part of the bog garden. It does not relish standing in water.

Primula aurantiaca

Height: 60-90cm (24-36in)
Situation: Full sun or partial shade
Flowering time: Early summer
Propagation: By sowing seed, immediately it ripens, in a good seed compost with the protection of a cold frame. Grow the young plants on in pots until ready for planting out in their permanent positions during the following spring. Established plants can also be divided during early spring.

A candelabra primula with bright reddish-orange blossoms. The leaves are green, long and rather coarse with a very distinctive aroma. This plant enjoys a richly-organic soil.

Primula beesiana

Height: 60-75cm (24-30in)
Situation: Full sun or partial shade
Flowering time: Early summer
Propagation: By sowing seed, immediately it ripens, in a good seed compost with the protection of a cold frame. Grow the young plants on in pots until ready for planting out in their permanent positions during the following spring. Established plants can also be divided during early spring.

Large, rosy-carmine flowers, each with a yellow eye, are produced in dense tiered whorls on strong stalks. The large, broad green leaves can often reach 30cm (12in) long. *Primula beesiana* prefers a cool spot with richly-organic soil.

Primula denticulata
Drumstick Primula

Height: 30-60cm (12-24in)
Situation: Sun or partial shade
Flowering time: Spring
Propagation: By sowing seed, immediately it ripens, in a good seed compost in a cold frame. Grow on in pots until ready for planting out in the autumn. Established plants can also be divided as they emerge during early spring, or immediately after flowering. Root cuttings can be taken during the winter and started in a cold frame.

This well-known primula is often grown in the herbaceous border, although it only fulfils its potential if given the constant moisture of a bog garden. Large globular heads of lilac, pink or purplish blossoms are borne on stout stems. The leaves are green, large and coarse, sometimes coated beneath with a yellow or white meal that often extends up the flower stems. There is also a white form, *P. denticulata* var. *alba*.

Primula florindae
Himalayan Cowslip

Height: 60-90cm (24-36in)
Situation: Full sun or partial shade
Flowering time: Summer
Propagation: By division of established plants during the early spring, just as the leafy shoots are emerging. Alternatively, by sowing seed, as soon as it ripens, in a good seed compost in a cold frame. Grow the young plants on in pots until ready for planting out in their permanent positions in spring.

A large, striking bog garden plant that will also grow satisfactorily in standing water or waterlogged conditions. Large heads of pendent, soft yellow flowers are produced on strong stems above clumps of coarse, green, strongly-aromatic leaves. This is a very hardy plant that is perfect for streamside planting.

Primula japonica

Height: 45-75cm (18-30in)
Situation: Full sun or partial shade
Flowering time: Early summer
Propagation: By division of established plants during the early spring, just as the leafy shoots are emerging. Alternatively, by sowing seed, as soon as it ripens, in a good seed compost in a cold frame. Grow the young plants on in pots until ready for planting out in their permanent positions in spring.

A strong growing primula with candelabra heads of deep red flowers on very stout stems. These arise from clumps of light green, cabbage-like leaves. A first-class bog garden plant that is also available in deep crimson, 'Miller's Crimson', and white with an orange-yellow eye, 'Postford White'.

Primula vialii
Orchid Primula

Height: 30-45cm (12-18in)
Situation: Full sun or partial shade
Flowering time: Early summer
Propagation: By sowing seed, immediately it ripens, in a tray or pan of good seed compost in a cold frame. Grow the young plants on in pots until ready for planting out in their permanent positions in the spring.

This is a remarkable plant that, at first sight, does not look much like a primula. Short stems support dense heads of small tubular flowers of red and bluish purple. These exotic looking blossoms emerge from among tufts of small, lance shaped, downy green leaves. Unfortunately, this is not a long lived plant, and it requires regular replacement. While enjoying moist soil, it does not relish waterlogged conditions.

Rheum palmatum
Ornamental Rhubarb

Height: 150-180cm (60-72in)
Situation: Full sun or partial shade
Flowering time: Summer
Propagation: By division of the large knobbly crowns during the dormant period, planting them in their permanent positions immediately.

Rheum palmatum is a wonderful architectural plant with broad spreading foliage and tall spikes of small, creamy-white flowers. There is a beautiful crimson-flowered cultivar, 'Bowles' Crimson', that has foliage with a purplish infusion. A cut-leaved variety, *R.p.* var. *tanguticum*, also has the same purplish hue.

Rodgersia tabularis

Height: 90-120cm (36-48in)
Situation: Full sun or partial shade
Flowering time: Summer
Propagation: By division of established plants during early spring, just before growth begins, planting the divisions in their permanent positions immediately.

The most interesting of the rodgersias, and the best for the bog garden, *Rodgersia tabularis* has pale green circular leaves held aloft on stout stalks. These are accompanied by dense panicles of creamy-white flowers. This plant loves really damp soil, but will not tolerate waterlogged conditions.

Trollius x *cultorum* 'Golden Queen'
Globe Flower

Height: 30-45cm (12-18in)
Situation: Full sun
Flowering time: Spring
Propagation: By division of established plants during the winter dormant period, planting the divisions in their permanent positions immediately.

Attractive, globular, buttercup-like flowers of rich golden-yellow are produced on strong wiry stems above compact mounds of finely-toothed foliage. There are several comparable cultivars in other shades, such as the reddish-orange 'Fireglobe', orange 'Orange Globe', and the canary-yellow 'Earliest of All'.

Cornus alba 'Sibirica'
Westonbirt Dogwood

Height: 90-120cm (36-48in)
Situation: Full sun or partial shade
Flowering time: Late spring or early summer. However, the flowers are not important; this plant is grown for its brightly coloured winter stems.
Propagation: By taking hardwood cuttings during the winter dormant period and rooting them in a cold frame, or in good soil in a sheltered position outdoors.

A handsome shrub that is grown for its winter colour. When cut back regularly, it produces naked winter stems of the most startling crimson-red. Enjoying damp boggy conditions, this most useful of waterside shrubs also produces small flat heads of creamy blossoms and has dull green foliage, which turns coppery-red during autumn.

Cornus alba 'Spaethii'

Height: 90-120cm (36-48in)
Situation: Full sun or partial shade
Flowering time: Spring or early summer. Sometimes the flowers are removed, as they detract from the variegated foliage. The plant is also grown for its coloured winter stems.
Propagation: By taking hardwood cuttings during the winter and rooting them in a cold frame, or in good soil in a sheltered position outdoors.

Like *Cornus alba* 'Sibirica', this thicket forming shrub has excellent bright red winter stems. However, instead of plain green leaves, the foliage is beautifully variegated in green and gold. It provides colour and interest throughout the year, enjoying damp boggy conditions, but not standing water.

Cornus stolonifera 'Flaviramea'

Height: 90-120cm (36-48in)
Situation: Full sun or partial shade
Flowering time: Late spring or early summer. However, the flowers are not important; this plant is grown for its brightly coloured winter stems.
Propagation: By taking hardwood cuttings during the winter dormant period and rooting them in a cold frame, or in good soil in a sheltered position outdoors.

This shrub makes an excellent complement to the bright-red-stemmed cornus. During the winter, when regular pruning and stooling take place, its naked stems are a striking yellow. The leaves are plain green, but colour at the approach of autumn, while the creamy-white flowers rarely appear if the plant is stooled. *Cornus stolonifera* 'Flaviramea' enjoys constantly damp soil.

Salix alba 'Chermesina'
Scarlet Willow

Height: 120-150cm (48-60in) if pruned annually
Situation: Full sun or partial shade
Propagation: By taking hardwood cuttings during the winter dormant period and inserting them into a good, friable soil in a sheltered part of the garden.

This lovely, reliable garden willow enjoys wet conditions. When stooled regularly, it is as versatile and colourful as the dogwoods. Vivid orange-red winter stems are followed by grey-green, lance shaped foliage. Cut to within a few centimetres of the base each spring, just as the stems begin to shoot. Stems that are older than a season do not retain the quality and colour of annually pruned growth. The same applies to the golden willow, *Salix alba* 'Vitellina'.

Taxodium distichum
Swamp Cypress

Height: To 20m (65ft)
Situation: Full sun
Propagation: By sowing seed during spring or early summer, in a soil-based compost in a cold frame, the plants being grown on in pots until the following season. Summer cuttings root fairly readily in a propagator, using equal parts peat and sand, or peat and perlite.

When mature, this splendid deciduous conifer is only suited to a large garden, but when young, it can be used for several years to provide interest in a small garden before removal. Of loose pyramidal habit, it has light green foliage that turns russet as autumn approaches. The trunk has a very fibrous bark, while the young branches are orange-brown and very attractive when lit by the winter sun. Unlike other conifers, this example will grow in standing water and on very wet land.

Vaccinium corymbosum
Swamp Blueberry

Height: 90-150cm (36-60in)
Situation: Full sun
Flowering time: Late spring
Propagation: By taking short cuttings with a heel during spring or autumn, and rooting them in a mixture of peat and sharp sand in a cold frame.

A dense-growing shrub with lance shaped or oval green leaves, which turn fiery scarlet or bronze during the autumn. The flowers are white or pale pink and are followed by large black fruits. This plant enjoys wet conditions, but must have an acid soil.

Althaea officinalis
Marsh Mallow

Height: 30-150cm (12-60in)
Situation: Full sun
Flowering time: Summer
Propagation: Easily raised from seed sown during spring or early summer, using a good seed compost in trays in a cold frame. Prick out seedlings into individual pots for growing on in a frame and plant out during late summer or early autumn.

This is a showy plant that is related to the garden hollyhock, having similar flowers and foliage, but on a much smaller scale. The flowers are somewhat rounded and flat, with bright pink petals, and are borne in irregular spikes among small leaves. The lower part of the plant is bushy with broad green leaves that are similar to those of a maple.

Fritillaria meleagris
Snake's Head Fritillary

Height: 15-30cm (6-12in)
Situation: Full sun
Flowering time: Late spring
Propagation: By lifting and dividing established clumps of bulbs every five or six years and replanting them. Seed sown immediately it ripens, in a soil-based seed compost, will germinate freely in a cold frame. The seedlings can be carefully pricked out, but will probably need another 12-18 months before being robust enough to be planted out in their permanent positions.

A small bulbous plant with narrow, blue-green leaves and attractive, pendent, bell-like flowers, which have a chequered pattern. The common species is a variable purple, but often white- or creamy-flowered forms appear. *Fritillaria meleagris* naturalizes well in grass, and usually seeds itself freely when flowering happily.

Geum rivale
Water Avens

Height: 10-30cm (4-12in)
Situation: Full sun
Flowering time: Summer
Propagation: By sowing seed during the summer, in trays of a good soil-based compost in a cold frame. Prick out seedlings into trays or individual pots and grow on in a frame for planting in their permanent positions in late summer or early autumn.

Geum rivale is an easy-going perennial with large, rough, rounded green leaves borne in tight clumps. Short, stout flower stems carry up to three charming nodding blossoms in shades of orange and pink.

Leucojum aestivum
Summer Snowflake

Height: 60-90cm (24-36in)
Situation: Full sun
Flowering time: Late spring and early summer
Propagation: By division of established bulbs immediately after flowering, and replanting them in their permanent positions without allowing them to dry out.

This is one of the few bulbs that enjoy very wet conditions. Although naturally a plant of the water meadow, it is usually found growing wild in grass at the streamside, rather than out in the meadow. Dark green, strap-like leaves surround slender stems bearing pendent heads of beautiful white blossoms, each petal being tipped with green. The individual blossoms look rather like small light shades.

Lotus uliginosus
Marsh Bird's Foot Trefoil

Height: 15-20cm (6-8in), but stems may trail to 120cm (48in)
Situation: Full sun
Flowering time: Summer
Propagation: By sowing seeds during the summer, in trays of a good seed compost in a cold frame. As soon as the seedlings germinate, prick them out into small pots for growing on, as they resent root disturbance.

Although an untidy scrambling plant, *Lotus uliginosus* is quite charming when grown among grass. It has a tough stoloniferous rootstock and spreads freely, producing trifoliate leaves and heads of yellow flowers on short wiry stems. The flowers are often tinged with red, and are followed by narrow fruits rather like tiny pea pods.

Lychnis flos-cuculi
Ragged Robin

Height: 23-50cm (9-20in)
Situation: Full sun
Flowering time: Summer
Propagation: By sowing seed during the summer, in trays of a good soil-based compost in a cold frame. Prick out seedlings into trays or individual pots, and grow on in a frame for planting in their permanent positions in late summer or early autumn.

A tough hardy perennial with narrow, green basal leaves and strong, wiry flower stems that bear starry and somewhat spidery red flowers arranged in loose groups. This plant grows well and looks its best in a grassy sward.

Nymphaea 'Aviator Pring'

Depth: 45-75cm (18-30in)
Spread: 75-150cm (18-60in)
Situation: Full sun
Flowering time: Summer
Propagation: By retaining young tubers and separating young plantlets in early spring.

This is a big, bold, day blooming waterlily with bright yellow, star-like blossoms held well above the water. The large, green toothed leaves have distinctive wavy margins.

Nymphaea 'Aviator Pring' can only be grown outside successfully during the summer when there is a consistent temperature of 24°C (75°F).

Nymphaea 'Blue Beauty'

Depth: 45-90cm (18-36in)
Spread: 90-150cm (36-60in)
Situation: Full sun
Flowering time: Summer
Propagation: By retaining young tubers and separating young plantlets in early spring.

One of the most popular day blooming tropical waterlilies, *Nymphaea* 'Blue Beauty' has fragrant, deep blue flowers, each with a central boss of golden stamens. The sepals are clearly spotted with black, while the large, rounded green leaves have brown surface freckling and purplish-green undersides. This waterlily can only be grown outside successfully in summer when there is a consistent temperature of 24°C (75°F).

Nymphaea x *daubenyana*

Depth: 15cm (6in)
Spread: 30-45cm (12-18in)
Situation: Full sun
Flowering time: Summer
Propagation: By retaining young tubers and separating young plantlets in early spring.

A fascinating, day blooming tub plant with small blue blossoms, rarely more than 5cm (2in) across. These have a spicy scent. The narrow petals have a greenish flush and surround a group of bright yellow stamens. The leaves may be oval or roughly arrow shaped, and are brownish green with chocolate splashes. A consistent temperature of around 19°C (66°F) is necessary to ensure successful flowering.

Nymphaea 'Emily Grant Hutchings'

Depth: 45-75cm (18-30in)
Spread: 75-150cm (18-60in)
Situation: Full sun
Flowering time: Summer
Propagation: By retaining young tubers and separating young plantlets in early spring.

This is one of the easiest night blooming waterlilies to flower in cooler climates under glass. In warm summer conditions, it is also very successful in the open. Large, deep pinkish-red blooms have deep amaranth stamens, which become rich mahogany with age. The sepals and foliage are green with a bronzed-crimson overlay. This plant requires a consistent summer temperature of 19°C (66°F) to flower successfully.

Nymphaea 'Panama Pacific'

Depth: 45-75cm (18-30in)
Spread: 75-150cm (30-60in)
Situation: Full sun
Flowering time: Summer
Propagation: By retaining young tubers and separating young plantlets in early spring.

A magnificent day blooming plant with large blossoms that open purplish-blue, but turn rich reddish-purple when fully expanded, and have golden stamens with violet anthers. The large rounded leaves are bronze-green with reddish veins. This is one of the hardier tropical waterlilies, but it still requires a consistent temperature of 19°C (66°F) to flower successfully.

Nymphaea 'Red Flare'

Depth: 45-75cm (18-30in)
Spread: 75-150cm (30-60in)
Situation: Full sun
Flowering time: Summer
Propagation: By retaining young tubers and separating young plantlets in early spring.

Nymphaea 'Red Flare' is a classic night blooming waterlily. It produces highly-fragrant, intense red, star-like blossoms, which are carried above the deep mahogany foliage. This tropical waterlily requires a consistent summer temperature of 25°C (77°F) if it is to flower successfully.

Nelumbo 'Baby Doll'

Depth: 45-75cm (18-30in)
Height: 90-150cm (36-60in)
Situation: Full sun
Flowering time: Summer
Propagation: By careful division of established clumps of the fleshy rootstock, these being replanted immediately in their permanent positions.

This lovely hybrid was developed in the United States. Silky white single blossoms are produced among handsome blue-green plate-like foliage on short stout stems.

This is a useful plant for a more exposed situation and makes an excellent addition to a tub garden, enjoying life in a raised container on a deck or terrace.

Nelumbo lutea

(Syn. *Nelumbo pentapetala*) Water Chinkapin

Depth: 45-75cm (18-30in)
Height: 90-120cm (36-48in)
Situation: Full sun
Flowering time: Summer
Propagation: By sowing seed in spring, in individual pots of soil-based seed compost, and just covering them with water in an aquarium. A temperature of 15°C (60°F) will ensure germination. Grow on until ready to plant out. Alternatively, divide and separate the banana-like rootstocks in spring.

An excellent plant for an indoor pool, being of modest size. Where the summer temperature remains around 24°C (75°F) for two or three months, it will grow outdoors. Large leaves, up to 60cm (24in) across, are borne on tall stems. The pale sulphur flowers are no more than 20cm (8in) across. A slightly smaller-flowered variety, *N. lutea* 'Flavescens', has a red spot at the base of each petal and in the centre of each leaf.

Nelumbo 'Momo Botan'

Depth: 15-45cm (6-18in)
Height: 45-75cm (18-30in)
Situation: Full sun
Flowering time: Summer
Propagation: By careful division of established clumps of the fleshy rootstock, these being replanted immediately in their permanent positions.

Nelumbo 'Momo Botan' is one of the shorter-growing forms of lotus. These are excellent for use in a tub or half-barrel, either under glass or, if the summer is hot (above 24°C/75°F), outside. The fully-double carmine blossoms are borne among bluish-green, plate-like leaves, which are held well above the water on strong stalks.

Nelumbo 'Mrs Perry D. Slocum'

Depth: 45-75cm (18-30in)
Height: 150-180cm (60-72in)
Situation: Full sun
Flowering time: Summer
Propagation: By careful division of established plants, separating the banana-like rootstocks and replanting them immediately in their permanent positions.

One of the most spectacular of the lotus cultivars, this plant produces large, fully-double flowers, up to 30cm (12in) across, which open rose-pink, but pass to creamy-yellow as they age. Bold, blue-green, plate-like foliage is held aloft on very strong leaf stalks. This is a really large plant that demands plenty of space.

Nelumbo nucifera
East Indian Lotus, Sacred Lotus

Depth: 45-75cm (18-30in)
Height: 180-240cm (72-96in)
Situation: Full sun
Flowering time: Summer
Propagation: By sowing seed in spring, in individual pots of soil-based seed compost, and just covering them with water in an aquarium. A temperature of 15°C (60°F) will ensure germination. Grow on until ready to plant out. Alternatively, divide and separate the banana-like rootstocks in spring.

In cool areas, this magnificent plant must be grown under glass; it will only thrive outside where the summer temperature is at least 24°C (75°F) for long periods and the light values are good. The large rounded leaves are held well above the water on strong stems. The blooms may reach 30cm (12in) across and change from deep rose-pink to flesh-pink with age. They are followed by decorative, pepper-pot-like seedheads.

Nelumbo nucifera 'Alba Grandiflora'

Depth: 15cm (6in)
Height: 30cm (12in)
Situation: Full sun
Flowering time: Summer
Propagation: By carefully lifting and dividing the creeping fleshy rootstock, replanting the divisions immediately in their permanent positions.

The finest large flowered traditional white lotus and widely planted in large pools in warm climates. Not well suited to greenhouse cultivation because of its stature.

Handsome bluish-green plate-like leaves, often with crimpled edges, are produced on strong stout stems. An old variety with its origins shrouded in mystery.

Acorus gramineus 'Variegatus'

Depth: To 10cm (4in)
Height: 35cm (14in)
Situation: Full sun
Propagation: By division of established plants during spring and early autumn.

Acorus gramineus 'Variegatus' is a semi-evergreen variegated plant with leaves rather like a small iris. It also grows in a similar fashion to an iris. The foliage is strikingly marked in green and cream. This plant will tolerate a little frost, but is best when grown in sub-tropical conditions with a minimum temperature of 13°C (55°F).

Colocasia esculenta 'Fontanesii'

Depth: To 30cm (12in)
Height: 90-100cm (36-40in)
Situation: Full sun or partial shade
Flowering time: Summer, but grown mainly for its foliage
Propagation: By division of tubers if the plants are lifted during the autumn, or just before coming into growth in the spring.

This is a very fine cultivar of the taro, having large, heart shaped, plain green leaves with dark green margins and veins. Under warm well-lit conditions, this plant will continue to grow throughout the year. The ideal temperature for year-round growth is 18°C (65°F). In cooler, but frost-free, conditions, it becomes dormant during the winter, and the tubers can be stored in sand.

Colocasia esculenta 'Illustris'

Depth: To 30cm (12in)
Height: 90-100cm (36-40in)
Situation: Full sun or partial shade
Flowering time: Summer, but mainly grown for its foliage.
Propagation: By division of tubers if the plants are lifted during the autumn, or just before coming into growth in the spring.

Another fine cultivar of the taro. Its large, heart shaped, dark green leaves are spotted with purple, while the leaf stems are vivid violet. Under warm well-lit conditions, this plant will continue to grow all year round. The ideal temperature for year-round growth is 18°C (65°F). In cooler, but frost-free, conditions, it becomes dormant during the winter, and the tubers can be stored in sand.

Cyperus haspan

Depth: To 15cm (6in)
Height: 60-90cm (24-36in)
Situation: Full sun or partial shade
Flowering time: Summer, but the flowers are insignificant
Propagation: By division of clumps of established plants during the active growing season.

A miniature version of the famous Egyptian papyrus, *Cyperus haspan* is an elegant plant with strong stems that support umbrella-like heads of very fine, bright green foliage. In warm conditions, this plant is reliably evergreen.

Thalia dealbata

Depth: To 60cm (24in)
Height: 120-150cm (48-60in)
Flowering time: Summer
Propagation: By division in early spring, or by sowing seed immediately it ripens. Place individual seeds, which are rather like brown peas, in pots of a soil-based compost standing in water up to the pot rim. If sown during the late summer, these may not germinate until the spring. The young plants can be planted during summer.

This large canna- or banana-like plant has leaves with long stalks and green oval blades rather like paddles. These have a natural white mealy covering. The violet blossoms are produced on a slender, long, wand-like stem. This quite spectacular plant is easily grown.

Zantedeschia aethiopica
White Arum Lily

Depth: To 30cm (12in)
Height: 60-120cm (24-48in)
Situation: Full sun
Flowering time: Spring and summer
Propagation: By lifting and dividing the tuberous roots during the dormant period, or by dividing growing plants early in the season.

The white arum lily is a striking plant with bold, heart shaped, bright green leaves and beautiful white spathes, each with a central yellow spadix. This has long been a popular plant, its blooms being widely used as cut flowers. The cultivar 'Crowborough' is tougher, but smaller, and well suited to garden use where it may be at risk of several degrees of frost.

Bacopa caroliniana

Depth: To 45cm (18in)
Situation: Full sun
Flowering time: Summer
Propagation: By taking stem cuttings when the plant is in active growth.

Bacopa caroliniana is an excellent, easy-going, scrambling submerged aquatic with pale green succulent foliage. The flowers are pale blue, but often they are not produced if the plant is grown in deep water.

Ceratopteris thalictroides
Floating Fern

Situation: Full sun or partial shade
Propagation: By removing the plantlets that develop on the edges of the leaves.

Although a floating plant, this species may occasionally root and grow as a submerged plant, unlike the almost identical *Ceratopteris pteridioides*. The attractive, soft green, heart or lance shaped foliage is arranged almost like a rosette.

Egeria densa
(Syn *Elodea densa*)

Depth: To 90cm (36in)
Situation: Sun or partial shade
Propagation: By taking short stem cuttings during the active growing season, fastening them together in small bunches with lead strips and placing them in their permanent positions.

This plant is very similar in appearance to the popular hardy submerged aquatic, *Lagarosiphon major*. Its dark green crispy leaflets are borne in dense whorls around strong green stems. *Egeria densa* is an aquatic that is much prized by fish keepers for its food value.

Eichhornia crassipes
Water Hyacinth

Situation: Full sun
Flowering time: Summer
Propagation: By removing the young plants that are produced on runners during the summer months. In areas where the plants cannot remain outside because of frost, these young plants should be overwintered; do not retain the old plants. Place fresh young stock in pans of mud, rather than allowing them to float in the water. They will survive low (but frost-free) temperatures and burst into growth in the spring.

This lovely floating plant has dark green shiny leaves with inflated bases that are honeycombed to give the plant buoyancy. From among this unusual foliage are produced strong spikes of blue and lilac blossoms, each with a peacock eye. *Eichhomia crassipes* is the best of the tender floating aquatic plants.

Pistia stratiotes
Water Lettuce

Situation: Full sun
Flowering time: Summer, but the flowers are insignificant
Propagation: By separating the young plantlets from the parent plant during the summer growing season.

This is a strange, but attractive, member of the arum family. It produces small green spathes among bold rosettes of downy, soft green foliage, which looks rather like a lettuce.

Vallisneria spiralis
Tape Grass

Depth: To 90cm (36in)
Situation: Full sun or partial shade
Propagation: By division of the rooted plantlets, which will spread freely during the active growing season.

A beautiful foliage plant with narrow, tape-like, translucent green leaves in clumps, although it does creep and eventually forms an extensive colony. The cultivar *Vallisneria spiralis* 'Torta' has leaves that are twisted like a corkscrew, while *V. gigantea* is a giant that will grow in water up to 120cm (48in) deep and has much broader leaves.

FISH

CHOOSING FISH

While plants make the major contribution to the appearance of the water garden, fish bring it to life. They also play an important part in the ecology of the pool, feeding on aquatic insect life and depositing detritus which, ultimately, will benefit the plants.

THE ROLE OF FISH

For the practical water gardener, the most important role for decorative pond fish is the control of mosquito larvae and damaging aquatic insect pests, such as caddis fly larvae. Even if you have no particular liking of fish or inclination to keep them, you should consider them carefully as an essential part of the biology of the aquatic environment.

In the pool, submerged aquatic plants in the presence of sunlight absorb the carbonic acid gas produced by fish and other aquatic fauna. Aided by the green chlorophyll in their leaves, the plants convert this into nourishment and, in the process, produce oxygen, which is dispersed into the water for the benefit of the fish. Therefore, for the well-being of a water garden, it is desirable to have reasonable and balanced quantities of both fish and plants.

Fish are an essential part of any water garden. Many pool owners make them a priority and, unfortunately, sometimes produce conditions in which plant life finds it difficult to survive.

Apart from the obvious ecological benefits of having fish in the pool, there are aesthetic ones, too. Watching colourful goldfish lazing in the sun or dashing among the floating foliage of waterlilies can be very therapeutic. The antics of the more lively characters like golden orfe, leaping for flies or playing in the spray of a fountain or the turbulent waters beneath a waterfall, are equally pleasurable, while the ritual of feeding can become compelling entertainment. After a period of feeding fish from one particular point at the pool edge, they will appear at the surface in response merely to a footfall or a shadow cast across the water.

WHICH FISH WILL LIVE TOGETHER?

One of the most troubling aspects of stocking a pool is selecting the fish.

Newcomers always seem to have heard horror stories of fish eating fish, and are fearful of an almighty power struggle in the pool if the inhabitants are not chosen with extreme care. In reality, however, there are few rules to worry about when it comes to choosing particular sizes or varieties, though it is probably a good

A BALANCED COMMUNITY

Careful observation of any pool will reveal that fish of various kinds occupy different zones. So-called scavenging fish live in the lower reaches of the pool and are rarely seen, although they will be performing a very useful function by cleaning up uneaten goldfish food and preying on troublesome aquatic insect pests. When selecting suitable scavengers, bear in mind that as you are unlikely to see them again until you clean out the pool, it is pointless introducing the more expensive and attractive golden tench when the common green species is perfectly adequate.

Goldfish and the various carp are middle-zone fish, for the most part swimming around in the central layer of the water, but because of their bright colouration being clearly seen. They are given to basking in the sun or, in very hot weather, seeking the shade of aquatic floating foliage, so they are very visible. This is particularly apparent when they are fed and come swimming around just beneath the surface of the water. Golden and silver orfe are essentially surface fish, being highly visible and swimming in shoals just beneath the surface of the water. Rudd will also make a similar appearance, but being of duller colouration are not so pleasing on the eye.

idea to steer clear of the various cold-water catfish.

Several species of 'catfish' are sold for ponds, and while all are innocuous when young, on attaining maturity they can cause carnage in the pool. They begin their lives eating aquatic insect life and snails, but end up eating fish fry and tearing at the tails and flowing fins of fancy goldfish. Even the common goldfish and shubunkins are not completely immune to their attentions. If introduced to the pool, they will lurk on the floor or among the submerged plants and be almost impossible to recapture unless the pool is emptied, so steer clear of these fascinating, but destructive, fish.

All the other fish will co-exist quite happily. It is true that an adult fish will eat spawn and sometimes small fry, but any fish over 5cm (2in) long should be completely safe from predation. This applies to all the carp family, including goldfish, shubunkins and tench.

All traditional domestic goldfish are suitable for an outdoor pool. There is a common misconception that the goldfish of the bowl or aquarium is, in some way, different from that of the garden pool. While size may play a part in this misunderstanding, in fact they are the same. A goldfish kept in a bowl may remain small, but that is because of the confines of the bowl. Once introduced to the garden pool, goldfish will soon grow and, irrespective of their size, will mix happily with their cousins.

WHEN TO INTRODUCE FISH

Most new pond owners will want to introduce fish to the pool quite quickly, especially if being pressured by children. However, resist adding fish to a new pool for at least a month after planting the last plants. They really need time to become established, even if you are only going to introduce small fish. These can still be extremely boisterous and may disturb freshly planted plants, especially submerged aquatics, as they dig in the substrate looking for food, or tug at tender new growth. Once plants have been disturbed, it is very difficult to re-establish them without emptying the pool and replanting the baskets. The deposit of soil or compost from the disrupted planting baskets will swirl continuously in the water as the fish dart about and dig for food, leaving a debilitating deposit on the foliage of submerged plants. So be patient and let the plants become properly established before choosing fish. Ideally, you should add only two or three at a time at approximately fortnightly intervals.

While there is a great temptation to introduce fish to the pool immediately it is filled with water, it is prudent to wait until the plants have become well established. The chances of disruption to either the plants or containers is then greatly reduced.

CHOOSING YOUR RETAILER

These days, the most common method of purchasing fish is by visiting an aquatics specialist or garden centre. It is as important to choose a good retailer as it is healthy and contented fish. Obviously, one goes with the other, but if you are buying fish for the first time, you may not necessarily recognize the most suitable establishment. If you have any doubts about where to purchase fish, visit a number of outlets. You may find considerable differences in housing methods, hygiene and price, the latter not necessarily being related to either of the former.

Most retailers of pond fish keep them in large fibreglass or plastic tanks or aquaria, the individual fish being graded according to size and variety. Often large numbers of fish are kept in relatively crowded conditions. Modern filtration and husbandry techniques ensure that the water quality is ideal and does not adversely affect the fish. Avoid buying fish from retailers where you have observed numbers of dead or unhealthy fish. Although you can select healthy looking fish from such tanks, they may be carrying disease organisms that can pass to your own collection.

Perhaps the most important factor to consider when selecting a retailer is his or her knowledge. This can be invaluable and will help you to choose the right foods, treatments and plants, as well as the right fish.

QUICK-REFERENCE GUIDE TO BUYING FISH

- Visit a number of retailers, comparing housing methods, hygiene and price
- Ask the retailer how long he has had the fish and avoid recent arrivals
- Look for erect fins and bright eyes; avoid small fish and those with scale damage
- Avoid lethargic fish and those that appear extremely lively
- Avoid fish displaying small white spots on fins and tails
- Avoid fish with unusually shaped bodies or unnatural (or very bright) colours

THE GUIDING PRINCIPLE

The majority of decorative pond fish sold for domestic use are imported. While some are bred in Italy, Germany and the UK, and considerable quantities raised in the United States, the leading producers are the Far East and Israel. The fact that they may have come from tropical climates does not have any effect upon their hardiness or suitability for the outdoor pool. However, it is worth asking how long they have been in the country, as a journey half-way around the world can be very stressful.

If the retailer has had the fish in stock for a week or more, they will probably be fine. Sometimes their body colour will give an indication of the amount of time spent with the retailer, especially in the case of goldfish and shubunkins. Usually, the brighter the colour, the more recent the stock. Always favour a pale red or salmon coloured goldfish, rather than one that is brilliant red, as the paler ones are likely to have been with the vendor longer, which means that they will have had time to become established and, therefore, are less likely to be troubled by their journey home with you.

It is preferable to select your fish personally from an aquatics specialist or the garden centre rather than to send by mail order. Modern filtration methods and techniques of storing fish mean that quite large numbers can be displayed together.

QUARANTINING NEW ARRIVALS

It is always a wise precaution to adopt some simple quarantine arrangements when introducing new fish. A small pond or aquarium, kept in a cool spot and ideally without any plants, makes an ideal quarantine tank. Plants tend to create problems when the fish are netted, and in some cases, if not handled carefully, can carry over various pests and diseases.

Treat all new fish with a precautionary dip in a general anti-parasitic medication. Observe the fish carefully for a period of three or four weeks. If disease is present, it will probably appear during this period, as the warmer spring and summer weather arrives, and should be treated with a proprietary treatment. You should also monitor the water quality in the quarantine tank with suitable test kits.

Many water gardeners merely place the fish directly into the main pool when they bring them home and experience few problems. In most cases, if you have carefully chosen your retailer and checked any fish for signs of ill-health or damage before purchasing them, they will be alright. However, if you have very special or expensive fish in your pool already, the inconvenience of quarantine is unquestionably worthwhile.

SELECTING INDIVIDUALS

There are certain principles that apply to selecting any healthy fish. Erect fins and bright eyes are the best indicators of good health, together with an absence of scale damage. Occasionally, large fish will lose a scale or two while being transported, but smaller fish should be intact. Do not worry too much if you buy a large fish that is missing some scales. Eventually, these will be replaced, and provided you treat the pool with a commercial fungus treatment, there is unlikely to be any secondary infection.

If the fish you are considering look very lively, this is not necessarily a sign of good health. Exceptionally lively antics, such as rubbing against underwater objects or jumping out of the water, may indicate that the fish is being irritated by an external fish parasite or that water conditions are poor.

Lethargic fish should be avoided, particularly those that sulk on the bottom of the container or remain isolated from the others. You should also avoid individuals that display small spots on the fins or tails. These are often associated with the disease called white spot which, unfortunately, is not uncommon in fish that are kept in crowded conditions, even though most responsible retailers maintain a regular treatment regime and are constantly vigilant. White spot disease is not a welcome ailment in any water garden, even though it can be controlled. However, do not confuse the white nuptial tubercles of mature adult male fish with this disease. The tubercles are white, measle-like spots that occuron the gills and head, and are particularly pronounced in male goldfish and shubunkins..

The shape, size and colour of the fish you select are very much a matter of personal choice. Avoid any fish with uncharacteristic shapes, such as carp that have larger than normal heads and tench with almost black bodies and a propensity to swim just beneath the surface of the water.

HOW TO INTRODUCE FISH

The important point to consider when introducing fish is the difference in temperature between the water in the bag and that in the pool. Usually, the water in the bag will be much warmer, and tipping the fish out into cold water can stress them, leaving them susceptible to disease.

It is important, therefore, to float the bag on the surface of the pool for 20-25 minutes before releasing the fish. If you leave the bag fastened with its rubber band while you do this, observe the fish carefully; the sun shining brightly on it can make the temperature inside soar in a matter of minutes, so the bag should be opened and the top of rolled down to make a float. Where possible, float the bag in a shaded area of the pool. Once you are satisfied that the water temperature has equalized, gradually add some of the pool water to the bag to equalise the chemical differences between your pool water and the water from your dealer, and then gently pour the contents of the bag into the pool.

On their release, the fish may well swim to the bottom of the pool and be reluctant to feed for several days, but don't worry – this is normal behaviour due only to the fact that the fish are not confident in their new surroundings.

Before introducing fish to your pond, acclimatize them to the new water temperature by floating the bag on the pool for 20 minutes.

Carp

Cyprinus carpio, *Carassius carassius* and varieties

Length: Up to 60cm (24in)
Conditions: Outdoor pool

The common carp and its varieties, such as the mirror, leather, crucian and Prussian carp, are only suitable for medium- and large-sized ponds; they tend to stir up the compost and plants in small pools. Ideal for the wildlife pond, they are chubby meaty fish with deep bodies, evenly-distributed fins and narrow tapering heads. All have strong lips and four pendent barbels.

The mirror and leather carp have distinctive dark silvery-grey bodies, which have only a partial or irregular covering of scales. The colour of crucian and Prussian carp, however, ranges from chocolate bronze to brown, and both fish are covered completely in scales.

Catfish

Ameiurus nebulosus, *Silurus glanis* and *Ictalyrus nebulosus*

Length: Up to 45cm (18in)
Conditions: Outdoor pool

There are certainly two, and occasionally three, different species that are sold as cold-water catfish: the horned pout (*Ameiurus nebulosus*), the wels or waller (*Silurus glanis*) and the brown bullhead (*Ictalyrus nebulosus*). All are superficially similar, having long barbels or whiskers. They prey upon aquatic insects while small, but graduate to tormenting young and fancy fish as they mature. None can be unreservedly recommended for the garden pool, although it is possible to keep them in a large tub water feature.

They are bottom feeding fish and, therefore, not often visible and of little decorative merit. They rarely breed successfully in the garden pool.

Comet Longtail and Shubunkin

Carassius auratus var.

Length: Up to 45cm (18in)
Conditions: Outdoor or indoor pool

Of all the goldfish varieties for the outdoor pool, the comet longtails must be the finest. They are truly beautiful fish with long flowing tails that, in some cases, are almost equal to the length of their body. They are available in almost any colour that is found among the true goldfish and shubunkins.

The shubunkin is a nacreous-scaled goldfish in which myriad colours intermingle. Its body is very smooth and appears to be scaleless, but scales are present. Almost any colour combination is possible: red, blue, violet, black and ochre all figure prominently. Under favourable conditions, they breed freely; they are also suitable for the indoor pool.

Dace
Leuciscus leuciscus

Length: Up to 35cm (14in)
Conditions: Outdoor pool

The dace is a beautiful fish for a large pool, or a small pool if the water is well oxygenated. It is a very active surface swimmer that tends to shoal and loves to leap for flies. This long slim fish is steely-grey in colour with a prominent head and cylindrical body. Young examples look rather like roach, but lack the red eye of that species.

Care should be taken when purchasing dace to ensure that they come from commercially bred stock; sometimes, wild fish are traded, which may be carrying diseases. While the dace can live with these, goldfish and other domestic species will succumb if they are introduced to the pool.

Dace are ideal for the wildlife feature. However, they are unlikely to breed except in the largest of pools.

Fantail, Veiltail, Moor and Telescope
Carassius auratus var.

Length: Up to 25cm (10in)
Conditions: Outdoor or indoor pool; not reliably hardy outdoors

These are lovely goldfish varieties with short, dumpy bodies and beautiful long tails. In the fantail, moor and telescope, the tail is divided into three, while in the veiltail, it is split into two fine segments. Because of their excessive finnage, these fish swim in an amusing, slow and somewhat erratic manner.

There are many different kinds of fantail, known as red, red and white or calico fantails, the last being a colourful variation of the shubunkin.

Moors and telescopes have bizarre protruding eyes. The latter are derived from the brightly-coloured goldfish, while moors are usually black, although calico moors have the colouration of a blue shubunkin.

Goldfish
Carassius auratus auratus

Length: Up to 45cm (18in)
Conditions: Outdoor or indoor pool

The common goldfish is a very familiar inhabitant of pools and aquaria. It is a tough character that will tolerate a wide range of conditions. Goldfish can vary in length considerably, their size being related to available space and genetics, rather than age. They are available in a wide range of colours: from pure white through yellow and orange to red, and all shades and combinations between. Under favourable conditions, they breed freely.

Higoi Carp
Cyprinus carpio var.

Length: Up to 60cm (24in)
Conditions: Outdoor pool

Thought to be a natural variation of the common carp, the higoi or Chinese red carp is a very attractive fish which, although given to boisterous behaviour, can be introduced sparingly to the garden pool. It is a hardy meaty fish of handsome proportions and of similar appearance to the common carp, but with a depressed head and strong, uniform, salmon- or orange-pink colouration. It is only likely to breed in a large pool.

Koi Carp
Cyprinus carpio var.

Length: Up to 60cm (24in)
Conditions: Outdoor pool

Of Japanese origin, there are literally dozens of different varieties of koi carp with special colour combinations. For the average garden pool, koi make an interesting addition, but do not be dazzled by the multitude of brightly coloured and often metallic-scaled beauties. Such is the diversity that it is tempting to introduce more than the two or three specimens that the average garden pool can support without disrupting the planting.

Although beautiful, koi carp are destructive, so if you become hooked on these lovely creatures, you must forsake the garden pool and make special provision for them with a proper filtration system. They may breed in the average outdoor pool, but this is more likely to occur in a specially prepared and dedicated tank.

Orfe
Idus idus (Syn. *Leuciscus idus*)

Length: Up to 45cm (18in)
Conditions: Outdoor pool

The common species of orfe is known popularly as the silver orfe. However, the pondkeeper is much more likely to come across the golden orfe. Both are of similar appearance, being long slender fish with small blunt heads and obliquely-cleft mouths. The silver orfe has a wonderful, glistening, silver-scaled body, while the golden form is a deep salmon-orange colour with a silvery belly and occasional markings of black on the back and head.

Both varieties of orfe are fast swimming, surface shoaling fish that enjoy leaping into the spray of a fountain or waterfall and snatching flies from the air. Occasionally, they will breed in a large outdoor pool.

Roach
Rutilus rutilus

Length: Up to 30cm (12in)
Conditions: Outdoor pool

The roach is essentially a river fish, but it will adapt readily to pond life, particularly if the water feature incorporates a fountain or waterfall. It is of similar appearance to the dace, having a silvery body that perhaps is a little meatier. Unlike the dace, however, it tends to mingle with goldfish in the middle zone of the pool, rather than dash around near the surface. It has very distinctive red eyes, which readily separate it from any similar species.

This is an excellent fish for the wildlife pool, but it is unlikely to breed except in a large expanse of water.

Rudd
Scardinius erythrophthalmus

Length: Up to 35cm (14in)
Conditions: Outdoor pool

The common rudd and its silver and gold colour forms are very attractive fish for both the garden pool and the wildlife feature. In the silver and gold varieties, the colouration takes the form of a flush, rather than a strong colour. The common species is a lovely creature, being a slender fish with a silvery-grey body and bright red fins, the dorsal fin being situated quite close to the tail.

Rudd prefer a heavily planted pool, although they will often be seen near the surface, basking in the sun. They will breed in large pools outdoors.

Tench
Tinca tinca

Length: Up to 45cm (18in)
Conditions: Outdoor pool

The common or green tench is normally added to the garden pool as a scavenging fish. It lurks on the bottom where it preys mainly on aquatic insect life and clears up uneaten fish food. However, it should not be seen as an animated vacuum cleaner that will clear up all manner of debris from the pool floor, although it will make an important contribution to pool hygiene.

The common tench has a short, broad, olive-green or greyish body and narrow tapering head. The male can be distinguished from the female as they develop by the presence of a strong ventral fin, extending almost to the anal orifice. In the female, the fin is short and weak. The golden tench has an orange-gold colour. Tench rarely breed freely in the garden pool.

Golden Shiner
Notomigonus crysoleucas

Length: Up to 30cm (12in)
Conditions: Indoor pool or aquarium; temperature range, 10-20°C (50-68°F)

This shoaling fish requires plenty of space, only small specimens being suitable for an aquarium. It is long and slender with a glistening silvery body, although the males take on an orange tinge towards the base of the lower fin during the breeding season. Golden shiners spawn in spring and benefit considerably from heavy submerged planting.

Guppy
Poecilia reticulata

Length: Up to 6cm (2½in)
Conditions: Indoor pool or aquarium; temperature range, 18-27°C (64-81°F)

This popular and widely kept fish is a favourite among beginners. The males are very colourful, being available in mixtures and shades of yellow, green, blue and red, while the females are mostly a dullish grey with occasionally some colour on the tail fin.

There are several very fine ornamental varieties, including the veiltail guppy, which has a tail approaching the length of its body that is normally splashed with vivid colours. Others are the gold guppy and lace guppy. The former is gold with splashes of red and blue, while the latter has a network of black circles enclosing various colours. They are live-bearers and breed freely.

Medaka
Oryzias latipes

Length: 3.5cm (1½in)
Conditions: Indoor pool. Temperature range 18-23°C (64-73°F).

A small and lively fish which enjoys life in either an aquarium or indoor pool. It is a tiny darting character with silvery and gold or white scales. These little fish seem happiest when swimming around in a group, upwards of a dozen creating a fascinating community.

Medaka will live happily with most other fish and breeds freely in well planted conditions with good filtration. It enjoys flaked and freeze-dried foods. However, this is not a long-lived species and will probably need to be replaced every season.

Molly
Poecilia sphenops

Length: Up to 6cm (2½in)
Conditions: Indoor pool or aquarium; temperature range, 18-28°C (64-82°F)

The most common molly is the black variety, although there are lyre-tailed kinds and the greenish-silver Mexican molly. The fancy mollies tend to prefer the higher end of the temperature scale. All live happily in a community and feed on small aquatic insects and algae, as well as fish flake. They are live-bearers and breed readily where there is plenty of plant cover.

Pumpkinseed Sunbass
Lepomis gibbosus

Length: Up to 20cm (8in)
Conditions: Indoor pool; temperature range, 5-21°C (41-70°F)
This deep-bodied handsome fish has dark brown vertical bands on a light brownish background. Its entire body is sprinkled with lighter spots. Although tolerant of most other species, it can be aggressive when breeding, the male sometimes actually killing the female.

The pumpkinseed sunbass prefers plenty of plant cover, but also enjoys swimming in open water. It feeds on worms, gnat larvae and other aquatic insects.

Shiner
Notropis lutrensis

Length: Up to 8cm (3in)
Conditions: Indoor pool or aquarium; temperature range, 15-24°C (59-75°F)

This is a handsome shoaling fish for cool conditions. It is a slender silvery character, the male having colourful orange patches when the breeding tubercules are present. It enjoys heavily planted conditions and moving water.

MOLLUSCS, AMPHIBIANS AND REPTILES

SNAILS

There is a multitude of freshwater pond snails, but for the majority of pond owners, only one species is worth considering: the ramshorn snail (*Planorbis corneus*), which has a flattened shell that is carried upright on its back. For the indoor pool or aquarium, there are both red- and white-bodied forms, but a black form is produced in large quantities for the pool owner. All three are hardy. If introduced with either the red or white variant, the black form would provide the dominant colour.

Ramshorn snails are extremely useful additions to the pool, feeding almost exclusively on algae, especially the tiresome, filamentous mermaid's hair, which so often coats planting baskets and the walls of the pool. In the balanced pool, they reproduce quite freely, producing flat pads of jelly containing several dozen eggs, which they stick beneath the floating foliage of waterlilies and other deep-water aquatics. If there is an over-population of fish, many of these eggs will be eaten; likewise, adult snails may be devoured.

The ramshorn snail, Planorbis corneus, *is a great addition to the water garden, as it will feed on filamentous algae, while leaving the aquatic plants alone.*

Sometimes, the freshwater whelk (*Limnaea stagnalis*) is sold as a pond snail. While it will graze on algae, it much prefers the floating foliage of waterlilies. In most pools, it is undesirable, creating more damage than benefit. In the wildlife pool, however, a few may be considered acceptable. A distinctive species, it has a tall, spiralled and pointed shell and a fleshy, greyish-cream body. It lays its eggs in a similar fashion to the ramshorn snail, but in long cylinders of jelly.

MUSSELS

Two species of freshwater mussel are considered useful additions to the garden pool: the swan mussel (*Anodonta cygnea*) and the painters' mussel (*Unio pictorum*). The former has a dull brownish-green shell, which is roughly oval in shape and contains a white fleshy body. It may grow as much as 10cm (4in) long. The painters' mussel is usually smaller and has a yellowish-green shell, marked with distinctive, dark brown growth rings. This may be introduced into a pool along with little fish called bitterling, the mantle cavity of the mussel being a refuge for the eggs and an essential part of the breeding cycle. However, this is very much the province of the fish keeper, rather than the water gardener.

The importance of the swan mussel to the ecology of the pool comes from its ability to remove suspended, single-celled algae from the water by sucking in green water and discharging clear. This will not make a significant difference to a very green pond, but the addition of a number of specimens to a well ordered water garden will be beneficial. It is not wise to introduce mussels to a new pool; they need a quantity of detritus on the bottom in which to settle down to a useful life. A new and relatively sterile environment is anathema to them.

FROGS, TOADS AND NEWTS

Whether you have the opportunity of introducing them or not, it is quite likely that these amphibians will eventually find their way to your water garden. Some fish keepers express concern over the introduction or presence of frogs in a pool, claiming that male frogs will occasionally attach themselves to fish during their mating period, clasping them around the head and gills, causing damage. In reality, however, this is likely to be a rare occurrence, and it is almost unknown if a suitable female frog is available. The common frog (*Rana temporia*) is the species that is most likely to arrive unannounced, although the edible frog (*Rana esculenta*) may also appear. Both are a muddy green colour and the edible frog has a distinctive pale stripe down its back.

Toads live a similar life to frogs, but are mainly nocturnal and often spend longer periods out of water. The number of species to be found is extensive, but for most pool owners, the common toad (*Bufo bufo*), is a favourite and almost certain to turn up. A dull olive or brownish creature with a somewhat warty skin, the common toad should be cherished, for it is the gardeners' friend, being a regular predator of slugs, snails and other pests. The natterjack toad (*Bufo calamita*) is also a friend, and a handsome one, having a distinctive yellowish or orange stripe down its back.

Newts are probably not as appreciated as frogs and toads, but they do make a valuable contribution to the life of the pool. The species most likely to be encountered are the common newt (*Triturus vulgaris*) and the tiny palmate newt (*T. helveticus*). Both are a similar brownish or olive colour, the males of each species having wavy crests and orange bellies.

REPTILES

Among the reptiles, the European pond tortoise (*Emys orbicularis*) is the most fun. Although it will eat small fish, it is a delightful character that will enjoy sunbathing on the edge of the pool. It may have a black or deep brown carapace with yellow spots and a black body, which is also freely marked with yellow. The closely related American pond tortoise (*E. blandingii*) is also good value, although generally of much duller appearance.

The Spanish terrapin (*Clemmys leprosa*) is an altogether different creature, being much less outgoing and quite reserved until familiar with its owner. Its shell, or carapace, can vary in colour from light olive-green to almost black, while the legs and head will be variations of these colours, liberally marked with yellow stripes. The Caspian terrapin (*Clemmys caspica*) is slightly smaller and has grey skin, delicately marked with a tracery of yellow lines, while the Reeves terrapin (*Geoclemys reevesii*) is of similar size, but has a dull brown shell and yellowish underside.

A well planted pool will attract frogs. Some fish keepers fear them, as they have been known to attach themselves to fish during their mating period, but they are generally well behaved.

Newts are not as readily appreciated as frogs and toads, but they do make an invaluable contribution to pool life, although they will only spend part of the year there.

Toads tend to use the pool as a breeding place and spend much of their time out in the garden where they devour slugs and all manner of troublesome insect life.

The European pond tortoise, Emys orbicularis, *is a friendly reptile. Although it will occasionally take a young fish, it is greatly valued for its otherwise friendly disposition.*

CHAPTER SIX

WATER GARDEN CARE

Having created a water garden, you can begin to enjoy the fruits of your labours – the splashing of the waterfall or fountain, brightly coloured goldfish gliding serenely beneath soft green waterlily pads – it is indeed a delight.

However, a water garden is not a static feature. Once constructed, planted and stocked with fish, a pool will not continue as a pleasant picture unaided. It will demand management, for it is both a natural environment, full of living plants and creatures, and an unnatural one, being a man-made ecosystem in what may be an alien setting, where normally those plants and creatures may never have existed together. If you have carefully thought through your water garden from the beginning, its management should be fairly simple; only the vagaries of nature may disturb it from time to time. For the most part, the care of a pool is routine, light and enjoyable work, which is very rewarding.

The important thing is observation. Remember that the pool is a living entity and, rather as a farmer who notices immediately if anything is untoward, so the pondkeeper should spot impending trouble. By regularly spending time at the poolside, you will minimize the opportunity for major problems developing, for relaxation beside a pool is often the removal of the odd dead floating leaf, faded blossom or small tangle of filamentous algae. If opportunities for lazy poolside days are few and far between, regard the water garden as you might the herbaceous or shrub border. Borders are regularly hoed and plants are staked, so with the pool, leaves and blanket weed should be constantly attended to, and when suspended algae appears, appropriate treatment should be provided. Consistency and observation are the keys to successful water garden maintenance.

Once established, a water garden is largely trouble-free. Regular manicuring is needed, but removing dead leaves and occasional blanket weed is usually a pleasure rather than a chore.

SEASONAL CARE

A considerable amount of routine work is necessary to ensure that a water garden functions efficiently during the summer – the active growing season, but before that a spring clear-up is essential.

SPRING CLEAN

After the winter, a lot of tidying up will be needed. The bog garden will benefit from having any lingering winter debris removed and the soil gently pricked over with a fork. This is the time to apply a mulch, but if the bog garden is connected directly to the pool, take great care in selecting the material for this. One that is rich in nutrients, such as well rotted animal manure, is undesirable, as it may release nutrients into the water which, in turn, will become green with algae. A well composted bark mulch is much better.

The marginal shelves should receive similar attention. Plants must be tidied up and, where appropriate, lifted, divided and replanted, utilizing only the vigorous outer portions. Mulching is not practical within the pool, but a fresh layer of pea shingle spread over the surface of the soil and around marginal plants, whether these are planted directly on the shelf or in containers, will be of great benefit in preventing the fish from stirring up the soil in their quest for aquatic insect larvae.

If the pool needs to be cleaned out, do it now, before the plants begin growing vigorously. At this time of the year, the plants will not suffer and any fish can be kept safely in containers in a garage or outhouse while the work continues. Only clean out the pool if the water has become an unpleasant black or blue colour, or if there is a substantial accumulation of silt and organic debris that is causing management problems. The regular use of proprietary products to break up sludge will reduce the frequency at which the pond will need cleaning out completely.

In the spring it is necessary to periodically lift and divide marginal aquatics and waterlilies to ensure that they retain their vigour. Use good clean garden soil or aquatic planting compost.

If a pool heater has been used during the winter, it should be disconnected, cleaned, dried and packed away until needed again in the autumn. If a pump is to be connected to the electrical supply, this must be done immediately. Make sure that the pump and any attachments, such as a filter, function properly before the season really gets under way. Use a suitable bacterial product to initiate the correct functioning of a biological filter.

PREPARING FOR SUMMER

Once the spring clean has been completed, preparations can be made for the summer season. It is very important to fertilize established plants, especially waterlilies, which often remain undisturbed for several years, yet are heavy feeders. To ensure that fertilizer reaches the roots where it is required without raising the nutrient level of the water, and thereby increasing the presence of algae, a certain amount of ingenuity must be employed.

There are proprietary tablet fertilizers and others that come in small sachets with a perforated section, through which the fertilizer is gradually released into the compost when dampened. Both the tablets and sachets are pushed into the compost right next to the plants with minimal disturbance. Some gardeners prefer to use traditional bonemeal and clay pills to fertilize their aquatics, and while this is not such an accurate method of supplying nutrients, it is still satisfactory. Each pill is made by mixing a handful of coarse bonemeal with sufficient wet clay to bind it together. Then it is thrust into the container next to the plant. Liquid fertilizers are also available and are very simple to use, but care should be taken when choosing to ensure that such a fertilizer is suitable for pond use, being rich in micro-nutrients, but without nitrates or phosphates.

SUMMER CARE

In warm weather, topping up the pool with water to replace that which has been lost through evaporation is very important. Any disturbance among the plants must be kept to a minimum. In the case of the bog garden, this should be restricted to weeding and dead-heading, and within the pool to dead-heading and the occasional thinning of submerged aquatics, although this should be for purely cosmetic purposes only at this time. Radical thinning of submerged plants during the summer months should be avoided, unless they are particularly overcrowded.

Provide support for any plants that require it, although by and large this will be restricted to the bog garden area. Staking will not look very attractive in the water garden, so as far as possible encourage plants to support each other by careful planting. Most floating aquatics grow rapidly during the summer months, and sometimes the carpeting types, such as *Azolla caroliniana*, need controlling. Remove excessive growth with a net and discard it on the compost heap.

FEEDING THE FISH

As the water warms up (above 10°C/50°F), the fish will become active and benefit from being fed a good-quality food. A well established pool will normally provide sufficient natural foods to support a small fish population, but feeding does allow their diet to be improved and balanced. It also encourages the fish to become more placid than usual. If fed regularly at one point in the pool, the fish will soon begin to respond to a cast shadow or even a footfall. Feed them twice a day, but only give enough food for them to consume in five minutes, then scoop up the remainder with a net and discard it. It is important to provide a good-quality diet that will be fully utilized by the fish with minimal waste.

At this time of the year, fish may start breeding, so keep an eye open for fry. You may not have any intention of encouraging breeding, but nature will take its course, and in many cases fry will be seen clinging to submerged plants following a session of frenzied activity by adult fish. If you want to keep a few fry, place them in a bucket of pond water with a substantial quantity of submerged plant, such as milfoil or Canadian pondweed. This will protect them from the predations of their parents and give them the opportunity to develop into valuable adult fish.

ALGAE CONTROL

Provided the pool is stocked in a reasonably well balanced manner, there should never be a serious algae problem. However, some of the filamentous kinds persist even when the pool water is completely clear, and while the algae can easily be killed with an algaecide, it still has to be removed to prevent deoxygenation of the water as it decomposes. A stick or cane with a hook or nail in the end is the simplest, and most effective, device for winding the algae in so that it can be discarded. Take care when using an algaecide, since it may also kill any waterlilies and oxygenating plants.

Warm weather will cause noticeable evaporation and the pool will require regular topping up with fresh water. During the heat of the day the fish will enjoy the gentle spray from a hosepipe.

ESSENTIAL TASKS FOR SPRING

- Tidy up bog garden and apply a mulch
- Tidy up pool margins, dividing plants as necessary
- Clean out pool if necessary
- Remove pool heater, overhaul and store
- Inspect pump and accessories and install
- Fertilize established plants
- Begin feeding fish

ESSENTIAL TASKS FOR SUMMER

- Keep pool topped up to allow for evaporation
- Keep bog garden free of weeds
- Dead-head bog garden and aquatic plants
- Stake plants that need supporting in bog garden
- Control carpet forming floating plants by netting off excess and discarding
- Check the water quality if fish are being kept
- Feed fish daily
- Watch for fish fry and remove any you wish to keep
- Watch for algae and treat as required

AUTUMN PREPARATIONS

Although the water garden appears to become dormant during the autumn and winter, there is still activity taking place. This must be catered for in the autumn, and sometimes adjustments made for it in the depths of winter.

Proper autumn preparations are vitally important for the survival of the pool's occupants during the winter, especially the fish. The first task is to clean up the marginal plants immediately the first autumn frosts have cut them back. On no account must they be permitted to fall into the pool and pollute the water.

Waterlilies can be allowed to die back of their own accord, except in small tub or container water gardens. Beginners to water gardening often feel concern for their waterlilies during the winter, but they need not fear, for hardy waterlilies do not suffer provided they remain submerged beneath 30-60cm (24-48in) of water. Small or pygmy kinds, growing in a shallow pool, can have the water drained off and their crowns protected by a generous layer of straw, the whole pool being covered with a plastic sheet to keep out the rain. They overwinter very well like this, especially where otherwise there would be very little water covering them. Waterlilies growing in tubs can be drained off, the plant, complete with mud, being stored in a frost-free place until the following spring.

Most floating plants disappear completely during the winter months, only the troublesome duck-weeds tending to linger. All the popular plants produce winter turions or, in the case of the water chestnut (*Trapa natans*), spiny seeds. These fall to the pool floor and do not reappear until the spring when the water starts to warm up. Obviously, the lower part of the pool is the coolest place, so sometimes it will be early summer before the turions surface and the plants burst into growth again.

To advance the plants' season, a number of turions should be gathered during the early autumn, before they sink to the bottom of the pool. Keep them in a bowl of water with a little soil sprinkled on the bottom. If stored successfully during the winter months, they can either be started into early growth with a little protection, or introduced to the warmer upper reaches of the pool much sooner. This may only make the difference of a week or two, but it is most important, especially when the foliage cover they provide is an essential part of the natural balance of the pool.

All the popular floating plants can also be stored successfully as plants in a cool light place, in bowls or jars of pool water with a little soil scattered over the base. When selecting suitable specimens, always choose the younger pieces of plants like the water soldier. Normally, the main plant will be brittle and will disintegrate in winter storage, but the soft young plantlets formed on runners will be perfectly happy under these spartan conditions.

Where there is an electrical supply to the pool, install the pool heater. If this replaces a pump, take this out of the water and give it a thorough clean. Remove the filter, and clean and dry it prior to storing the pump for the winter. Even if you do not have a pool heater, there is little point in allowing the pump to remain in the pool throughout the winter.

Fish will be perfectly happy and able to overwinter if they are in good condition in the autumn. Generally, they will experience few problems if they have had sufficient food during the summer months, and they will pass through severe weather unscathed. If possible, it is worth feeding them on a wheatgerm-based food before the onset of winter. Such foods

It is very important to keep leaves out of the pool in autumn. Not only do they fall directly into the pool, but are often blown into the water from other parts of the garden.

ESSENTIAL TASKS FOR AUTUMN

- Clean up marginal plants after the first frosts
- Drain shallow pools containing small waterlilies, protect crowns with straw and cover with polythene
- Drain tubs containing waterlilies and store plants in a frost-free place
- Collect turions of floating plants and store for the winter
- Collect young plantlets of floating plants and store for the winter
- Remove pool pump and accessories, clean and store; or move pump closer to the filter (see page 275)
- Install pool heater
- Feed fish wheatgerm-based foods.

ESSENTIAL TASKS FOR WINTER

- If no pool heater is used, vent pool if it freezes over by melting the ice with pans of hot water
- Float a piece of wood or rubber ball on the water of concrete pools to absorb ice pressure
- Feed fish wheatgerm-based foods during mild weather.

During frosty periods it is important to retain a small area of ice-free water to allow the accumulating gases in the pool beneath to escape freely into the air. The safest method of creating a hole is to stand a pan of boiling water on the ice and allow it to melt through.

are specially manufactured and are rapidly digested by the fish, even in cool weather.

COPING WITH WINTER

Although the pool is not as lively and vibrant during the winter as it is in the summer, life goes on, especially the steady decomposition of organic material in the murky depths on the floor. Under normal circumstances, the gases that are produced by this year-round decomposition escape freely into the air, but if the pool ices over in severe weather, they become trapped between the water surface and the ice, putting the fish at risk of being asphyxiated.

So of all the tasks in winter, venting the pool when it ices over is crucial. If you have a pool heater, there will be no problem. The heater will comprise a brass rod containing a heating element and a polystyrene float. The term 'pool heater' is a bit of a misnomer, for it does not heat the entire pool, but rather keeps a small area free of ice and allows the ready escape of gases.

Never break the ice with a hammer or similar blunt instrument. This creates shock waves that can concuss or even kill the fish. Even running across a frozen pond can cause extreme distress to the fish beneath. A pan of boiling water stood on the ice and allowed to melt through is the best solution, although infinite patience is required, as it will take several panfuls to have an effect upon any but the thinnest layer of ice.

Modern pool construction materials are usually quite resistant to frost and ice problems, but not so concrete. Ice can exert tremendous pressures that are capable of cracking the most expertly laid concrete if precautions are not taken. The best way to overcome the problem is to float a piece of wood or a rubber ball on the surface of the water, so that the pressure is absorbed by an object that is capable of expanding and contracting.

If fish become active during mild spells, feed them on a wheatgerm-based food, as this will prevent them from using up their valuable stored food reserves.

MAINTAINING KOI POOLS

The care and maintenance necessary for a koi pool differs considerably from that required by a conventional garden pool, for the focus is very much on the fish. Although the aquatic environment must be right, the condition of the fish and their behaviour will be of the greatest concern.

Spring is the most difficult time for the koi keeper, for having come through the winter, the fish are likely to be run down, despite any hearty feeding and preparation in the previous autumn. Koi always give of their best in a water temperature of 18-24°C (65-75°F), and much prefer the shorter winters of their Japanese homeland to the extended cold and fluctuating temperatures of short winter days in northern latitudes. Although they will survive most winters without difficulty, inevitably they will be in poor condition and will not improve until the water temperature rises and they begin to feed actively again.

Koi that are not in the best of spirits will be vulnerable to infections. As they become more active, inspect them carefully. Provided the water quality has been maintained to a high standard throughout their period of winter torpor, you are unlikely to find anything untoward, but if a problem is spotted, it must be dealt with promptly.

SUMMER CARE

As spring moves on and slowly turns to summer, the fish will demand more food. However, do not simply feed greater amounts at a specific time each day, but rather dispense it more often. When possible, feed five or six times a day, using a good high-protein food. Do not skimp on its quality; large quantities of mediocre food will not have the same effect as the controlled feeding of a scientifically formulated food.

Koi sticks are the most popular artificial food, but this diet can be supplemented with occasional treats. If you come across earthworms when digging the garden, throw them into the pool, as the koi will be very appreciative. They will feed on all manner of aquatic insect life too, and also enjoy

To ensure water clarity and quality in a koi pool it is recommended that during summer up to 20 per cent of the water volume should be changed each week. This should be reduced according to temperature to as little as five per cent in winter.

Koi will enjoy a summer treat of green food and will consume a lettuce with relish. Tie a string to it to anchor it in the pool and remove any that has not been eaten after about fifteen minutes.

Once water temperatures drop below 5°C (41°F), fish will stop feeding. Koi that are in good health, and that have been well fed during the autumn, should not be harmed by such cold weather.

eating vegetable matter. This is why there is little point in introducing good aquatic plants, for the koi will simply destroy them. However, aquatic plants are not necessary to provide the green stuff in their diet; any succulent leafy material will do. For example, tie a string to the stalk of a lettuce, so that it can be anchored, and place it in the pool. The fish will take a little time to get used to it, but eventually will eat it with relish.

Apart from improving the health of the koi, providing a varied diet and controlling their method of feeding make it more likely that the fish will become hand tame. Once this has been achieved, netting and inspecting the fish, when necessary, will be much easier.

The quality of water in the summer is particularly critical. Everything seems to happen much more quickly during hot weather, which means that problems can occur almost instantaneously. Regular maintenance is vital: settlement areas must be flushed daily, while once a week the floor of the pond must be vacuumed to clear those areas beyond the influence of the bottom drain. Other weekly tasks are back flushing the filter chambers and the routine testing of the water for pH, nitrite and ammonia levels.

Most koi keepers believe that, in hot weather, up to 20 per cent of the water volume should be changed each week. This should be reduced to 10 per cent in cooler weather, and as little as 5 per cent during winter. The fresh water must always be fed through a purifier or treated with a tap water conditioner to prevent any unexpected pollutants in the water from harming the fish.

Throughout the spring and summer season, check the water quality carefully. All may seem well, but if the fish start to flick and turn themselves over in flashes on the floor of the pool, it may not be the case. This distinctive behaviour may be a sign of parasites, but it is much more likely to be due to a temporary shift in water quality. Test for pH, ammonia and nitrite, for the last in particular can occur through increased feeding in warm conditions. In this case, the filter system may need improving. In warm weather, oxygen may also be in short supply, and it may be necessary to use a pond air-pump to increase the oxygen level.

PREPARING FOR WINTER

As autumn and winter approach, it is essential to prepare koi for their ordeal. Temperatures below 10°C (50°F) create stress in koi, and once they drop below 5°C (41°F), the process that controls digestion and the absorption of food ceases altogether. Once water temperatures have reached these levels, continued feeding is pointless. Until then, it is important to feed liberally and regularly, with high-quality wheatgerm foods, to build up the fish for the winter. In some cases, freshly purchased young koi will not survive their first winter, but larger fish, which have become acclimatized to the pool during an entire season, usually present few problems if they feed properly before the chill weather descends. You should continue to feed wheatgerm foods when the fish are active during the winter period.

POND REPAIRS

It is unfortunate that no matter how carefully a pond is constructed and maintained, occasionally a leak will develop. This can have a devastating effect upon pond life, and remedial action must be taken swiftly. Sometimes, the decision should be taken to start again, for in the case of polythene, PVC and LDPE liners, repairs are rarely satisfactory.

RUBBER LINERS

However, the same does not apply to rubber liners, such as the butyl type. These are as easy to repair as a cycle tyre if you can locate the puncture. Repair kits for this kind of liner are readily available.

Once the problem has been located, the liner in the immediate vicinity must be allowed to dry out. Then the surface should be cleaned thoroughly with a scrubbing brush and, if necessary, roughened a little with a piece of glasspaper. This will help ensure a good bond once the adhesive has been applied. Cut a patch at least one-and-half-times the size of the damaged area, apply the adhesive and press down firmly. Leave the patch to dry for 12 hours, preferably longer, before refilling the pool with water. Some repair kits have self-adhesive patches which, once applied, can safely be subjected to water within half an hour.

PRE-FORMED POOLS

Pre-formed pools that are made from any kind of plastic or PVC material are almost impossible for the home gardener to repair, but those made from fibreglass can be patched if necessary. For the most part, fibreglass pools should be immune to damage, but sometimes problems will occur in an inadequately supported pool if anyone stands in it while cleaning it out, or if a pool is being moved to another part of the garden and reinstalled.

When damage does occur, it is not too difficult to repair with an automotive repair kit containing fibreglass matting (follow the manufacturer's instructions carefully). However, as it is best to repair the underside of the moulding, it will need removing from the ground and inverting.

CONCRETE

Although regarded as permanent strong structures, concrete ponds can suffer, especially during the winter. While it is rare for a professionally constructed pool to leak badly, this still can occur in very severe weather if you do not take suitable precautions. The pressure of ice over a protracted period on a concrete pool structure can cause fracturing. To alleviate this risk, float a large piece of wood or several rubber balls on the pool during the winter months. If severe frost occurs, they will absorb some of the pressure, rather than the rigid walls of the pool.

Sometimes, a concrete pool will suffer from flaking: the frost gets under the surface layer of concrete, causing it to bubble and lift. Rapid deterioration then sets in. In practical terms, little can be done by way of concrete repairs. However, it is often possible to reline such a pool with a rubber liner. This should be installed and secured in much the same manner as lining an excavation in the ground.

Fractures can usually be repaired satisfactorily, although even a good repair will be a potential site of weakness, and sometimes problems can recur. Clean the area of the leak

REPAIRING A HOLE IN A RUBBER LINER

1 Allow the liner to dry out and then clean the surface thoroughly with a scrubbing brush. In order to ensure a good strong bond for the adhesive, rough the surface of the liner with sandpaper.

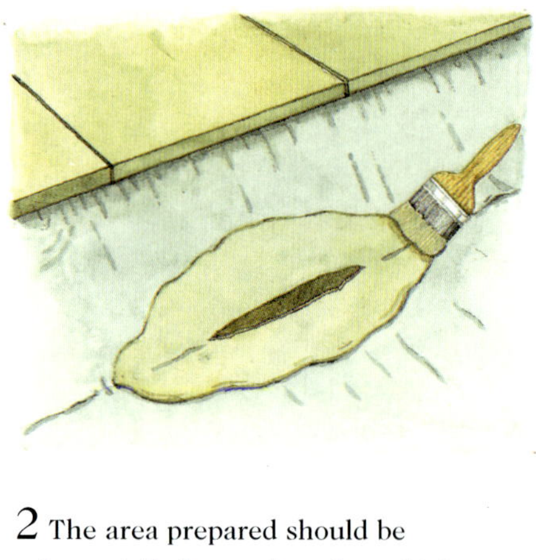

2 The area prepared should be substantially larger than that which is damaged. Use an adhesive which is specifically recommended for the purpose and apply liberally.

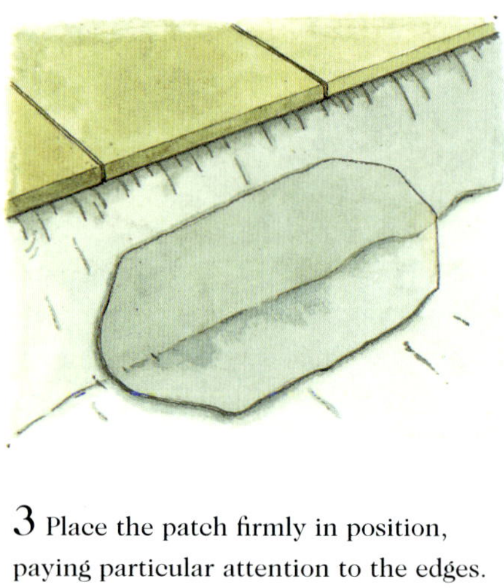

3 Place the patch firmly in position, paying particular attention to the edges. These must be stuck down firmly. Allow the patch to dry for at least 12 hours before refilling the pool with water.

REPAIRING A FRACTURE IN A FIBREGLASS POOL

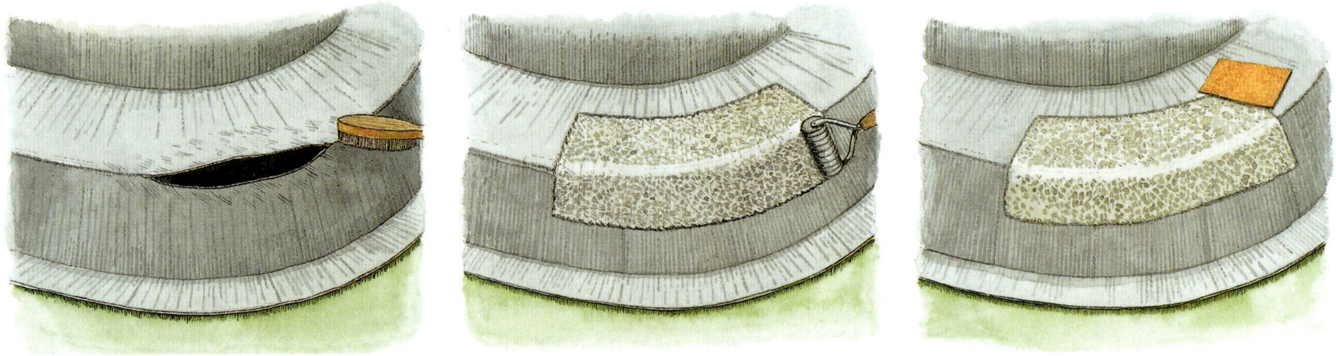

1 Remove the pool unit from the ground and invert. Clean the whole area with a wire brush. Rub around the damaged area with glasspaper, then brush thoroughly to remove any dust.

2 Cut a piece of fibreglass matting up to twice the size of the damaged area and, carefully following the instructions, mix the resin and hardener. Then apply it with the ridged roller provided.

3 It could take a couple of days for the matting to set hard, so it is a good idea to carry out this job in a garage or similar outbuilding. Sand off any rough edges before reinstalling the pool.

with a stiff brush and wash off the dust and debris. Cut out the crack with a cold chisel, making a V-shaped groove along the fracture line, at least 2.5cm (1in) deeper than the obvious crack. Roughen the surface of the concrete with the chisel so that fresh concrete will adhere to it successfully.

Mix by volume one part cement, two parts sand and four parts gravel. Then add waterproofing compound and, when thoroughly mixed together, combine with water until you achieve a workable consistency. Apply the mixture with a plasterer's trowel. This is a good strong mixture that should provide a seal. Some builders will recommend that the gravel content of the mixture be reduced to make it easier to fill the crack and to smooth, but for the amateur pond repairer, the full concrete mix, even if more difficult to lay and to smooth, will ensure an efficient repair.

The concrete must be allowed to dry out for several days. However, it must not be allowed to dry out too quickly, otherwise hairline cracks may appear in the surface. To prevent this, cover the repaired area with damp sacking and keep it damp until the concrete has set firmly. Then treat it with a sealing compound to prevent free-lime escaping into the pool when water is added, as this can harm the fish.

REPAIRING A FRACTURE IN A CONCRETE POOL

1 Cut out the Concrete around the crack, being sure to remove any damaged material. Cut a V shape which is sufficient to take enough concrete for proper uniting of new with old.

2 Fill with a strong concrete mix ideally with a water proofing compound incorporated. Apply with a plasterer's trowel to ensure a smooth finish and tamp down firmly.

3 After the concrete has haf an opportunity to dry thoroughly, paint with a sealing compound. It may be necessary to use a primer first in order to ensure that the sealant sticks.

MAINTAINING WILDLIFE POOLS

There is a common assumption that if you establish a wildlife pool with native plants, it will become a biologically stable environment, which can be enjoyed without having to be managed. However, even if a wide range of native plants is established and local fauna attracted, it must be remembered that a wildlife pool in a garden is largely an artificial environment. Given the constraints of scale, it will need as much care and attention as the manicured pool.

With little competition and an ideal environment, plants will flourish in the wildlife pool. Careful pond profiling helps to restrict their spread to the areas desired.

CONTROLLING GROWTH

The major problem that faces the wildlife pond owner is keeping the plants within bounds. With little competition and an ideal environment, they will flourish. Some control can be exercised by creating careful containment at planting time, and also by pond profiling, that is making some areas of water deep enough to provide a natural barrier to further encroachment. These measures will not solve the problem completely, however.

One of the most difficult aspects of plant control in a wildlife pool is seeding. On the one hand, the seeds of many species attract wildlife, but on the other, those very same seeds establish indiscriminate colonies of plants wherever they find a convenient niche. Really troublesome species, like the water plantains or alismas, which do not greatly benefit wildlife, but have extremely numerous and viable seeds, should have their flower stems removed immediately the tiny blossoms fade. The same applies to the coarse species of sedge and, where practicable, the rushes. Both groups can become invaders if not controlled very carefully. In these cases, the removal of old flowering material is beneficial, but does not detract from the overall well-being of the feature.

Invasive rhizomes or stolons, especially of plants like the manna grass (*Glyceria fluitans*) can cause serious management problems in a small wildlife pool, even when planted in a container. This plant often appears of its own accord and is to the water garden what couch grass is to ordinary beds and borders. Despite what the natural history books may tell you about its benefits to wildlife, if you find any hint of this plant in your wildlife pool, remove it, as it can be the cause of perpetual heartache. It looks similar to couch grass, but is of a much lighter green and tends to have soft downy foliage.

The methods for dealing with other invasive wildlife plants will depend on their mode of growth. If reedmace, or typhas, become a problem, they should be cut below water level in the autumn, allowing the hollow cut stems to fill with water during the winter and rot. Sometimes the main terminal growth of the rhizome, which is yet to appear above water, will survive, but it will produce an individual plant that is easily removed. Burreeds, on the other hand, are easier to dispose of during late summer. If the main plants invading the pool are removed, it is almost certain that the remainder of the spreading root system will die.

THE IMPORTANCE OF CONTROLLING GROWTH

Visually, it is important to have a variety of species and not to allow one dominate the others, but there are also very practical ecological reasons for control. Since the wildlife pool is a naturally planted feature in an unnatural environment, it will require management, particularly as most water gardeners will want to achieve an ecosystem that is at a particular stage of succession: the stage at which it is visually appealing, with a range of plants offering a diversity of opportunities to as much aquatic life as possible. Indeed, we have to consider that what we are attempting is comparable with, for example, the maintenance of a natural heathland area which, if not tended properly, would revert to scrub.

By maintaining a wildlife pool in this manner, the diversity of plants satisfies our desire for cultivating different species, but also offers special riches to individual groups of aquatic life. If a small area is maintained clear of tall vegetation, it can serve as a spot for birds that want to bathe or, if the feature is large enough, as a nesting site.

Reducing the amount of plant growth also admits light, which is not only vital for the successful growth of some of the valuable smaller species that otherwise may be shaded out, but also beneficial for creatures such as dragonflies that prefer open sunny conditions. Live green plant growth should be rationalized together with any that is showing signs of decomposing in the water. Decaying vegetation creates most unpleasant conditions for any wildlife, deoxygenating the water and often impairing the growth of adjacent desirable aquatic plants.

Submerged aquatics rarely present the same problems in the wildlife pool, unless planted unrestricted on a muddy pond floor. Here they may invade the territory of other emergent deep-water aquatics, but for the most part, it is a case of the more, the merrier. Any submerged plants that produce vast quantities of foliage, which will either create serious oxygen depletion problems at night or restrict the activities of true aquatic life, can be cut back at will. However, do not shear them heavily during the summer, as you may induce a green algal bloom. When removing such debris, shake it carefully over the pond to dislodge and preserve many of the tiny creatures to which it will almost certainly be home.

WELCOME INHABITANTS

A wildlife pool must be tended in the same way as a manicured garden pool, but greater attention should be paid to its inhabitants. In an ordinary garden pool, some of the creatures that the wildlife gardener may welcome, such as caddis flies, will be anathema to the true gardener, since their larvae will demolish waterlilies. Frogs and toads may inhabit either pool, and both the water and wildlife gardener should be aware of the implications of spawning. In the wildlife pool, such an invasion will be seen as desirable, but in the garden pool, it may be regarded as a nuisance, although doubtless the resultant young frogs will be welcome, if not devoured while still tadpoles by hungry goldfish.

Although it is desirable to maintain a wildlife pool to look as natural as possible, this does not mean leaving it to its own devices. In order to create a natural appearance, regular and subtle manicuring is essential, especially in the latter part of the growing season.

SEASONAL CARE

SPRING ROUTINE

The activities of frogs, toads and newts must be taken into account when giving the pool its spring manicure. Any over-wintering vegetation should be cut back carefully, even that of so-called evergreens such as the pendulous sedge (*Carex pendula*). If it is allowed to remain, the new growth will be produced on and among the old winter-damaged vegetation and will always look untidy.

All marginal plants can be cut to within 5cm (2in) of the base, with the exception of any hollow-stemmed kinds that may 'drown' if their cut stems fill with water. The reedmaces are particularly vulnerable to this, although more so in winter than spring. This is also the time to make adjustments to planting arrangements and, where appropriate, lift and divide any plants that are overcrowded.

Plants growing in aquatic planting baskets need very regular attention. Few species that are popularly grown in the wildlife pool will remain within the confines of even a large container for more than two growing seasons. When placed close together on a marginal shelf, reeds and rushes will often travel from one basket to another. Ideally, half the total number of plants should be divided and replanted each year, which will ensure consistently good cover. If everything is lifted and divided every other season, the pool changes from spartan to crowded every two years, which makes for an unstable ecology.

Some of the more rampant scrambling plants, such as brooklime (*Veronica beccabunga*) and water mint (*Mentha aquatica*) benefit from being replaced each season. As soon as the new growth is 5cm (2in) long, remove some of the stronger shoots and root them in a tray or pot of mud. Roots will be produced rapidly, and within a couple of weeks, rooted cuttings will be available to plant back. The adult plants can then be discarded. Young plants make much more vigorous growth, yet still flower freely during the summer.

Spring is the time to make adjustments to plantings. The new shoots of marginal aquatics, which will be clearly visible, can be removed and used for propagation purposes.

SUMMER CARE

Apart from controlling plants and keeping them within bounds, there is little to be concerned about during the summer. If there are fish in the pond, sufficient open water should be retained to ensure that they can live happily and breed if they feel the urge. Often, submerged aquatics are allowed to become rampant when the pool is considered to be natural, but open water is just as important as an abundance of submerged growth for all manner of aquatic life.

Pest and disease control must not be neglected, either, for although a pool may be dedicated to wildlife, this does not mean that epidemics of aphids or mildew can be tolerated. A severe attack of waterlily aphids among succulent aquatics like the arrowhead or flowering rush, can cause such debilitation that they do not grow and flower properly, which, in turn, can affect the well-being of other insect species, which may depend upon these plants for food or shelter.

The likelihood of severe problems is remote, but attacks can come from unexpected quarters: some insect life, which in small numbers can be fascinating and perfectly acceptable, may get out of hand. For example, large numbers of caddis fly larvae and the caterpillars of brown china mark moths can cause devastating damage, so vigilance is essential.

AUTUMN ROUTINE

The removal of the bulk of fading vegetation is desirable, especially in areas where the waterlily beetle is endemic. It loves nothing better than the dying foliage of marginal plants,

The vigorous free-seeding nature of many reeds, rushes and grasses is of enormous benefit to wildlife. There is a balance to be maintained in order to preserve pool hygiene and at the same time satisfy the requirements of birds and small mammals.

ESSENTIAL TASKS FOR SPRING

- Cut back overwintering vegetation
- Cut back all marginal plants, except hollow-stemmed species, to within 5cm (2in) of their base
- Lift and divide overcrowded plants
- Every other year, divide half of marginal plants growing in aquatic planting baskets
- Remove shoots of rampant scrambling plants, root them in mud and use to replace adult plants

ESSENTIAL TASKS FOR SUMMER

- Cut back plants to keep them within bounds
- Cut back submerged aquatics to ensure sufficient open water for fish
- Watch for pest and disease attack

ESSENTIAL TASKS FOR AUTUMN

- Remove as much fading foliage from marginal plants as possible
- Collect winter buds and small plantlets of floating plants and store for the winter

ESSENTIAL TASKS FOR WINTER

- Vent pool if it freezes over by melting the ice with pans of hot water

where it can hide for the winter. Some species may be allowed to remain if their seeds provide food for wildlife, but the tidier you can make the wildlife pool for the winter, the fewer potential problems there will be in the following year.

While floating plants like the water soldier (*Stratiotes aloides*) and frogbit (*Hydrocharis morsus-ranae*) will survive quite happily outdoors, they will achieve a better start in the spring if either winter buds or small plantlets are given a little protection by being placed in a bucket of water with a layer of soil in the bottom. This should be stored in a light place. Usually, hardy floating plants fall to the bottom of the pool for the winter, taking a long time to break into growth and reappear in the spring. If you afford some protection to them in this way, their growth can be advanced and a much longer season enjoyed.

WINTER CARE

Although the wildlife pool is likely to contain native species of fish, they will still be vulnerable to the effects of being frozen in the pool. It is not the cold that kills them, but asphyxiation by the noxious gases that are produced by decomposing vegetation on the floor of the pool, which becomes trapped beneath the ice. Venting the ice cover is as important for a wildlife pool as it is for the manicured goldfish pond. Otherwise, there is little to be concerned about in winter, for all the plant species that are commonly grown in the wildlife pond are likely to be perfectly hardy.

ATTRACTING WILDLIFE

Planting suitable native aquatic plants will encourage the arrival of a diversity of species which, to some extent, rely upon them. These may not be exclusively aquatic fauna, but other species that depend upon aquatic plant life, such as the large copper butterfly, which needs to lay its eggs on the great water dock (*Rumex hydrolapathum*). The introduction or 'inoculation' of the pond with local species and, perhaps, a little detritus from an established pond will also help to develop the ecological system. Starting a wildlife pool and initially attracting desirable creatures is one thing; keeping them all living in harmony, and at appropriate stocking rates, is quite another.

MAINTAINING BALANCE

As with the conventional garden pool, the wildlife feature must have a proper balance of plants to keep the water free from algae. The regular removal of excess growth, or introduction of fresh plants should ensure that this is achieved. It is tempting to leave a wildlife pool to take care of itself so that it develops a natural balance of its own, but this does not work; either the submerged plants swamp all the open water space, or duckweed (*Lemna minor*) smothers the surface, kills the submerged plants, and the water becomes black and unpleasant.

If the plant balance can be maintained by regular attention, most other species will live happily. Fish eventually grow and breed to suit the amount of available space, but this can have a devastating effect on other species, such as caddis flies, the larvae of which are regularly devoured by fish. If the interesting aquatic insect life disappears, fish stocks may need to be reduced. A good indicator of overstocking, in the context of a wildlife pool, is the regular occurrence of empty water snail shells floating on the surface. On some occasions, their demise may have been caused by birds, but the greater likelihood is of fish sucking the creatures from their shells and eating them. This usually only happens in a pool that is close to its maximum stocking rate.

A healthy balance of native aquatic plants encourages a wide diversity of fauna. The large copper butterfly, for example, requires the foliage of great water dock on which to lay its eggs.

DEVELOPING FULL POTENTIAL

On the other hand, conditions have to be really good for fish to develop to their full potential. Adequate food must be provided. Although the pond may be planted for wildlife, this is no guarantee that sufficient natural food will be present to ensure excellent growth, so supplementing their diet with a manufactured fish food will be beneficial. Not only will the latter provide essential nutrients, but it will protect some of the aquatic insect life which, otherwise, might find its way into the fishes' diet. A combination of a sound feeding programme and a water pH between 7.5 and 8.0 produces the best results.

While the ecology of any pool is vulnerable, that of the wildlife feature is particularly at risk. Unlike the garden pool, where the plants and decorative fish are the most important elements, in a wildlife pool, everything is important, from the dragonfly larvae to the diving beetles. As a result, two slightly different pond management regimes apply.

In the wildlife pool, maintenance must be carefully undertaken in stages to ensure the minimum of disturbance to aquatic life. In the garden pool, however, a complete clear-out can take place whenever the gardener wishes, and apart from the possibility of an early problem with a green algal bloom when the plants are put back, life with the goldfish and orfe continues. The wildlife feature is much more vulnerable: the wholesale clearance and scrubbing out of a wildlife pool will set its ecology back at least two years.

Under such circumstances, when establishing the pool, it is useful if plantings can be phased over a two-year period, so that lifting and dividing can follow a similar programme. In this way, the pool is never naked, and at least half of the plant habitats remain undisturbed for two years. In the soil-bottomed pond, where plants are established directly into the mud, the restriction and reduction of invading species can be undertaken in a similar manner.

UNDERSTANDING WILDLIFE NEEDS

Cleaning out the pond should be resisted as much as possible. Even if a layer of detritus starts to build up on the floor of the pool, it should be allowed to remain, unless it is turning the water putrid, for it will be home to myriad invertebrates. In the autumn, keep as many fallen leaves as possible out of the pool to minimize the build-up of organic material on the bottom. This should restrict the need to clean out the pond to once every eight or ten years. It also allows the micro flora and the fauna, which live in the lower reaches of the pool, to develop fully and make a major contribution to the pool's ecology.

While carrying out maintenance within the pool is vital, caring for the surroundings is very important if wildlife is to be attracted and encouraged to stay. Although trees are not a good idea beside pools, shrubby planting in close proximity is essential, especially for birds. One of the major attractions of any pond is being able to watch the birds use it for bathing and drinking. If palatable berries can be produced on shrubs nearby, the birds will have everything they require for sustenance, as well as cover in which to hide. Encourage those plants which produce edible seeds so that wildlife can feast on the autumn bounty.

A wildlife pool should remain largely untouched, except for careful and regular manicuring. Resist the temptation to periodically clean it out, for even the build up of detritus can itself provide a home for myriad fascinating aquatic invertebrates.

MAINTAINING INDOOR POOLS

An indoor water feature requires different maintenance techniques to a normal outdoor pool, although the underlying principles are the same. The major problems arise from often uncontrollably high summer temperatures and the difficulty of maintaining winter growth owing to poor light levels.

ROUTINE MAINTENANCE

Everything happens much more quickly in an indoor pool: pests and diseases are likely to appear sooner and be more persistent, while the compost will become more exhausted. As a matter of policy, all indoor aquatic plants should be repotted and provided with fresh compost early each spring. Remove as much of the old compost as possible without disrupting the root-ball. If any plants need dividing, treat them in the same manner as hardy aquatics.

Many submerged aquatics should be replaced each year. The individually planted, non-bunching species, such as vallisneria, are usually alright, but may need occasional thinning. However, bunched plants should be replaced. Remove the young growing shoots, re-bunch them and plant them in fresh compost.

Watch all plants carefully for signs of pests and diseases. Spraying is impossible because chemicals must be kept out of the water, but a systemic insecticide, or the equivalent fungicide for a disease, can be applied directly to the foliage. Wear rubber gloves and use an absorbent cloth to wipe the chemical over as much of the emergent foliage as possible, being careful to avoid causing damage or permitting drips of the chemical to enter the water.

As with all aquatics, dead-heading is vital, but so is the removal of discolouring leaves. It is essential to keep as much decomposing organic matter as possible out of the pool.

An indoor water feature can be a delight. Problems arise mainly from high temperatures in summer and poor light during winter. Carefully contrived planting can contribute much to success.

CARING FOR FISH

An indoor pool offers a great opportunity to enjoy fancy goldfish. All require the same care as the common goldfish, but because the environment will be much more hospitable during the winter, they can be guaranteed to survive. The major hazard is the prospect of oxygen depletion. This may occur if the pond is close to the limits of its capacity, when the fish may be seen mouthing for air at the surface. A gentle spray of cool water from a hosepipe should rectify the situation. In the long term, however, it will be necessary either to reduce the stocking level or install a pond airpump to increase the oxygen content of the water.

Feeding will be more necessary than outdoors, as the true ecology of the pond, with all its myriad creatures, will not evolve. Feed more regularly and over a longer period, as indoor fish will burn more energy. Give enough food for the fish to feed for ten minutes. After that, remove and discard any that remains afloat. Start feeding early in the year, immediately the fish swim about actively, and continue well into the autumn. During the winter, provide them with a pinch of food every week. If they eat it, continue to do so, but if they ignore it, desist until they appear active and hungry.

OVERWINTERING PLANTS

If the pool is warm enough to sustain active growth and it is possible to maintain a reasonable day length with high-quality light, the plants will continue growing as if it is summer. A regular manicure, and removal of faded flowers and foliage, is all that will be required, along with a careful check for pests and diseases.

OVERWINTERING TROPICAL WATERLILIES

1 As autumn arrives, remove waterlily containers, cut back the waterlily foliage and allow the plants to dry out and die back naturally. Do not lift them immediately.

2 Separate out the tubers and spread them out in a tray of damp sand. Be selective and only store those tubers which are strong, vigorous and appear generally healthy.

3 In the spring carefully pot the tubers individually in a good aquatic planting compost. Stand them in water, soaking the compost but submerging them completely once growth is observed.

If the pool is to become more or less dormant during the winter, a similar maintenance programme to that used outdoors should be implemented. Remove all faded foliage from marginal aquatics and discard it. Cut back any tangled submerged plants, especially those congested with algae, and discard them. Floating plants, like fairy moss, are best removed, a small portion of the healthiest growth being placed in a bowl of pond water with a little soil in the bottom. This should be kept in light, frost-free conditions. Water hyacinth can be overwintered by removing the healthy young plants clustering around the adult and placing them in a deep tray of mud or very wet compost. This should be kept at room temperature.

Tropical waterlilies rarely continue to prosper in winter. Most grow from tubers in a similar fashion to begonias, and they benefit from being stored in controlled conditions. As autumn approaches, remove the containers, cut off the fading foliage and allow the mud to dry out. Do not lift the plants immediately; give them a little time to come to rest naturally. Then separate the tubers and pack them in damp sand.

The rootstocks of nelumbos should also be overwintered in damp sand. Lifting them in the autumn ensures that only a vigorous rootstock is replanted the following year.

STARTING PLANTS INTO GROWTH

Once the winter has passed, check that each waterlily tuber is sound, then pot them individually in pots filled with a good aquatic planting compost. Stand the pots in an aquarium or a bucket of water in a warm light place. Warming the water with an aquarium heater will encourage the tubers to sprout quickly. Within a few days, juvenile underwater leaves will appear, followed a couple of weeks later by the adult floating leaves. At this stage, the waterlilies can be planted in their containers and moved to the pool.

Plant nelumbo rootstocks in fresh aquatic compost in the spring, placing them horizontally in planting baskets. Stand these in a container of water that just covers the surface, and as growth commences, raise the water level. Once the plants are growing vigorously, place them in the pool.

Spring is also the time when floating plants are introduced to the pool. Remove any dead pieces from the overwintered portions and place the live green material into the pool as soon as the marginal plants break into growth. Carefully remove the water hyacinths from their trays, gently washing the roots free, then float them in the pool. If unbalanced by unnatural root development, carefully cut their roots back with a knife.

THE ALGAE PROBLEM

Indoors, the combination of higher water temperatures, consequent evaporation and topping up with nutrient-laden water adds to the potential for abundant algal growth. Unfortunately, however, most algicides that are recommended for outdoor use will create inhospitable and often toxic conditions in the warm environment of an indoor pool.

Suspended green algae should be controlled by balancing submerged and floating aquatic plants. However, filamentous algae, especially silkweed, creates the greatest problem. This must be removed by hand the moment it is observed. Do not use an algaecide, as apart from the risks of toxicity, the dead silkweed will rapidly decompose and pollute the water.

WATER QUALITY

Water is the most important element in a garden pond, and its effective management is vital to ensure the good health of all the living organisms that depend upon it. The water in a pond is required (by fish, at least) for every aspect of life: to carry oxygen from the atmosphere to the gills, so that the fish can respire; to remove carbon dioxide; to carry away ammonia; to enable the fish to move; and to prevent them from becoming dehydrated. As you can see, the water in a pond is almost a self-contained ecosystem, only interacting with the atmosphere to exchange gasses such as oxygen and carbon dioxide. The toxic wastes that are released into the water must be broken down in the water, otherwise they will quickly reach dangerous levels and will kill the creatures living in the ecosystem.

THE NITROGEN CYCLE

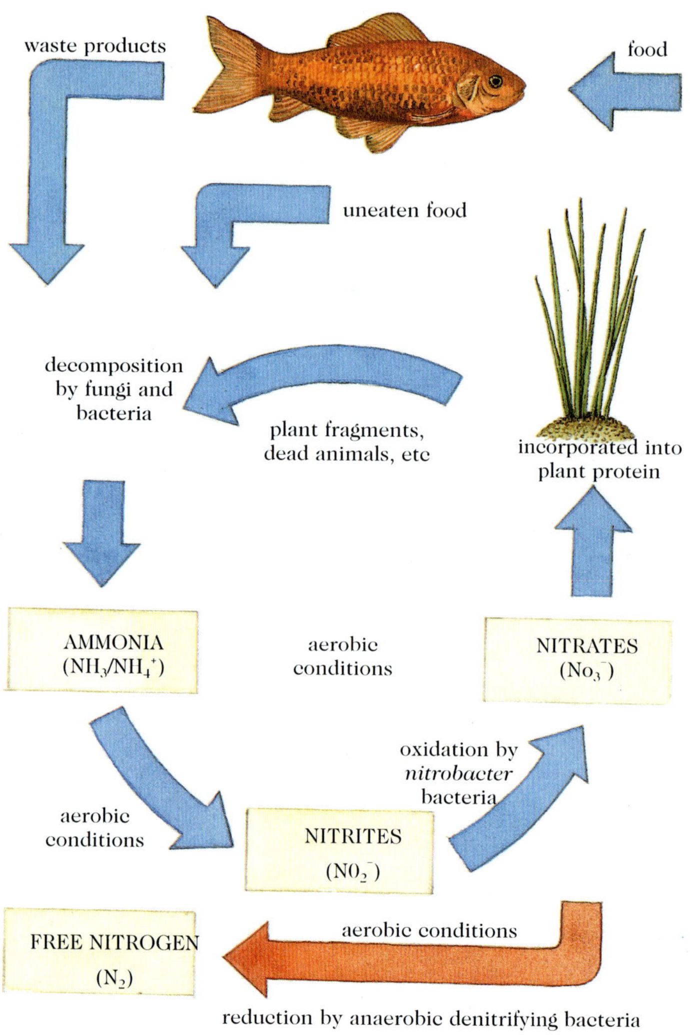

The nitrogen cycle is the process by which potentially dangerous fish wastes and uneaten food are converted into less toxic products, such as nitrate, which is used as a fertilzer by plants.

Fortunately, there is a naturally occurring process, known as the nitrogen cycle, that will prevent the build up of toxic waste, provided everything is working correctly. However, it is a wise precaution to monitor the levels of key chemicals, especially during the summer.

TEST KITS AND SOLUTIONS

There are many test kits and water quality rectifying products available, and the novice may be excused for being daunted by the prospect of testing pond water for the first time, especially if not scientifically minded. However, those fears should prove unfounded. The best test kits are easy to use and come with full instructions on how to resolve any of the problems that testing identifies. Often, the solution to a water quality problem can be achieved before it becomes serious enough to cause death or disease in the fish. This is a very real threat if a water quality problem is allowed to deteriorate. Therefore, testing and maintaining water quality should be viewed as essential preventative action.

STILL WATER

The balance of plant growth, which should ensure water clarity from the outset, and the responsible introduction of fish generally ensure that still water will be of acceptable quality. How stable this balance remains will depend upon the size of the pool. It is much easier to keep a stable balance in a large pool than in a small body of water.

Still water becomes thermally stratified during the heat of the summer, because the sun's warmth is absorbed near the surface and cannot penetrate the depths. Small shallow pools may stratify when the day is warm, but return to a uniform temperature at night as the surface layers cool and sink to mix with lower layers. These rapid changes can cause problems in both the supply of oxygen and the blooming of algae.

In very deep pools, the changes are seasonal rather than daily. In early spring, a clear distinction develops between the upper, warm epilimnion layer and the lower, cold hypolimnion layer. Between these layers is a transitional zone called the thermocline. These all have an influence on the behaviour of aquatic life, as the layers do not mix.

The lower layer receives no oxygen, but does benefit from organic debris scattered into it from the upper layer. Conversely, the topmost layer receives none of the results of decay and, by the end of the summer season, will be short of nutrients. This, in turn, can affect plants like floating aquatics, which only occupy that zone. This is why, in larger bodies of water, floating plants sometimes appear to go into decline towards the end of the summer. These distinct zones continue until the turbulence created by autumn gales mixes them and, of course, they cool down naturally.

Not only is water clarity important, but also the unseen acidity or alkalinity. Pure water has a neutral pH of 7.0, but in a pond there are many dissolved chemicals and these can have a marked effect upon the condition of the water.

ACIDITY AND ALKALINITY

The importance of acidity and alkalinity in a conventional garden pool cannot be overestimated. A test kit is an essential tool, which should be used at least once a month during the summer.

The acidity or alkalinity of the water is indicated by its pH value. Pure water has a pH of 7.0, which is neutral, being neither acid nor alkaline. In a pond, many chemicals dissolve into the water, and all of these chemicals will have an influence on the pH. A pH value between 0.0 and 7.0 indicates acid conditions, while a pH between 7.0 and 14.0 is alkaline.

Pond fish will thrive best in a pH of 7–8, although anywhere between 6.0 and 8.5 is acceptable. If the pH falls outside this range, pH adjusters should be used to achieve a suitable level. If the pH is consistently high, you should investigate and find the cause. In many cases, it can be traced to untreated concrete on the pond surround, a statue in the pond, or even an old house brick used to support a planting basket.

Algae also has an influence on pH: if the pond is heavily infested with algae, the pH value may change by as much as 3.0 between morning and evening. This is because the algae use carbon dioxide and remove carbonic acid from the water during the day, thus raising the pH. After dark, the algae stop photosynthesizing and produce carbonic acid, thus lowering the pH.

Some natural indicators of acidity and alkalinity can also be observed. For example, if the water soldier (*Stratiotes aloides*) floats freely with its spiky leaves projecting well above the surface of the water, the conditions are alkaline; if it does not float properly and becomes suspended in the water, acid conditions prevail. Likewise, if snails have shiny unblemished shells, the water is alkaline, if they become pitted or thin, it is acid.

To ensure a stable pH, the filtration must be good, and neither organic nor inorganic elements must be allowed to build up.

The water soldier is a fine indicator of pH. In alkaline water it floats with its leaves partially above the surface.

MOVING WATER

Aside from the decorative benefits of moving water, there is a practical bonus in that it not only provides the ability to filter water, but also assists in the exchange of gases, especially oxygen and carbon dioxide. Its only disadvantage is the constraint it places upon the cultivation of waterlilies and other deep-water aquatics in the smaller pool. The circulation of water is invaluable in the smaller pool, however, for the lower layers of water are brought to the surface and gaseous exchange is enhanced. The surface water of a still pond has a limited ability to create such an exchange, and problems can result at night when heavily planted pools may become almost depleted of oxygen.

Care must be taken with the movement of water, for in some circumstances (though not generally in a garden pool), such as in deep water where deoxygenation has taken place during the summer and all but the anaerobic bacteria have disappeared, dragging this into the upper layer of water will be counter-productive. Instead of retaining high-quality water within the epilimnion layer, it becomes contaminated by the toxic by-products of anaerobic decomposition, resulting in very unpleasant pollution.

If you are contemplating keeping koi carp, moving water will be essential, but the whole set-up will be very different from that found in the garden pool. While the koi will greatly enjoy swimming and leaping about in swirling water, the water movement will be an essential part of the entire filtering process and the maintenance of high-quality water.

CHLORINE

Chlorine is added to domestic water supplies to reduce bacteria levels and make the water suitable for human consumption. It is best removed either by filtering the water through a carbon filter or, more commonly, by using a proprietary dechlorinator. Increasingly, water authorities are using chloramine, as it is more stable than chlorine. This will be removed by traditional dechlorinator products, but in the process ammonia will be released into the water. Therefore, it is advisable to treat the water with a bio-start product soon after using the dechlorinator to breakdown the ammonia.

The circulation of water is invaluable in a well stocked pool, for the lower layers of water are brought to the surface and gaseous exchange is enhanced. The surface water of a still pond has little ability to create such an exchange.

COPING WITH ALGAE

There are many different species of aquatic algae, but for practical purposes, all can be divided into two groups: free floating or suspended and filamentous. The former are often minute, single-celled species that cause an algal bloom in the pool, turning the water like pea soup; the latter include silkweed, blanketweed and mermaid's hair. Although rarely a sign of an unhealthy pool, algae can cause the pool owner considerable distress, totally ruining the visual effect.

SUSPENDED ALGAE

Free floating and suspended algae, of the kind that turn the water green, are most prevalent in spring, but may be found at other times if the pool is too rich in nutrients. At the start of the growing season, even a well balanced pool may suffer from a temporary algal bloom as the water begins to warm up. Algae will appear very rapidly in such conditions and proliferate until the higher plants, such as the submerged aquatics, begin to grow actively and the waterlilies and other floating foliage plants develop to produce surface shade. Once all the aquatics are established in the pool and growing freely, the nutrients that cause the problem will be mopped up and the algal bloom will disappear almost as quickly as it arrived.

The pea soup effect in water is created by myriad tiny single-celled algae. This can be controlled by the restricted use of fertilizers and the encouragement of submerged aquatics.

It is essential to be patient during the spring and to wait for nature to take its course. Provided you have a suitable balance of plants, eventually all will be well. Whatever you do, resist the temptation to empty the pool of water and refill with fresh. This may produce a temporary alleviation of the problem, but after a few days, the water will be greener than ever. Fresh water, even from the tap, is loaded with mineral salts, which will take much longer to be absorbed, especially as the higher plants that resolve the problem will have been disturbed and, therefore, checked in their growth. Never change pond water that is green if you have a balance of other aquatic life in the pool. Just be patient. However, it is a good idea to use a flocculating product, which will temporarily sink the algae out of suspension, allowing light to reach the submerged plants and thus accelerating their growth.

ARTIFICIAL CONTROL OF ALGAE

Every pond owner will encounter green water at some point. Algaecide products are available that will kill green water algae, but care must be taken to remove the dead algae, otherwise it may decompose, harming fish and plants. An alternative way to deal with green water algae is to use a flocculating product that will clump the single-celled algae together, making them heavier and causing them to sink. This will allow light to reach the submerged plants in the water. You may need to repeat the treatment several times, as flocculating products will not prevent the green water from reforming.

If you suffer an ongoing problem of green water, you should consider installing an ultraviolet (UV) filter. Essentially, this comprises a fluorescent tube that emits ultraviolet light rather than visible light. Because UV light is harmful to the human eye, such a filter will be enclosed in a dark tube. The water passes through this and around the UV tube, and the UV light kills the algae. A UV filter should be used in conjunction with a mechanical filter to collect the dead algae.

The methods of removing filamentous algae, such as blanketweed, are completely different to those used to combat green water. Algaecides are available, but as with green water, the dead algae should be removed to prevent water pollution. Alternatively, a pond balancing product, which adjusts the balance of nutrients in the water, can be used. Although these products tend to take longer to work, they increase the nutrients available to the desirable pond plants, while restricting nutrients to the algae.

Whatever product you use, remember that if you kill a large population of filamentous algae, it will start to decompose and contaminate the water. Therefore, after treatment has proved effective, it will still need removing from the pond, although it is safe to leave any small pieces that break.

FILAMENTOUS ALGAE

Filamentous algae come in several different forms. The most persistent and troublesome is blanketweed, a thick, mat forming kind that is coarse and fibrous, and which tangles itself around all manner of aquatic plants. In bad cases, it often forms large floating mats or colonies, the lower parts frequently becoming dense accumulations that begin to decompose through lack of light and create an unpleasant smelling brown or black mass. One of the most irritating aspects of blanketweed is that it often grows lustily in a pond that otherwise is completely clear. Rarely does it seem to prosper in green water.

Silkweed is a similar proposition. This is a more slimy growth that tends to cling around submerged aquatics and the leaf stalks of waterlilies and other deep-water plants. Usually, it is a very dark green. Unlike blanketweed, which can be lifted easily from the water by hand, it tends to slip through the fingers and is more difficult to remove.

Mermaid's hair, the hairy, pale green algae that clings to planting baskets and to the walls of the pool, is quite innocuous and can actually help to give the pool a natural look. Provided it does not start to invade the stems of waterlilies or become tangled among submerged aquatics, it should not present a serious problem.

Green water, which is caused by filamentous algae, often accompanied by an abundance of duckweed, is very difficult to control. A balanced planting assists, but does not guarantee, a cure. While chemical control is possible, manual removal is the safest option.

NATURAL CONTROL

The ideal method of algae control is a biological one: the creation of a balance that will not permit it to develop freely. This has been outlined already and embraces the principle that if there are sufficient submerged plants to utilize the major plant foods in the water, and enough surface shade provided by floating foliage to reduce the light penetrating the water to a level that only the submerged plants can tolerate, clear water will occur quite naturally.

This is a very good theory, and for the most part it works, although occasional setbacks will occur. A pond is a natural and evolving environment, so inevitably changes take place, and constant monitoring will be required if a natural balance is to be maintained. Simply introducing a fresh container of aquatic plants in compost, which may add a few more nutrients to the ecosystem, can be enough to tip the balance.

The natural way is certainly the best method of coping with algae. Having the right plant balance is the key, but this must be linked with the sensible introduction of fish. An over-population of the latter can quickly tip the balance back in favour of the algae, especially the green water discolouring kinds. If fish become a significant interest and you want to steadily increase your stock, it may be worth abandoning natural algal control in favour of a filter.

The ideal solution for water clarity is a natural balanced planting where submerged plants utilize excess nutrients, the leaves of the waterlilies provide underwater shade and restrict the development of algae and the marginal plants frame the watery picture.

FILTERS AND FILTRATION

If a garden pond is designed and built purely for plants and naturally occurring wildlife, a filter will not be necessary, as the biological systems will establish naturally, and the pond will develop at its own pace, without producing undue waste products. However, if the pond will be a home for fish, a filter should be seriously considered.

WHY FILTER?

The main reason for filtering your pond is to clean up the environment. As described earlier in this chapter, a pond is almost a self-contained ecosystem, and like any ecosystem, it needs a mechanism for removing the toxic waste. Since the garden pond is an artificial environment, it requires artificial methods to keep it free of waste. This enables you to keep reasonable numbers of fish in the pond. Before you can install a filter, however, you will need a suitable pump to force the water through the filter. The pump and water outlet positions should be considered carefully in relation to any waterlilies, which will not thrive in moving water. Where possible, an area of still water should be set aside for them.

FILTRATION SYSTEMS

There are three major kinds of filtration system: mechanical, chemical and biological. Mechanical filtration pushes water through a system incorporating gravel, clinker or foam, catching and removing all suspended particles as it does so. This is useful where there is a problem of plants or compost being stirred up, but it does nothing significant to improve the quality of the water. It simply cleans the water physically.

Chemical filtration removes toxic and undesirable chemicals from the water by using the absorbent properties of substances like carbon and zeolite. The latter is commonly employed in newly established aquatic systems to remove ammonia. It is a natural ion exchange resin, which replaces ammonia with sodium, so it is rechargeable with salt. Carbon can be used to remove chlorine, heavy metals, organic dyes and odours. Organic dyes, such as phenol and tannin, can be responsible for much of the brown discoloration in the pond, and they cannot be removed by mechanical filtration.

Chemical filtration is not a replacement for biological filtration; you will still need to provide a site for biological decay. If carbon is allowed to remain in the filter for a long period, it will become biologically active, which will cause a problem when it is removed, as the biological filtration capacity will be reduced, which will result in an increase of ammonia and nitrite.

It is possible to include both mechanical and chemical filters in the same unit, or they can be separate and connected to one another. Where two or more filter chambers are used, it is worthwhile fitting a by-pass pipe so that when one is replaced or cleaned, the other will continue to function. With new advances being made all the time, chemical filters are constantly being improved, and for the latest information, it is essential to visit your local aquatic supplier.

The most popular kind of filter is the biological type. This depends upon bacteria in the filter medium breaking down

In a heavily stocked pond where there are limited opportunities for the successful establishment of plants, artificial filtration is essential. There are several very successful systems which can ensure water clarity all the year through.

FILTER MEDIA

The success of a filtration system is very dependent upon the kind of filter medium used. These are very diverse, and each has its advocates. Gravel is one of the most widely used, largely because it is readily available and comes in various grades, although most filters function best on a particle size of 6mm (¼in). Some gravels have irregularly shaped grains and are of a porous nature. Their larger surface area provides accommodation for bacteria, as well as producing good straining properties.

Processed lava granules are excellent, too. These are almost sponge-like, having a large surface area and a web of capillaries inside. This structure is a very efficient physical filter and also provides plenty of space for beneficial bacteria to colonize. It is inert, sterile, of neutral pH and also very light.

Baked clay granules are another medium that is sometimes used and, in fact, is favoured by a number of manufacturers. This material is similar to that used in hydroculture for the cultivation of house plants. It is clean and very easy to use, unlike sand, which is often recommended, but which in practice creates awful problems. The only role for sand is in a sand-fed filter, which is more the prerogative of the koi keeper.

Apart from natural and enhanced granular materials, some artificial filter mediums are very popular. Foam is among the favourites, although it does tend to clog frequently and require regular maintenance. Fortunately, it is very easy to clean. Only use foam that is recommended for the filter; do not try to economize by purchasing foam from a home-improvement store. The latter may be treated with a fire-retardant chemical which, when installed in the filter, could kill the fish.

Filter brushes are currently quite popular, too. These look like very large bottle brushes, being of cylindrical shape, and fit snugly into the system. Like foam, they need regular cleaning. In addition, they also provide an excellent home for bacteria.

High-surface-area scintered glass is becoming increasingly common as a filter medium, probably due to its ability to remove nitrate from the water.

The most bizarre filter medium is what are termed plastic mouldings. These are pieces of shaped plastic with large surface areas, which provide excellent homes for bacteria. The most common shape looks rather like a plastic spring or hair roller, the latter being a perfectly acceptable substitute.

Gravel is one of the most widely used filter materials as it is readily available and comes in various grades and sizes.

Baked clay and processed lava granules have a large surface area and a web of capillaries inside.

Foam is widely used, but it clogs easily and requires regular maintenance. Only use special filter foam.

Filter brushes are very popular and are easy to clean. They fit neatly into a modern filtration system.

Scintered glass pellets provide a high surface area and are excellent for remoing nitrate from the pool

Shaped plastic mouldings have large surface areas and provide an excellent home for the all essential bacteria.

toxic substances, such as ammonia, into nitrites and then into nitrates that are readily utilized by the plants (see *The Nitrogen Cycle*, page 268). This is quite a long-term project, for it takes some time for the beneficial bacteria to become sufficiently established to work effectively. Being part of the pond's ecological system, albeit in a slightly artificial situation, they are also vulnerable to changes in water conditions. For example, they can be severely damaged by some pond cures intended to combat bacterial problems, for when the solution enters the filter, the beneficial organisms may also be attacked. It is worth checking whether this is likely to occur before buying such a remedy.

In a biological filtration system, some bacteria, which do not need oxygen, derive energy from being involved in a partial break-down of organic matter and, in doing so, release ammonia or ammonium compounds into the water. In confined conditions, these would be quite capable of killing fish, but other bacteria are also present and convert such harmful ammonia compounds into less noxious nitrites and nitrates, which are not all that harmful to fish and are readily assimilated by plants. These beneficial bacteria do require oxygen to survive and live happily in the oxygenated water that passes down through the filter from the upper layers.

Pure mechanical filtration, although limited in its ability to improve water quality, can be quickly activated. Merely switching on the pump ensures instant improvement. However, for long-term economy and success, the biological filtration method is preferable.

TYPES OF FILTER

There are two main types of filter: internal and external. An internal filter has to be immersed in the water and, with careful planting, can be disguised. Ideally, a decision on its use should be made before the pool is constructed so that provision can be made in the excavation to incorporate it sympathetically, otherwise it may prove intrusive. For most pool owners this should not be a problem, for the modern portable internal filter is easily disguised and connects very neatly to the pump system. However, the filtration requirements of the koi keeper are likely to be significantly greater than the ability of even the newest, most efficient, portable internal filtration systems.

Of course, by employing an external filter, the pool will not be cluttered, but it does need to be in close proximity to the pool to function properly, and regular access for maintenance will be required. So an appropriate planting around the pool to disguise its presence is essential. If a rock garden is being incorporated as part of the overall feature, the filter system can often be hidden within it, though, of course, this will need to be planned from the outset.

For a filtration system to operate effectively, it should be connected to a pump with more capacity than the manufacturer recommends. It is always preferable to have spare pump capacity, despite the additional cost, rather than discover that a complete change to pumping arrangement proves necessary later on. However, the flow rate through the filter itself should match the manufacturer's specification. The size of pump is also critical if you want to incorporate a waterfall or fountain, for a much more powerful unit will be necessary if filtration is part of its role as well. However, in some circumstances, there are advantages to using a separate pump for each purpose. (For more information on pumps, see pages 122-123.)

Although apparently trouble-free, filters do require regular maintenance if they are to function efficiently. The frequency of maintenance will depend upon the kind of filter medium employed, together with the condition of the water, but a weekly check during the peak summer months will ensure that all continues safely.

NATURAL FILTRATION

Filtering with plants is all the rage at present. Such a system can be adapted to the garden pool, too, and has long been practised by Chinese and Japanese fish breeders. It simply involves establishing a small subsidiary pond, or a filter box, with vigorous plants that will absorb harmful chemicals, such as phosphates and nitrates, from the water, then running that water through a conventional mechanical filter and back into the pool. The plants absorb all manner of excess mineral salts, in addition to nitrates and phosphates, all of which become locked up in their systems. Thinning the plants periodically removes the chemicals from the pond's life cycle. Unfortunately, using plants in this way will not remove significant quantities of ammonia and nitrite.

Any filtration system should be of sufficient capacity for the pool to be treated and must incorporate a pump that has more power than is necessary to cope with the basic requirements.

DOWNFLOW FILTER

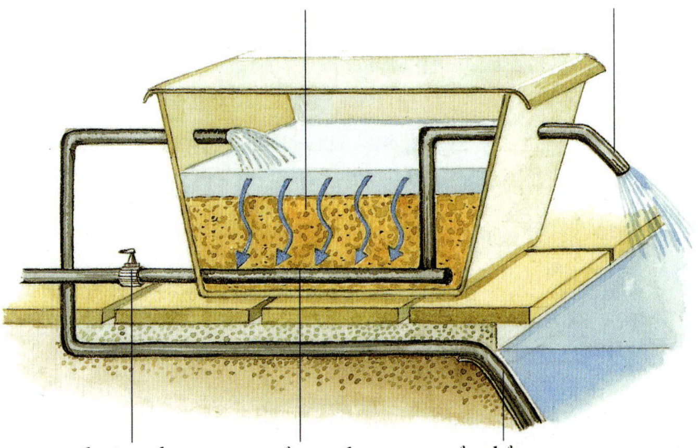

In a downflow filtration system the water enters at the top of the chamber, then percolates through the filter medium to the outlet pipe. This system is easier to maintain than an upflow one.

UPFLOW FILTER

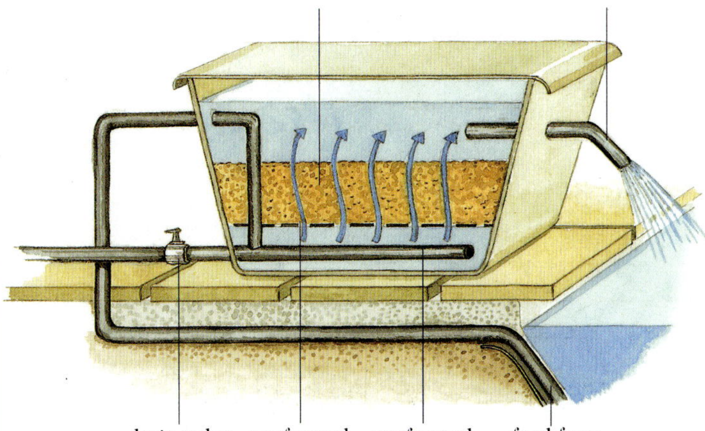

In an upflow filter, the pond water enters at the base of the filter chamber and is pumped up through the filter medium. A variety of filter media may be used, gravel being typical.

THE FILTER

Most pond owners who decide to buy a filter would be well advised, initially, to purchase one that will suit their needs, rather than attempt to build one, unless they plan to keep large numbers of koi. Whatever configuration it takes, the ready-made filter will require careful placing, not only to function efficiently, but also to be as unobtrusive as possible. While a specially tailored filter would be easier to accommodate, until considerable experience has been gained, or expert advice sought, it is a route that is best avoided.

UNDERGRAVEL FILTER

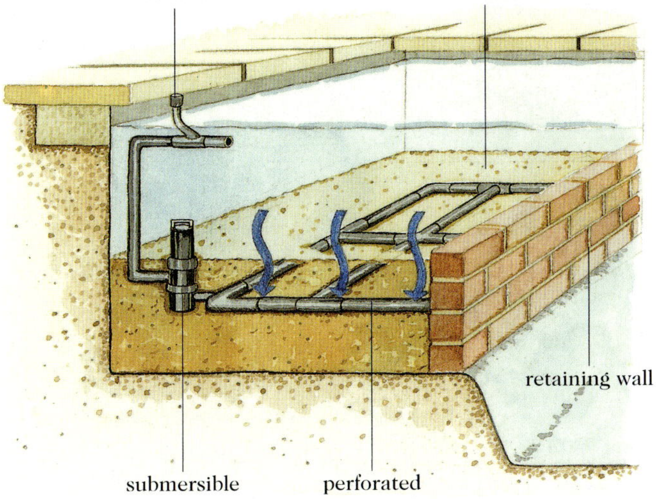

A typical under-gravel filter located on a marginal shelf. A gridwork of pipes draws in water from the entire gravel bed. Such a filter is not usually an option for a beginner.

In addition to the mechanical and biological functions of a filter, there are two modes of operation: upflow and downflow. These refer to the route taken by the water as it passes through the filter medium. The upflow system has a pipe that leads the water into the bottom of the filter chamber, where it permeates up through the filter medium. Conversely, the downflow system permits the water to enter at the top of the chamber, then percolate through the filter medium to the outlet pipe and back into the pool. In a garden pool situation, there is little to choose between the two systems, although the downflow type is easier to maintain, as the large debris collects at the top of the filter. Each would benefit from a prefiltration chamber to remove large organic debris.

Apart from the box-style filter, it is also possible to introduce an under-gravel filter. This is an adaptation of the method widely used by aquarists, comprising a series of perforated pipes beneath a layer of gravel that is contained in some convenient manner, perhaps on a marginal shelf. It depends upon constantly moving water to keep the aerobic bacteria happy, allowing them to work on the organic debris and make it harmless. Such a filter must be made at home, and it is not the best option for a newcomer. Although it is quite efficient and easily disguised, it is difficult to maintain.

SEASONAL ADAPTATIONS

While filters function in various different ways, each has an outflow that discharges clean water back into the pond. During summer, it is beneficial for the pump to be some distance from the filter chamber so that water currents are created that mix the water zones and improve quality. To aid oxygenation, the water should also be returned to the pond above the surface. In winter, the pump can be moved closer to the filter and the surface of the water, the return being beneath the water to create a much smoother effect.

PROBLEM-SOLVING

WATER QUALITY AND FILTRATION

I am contemplating constructing a koi pool and have been told that it is important to have a drain in the floor, and to flush out regularly. How often do I need to do this?

A bottom drain is used frequently by some koi keepers as a means of flushing out accumulated debris from the pool floor. Other fish keepers will use a special vacuum cleaner regularly to clear up organic debris. The density of the fish population will have a bearing on how often you need do this. In a moderately populated pool, there is unlikely to be too much organic waste material, so flushing need only be carried out occasionally.

Bottom drains are a useful addition to a koi pond, enabling debris to be removed from the pool floor. They will need to be considered before the pond is constructed.

How do I test my pond's water to ensure that it is of good quality?

There are many tests that can be conducted on pond water. However, the most significant are for pH, ammonia and nitrite. Easy-to-use test kits are available, either in tablet or liquid form, which change the colour of the water. By comparing this with a chart supplied in the kit, it is possible to determine the quality of the water. Good test kits will explain how to interpret the results and resolve any problems. Testing the water regularly will enable you to identify problems in your pond before they become serious enough to cause fish to die.

What happens if my pond becomes too acid or alkaline? How will it affect the plants and fish?

In ponds where the water is excessively alkaline, the fish will pick up fungal diseases more readily, as their natural mucus protection will be damaged. The gills of fish can also be damaged by alkalinity, causing them to die, apparently without cause. Ammonia compounds in the water also become more toxic, while the ability of a biological filter to work effectively will be reduced. Most plants dislike excessive alkalinity, and often submerged aquatics will become coated with a limy deposit.

Many of the same, or similar, symptoms occur in water that is too acid, although this is a less common condition. Fish will look unhappy and die without apparent reason, although they may show some reddening of the fins. Biological filters also do not perform properly under acid conditions, while many plants do not prosper, especially the submerged aquatics. However, acid-loving marginal plants, such as the cotton grasses, will enjoy the conditions.

Cotton grass is one of the few marginal aquatics that enjoys acid conditions.

The sort of green water seen here, which muddies the colours of koi, is only really effectively removed with an ultra-violet filter. Exposing algals cells to UV light causes them to unite into larger bodies, which can then be removed by a normal filter medium.

In most established pools, where there is a balance of plants and fish, neither excessive alkalinity nor acidity is likely to be a problem. However, in a koi pond, a much closer check must be kept on the situation, for the quality of water in such an environment is more finely balanced and can easily be tipped either way unexpectedly. If necessary, use a proprietary pH adjuster to correct the pH level of the water, at the same time taking action to identify and correct the cause of the problem.

Which is the best kind of filter to use to rid my pool of green water?

The only form of filtration that will provide a reliable cure for green water is an ultra-violet (UV) system. Most other filters are unable to remove tiny, often uni-cellular, algae by straining them out. However, exposing them to ultra-violet light causes the algal cells to unite into larger bodies, which can be captured by a normal foam filter medium.

I believe that the flow rate of water through a filter is quite critical. How does this affect its performance, and how do I know that I have got it right?

The correct flow rate largely depends upon the manufacturer's recommendation. It is not something that is easily calculated by the domestic gardener, although it is important to understand the effects of too slow or fast a flow rate.

If the flow rate is too rapid, it will disturb the aerobic bacteria in the biological part of the system, and in natural filters, it will create inefficiencies by stunting vegetative growth. When the flow rate is sluggish, the weak current is unlikely to be sufficient to move debris towards the drains. A weak flow rate also creates layers in the water, reducing the efficiency of the filter as well as affecting the oxygen content of the pool depths.

What is a venturi? I have been told that I need one for my koi pool, but what does it do?

A venturi is a gadget that can be attached to the outflow of a pool filtration system to increase the water's oxygen content. It creates a vacuum that sucks in air, which is mixed with the water, this being regulated quite simply. As koi have a very high oxygen requirement, the addition of such a device will prove very useful, but it is not essential.

PLANT PROPAGATION

RAISING AQUATICS BY VEGETATIVE METHODS

The normal vegetative methods of increasing aquatic plants (by division or from cuttings and eyes) are all quite easily executed, even if your facilities are quite basic. For the most part, a good light window ledge is all that is necessary to raise good-quality plants.

DIVISION

Almost all aquatic and bog garden plants can be increased by division in the spring. This is simply the process by which the crown of the plant is divided into two or more pieces, which are potted or planted individually. With aquatic plants such as reedmaces and rushes, which have creeping root systems, this involves removing a length of rootstock with a terminal shoot attached and planting it separately. Plants like iris, water plantain and marsh marigold, which grow in clumps, can simply be separated by hand or with a trowel, rather like herbaceous plants.

This applies to most of the bog garden plants, too, established clumps being prised apart during the dormant season and the outer, more vigorous, young pieces being replanted.

ROOT CUTTINGS

A number of bog garden plants can be readily increased by taking root cuttings. This can be done in addition to division or, in some cases, as a substitute if a plant has not developed to the stage where it requires dividing. Of all the bog garden plants, it is the drumstick and candelabra primulas that benefit most from being increased by root cuttings. However, many vigorous perennials with fleshy, thong-like roots may also respond to this propagation method.

Root cuttings should be removed during the dormant season, the parent plant being lifted and suitable pieces of root removed. Then the adult plant is returned to the garden. The best roots to use are those that are no thicker than a pencil, but not so thin that they are likely to dry out before sprouting. Place pieces of root, about 2.5cm (1in) long, horizontally in trays of good seed compost, cover lightly with more compost, water, then place them in a cold frame. Within a few weeks, the root cuttings will start to sprout. At this stage, they can be lifted carefully and potted individually in small pots for growing on, ready to be planted out in the following autumn or spring.

STORAGE ORGANS

A number of aquatic plants produce turions or winter storage buds. In some cases, such as with the arrowhead or flowering rush, these are primarily food storage organs. However, they are produced freely and can be separated and allowed to develop as new plants, rather than remain in clumps. With some floating plants, and several submerged aquatics, turi-

PROPAGATION BY DIVISION

1 Established plants should be carefully divided and the youngest, most vigorous portions used for propagation purposes. Old material should be discarded, even though it may be more substantial.

2 Trim the foliage of the plant back hard – this will in all probability die anyway. Cut back the roots prior to planting and remove any suspect decaying rootstock.

3 Replant the prepared division in good clean aquatic planting compost in an appropriate aquatic planting basket. Water well, driving all the air out of the compost before placing in the water.

ons are a means of dispersing and redistributing the plants around the pond, a natural means of propagation with which the water gardener need not interfere.

STEM CUTTINGS

While most marginal and bog garden plants are readily divisible, a number are much better propagated from stem cuttings. Indeed, some perennial plants, like water mint and brooklime, which can be divided successfully, make better plants if propagated each spring from short stem cuttings.

Such cuttings should be of non-flowering shoots, about 5cm (2in) long, which should be removed from the parent plant in late spring when actively growing. If inserted into a tray or pot of sandy loam, or indeed good, friable, stone-free muddy soil, and partially or completely submerged in water, rooting will take place within 10-14 days. The young plants can then be lifted, potted and grown on individually.

Submerged aquatic plants are mostly increased by taking stem cuttings during the growing season. These should be gathered into bunches and fastened together with a thin strip of lead. This is allowed to remain around the bunch of cuttings, which should be pushed into their permanent position in the compost.

WATERLILIES FROM EYES

All hardy waterlilies, except *Nymphaea* 'Pygmaea Alba', which must be reproduced from seed or occasionally by division, are best propagated from eyes. These are tiny growing points that occur with varying frequency along or around the rootstocks of mature hardy waterlilies. In most cases, they are rather like smaller versions of the main growing point, often with their own complement of juvenile foliage, although with *Nymphaea tuberosa* and its cultivars, they take the form of readily detachable, brittle rounded nodules.

Adult hardy waterlilies should be lifted during the spring or early summer, and the required number of eyes removed with a sharp knife. The wounds of both the rootstock and the eye should be dusted with powdered charcoal to reduce the risk of fungal infection. The eyes may be potted into small pots or modular trays, using a soil-based compost, and stood in a shallow container. This should be filled with water until it covers the rims of the pots. If the eyes are tiny, they will benefit from the protection of a cold frame or greenhouse during their early life. As they start to root and grow, they should be moved into progressively bigger pots and deeper water until large enough for planting in the pool.

WATERLILIES FROM OTHER METHODS

Some of the tropical waterlilies are increased from seed, but by and large, the named cultivars are best propagated by separating young plants in the spring. The tubers should be potted and placed in a temperature of around 21°C (70°F) in a sunny spot. Within a couple of weeks, the first true floating leaves will have appeared. With finger and thumb, locate the stem-like growth connecting the young plant to the tuber. Pinch it off next to the tuber, removing the young plant with the roots intact, but leaving the tuber in its pot. The young waterlily plant should be potted up and the tuber allowed to regrow. This can be done two or three times with a tropical waterlily tuber, before a single final growth is retained for the coming season.

A number of tropical waterlilies are also viviparous, producing young plantlets on their leaves. These can be regularly removed and potted up as fresh plants.

PROPAGATION BY STEM CUTTINGS

1 Remove good healthy stems of non-flowering shoots from actively growing plants. This is best done during spring and summer when the plants are growing vigorously.

2 Clean up the foliage and gather together in small bunches up to 5cm (2in) long. Fasten neatly around the base of the stems with a thin lead strip to hold them together.

3 Plant the bunches of cuttings in aquatic planting baskets filled with compost. Bury the lead weight beneath the compost or else it will rot through the stems and the tops will float away.

RAISING AQUATIC PLANTS FROM SEED

As with many land plants, a considerable number of aquatic plants can also be raised from seed. For the most part, these are natural species, although strains of one or two subjects, such as iris and mimulus, can also be increased in this way to advantage. Named cultivars rarely come true and must be increased vegetatively.

WATERLILIES

Although there is currently a trend towards growing some of the large-flowered waterlilies from seed, their progeny will always differ from the parents, being mostly inferior and rather difficult to grow to flowering size. Recent developments in techniques and knowledge of the behaviour of a select group of hardy waterlilies has spawned this unfortunate trend, for rarely will the expectations of the pool owner be realized. For a high-quality, large-flowered waterlily, vegetatively propagated stock is essential.

The only waterlilies that justify raising from seed, and indeed, apart from occasional division, cannot be increased in any other way, are *Nymphaea* 'Pygmaea Alba' and its progenitor, *N. tetragona*. *N.* 'Pygmaea Alba' is a very small cultivar that, after flowering, often produces greenish-white fruits, which are filled with viable seeds. If gathered and sown immediately, they ripen and germinate very freely. The trick is to gather the seed when it has developed sufficiently and before it is distributed in the water. To ensure that all the seeds are captured from the rupturing fruits, place a tiny muslin bag over each developing pod.

Waterlily seeds are very small and embedded in a sticky gelatinous material. If you try to separate the jelly from the seeds, damage can occur. It is far better to sow both the seeds and jelly together, spreading the sticky mess as evenly as possible over the surface of the compost. For waterlilies, a good soil-based compost is preferable to any of the wide range of soil-less types that are available. Spread the seed over the surface of the compost, using a pair of tweezers, then lightly cover them with more compost. Spray the pots of seeds gently from overhead with water to settle the compost. Then stand the pots in a warm light position in a bowl or aquarium, making sure that the water level is just above the level of the compost.

Seedlings should start to appear after three weeks. They will have translucent, more or less lance shaped leaves that, at first glance, look as if they could be an aquatic liverwort. At this stage, they are very vulnerable to becoming entangled in fine filamentous algae. At the first sign of trouble, administer one of the reputable algae controls. If algae is allowed to accumulate, then killed, it must be removed promptly so that it does not begin to rot and damage the seedlings.

As the waterlily seedlings develop, the water level should be raised very slightly. As soon as the first two or three floating leaves come to the surface, the plants can be pricked out. They should be lifted in small clumps, washed thoroughly to remove any compost, then gently teased apart. Prick the seedlings out into a seed tray or pan, then immerse it in a container of water so that the water level is approximately 2.5cm (1in) above the surface of the compost. As the floating leaves of the seedlings grow and develop, the water level can be raised gradually. After a season, the seedlings will be large enough to plant out in their permanent positions.

SOWING SEEDS

1 Always use a good clean seed compost and thoroughly soak before sowing seeds. Spread the seeds sparingly over the surface of the compost. Crowded seedlings are subject to disease.

2 Cover the seeds with a thin layer of compost or sand. The use of sand is particularly beneficial for waterlily seeds and helps to discourage the proliferation of troublesome algae.

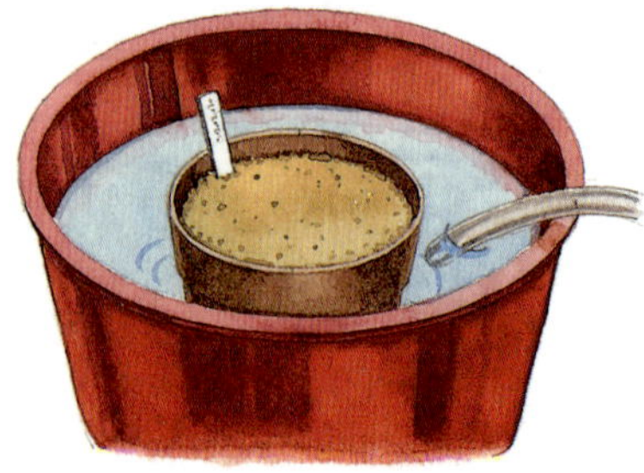

3 Stand the pot in a container of water. For waterlilies fill the container so that the water level is just above that of the compost. With bog and marginal plants it should be just below compost level.

Candelabra primulas are among the easiest plants to raise from seed. Freshly gathered seed germinates freely, many of the named varieties of primula, like 'Postford White', coming true to type.

The water hawthorn, Aponogeton distachyos, *is easily raised from seed providing that it is fresh, green, and sown in a loamy compost immediately. It must never be permitted to dry out.*

OTHER AQUATICS AND BOG PLANTS

Seed is the readiest means of raising many of the most popular marginal aquatics and the vast majority of bog garden plants. For the most part, it should be remembered that only the species will come true from seed, although there are notable exceptions, such as the *Primula japonica* cultivars 'Postford White' and 'Miller's Crimson'. While the majority of marginal and bog plants can be increased by vegetative means, raising from seed is generally the most reliable and economic method, especially when more than two or three plants are required.

Almost without exception, marginal subjects and deep-water aquatics, such as the water hawthorn (*Aponogeton distachyos*), should be sown when the seed is fresh and sometimes still green. Indeed, seed of the water hawthorn should not be allowed to leave the water until ready for sowing, otherwise it will perish.

Sow the seed of true aquatics in a wet, heavy loam compost, although plants that will have floating leaves, such as water hawthorn, appreciate a few centimetres of water over their crowns once through the soil. Initially, it is inadvisable to submerge freshly sown seeds, as they are often light and will float right out of the compost. A thin layer of silver sand will help hold them down and also assist in preventing the rapid development of algae on the surface of the compost. Once the seeds germinate and the seedlings have become established, they can be pricked out and treated rather like young waterlily plants.

Bog garden plants are dealt with in a similar manner, although some gardeners raise young plants in the open ground. However, this can be fraught with difficulty, for the seed is often fine, the soil conditions likely to be quite hostile, and watering difficult to control. Raising plants in seed trays or pans, within the protection of a cold frame, is much easier to manage, and the quality of plants produced is almost inevitably better.

The seed of most bog garden plants is best sown fresh, which is fine if you can collect your own, but a bit of a problem if you have to depend upon the seedsman. Collected seed is usually sown during mid- to late summer, while packeted seed has to wait until the spring. In some cases, seed that is not fresh requires chilling to break its dormancy; this is quite common with primulas.

Sow the seed in a good soil-less seed compost in clean pans, in the same manner as when fresh. Then place the containers in the freezer, allowing them to remain there for a couple of weeks before bringing them out into the light and warmth. Germination will follow quite rapidly. Once the seeds of bog garden plants have germinated and the seedlings have been pricked out, they should be grown on in individual pots for the remainder of the season, ready for planting out in the following spring.

PLANT PESTS AND DISEASES

Several pests and diseases afflict aquatic plants, but unlike elsewhere in the garden, these cannot be sprayed with chemicals, for they would kill the fish. Therefore, in the water garden, more than anywhere else, the gardener needs a comprehensive understanding of the life cycles of the various pests and diseases so that they can be attacked at the most appropriate time. In addition, garden hygiene must be of the highest standard.

WATERLILY APHID

The most troublesome pest of waterlilies and other succulent aquatic plants is the waterlily aphid. In warm humid weather during summer, it reproduces at an alarming rate, smothering the plants and causing widespread disfigurement of both flowers and foliage.

Understanding the aphid's life cycle is the only way by which effective control can be implemented. During early autumn, eggs from the late summer brood of aphids will be laid on the branches and in fissures of the bark of plum and cherry trees. These will overwinter, hatching in the spring, when winged female adults will fly to the host plants. Here they live happily, reproducing asexually and giving birth to live wingless females, which continue the process every few days. As autumn approaches, a winged generation of adults unites sexually, the females flying to the winter host trees to deposit their eggs.

From this, it will be apparent that only in their overwintering stage are they vulnerable to attack by the gardener. During the winter, when the trees are completely dormant, spray with a tar oil winter wash. This is specifically manufactured as an ovicide for destroying the overwintering eggs of insect pests on fruiting and decorative trees. A winter wash will effectively break the life cycle of the aphid, and any reinfection will have to come from afar.

During the summer, if waterlily aphids return, the only way of coping with them is to spray infested plants with clear water from a hosepipe, which should knock the creatures into the water, where many will be devoured by fish. Although, inevitably, some will crawl across the surface tension of the water and back onto the plants, with luck, the majority will be eaten.

WATERLILY BEETLE

An extremely destructive pest, the waterlily beetle can spread with impunity in warm areas. Where there are severe winters, however, its progress will be impeded. It is a very

Waterlily aphids are troublesome pests of aquatic plants, infesting not only waterlilies, but also most other succulent marginal plants. Once established they are difficult to eradicate.

Waterlily beetle, greater pond snails and false leaf mining midge can all cause severe disfigurement of the foliage of waterlilies and other deep water aquatics such as nuphars.

specific pest, only attacking waterlilies, but where it does take hold, it becomes a major problem.

The small, dark brown beetles and shiny black larvae are usually found on waterlily pads, where they strip away the epidermal layer of tissue, leaving the slimy tattered remains to decay. Opening blossoms and buds are also attacked. Severe infestations will leave little except flower stalks and skeletonized leaves.

The adult beetle hibernates in pondside vegetation during the winter, emerging in late spring and early summer, just as the waterlily pads reach the surface of the water. They migrate to the waterlilies, depositing clusters of eggs on the leaf surfaces. After a week, curious black larvae with distinctive yellow bellies emerge and feed on the foliage until pupation takes place, either on the waterlily pads or in surrounding vegetation. Under warm conditions, there may be three or four broods in a season.

Apart from ensuring good pond hygiene, little can be done to control this pest, except to spray the plants with clear water to knock the larvae into the pool where, hopefully, the fish will feed on them. Clearing up the marginal vegetation thoroughly in the autumn, to remove any hiding places where the beetles can overwinter, is the most useful means of exercising some control. However, once the pest is established, constant vigilance will be required. If necessary, they may have to be picked off by hand.

BROWN CHINA MARK MOTH

The larvae of this insignificant looking, brown patterned moth is one of the most destructive pests of aquatic plants, especially waterlilies. Not only does it cut and shred the floating foliage of aquatic plants, but it also makes a shelter for itself, prior to pupation, by sticking down two pieces of leaf within which it weaves a greyish silky cocoon. Damaged plants look very unsightly, their chewed leaves crumbling at the edges and surrounded by pieces of floating and rapidly decaying foliage.

The brown china mark moth lays its eggs on the undersides of floating leaves during the summer. They hatch and the caterpillars burrow into the undersides of the juicy foliage, later making oval cases out of pieces of leaf. They continue to feed and grow, passing the winter before pupating. Small infestations can be picked off by hand, but do not forget to net off any floating leaf debris, as this may have cocoons attached. In severe cases, it is worth defoliating the plants completely, removing all the leaves and allowing fresh submerged foliage to emerge unscathed.

The beautiful china mark moth is a species that behaves in a very similar manner, except that the caterpillars burrow into the stems of aquatic plants in the early stages of their life. Here they hibernate, eventually emerging to make leaf cases and their silky cocoons. Again, picking them off by hand is the only reasonable option.

CADDIS FLY

Most of the caddis flies produce larvae that feed on the foliage of aquatic plants, many of them being totally submerged in their larval stage. The flies lay their eggs during the summer in long strings, which are often wrapped around aquatic plants in the water. When the larvae have hatched, they start to spin their silken cases, to which are attached small stones and plant debris. The larvae live in these hollow

Although not a particularly noticeable species in its adult form, the brown china mark moth produces larvae which can cause extensive damage to the floating foliage of aquatic plants.

Caddis flies produce larvae that feed on the foliage of aquatic plants. They are difficult to detect as they live in tubular cases produced by sticking together small stones and plant debris.

cases while they devour the foliage of aquatic plants. When large populations are present, they can be quite destructive, but the presence of fish helps to exercise some control over them. Otherwise, the only option is to pick them off by hand.

FALSE LEAF MINING MIDGE

A most irritating pest that can be seen in many garden pools, the false leaf mining midge seems to be particularly troublesome with small waterlilies cultivated in tubs and containers. The minute larvae of this pest eat a narrow tracery of lines over the surface of floating foliage. This eventually turns brown and rots. There is no control, except regularly spraying affected plants with clear water to dislodge the pests. However, in severe cases, it is a good idea to remove all the floating foliage, together with the pest, to give the replacement growth a fresh start.

POND SNAIL

While the ramshorn or planorbis snail is a valuable consumer of algae, which rarely if ever devours desirable garden plants, this is not true of many other snails. Species like the greater pond snail, or freshwater whelk, and the fountain bladder snail can be extremely destructive, damaging aquatic plants in the same manner as garden snails attack land plants. Aquatics with floating foliage are particularly vulnerable to being grazed upon, and severe infestations can cause complete defoliation. For the most part, snails with tall pointed shells, which produce eggs in cylinders of jelly, are the most destructive; flat rounded snails, which lay their eggs in flat pads of jelly, are generally quite innocuous. Unfortunately, gardeners sometimes mistake the cylinders of jelly for fish spawn, especially when they arrive attached to plants. In this case, a population will quickly take hold in a pool.

Small tubs and planters can be rid of snails by mixing a proprietary aquatic snail killer into the water, but this would be impractical for a garden pool. Therefore, physical methods must be relied upon. Picking off by hand is a tiresome occupation, but it can be made easier by floating fresh lettuce leaves on the surface of the water overnight. By the morning, there is likely to be a considerable congregation of snails beneath them, which can be collected and destroyed.

WATERLILY LEAF SPOT

There are two species of leaf spot disease that damage waterlily leaves. One causes dark patches to appear on the surface of the leaves, which eventually rot through; the other tends to start at the outer edges of the leaves, causing them to turn brown and crumble. Both are debilitating and disfiguring, but they are not very serious problems. Their incidence will vary considerably from year to year, depending upon the prevailing conditions.

Removing damaged foliage, and discarding it safely elsewhere in the garden, will do much to prevent their spread. In decorative pools where there are no fish, a copper fungicide, like Bordeaux mixture, can be utilized effectively.

WATERLILY CROWN ROT

There are two distinctive forms of waterlily crown rot, which is believed to be caused by at least two different organisms. One has been known variously over the years as waterlily crown or root rot. It is believed to be a phytophthora, a relative of potato blight, and is specific to waterlilies and their

The greater pond snail is a very destructive creature which is often mistakenly introduced to the pool in the belief that it will graze on algae. It will do so, but much prefers waterlily leaves.

Waterlilies growing in unhygienic and stressful conditions will soon succumb to fungal diseases. One of the first to invade is waterlily leaf spot, which causes dark patches on the leaves.

PLANT PESTS AND DISEASES

Symptoms	Cause	Cure
Foliage distorted; masses of tiny black insects on waterlilies and other emergent plants	Waterlily aphid	In winter, wash nearby plum and cherry trees to destroy overwintering populations. In summer, wash aphids into the pool with a strong jet of water; the fish will devour them.
Epidermal layers of leaves and flowers stripped away; small brown beetles and shiny black larvae present	Waterlily beetle	In summer, knock the creatures into the pool with a strong jet of water and allow the fish to devour them. Good pondside hygiene in autumn denies them a place to overwinter.
Floating foliage cut and shred, floating on water surface	Brown china mark moth	Pick off larvae by hand and net all floating debris, which may have larvae attached.
Pieces of floating foliage neatly removed	Caddis fly	No cure, but a good fish population will keep the pest under control.
Badly chewed floating foliage, often with cylinders of jelly beneath	Pond snail	Pick off snails and jelly containing eggs by hand. Float a fresh lettuce leaf on the water overnight to attract the pests, then remove and destroy them.
Tracery of lines on floating foliage, which eventually rots and crumbles	False leaf-mining midge	Spray foliage with clear water to remove the pests so that the fish can devour them.
Dark patches on waterlily leaves that eventually rot	Waterlily leaf spot	Remove badly affected foliage and destroy. In pools containing no fish, spray with Bordeaux mixture.
Blackening and rotting of waterlily crowns	Waterlily crown rot	No cure; destroy affected plants and sterilize the pool with a solution of sodium hypochlorite. Remove all fish first, then flush out the pool with clean water before refilling.

allies. It has a preference for attacking yellow-flowered cultivars like *Nymphaea* 'Marliacea Chromotella', although it does attack others on occasion. Apparently healthy plants suddenly develop a blackening of the leaves and flower stems, which become soft and rotten, the rootstocks turning evil smelling and gelatinous.

All affected plants should be removed and destroyed, the pool being cleansed and sterilized by swirling a muslin bag filled with copper sulphate crystals through the water. All fish must be removed before any such treatment begins, and not returned until the pool has been emptied, swilled out and refilled with fresh water.

The more recent strain of crown rot disease is believed to be caused by a number of pathogens, which have not yet been fully identified. This disease is believed to have been introduced from the Far East on imported waterlily plants. It attacks all cultivars with impunity, causing the crowns to decompose rapidly into an unpleasant brown mass. At present, there is no cure, so it is vital to remove and destroy any infected plants. Then the pool should be cleaned thoroughly and sterilized with a solution of sodium hypochlorite before being flushed out with fresh water. Once clear water has been run back in, new plants can be safely introduced.

Yellow waterlilies such as N. *'Marliacea Chromatella' are prone to attack by the crown rot believed to be caused by phytophthora; the more virulent modern crown rot disease kills all varieties.*

FEEDING FISH

One of the most enjoyable, yet controversial, issues for the pool owner is the feeding of fish. Is it necessary? How often should you do it? And what should you use? If you are a fish enthusiast, your choice of foods may be as diverse as those for a pet cat or dog, but if the pool is essentially a wildlife habitat, provided all is well, the fish may not require much feeding at all.

SELECTING FISH FOOD

While it is not necessary to feed decorative fish in a well balanced pool, there can be few water gardeners who are not fascinated by the prospect of regularly feeding them and watching their antics. Like most other domesticated creatures, fish will not go seeking food if it is provided for them; once a routine has been established, a footfall close by the pool or a shadow cast across the water will bring the fish to the surface in the expectation of being fed. However, if you intend feeding them regularly, it is important to use a balanced and nutritious food.

Unquestionably, stick fish foods are the easiest to handle and, if you select a quality brand, the best balanced for pond fish. They have the advantage of floating on the water for a considerable period of time, so if the fish have not devoured them within ten minutes, any remaining food can be netted and removed. This prevents uneaten food from settling on the floor of the pool, where it will decompose unpleasantly. Although the sticks may seem rather large for some of the smaller fish, remember that the fish will suck at them rather than gulp them down in one go, although this inevitably happens with some of the larger fish.

Flaked fish food is also excellent and mostly scientifically balanced. There are specific cold-water flakes, and some companies manufacture a special formulation for the pool. They are much loved by goldfish, and easily taken by very small fish, but unless feeding is undertaken on a still day, the flakes can end up in the herbaceous border, rather than the pool. They also float for much less time than the sticks, yet are likely to cause almost as much contamination of the water if allowed to sink. A careful eye needs to be kept on the flakes to ensure the prompt removal of any that remain uneaten.

Feeding fish is one of the great delights of pool ownership. In a well maintained, balanced pool it is not normally essential, unless there is a large population of fish, such as in a koi pond.

LIVE FOODS

Enthusiastic fish keepers occasionally like to feed some live food during the summer months. If you can spare a little time, feeding live food to your fish will certainly be worthwhile from their point of view. Most fish have regular access to live food, although this is often obtained naturally by preying on aquatic insect life in the pool. The occasional provision of a tasty morsel of earthworms or daphnia, however, will be much appreciated. Earthworms are a natural treat that can be easily collected in most gardens. Avoid worms from areas that have been treated with chemials, however, as these could harm the fish.

Daphnia, or water fleas, are a very different proposition. These can be cultured quite easily, making it possible to maintain a fresh supply of live food throughout the summer with little effort. Daphnia may often be found naturally in ponds, water butts and, on occasion, even large puddles. However, a culture can be purchased from an aquatics supplier and perpetuated in a tub or barrel. All that is required is a layer of soil about 2.5cm (1in) deep, the addition of rainwater, although conditioned tap water will also suffice, and the introduction of the daphnia. Under such conditions, they will prosper, and small quantities can be gathered with a fine muslin net each week as a live treat for the fish.

WHEN TO FEED

The necessity of feeding fish is a continual bone of contention among fish keepers, and there is no consensus of opinion. By and large, however, in a sparsely stocked pool, if you want to feed the fish, there will be benefits, but if you do not, the fish are still likely to grow and flourish on the natural food within the pool.

During the winter, the metabolism of pool fish slows down and they do not require regular feeding when the temperature is below 5°C (41°F). During this cold period, the fish rely on their stored food reserves. However, recent research has shown that feeding a wheatgerm-based food during mild spells, when the temperature rises above 5°C (41°F), will preserve their food reserves and ensure that they are strong and healthy at the end of the cold period. Feed the fish on a few food sticks whenever they are active and rise to the surface in search of food.

As the water temperature rises in the spring, the fish will become more active and should be fed more regularly. Feed as much as they will consume within ten minutes each day.

In the summer, the fish will feed actively and can be given higher-protein foods to encourage growth, and foods containing colour enhancers to promote good body coloration. Again, feed as much as the fish will consume in ten minutes, once or twice a day. This amount will be much greater than in the spring.

Great enjoyment can be derived from feeding fish, but a well balanced food must be selected and no more given to the fish than can be comfortably cleared up in twenty minutes. Feeding should only be undertaken during spring and summer when the fish are active.

FISH PESTS AND DISEASES

There are many pests that can afflict fish, but the majority are readily controlled. Most outbreaks are caused by stress in the fish and rarely do any infestations simply break out in the well ordered pool. Fish can also suffer from a number of debilitating diseases, which can look quite frightening, but they rarely appear in the well managed water garden. Many infections in ponds break out as a result of the fish being stressed due to poor water quality, so check the water quality as a matter of course (see page 268).

ANCHOR WORM

This is a very tiresome and unpleasant crustacean that is a common parasite of the goldfish and carp family. It is a small creature, rarely more than 6mm (¼in) long, with a slender tubular body and a barbed head, which it embeds in the flesh of its host, causing unsightly lesions and tumour-like growths. It often looks particularly hideous, as it develops a light covering of green algal growth.

Treatment: The most practical method of dealing with anchor worm is to capture each infested fish, hold it in a wet cloth and dab the parasite with a 0.1 per cent solution of potassium permanganate, using a small paint-brush. This will kill the creature, which can then be gently withdrawn with tweezers. Finally, treat the wound with a proprietary fungicide. There are also several proprietary parasite cures, which can be added to the water of the pool to destroy anchor worms at the free swimming stage of their life cycle.

DIVING BEETLES

Young fish may be devoured by the various diving beetles and their larvae, or naiads. The beetles vary in size and colour, but the great diving beetle (*Dytiscus marginalis*), which is about 5cm (2in) long and has a yellow-bordered, dark brown body, is the commonest. Most pool owners tolerate the activities of diving beetles, regarding them as part of the natural fauna of the water garden and living with the minimal destruction they cause.

DRAGONFLIES

Some water gardeners are concerned about dragonfly attacks on young fish, for these vicious predators are killers. Although adult dragonflies are beautiful to watch, their larvae, or naiads, which spend up to five years living and eventually pupating in the pool, are very destructive, posing a threat particularly to young fish. Rarely is a fish killed in one go, but serious injury can be inflicted. The naiads live among submerged aquatic foliage. As soon as suitable prey comes into view, this keen-eyed predator will shoot forward its strange face mask. This is like a pair of hooked jaws, which grip the prey and bring it back to the gaping mouth.

Treatment: There really is no satisfactory way of dealing with this problem. As the adult stage of the life cycle is so lovely, and most pond owners enjoy the presence of dragonflies flitting above the water, the unfortunate dietary habits of their young are best tolerated.

Diving beetles can fly into the pool from the surrounding countryside. Although handsome and fascinating creatures, their unpleasant larvae prey freely on young fish.

Dragonfly larvae or naiads attack and kill young fish. However, adult dragonflies are beautiful and provide so much enjoyment that most pool owners feel that this is a small price to pay.

DROPSY

Fish that are suffering from this disorder become distended, the scales standing out from their body and resembling the needles of a pine cone. This can be caused by an internal bacterial infection, a kidney disorder, or an influx of water.

Treatment: Controlling dropsy is possible if the cause of the swelling is known. Placing the fish in a salt bath (25g/1oz rock salt per 4.5 litres/1 gallon of water) for seven days will often reduce the swelling. Treating with an antibacterial remedy can also be effective if bacteria are responsible. The best remedies are those sold for treating ulcers, as these are caused by the same types of bacteria.

FIN AND TAIL ROT

Caused in most cases by a combination of bacterial organisms, this infection usually begins on the edge of the tail or fin, which slowly rots away until nothing but a stub remains. The first indication of trouble is a distinctive white line running along the outer margin of the fin, which gradually progresses downwards to leave the outer margin badly frayed, the soft tissue between the hard rays of the fin disintegrating.

Treatment: If the disease is caught early enough, a proprietary fin rot cure can be used. In most cases, the fin tissue will heal satisfactorily and regeneration will take place. Where the disease is so bad that the rot has reached the base of the hard rays and is beginning to invade the main body tissue, the use of antibiotics may be necessary.

FISH LOUSE

There are several species of fish louse, which cause distress to pond fish. They are parasitic crustaceans that cling to the bodies of fish to feed and then drop off to digest their blood meal. Although some have specific host requirements, they all look much the same, having a strange flattened circular carapace with a diameter of up to 1cm (3/8in) and feelers.

Treatment: There are specific proprietary parasite remedies, containing the active ingredient dimethyl-trichlorohydroxyethl phosphonate, which can be used to control this parasite. However, in some countries, including the UK, these are only available from a veterinarian. Such treatments are harmful to orfe and rudd. It is important to treat the whole pond to control the parasites that are not on the fish.

FUNGUS

The various fungal diseases that afflict fish usually appear as a downy cotton-wool-like growth on the fins, tail or body. They normally occur as a secondary infection on wounds caused by the fish colliding with a sharp object or rough handling by the pool owner, as a result of the fish becoming run down during a mild winter, following attacks by pests such as anchor worm or white spot, or due to poor water quality. There is also an unrelated 'fungus', which is caused by a bacterium and referred to commonly as mouth fungus. This appears around the mouth as small cotton-wool-like growths that eventually destroy the tissue.

Treatment: The true fungal diseases are easily treated, provided they are not allowed to become deep seated and widespread. Proprietary fungus cures are very effective when added to the pool. Sometimes, several treatments may be needed, but they are generally very effective. A salt bath, (25g/1oz rock salt per 4.5 litres/1 gallon of water) is the traditional method of coping with fungus. However, although effective, it is a long-term process and, in severe cases of the disease, usually does not act quickly enough. Because fungal disease normally occurs as a secondary infection, it is important to identify and correct its primary cause to prevent recurrence soon after treatment is complete.

Provided that it is identified in the early stages, mouth fungus can be controlled effectively using a commercially available bacterial treatment.

The bacteria reposonsible for fin rot are common in pond water and, like many potential pathogens, they form a constant threat to fish. Treatment with a proprietary cure is generally effective.

The fungus diseases which afflict fish usually appear as a white cotton-wool-like growth. If symptoms are noticed in the early stages and the diseas treated promptly, most fish will recover.

GILL & BODY FLUKES

These are minute creatures that infest the gills and bodies of decorative pond fish, causing them to swim about haphazardly or gasp at the water surface. They rush around the pool, banging themselves against the sides and rising to the surface in sudden fits. The rate of respiration increases, while the fins constantly twitch.

Treatment: Use one of the many good parasite cures on the market. Ensuring that the water is well oxygenated during treatment will ensure that the fish survive while damaged gill tissue regenerates.

LEECHES

These are well-known predators of creatures of all kinds, and fish have their very own species. In common with other bloodsucking leeches, they have a sucker at both ends of the body, which are powerful attachment organs. They also have sharp, cutting mouthparts, and secrete an anti-coagulant to prevent the blood from clotting. A single leeche can, in a single meal, take in ten times its own weight of blood. This can last for a very long time and be very distressing for the fish. Before treating the fish, check that the leech is actually attacking it; most species depend on snails and similar creatures for their nourishment.

Treatment: Removal of leeches is simple: immerse troubled fish in a salt bath, such as that traditionally employed for treating fungal diseases (25g/1oz per 4.5 litres/1 gallon of water). The leeches usually drop off after this treatment. Never try to remove them without treating them first, as they will create very unpleasant wounds if withdrawn forcibly. Apply a proprietary fungus cure after the leeches have been removed to protect against secondary infection. Unfortunately, this does not control any leeches that are not actually attached to the fish. Therefore, several treatments are usually necessary.

The fish leech attaches itself to its host and gorges on blood before dropping off and digesting its meal. It is important to protect damaged host fish from secondary attacks of fungus disease.

RED PEST

This disorder causes the fish to become sluggish and rise to the surface of the water. They show reddish-brown on their sides and bellies, and occasionally on their anal or pelvic fins. If left untreated, it will spread throughout the pool. It is a bacterial infection usually associated with overcrowding or poor water quality.

Treatment: If caught in the early stages, improving the water quality through a partial water change, followed by treatment with a general external parasitic remedy will be effective. More advanced cases require antibacterial or antibiotic treatment. This may also be the initial stage of ulcers and should be treated with an ulcer remedy.

ULCERS

Ulcerated patches appear on the bodies of affected fish in a random manner, exposing raw tissue that may be streaked with blood. It is a distressing disorder for the fish and for the pond owner to witness. In the main, it appears to be caused by the same, and related, bacteria that cause fin and tail rot. Ulcers often occur in fish that are weakened or stressed in some way. Therefore, it is important to identify and correct the primary cause, as well as the ulcers themselves.

Treatment: Proprietary treatments are available that can control ulceration in its early stages. In more advanced stages, it is necessary to apply the remedy directly onto the wound, or to use antibiotics, either in a medicated food or, for larger fish, by injection.

WHITE SPOT DISEASE

Badly infested fish look as if they have white measles, take on a pinched appearance and swim in a drunken fashion. If left untreated, the fish usually die. This is a widespread parasitic disease that usually appears in freshly introduced or stressed fish. High stocking levels in the pool wil increase the

White spot disease is a debilitating affliction which usually results in death. It is a widespread disease which is usually associated with freshly introduced or stressed fish.

likelihood of transmission of these parasites. White spot disease is caused by a member of the group of single-celled creatures known as protozoa. This is tiny, scarcely 1mm (1/24in) across, and spends part of its life cycle embedded in the skin of fish, causing extreme discomfort and often death.

Treatment: Fortunately, white spot is easily cured using proprietary treatments. These must be introduced to the pool to control the white spot parasite in its free swimming stage, as well as on the fish. The treatment may take effect in anything from three to 14 days, taking longer at low temperatures.

SLIME AND SKIN DISORDERS

These are often referred to as diseases, although in fact, they are either caused by tiny, single-celled organisms, known variously as costia, cyclochaete and chilodonella, or by poor water quality. Affected fish often swim on the bottom of the pool with their fins folded and rub against underwater objects. Their bodies become covered with a bluish-white deposit – a mixture of the parasites and an excess of slime.

Treatment: A proprietary parasite cures will usually be effective. Combine treatment with improved water quality.

FISH PESTS AND DISEASES

Symptoms	Cause	Cure
Small lesions and tumour-like growths, often with algal covering	Anchor worm	Dab affected areas of fish with a 0.1 per cent solution of potassium permanganate, remove parasites and treat wounds with a proprietary fungicide. Treat the pool with a proprietary anti-parasite remedy.
Bloated body with distended scales	Dropsy	Place fish in a salt bath (25g/1oz per 4.5 litres/1 gallon) for one week to reduce swelling. Treat the pool with an antibacterial (ulcer) remedy.
Fins and tails rotting away	Fin and tail rot	Use a proprietary fin rot cure or, in advanced cases, antibiotics.
Small, almost transparent, disc-like creatures clinging to the body	Fish louse	Treat the pool with a proprietary anti-parasite remedy containing dimethyl-trichlorohydroxyethl phosphonate.
Fish swim around frantically, banging against the sides and bottom of the pool	Gill flukes	Use a proprietary anti-parasite cure.
Small, brownish worm-like creatures clinging to fish body	Fish leech	Immerse affected fish in a salt bath (25g/1oz per 4.5 litres/1 gallon) and treat wounds with a proprietary fungicide.
Greyish patches of cotton wool-like-growth on body	Fungus	Treat with a proprietary fungicide.
Sluggish movements and a tendency to keep near the surface of the water; reddish brown colouration of sides and bellies	Red pest	In the early stages, a partial water change plus proprietary parasite remedy should prove effective.More advanced cases require antibacterial (ulcer) or antibiotic treatment.
Patches of raw tissue and ulcerated sores	Ulcers	In early stages, add a proprietary treatment to the pond. In more advanced cases, apply this directly to the wound or use antibiotics.
Whitish slime over the body and the fish swimming erratically	Slime and skin parasites	Use a proprietary anti-parasite product combined with a partial water change to improve water quality.
Spots like white measles over the body, head and fins	White spot disease	Treat the pool with a proprietary white spot cure.

PROBLEM-SOLVING

FISH CARE

If I have a very sick fish, which is the most humane way to kill it?

Many pond owners are squeamish about killing a fish, even when obviously it is in terrible agony and at death's door. However, it is a responsibility that must be faced. The safest way to dispatch a sick fish is to hold it firmly in a dry cloth and deliver a sharp blow to its head. Death will be instantaneous. A fish can also be over-anaesthetized by your veterinarian.

I have a large goldfish that appears to be very swollen and distressed. What could be wrong with it?

Goldfish with distended bodies can be suffering from several disorders. If the fish is large and female, it could be spawn bound. A female goldfish can normally control whether or not she spawns, depending upon prevailing conditions. Sometimes, the body begins the process of preparing for the breeding season and circumstances change so that the fish begins to re-absorb the eggs that were being developed.

If this is unsuccessful, which can occur if the fish is undernourished or stressed, the eggs become hard and cannot be expelled. They may then begin to decay within the body and an accumulation of gas occurs, which leads to death. Stripping the fish by gently massaging its flanks while holding it in wet hands sometimes helps, but more often than not, the fish dies. Prevention is better than cure; a healthy environment rarely gives rise to such a problem.

Another possible cause of the swelling is dropsy. This is bacterial in origin, and a tell-tale sign of the condition is the accompanying protrusion of the scales on the swollen body. Some fish keepers refer to dropsy as pine cone disease because of the prominence of the scales. Use of a salt bath (25g/1 oz rock salt per 4.5 litres/1 gallon of water), combined with a proprietary antibacterial remedy, may be successful.

If the swelling is on one side of the body only, it could be a tumor. There is no cure, but the fish will probably live for several years.

My beautiful fantail goldfish is swimming alternately on its back and nose downwards. Every so often, it swims down to the bottom of the pond in a drunken spiral fashion, but soon returns to the top again. What could be causing this apparent loss of balance?

Unfortunately, this disorder is quite common in fancy goldfish, and is usually associated with a derangement of the swim bladder, which is the balancing mechanism of the fish.

The usual cause of swim bladder disorders is a sudden change of water temperature, which may be caused by a number of different factors, for example stress when fish are introduced into the pool, after a large water change, or during periods of clear frosty weather. Providing the fish with a period of steady water temperature will usually control the problem, although afflicted fish may show similar symptoms if a sudden temperature change occurs.

A similar problem may occasionally occur with fancy goldfish if they are fed an unsuitable diet, and will be apparent for a few

Fancy goldfish are prone to a derangement of the swim bladder, which affects their balance. This is usually caused by a rapid change in water temperature.

hours immediately after feeding. Using a good-quality flake or stick diet should prevent this.

How can I deter a heron? It visits my small pond regularly, but I am reluctant to cover the pool with a net, as this spoils the plants.

Herons are not just predators of the countryside; even small ponds in urban gardens are vulnerable to their attentions. While netting will certainly keep them out, it will more often than not detract from the beauty of the pond and can make even the simplest routine pond management difficult.

Providing hiding places for the fish in the pool is a useful idea: perhaps a piece of flat stone supported on a couple of other stones, under which the fish can take refuge. This can usually be arranged without looking unsightly. Otherwise, the only sure way of keeping herons out is to erect a series of short stakes, about 30cm (12in) from the edge of the pond and projecting 15cm (6in) from the ground, and attach a strand of fishing line to them. Herons usually walk into the water to fish and are known to have quite sensitive legs. As the bird walks towards the water, its legs will touch the fishing line, which will tend to deter it from proceeding further.

When fish die in a pond, do they always come to the surface?

In the majority of cases they do, so if you have not seen some of your fish for a week or two, it is more likely that they are hiding away among the plants, rather than having died. This is particularly so in spring and autumn. The only occasion when dead fish are unlikely to surface is if they become entangled in submerged plant life. On occasion, this may cause some pollution of the water when they begin to decompose. However, a single fish is unlikely to cause a serious pollution problem, unless it has died from a disease.

If netting is used to deter herons, construct a frame that is pleasing to the eye and which lifts the net well clear of the plant foliage. Netting stretched across the pool with plants growing through is ugly and awkward to manage.

GENERAL INDEX

Page numbers in *italic* refer to illustrations; those in **bold** to main references.

PLANT INDEX

Page numbers in *italic* refer to illustrations; those in **bold** to main references.

PICTURE CREDITS

The publishers wish to thank the following photographers and picture agencies who have supplied photographs for this book. Photographers, picture agencies and, where known, designers, have been credited by page number and position on the page: (B) Bottom, (C) Centre, (T) Top, (L) Left, (R) Right etc. The following abbreviations have been used: Garden Picture Library: GPL; Chelsea Flower Show: CFS; Harry Smith Horticultural Photographic Collection: Harry Smith; Stapeley Water Gardens: SWG; Elizabeth Whiting Associates: EWA.

Half-title page Bob Challinor/GPL; Frontispiece John Glover/GPL; **Title page** Brian Carter/GPL; **Title verso** Ron Sutherland/GPL (Anthony Paul); **6** Ron Sutherland/GPL; **9** Brigitte Thomas/GPL; **10** John Glover/GPL; **12** Ron Sutherland/GPL (Anthony Paul); **13** Gary Rogers/GPL; **14** The Bridgeman Art Library, courtesy of The British Museum; **15** The Bridgeman Art Library, courtesy of the Board of Trustees of the V&A; **16** (L) James Allison (Julian Dowle Partnership), (R) Marie-Louise Avery © Salamander Books Ltd; **17** John Bethell/GPL; **18** (T) Gerard Liston/GPL, (B) Clive Boursnell/GPL; **19** John Bethell/GPL; **20** Steve Wooster/GPL; **21** Ron Sutherland/GPL; **22**(L) Marie O'Hara/GPL (John Hill Design), (R) Lamontagne/GPL; **23** Ron Sutherland/GPL; **24** Clive Nichols/GPL (Douglas Knight/CFS); **25** (L) Ivan Ruperati/GPL, (R) Ron Sutherland/GPL (Myles Challis Design); **26** Brigitte Thomas/GPL; **27** Ron Sutherland/GPL (Myles Challis Design); **28** Steven Wooster/GPL; **29** (L) John Glover/GPL (Hampton Court International Flower Show), (R) Juliette Wade/GPL; **30** Ron Sutherland/GPL (Anthony Paul); **31** James Allison (Waterford Gardens, NJ); **32** Ron Sutherland/GPL (Beth Chatto); **33** John Glover/GPL; **34** Geoff Dann/GPL; **35** James Allison; **36** James Allison; **37** (T) Heather Angel, (B) Ron Sutherland/GPL; **38** James Allison; **39** Christine Douglas; **40** Ron Sutherland/GPL (Anthony Paul); **41** Steven Wooster/GPL; **42** John Glover/GPL; **43** John Glover/GPL (Askham Bryan College/CFS); **44** James Allison; **45** Ron Evans/GPL; **46** Lynne Brotchie/GPL; **47** James Allison (Oak Leaf Conservatories/CFS); **48** Gerard Liston/GPL; **49** Gary Rogers/GPL; **50** (T) John Glover/GPL (Daily Telegraph Garden/CFS), (B) J.S. Sira/GPL; **51** Roger Hyam/GPL (Nicola Fox/CFS); **52** Ron Sutherland/GPL (Douglas Knight); **53** (T) Brian Carter/GPL (CFS), (B) Vaughan Fleming/GPL (David Stevens/CFS); **54** GPL; **55** Clive Boursnell/GPL; **56** John Baker/GPL; **57** John Glover/GPL; **58** Steven Wooster/GPL; **59** Henk Dijkman/GPL; **60** Steven Wooster/GPL (Tim Newbury/CFS); **62** Steven Wooster/GPL (Sir Mylles Warren); **63** (T) Henk Dijkman/GPL (D. Beyer), (B) Jane Legate/GPL; **64** Gil Hanly/GPL; **65** John Glover/GPL; **66** James Allison; **67** (T) Brigitte Thomas/GPL; (B) Ron Evans/GPL; **68** J.S. Sira/GPL; **69** Heather Angel; **70** Bob Challinor/GPL; **71** Alan Mitchell/GPL; **72** Lynne Brotchie/GPL; **74** John Glover/GPL (Christopher Costin Design); **75** Ron Evans/GPL; **76** Ron Sutherland/GPL; **78** Nigel Francis/GPL; **79** John Glover/GPL; **80** Gil Hanly/GPL; **83** Marie O'Hara/GPL (Julian Dowle Partnership); **84** Brigitte Thomas/GPL; **85** Brian Carter/GPL; **86** Jerry Pavia/GPL; **88** Brigitte Thomas/GPL; **90** Geoff Dann/GPL; **91** (T) Clive Boursnell/GPL, (B) Jerry Pavia/GPL; **92** Ron Sutherland/GPL; **96** Ron Sutherland/GPL (Lucy Huntingdon/CFS); **97** Brigitte Thomas/GPL (Chevalier & Frinault); **98** Gary Rogers/GPL; **99** John Glover/GPL; **100** Marianne Majerus/GPL; **102** Juliette Wade/GPL; **103** Ron Evans/GPL; **104** James Allison; **105** Michael and Lois Warren/Photos Horticultural; **106** Geoff Dann/GPL; **107** EWA; **108** Brian Carter/GPL (Ray Forder-Stent/CFS); **110** Marie-Louise Avery © Salamander Books Ltd. (Douglas Knight/CFS); **112** Martine Mouchy/GPL; **115** James Allison; **116** GPL; **117** J.S. Sira/GPL; **118** Henk Dijkman/GPL; **120** Clive Boursnell/GPL; **121** Bob Challinor/GPL; **122** James Allison; **123** J.S. Sira/GPL; **124** Steven Wooster/GPL; **126** Ron Sutherland/GPL; **128** Linda Burgess/GPL; **129** Lamontagne/GPL; **130** J.S. Sira/GPL; **132** Lamontagne/GPL; **133**(L) John Glover/GPL (Barbara Hunt), (R) Mark Holt (Karen Stoltzman); **134** (L) Howard Rice/GPL, (R) John Glover/GPL; **136** Clive Nichols (Roger Platts); **137** Kate Zari Roberts/GPL; **138** (T) Steven Wooster/GPL, (B) Ron Sutherland/GPL; **139** Ron Sutherland/GPL; **140** Brian Carter/GPL; **142** Henk Dijkman/GPL; **143** Ron Sutherland/GPL; **144** Jerry Pavia/GPL; **145** (T) Ron Sutherland/GPL, (B) Bob Challinor/GPL; **146** Ron Sutherland/GPL; **147** Brian Carter/GPL; **148** Clive Nichols; **150** (T) Ron Sutherland/GPL, (B) Roger Hyam/GPL; **152** Brian Carter/GPL; **154** Ron Sutherland/GPL; **155** Neil Holmes/GPL; **156** Steven Wooster/GPL; **157** Bob Gibbons/Natural Image; **158** Clive Nichols; **159** Clive Nichols; **160** Nigel Francis/GPL (Hidcote Manor Garden); **161** Jerry Pavia/GPL; **162** John Glover/GPL; **163** (T) Gary Rogers/GPL, (B) Ron Evans/GPL; **164** James Allison; **165** James Allison; **166** James Allison; **168** Brian Carter/GPL; **169** Ron Sutherland/GPL; **170** Steven Wooster/GPL (Anthony Paul); Brigitte Thomas/GPL; **172** Steven Wooster/GPL; **173** Ron Evans/GPL; **174** Geoff Dann/GPL; **175** (T) Lamontagne/GPL; (B) Gillian Beckett/ Natural Science Photos; **176** Brian Carter/GPL; **177** (T) Marijke Heuff/GPL; (B) Anne Hyde; **178** Tommy Candler/GPL; **179** Linda Burgess/GPL; **180** (T) Geoff Dann/GPL, (B) James Allison; **181** John Glover/GPL; **182** (T) Reg Henley, (C) James Allison, (B) SWG; **183** (T, B) James Allison, (C) Howard Rice/GPL; **184** (T) Harry Smith, (C) James Allison, (B) Densey Clyne/GPL; **185** (T, C) SWG, (B) James Allison; **186** (T, B) James Allison, (C) Christine Douglas; **187** (T) Densey Clyne/GPL, (C, B) SWG; **188** (T) Harry Smith, (C, B) James Allison; **189** (T) Christine Douglas, (C, B) SWG; **190** (T, C) SWG, (B) Christine Douglas; **191** (T) James Allison, (C) Brian Carter/GPL, (B) SWG; **200** (T) Brian Carter/GPL, (C, B) James Allison; **193** (T) James Allison, (C) Gary Rogers/GPL, Christopher Fairweather/GPL; **194** (T) Didier Willery/GPL, (C) Brian Carter/GPL, (B) Bob Gibbons/Natural Image; **195** (T) Didier Willery/GPL, (C) James Allison, (B) Christine Douglas; **196** (T) David England/GPL, (C) Clive Nichols/GPL, (B) Ron Sutherland/GPL; **197** (T, C) Harry Smith, (B) Howard Rice/GPL; **198** (T) Smith/Polunin Collection, (C) James Allison, (B) Brian Carter/GPL; **199** (T, C) James Allison, (B) Didier Willery/GPL; **200** (T) Michael Howes/GPL, (C) Harry Smith, (B) Howard Rice/GPL; **201** James Allison; **202** (T) Brian Carter/GPL, (C) Harry Smith, (B) James Allison; **203** (T) Neil Holmes/GPL, (C) James Allison, (B) Perry D. Slocum; **204** (T) John Glover/GPL, (C) SWG, (B) James Allison; **205** (T, C) Harry Smith, (B) James Allison; **206** (T) Harry Smith, (C) James Allison, (B) Smith/Polunin Collection; **207**(T) Smith/Polunin Collection, (C) Brigitte Thomas/GPL, (B) Bob Gibbons/Natural Image; **208** (T) Smith/Polunin Collection, (C) James Allison, (B) Harry Smith; **209** (T) Andrew Lawson, (C) Heather Angel, (B) Harry Smith; **210** (T, B) James Allison, (C) Harry Smith; **211** James Allison; **212** (T) Harry Smith, (C) James Allison, (B) Peter Wilson/Natural Image; **213** (T) Michael Howes/GPL, (C) Harry Smith, (B) Bob Gibbons/Natural Image; **214** (T) Steven Wooster/GPL, (C) SWG, (B) Geoff Dann/GPL; **215** (T, B) Brian Carter/GPL, (C) Christine Douglas; **216** (T) Didier Willery/GPL, (C) John Glover/GPL, (B) Christopher Fairweather/GPL; **217** (T) Steven Wooster/GPL, (C) Jerry Pavia/GPL, (B) James Allison; **218** (T) Philippe Bonduel/GPL, (C) Peter Styles, (B) Marijke Heuff/GPL; **219** (T) John Glover/GPL, (C) Bob Challinor/GPL, (B) James Allison; **220** (T) Vaughan Fleming/GPL, (C) John Glover/GPL, (B) Brian Carter/GPL; **221** (T) James Allison, (C, B) Harry Smith; **222** (T) Didier Willery/GPL, (C) David Russell/GPL, (B) James Allison; **223** (T) Michael and Lois Warren/Photos Horticultural, (C, B) John Glover/GPL; **224** (T) James Allison, (C) Harry Smith, (B) Christopher Fairweather/GPL; **225** (T) David England/GPL, (C, B) James Allison; **226** (T) John Glover/GPL, (C) Brian Carter/GPL, (B) Christopher Fairweather/GPL; **227** (T) Brigitte Thomas/GPL, (C) Michael and Lois Warren/Photos Horticultural, (B) Harry Smith; **228** (T) Roger Hyam/GPL, (C) Howard Rice/GPL, (B) David England/GPL; **229** (T)Harry Smith, (C) Bob Gibbons/Natural Image, (B) Dennis Davis/GPL; **230** (T) Perry D. Slocum, (C) John Glover/GPL, (B) Christine Douglas; **231** (T) John Glover/GPL, (C) Christine Douglas, (B) James Allison; **232** (T) Perry D. Slocum, (C, B) James Allison; **233** (T) Perry D. Slocum, (C) Rex Butcher/GPL, Harry Smith; **234** (T) Christine Douglas, (C) James Allison, (B) Michael and Lois Warren/Photos Horticultural; **235** (T, C) James Allison, (B) Brian Carter/GPL; **236** (T, B) Perry D. Slocum, (C) Peter Styles; **237** (T) Christine Douglas, (C) SWG, (B) Harry Smith; **238** James Allison; **239** Michael and Lois Warren/Photos Horticultural; **240** James Allison; **241** Jane Legate/GPL; **242** (T) D.B. Lewis/Natural Science Photos, (C) Mike Sandford, (B) James Allison; **243** (T, C) Hans Reinhard/Bruce Coleman Ltd., (B) Mike Sandford; **244** (T, C) Jonathan Kelly © Salamander Books Ltd., (B) Natural Science Photos; **245** Hans Reinhard/Bruce Coleman Ltd., **246** (T) William A. Tomey, (C) Hans Reinhard/Bruce Coleman Ltd., (B) Richard T. Bryant; **247** (T, B) Mike Sandford, (C) Hans Reinhard/Bruce Coleman Ltd.; **248** Richard Revels/Natural Science Photos, **249** (TL) Heather Angel, (TR) Bob Gibbons/Natural Image, (BL) O.C. Roura/Natural Science Photos, (BR) N. Barltrop/Natural Science Photos; **250** Jane Legate/GPL; **252** John Glover/GPL; **253** Michael Howes/GPL; **254** Michael Howes/GPL; **255** Jane Legate/GPL; **256** Ron Sutherland/GPL; **257** (L) Jonathan Kelly © Salamander Books Ltd., (R) David Twigg; **260** Roger Hyam/GPL; **261** Henk Dijkman/GPL; **262** John Glover/GPL; **263** Jerry Pavia/GPL; **264** Ron Sutherland/GPL; **265** Ron Evans/GPL; **266** EWA; **269** (T) Gary Rogers/GPL, (B) SWG; **270** J.S. Sira/GPL; **271** Marie-Louise Avery © Salamander Books Ltd., **272** Michael Howes/GPL; **273** Gary Rogers/GPL; **274** Eric Crichton © Salamander Books Ltd., **275** (TL, TC, TR, BL, BR) Jonathan Kelly © Salamander Books Ltd., (BC) Interpet Ltd.; **276** Eric Crichton © Salamander Books Ltd.; **278** James Allison; **279** David Twigg; **283** (L) Ron Evans/GPL, (R) John Glover/GPL; **284** (L) Vaughan Fleming/GPL, (R) Brian Carter/GPL; **285** (L) Bob Gibbons/Natural Image, (R) Heather Angel; **286** (L) Heather Angel, (R) Philip Swindells; **287** Harry Smith; **288** Eric Crichton © Salamander Books Ltd., **289** Jane Legate/GPL; **290** Andy Purcell/Bruce Coleman Ltd., **291** (L) Dr. James Chubb, (R) Heather Angel; **292** Heather Angel; **294** Jane Burton/Bruce Coleman Ltd., **295** Howard Rice/GPL.